Inheritance Act Claims

SECOND EDITION

Other titles available from Law Society Publishing:

Conveyancing Checklists (2nd edn)
Frances Silverman and Russell Hewitson

Conveyancing Handbook (23rd edn)
General editor: Frances Silverman

Environmental Law Handbook (7th edn)
Valerie Fogelman, Trevor Hellawell and Andrew Wiseman

Leasehold Enfranchisement and the Right to Manage (3rd edn)
Christopher Sykes

Property Development
Gavin Le Chat

Stamp Duty Land Tax (9th edn)
Reg Nock

Titles from Law Society Publishing can be ordered from all good bookshops or direct (telephone 0370 850 1422, email **lawsociety@prolog.uk.com** or visit our online shop at **bookshop.lawsociety.org.uk**).

INHERITANCE ACT CLAIMS

A Practical Guide

SECOND EDITION

Miranda Allardice, Tracey Angus, Paul Hewitt and Penelope Reed

The Law Society

Crown copyright material is reproduced with the permission of the Controller of Her Majesty's Stationery Office
The material in Appendix C is reproduced with the kind permission of the Association of Contentious Trust and Probate Specialists

ISBN-13: 978-1-78446-080-8

First published in 2007
This second edition published in 2017 by the Law Society
113 Chancery Lane, London WC2A 1PL

Typeset by Columns Design XML Ltd, Reading
Printed by TJ International Ltd, Padstow, Cornwall

The paper used for the text pages of this book is FSC® certified. FSC (the Forest Stewardship Council®) is an international network to promote responsible management of the world's forests.

Contents

About the authors

Miranda Allardice is a barrister at 5 Stone Buildings where she has a general chancery practice with an emphasis on family provision, contentious probate, administration of estates, and complex matrimonial finance claims. She has a track record in 1975 Act claims that takes in *Re Myers*, the *Ilott* v. *Mitson* litigation and *Holliday* v. *Musa*, among others. She has a well-established succession mediation practice and is a member of ACTAPS.

Tracey Angus QC is a barrister at 5 Stone Buildings. Her practice is focused on contentious trusts and probate claims (and professional negligence claims arising in that context) as well as Court of Protection work. She has appeared in a number of 1975 Act claims, including *P* v. *G, P and P* (the first 'big money' claim by a surviving spouse post *White* v. *White*) and *Dellal* v. *Dellal* which is the only reported decision concerning the anti-avoidance provision in s.10 of the Act. She is a member of ACTAPS and the PNBA.

Paul Hewitt is a partner in Withers LLP's top ranked Contentious Trust and Probate team. He has a long list of reported successes in the Court of Appeal and elsewhere (including the Royal Court in Jersey), such as *Burgess* v. *Burgess*, *RSPCA* v. *Sharp*, *Re Turquand Young*, and *Pakistan* v. *NatWest*. Paul has a significant 1975 Act practice advising both claimants and defendants, and he lectures on contentious trust and probate matters. He is a member of STEP and ACTAPS.

Penelope Reed QC is a barrister at 5 Stone Buildings where her practice concentrates on trusts, wills, contentious probate, family provision claims and equitable remedies. She is a member of STEP, ACTAPS and the Chancery Bar Association. Penelope is also author of several trust and will books. She has appeared in many family provision claims, including *Cunliffe* v. *Fielden*, *Berger* v. *Berger* and for the successful appellant charities in the Supreme Court in *Ilott* v. *Mitson*.

Preface

The first edition of *Inheritance Act Claims* was published in 2007. Since then, the number of claims made under the 1975 Act has continued to grow generating significant decisions on virtually every aspect of the 1975 Act. These have clarified the court's approach to domicile, applications for permission to make a claim out of time, the anti-avoidance provisions, the divorce comparator and applications made by cohabitees, dependants and adult children. Most significantly, *Ilott* v. *Mitson* became the first ever claim under the 1975 Act (or its 1938 predecessor) to reach the highest court in the land.

The 1975 Act has been a barometer of social change: the introduction of claims by adult male and female children in the 1975 Act itself, cohabitees in 1994, civil partners in 2005 and, most recently, the introduction of same-sex spouses as applicants in 2014. In October 2014 significant amendments were made to the 1975 Act by the Inheritance and Trustees' Powers Act 2014. These amendments affect the categories of persons who can apply for relief under s.1, the types of orders the court can make under s.2, the factors to be taken into account under s.3, the time limit for applications in s.4 and the court's powers in respect of property passing by survivorship in s.9.

Since the first edition of this guide, Anna Clarke has left the Bar to go into academia and we owe her a debt of gratitude for the work she did on the first edition. We are delighted to welcome Miranda Allardice in her place.

Thanks are also due to Eliza Eagling, Lucy Johnson and Steven Kempster for help with the text.

The law is correct as at August 2017.

Table of cases

Table of statutes

Table of statutory instruments

Table of international instruments

Abbreviations

'the Act' or 'the 1975 Act'	Inheritance (Provision for Family and Dependants) Act 1975
ADR	alternative dispute resolution
AID	artificial insemination by donor
CPR	Civil Procedure Rules
ECHR	European Convention on Human Rights
EU	European Union
FDR	financial dispute resolution
HFEA 2008	Human Fertilisation and Embryology Act 2008
HMRC	Her Majesty's Revenue and Customs
MCA 1973	Matrimonial Causes Act 1973

CHAPTER 1

Overview

Many clients who are told that the court can interfere with what they put in their wills react with indignation. However, English law is relatively unusual in recognising the concept of complete testamentary freedom. Many jurisdictions have rules about forced heirship which are unknown in England and Wales.

English law does now recognise the need for testators to make provision for those to whom they owe an obligation. Quite apart from anything else, there is a social reason for ensuring that those who die provide for those dependent on them and do not leave them to fall back onto the State for support.

The court's jurisdiction under the Inheritance (Provision for Family and Dependants) Act 1975 ('the Act' or 'the 1975 Act') is the only exception to the principle that a person is free to dispose of his property as he chooses or to let the intestacy provisions apply to his estate.

The 1975 Act's predecessor, the Inheritance (Family Provision) Act 1938, was fairly limited in form, excluding several of the categories of applicants who can apply under the 1975 Act. In 1974 the Law Commission produced *Family Law: Second Report on Family Property, Family Provision on Death* (Law Commission Report 62) which led to the enactment of the 1975 Act. That Act was hailed in some quarters as a 'mistresses' charter', in that dependants could for the first time apply for provision. The Act also allowed for the first time adult children (beyond the original limitation to unmarried daughters and disabled adult children) to apply for provision which has, over the years, spawned a considerable amount of litigation. It also linked the provision made for a widow or widower to the provision which they might have expected to receive on divorce – as it had been observed that divorcing wives were doing better in terms of provision than widows under the 1938 Act.

The Act has in many ways provided a barometer of social change.

In 1995 the Law Reform (Succession) Act introduced a new category of applicant – the cohabitant. This meant that applicants who had lived with the deceased for more than two years, but might not be able to show dependency within the terms of the Act, could still make an application. The change recognised the fact that many more couples were living together rather than marrying.

In 2004 the Civil Partnership Act was introduced which put registered civil partners on the same footing as spouses as far as the 1975 Act was concerned. Those cohabiting as if they were civil partners are included in the class of applicants who can apply, as well as children treated as a child of the family where there was a civil partnership and former civil partners.

In December 2011 the Law Commission published its report on *Intestacy and Family Provision Claims on Death* (Law Commission Report 331) and some of its provisions made their way into the Inheritance and Trustee Powers Act 2014. Amongst other things that Act made substantial amendments to the 1975 Act. The changes made are dealt with in the relevant parts of this work. What is perhaps more interesting is what was not included in the final legislation: a right for cohabitees on intestacy, which might have significantly reduced the number of 1975 Act claims by cohabitees, and changes to the rules about the required domicile of the deceased at the date of death, which again could have considerably simplified what is a troubled aspect of this jurisdiction.

There is little doubt that this is an area of law where family and chancery law meet; where the chancery practitioner needs to understand family law concepts such as a child of the family and what provision might be expected on divorce, and the family practitioner needs to understand concepts of succession law such as domicile, the meaning of the net estate and the tax implications of any order made or compromise reached.

In approaching any claim under the Act, it is wise to adopt a step-by-step approach. The following chapters of this book take the reader through those steps in detail, but the following is a summary of the questions which the practitioner needs to work through:

1. Did the deceased die domiciled in England and Wales? This may be self-evident in many cases, but domicile and residence/nationality are often confused. The world is now a much smaller place and many people live and work in a country which is not their country of domicile.
2. Does the potential claimant fall within one of the classes of applicant set out in s.1 of the Act? This can pose particular difficulties in the case of a dependant, for example, or a child where paternity is disputed.
3. If the claimant does qualify as an applicant, does the will fail to make reasonable financial provision for him or her having regard to the factors listed in s.3 of the Act? It is important to undertake this test first. There will be cases where, for example, the financial resources of the claimant will mean that it was reasonable for him or her to be completely excluded from benefit under a will or on intestacy.
4. If the will or the provision on intestacy do not make reasonable financial provision for the claimant, what is the appropriate provision for the claimant? It is likely that all that can be advised is a range of possible awards.
5. Both stages (3) and (4) require the practitioner to look at the size and nature of the net estate. This is a crucially important part of the overall picture. It is perhaps trite to point out that if the estate is small and there are a number of competing claims on it, the task of making adequate provision for a claimant

may be a very difficult one. A large estate makes the task far easier and so a claimant who might not be able to succeed against a modest estate might have a better chance against a more substantial one. This is the point where the issue of whether there is joint property which has passed by survivorship needs to be considered. The question of property which is subject to a nomination arises less often. It is also at this point that it needs to be decided whether any of the anti-avoidance provisions need to be addressed – can property of which the deceased disposed in his lifetime be recovered for the net estate?

6. If a claim is to be made then time limits need to be addressed and a standing search (not a caveat) entered at the Probate Registry to alert the practitioner to when a grant has been issued.

It is important to stress that this jurisdiction is an objective one. The court cannot do what it thinks would be fair in the circumstances. Sometimes clients see the Act as a method of bringing into effect the unexecuted testamentary wishes of the deceased, but the court cannot use it for that purpose. The question for the court is not, was the deceased reasonable in failing to make provision for a particular applicant? The answer to that question might well be no, because it seems unfair to the judge that, for example, a particularly deserving person has been omitted from the will. The issue is whether objectively it is reasonable having regard to the factors in s.3 of the Act that the will or the intestacy makes no provision for the applicant.

Assessing the likely quantum of awards is one of the most difficult tasks both for the practitioner and the court. In practice, lump sum awards are most frequently made, although sometimes a claimant will, for example, be given a life interest in a fund or a property in which to live. In the case of all claimants except for spouses, civil partners and those whose relationship has been dissolved less than one year before the death and are treated as spouses or civil partners, it is a question of what is required for their maintenance. In the case of spouses, civil partners and those who have been treated as such, the provision is what would be reasonable in the circumstances and the court is required to cross-check the provision it is envisaging making against the provision which the court would have awarded if the relationship had been terminated by divorce or the dissolution of the civil partnership rather than death. It is therefore necessary in those cases to have regard to recent developments in ancillary relief applications.

While there is a considerable amount of case law on this area by now, the reality is that the vast majority of these cases never reach trial but are settled beforehand. Such compromises may present as many challenges as taking the case to hearing. There are tax considerations in many if not most cases, and particular difficulties may arise where there are children involved in the claim or those lacking capacity.

This book is designed to take the reader through the step-by-step process with reference to the Act and the most important case law.

CHAPTER 2

Threshold jurisdiction

2.1 INTRODUCTION

Section 1 of the Inheritance (Provision for Family and Dependants) Act 1975 sets out the circumstances in which an application may be made to the court. It provides that, where a person

(a)   has died;
(b)   was domiciled in England and Wales; and
(c)   was survived by one or more of the persons listed in s.1(1)(a)–(e);

any of the persons listed may apply.

The Inheritance and Trustees' Powers Act 2014 amended s.4 of the Act to expressly allow an application before any grant of representation. There had previously been some doubt as to whether this was permissible.

2.2 ESTABLISHING THE FACT OF DEATH

In most cases there will be no difficulty in establishing that there has been a death.

An official copy of the grant of representation is normally exhibited to the written evidence in support of the claim (see **Chapter 8**). This will specify the date of death and the court does not normally look for any further proof.

In the event that the grant of representation has not been issued, an official copy of the death certificate, or evidence of death from a foreign country, should suffice.

In rare cases there may be a question as to whether a person has died. The Presumption of Death Act 2013 provides for the possibility of a court declaration that a missing person is presumed dead. The application is brought under the Civil Procedure Rules 1998 (CPR), rules 57.17–57.23 and accompanying Practice Direction 57B.

2.3   DOMICILE – CONTEXT AND PRINCIPLES

The court can only make an award out of the estate of a person who was domiciled in England and Wales at the time of death.

However, migration and, in particular, freedom of movement of persons within the EU mean that practitioners very often deal with estates where the deceased was either born outside the jurisdiction or lived outside the jurisdiction for a significant part of his life.

In *Agulian* v. *Cyganik* [2006] EWCA Civ 129 Longmore J expressed surprise in para.8 that 'the somewhat antiquated notion of domicile' is a prerequisite to the court's jurisdiction under the Act. In many family disputes, the court's jurisdiction is determined by reference to habitual residence.

The Law Commission described domicile as 'a highly technical concept' and recommended that 'it should no longer be the sole precondition to an application under the Act that the deceased died domiciled in England and Wales' (Law Commission Report 331 *Intestacy and Family Provision Claims on Death*). However, the Inheritance and Trustees' Powers Act 2014 made no change to the domicile requirement.

Domicile is not the same thing as residence or nationality.

If the deceased had a foreign domicile of origin (whether or not born in England and Wales) but did not form an intention to permanently reside here, he generally remains domiciled in his country of origin, no matter how long he lived here. Conversely, if the deceased's domicile of origin was England and Wales and he or she left many years ago but with the intention of returning one day, he or she will remain domiciled here.

Domicile is therefore a potential issue in many estates. Indeed, it is easily overlooked where the deceased was domiciled in Scotland, Northern Ireland, the Isle of Man or the Channel Islands.

If domicile is in dispute, it will usually be appropriate for it to be determined as a preliminary issue. The onus is on the person disputing jurisdiction to raise it at the earliest possible stage. Failure to do so may result in an order to pay the costs relating to the issue even in the event of success on the domicile issue.

The question must be decided in accordance with the law of England and Wales. Under that law a person must have a domicile and can only have one domicile at any given time. It must be one of the following:

(a)   a domicile of origin;
(b)   a domicile of choice; or
(c)   a domicile of dependency.

An existing domicile is presumed to continue until it is proved that a new domicile has been acquired. The presumption is weakest in the case of a domicile of dependency and strongest where the domicile is one of origin.

2.4 DOMICILE OF ORIGIN

Every individual acquires a birth domicile known as a domicile of origin. In the case of a legitimate child born during his or her father's lifetime (whether or not the parents are separated), it will be the domicile of the father at the time of the child's birth. In the case of an illegitimate child or a legitimate child born after the father's death, the child's domicile will be the domicile of the mother at the time of birth.

Where a legitimate child's parents are separated but not divorced, his domicile of origin will be the domicile of his father, but his domicile of dependency will, generally, be the domicile of his mother if living with her (see below at **2.6**). It is unclear whether the domicile of a legitimate child born after the divorce of his parents will be his mother's domicile.

A domicile of origin may only be altered as a result of adoption or a parental order under the Human Fertilisation and Embryology Act 2008 (HFEA 2008), s.54. In either case, the child is treated as the legitimate child of his or her parent(s) under the order, even if the relevant order was obtained by a single person or an unmarried couple (Adoption and Children Act 2002, s.67(2); Human Fertilisation and Embryology (Parental Orders) Regulations 2010, SI 2010/985, Sched.1). Where the parents are of the opposite sex, the rules on domicile of origin described above will apply. Therefore, if an unmarried couple adopt a child, the adoptive father's domicile will determine the child's domicile of origin.

Where there are same-sex parents or civil partners then following the passing of HFEA 2008:

1. In the case of a male couple, the child will be illegitimate (as the biological father will not be married to the mother) unless the child has been adopted or there is a parental order. Therefore the domicile of the mother of the child will apply under general principles.

   If there is a parental order or adoption, the child is treated as the child of the adoptive parents. It is thought that the biological father's domicile will determine the domicile of the child, but there is no authority on the issue.

2. In the case of a female couple, the mother who bore the child is always treated as the mother (HFEA 2008, s.33) unless there is adoption or a parental order.

   A child born by artificial insemination (AID) or in vitro fertilisation (IVF) of female civil partners or spouses is treated as having no father and therefore the domicile of the birth mother will determine the child's domicile.

   Where a child is born by AID or IVF of a female same sex couple (not in civil partnership or same sex marriage) the child will be deemed to have no father if certain conditions as to consents and treatment are met, so again in such cases the birth mother's domicile will determine the position (HFEA 2008, ss.43, 44 and 45).

A domicile of origin may be supplanted by domicile of choice. However, the domicile of origin will revive if, having acquired a domicile of choice, a person loses that domicile of choice without acquiring an alternative domicile of choice.

A domicile of origin may also be displaced by a domicile of dependency. However, if a minor child, having acquired a domicile of dependency which differs from the domicile of origin, later acquires a new domicile of choice and then abandons that domicile of choice, it will be the domicile of origin and not the domicile of dependency which revives.

2.5 DOMICILE OF CHOICE

Every independent person can acquire a domicile of choice by the combination of residence and an intention of permanent or indefinite residence (Dicey, Morris and Collins, *Conflict of Laws* ('*Dicey and Morris*'), 15th edn, Sweet & Maxwell, 2016, pp.133–8). The intention must be fixed and must be for the indefinite future. It must be formed independently of external pressures.

If the deceased intended to return to his domicile of origin on the happening of a clearly foreseen and reasonably anticipated contingency (e.g. the termination of employment), the intention required to establish a domicile of choice will be absent. However, if he only had in mind to return to his domicile of origin in the event of a vague possibility (e.g. winning the lottery) or some sentiment about dying in the land of his fathers then he may have had sufficient intention to acquire a domicile of choice.

Even if the deceased has left his domicile of origin with the intention of never returning, the domicile of origin will adhere unless there is affirmative proof of an intention to reside permanently in another territory with a different legal system.

A domicile of choice can be abandoned. If someone ceases to reside in the territory of the domicile of choice and has no intention of returning to it, then his domicile of choice will be abandoned. In such circumstances, his domicile of origin will revive unless and until he acquires a new domicile of choice (*Re Flynn* [1968] 1 All ER 49). The burden of proving abandonment of a domicile of choice is said to lie upon the person asserting it and requires cogent proof (*Inland Revenue Commissioners* v. *Duchess of Portland* [1982] Ch 314; *Irvin* v. *Irvin* [2001] 1 FLR 178).

2.6 DOMICILE OF DEPENDENCY

Special rules determine the domicile of dependent persons. Dependent persons are incapable of acquiring a domicile of choice. Thus, it is possible for dependent persons to be domiciled in countries where they do not have their permanent home.

The class is now restricted to unmarried children under the age of 16 (Domicile and Matrimonial Proceedings Act 1973, s.17(5)) and to persons suffering from a relevant mental disorder (*Dicey and Morris*, rule 16). The reference to unmarried children is because certain jurisdictions permit children to marry under the age of 16 (see: Domicile and Matrimonial Proceedings Act 1973, s.3(1)).

Until the Domicile and Matrimonial Proceedings Act 1973 came into force on 1 January 1974 married women were dependent on their husbands for their domicile. A woman who was married immediately before 1 January 1974 is treated as retaining her husband's domicile as a domicile of choice (if it was not also her domicile of origin) until it is changed by acquisition or revival of another domicile.

The domicile of a legitimate child under the age of 16 is the same as, and changes with, his father's domicile (*Re Duleep Singh ex p. Cross* (1890) 6 TLR 385 (CA); *Henderson* v. *Henderson* [1967] P 77). It is thought that this rule would apply to a legitimated child from the date of his legitimation (*Dicey and Morris*, rule 15(2)).

If the dependent child is illegitimate or if the father is dead, then his domicile will generally be the same as, and will change with, his mother's domicile. However, whether or not the child's domicile will alter with that of the mother depends on whether, in any given case, she has exercised her power to change the child's domicile with her own. For example, a mother who moves to a different country and acquires a new domicile but leaves her child behind is unlikely to have exercised the power to change the child's domicile (see *Re Beaumont (Deceased)* [1893] 3 Ch 490 at 496–7). It is thought that the domicile of a child with no living parents cannot be changed (*Dicey and Morris*, 6-094).

An adopted child under the age of 16 will acquire a domicile of origin (not dependency) as if he was the child of his adopted parent or parents (Adoption and Children Act 2002, s.67(1)). An adopted child will be treated as a legitimate child, whether adopted by a single person or an unmarried couple (Adoption and Children Act 2002, s.67(2)). Likewise a child who is the subject of a parental order under HFEA 2008, s.54, is treated as the legitimate child of the person(s) who obtained the order (SI 2010/985, Sched.1). See **2.4** for children of same-sex couples.

Different rules apply if a legitimate or legitimated child aged under 16 has parents who are currently living apart, or who were living apart when that child's mother died (see Domicile and Matrimonial Proceedings Act 1973, s.4). If the child has a home with his mother and no home with his father, the child's domicile will be the same as, and change with, the domicile of his mother. The same applies if the child's last home was with his mother and he has not since had a home with his father. If at the time of death of a child's mother the above rules applied and that child has not since had a home with his father, the domicile of the child will be the domicile his mother had at the date of her death. In any other case, the domicile of the child is the same as, and changes with, the domicile of the father. Thus if, since the parents have been living apart, the child has had no home with either parent (for example, he has been living with his grandparents), his domicile will be the same as, and will change with, the domicile of his father.

A person who suffers from a mental disorder may be incapable of forming the necessary intention to acquire a domicile of choice. If he is incapable of forming such an intention, he cannot change his domicile. If a person's disorder dates from birth or from a time when he was a dependent child, his domicile will remain that of his dependency unless and until he recovers capacity. In all other cases, his domicile will remain the same as when the relevant disorder began.

On ceasing to be dependent, a person will continue to be domiciled in the country of his last domicile of dependency until acquisition of domicile of choice or revival of domicile of origin.

2.7 FACTORS ESTABLISHING DOMICILE

The claimant has the burden (on the usual civil standard of probability) of proving that the deceased died domiciled in England and Wales.

Disputes tend to turn on whether or not a domicile of origin has been displaced by a domicile of choice. The court is not prepared to infer the acquisition of a domicile of choice lightly. It requires cogent and convincing proof of the necessary intention on the part of the deceased to establish his permanent home in a different territory.

The grant of representation will usually contain a statement as to the deceased person's domicile. It will be based on the information provided in the oath sworn in support of the application for the grant. However, a statement of domicile contained in the grant of representation will not determine the issue in any proceedings under the Act (although the person swearing the oath may be expected to explain any alteration in his position).

Similarly, the fact that Her Majesty's Revenue and Customs (HMRC) may have formed a view as to a deceased person's domicile for tax purposes will not bind the court when it comes to determine the issue of domicile in proceedings under the Act (*Agulian* v. *Cyganik* (see **2.3**)).

Agulian v. *Cyganik* concerned a (Greek) Cypriot who had been in England for all his working life and died here. Nevertheless, it was held that he had not changed his domicile of origin from Cyprus to England. The Court of Appeal emphasised the adhesive nature of the domicile of origin. In contrast, *Holliday* v. *Musa* [2012] EWCA Civ 1268 concerned a (Turkish) Cypriot who spent most of his adult life in England yet maintained significant links with Cyprus. The Court of Appeal upheld the first instance decision that he had acquired a domicile of choice here.

Any circumstance that is evidence of a person's residence, or of his intention to reside permanently or indefinitely in a country, must be considered in determining whether he has acquired a domicile of choice (*Dicey and Morris*, pp.138–43). Megarry J stated in *Re Flynn* (see **2.5**) that:

> in one sense there is no end to the evidence that may be adduced; for the whole of the man's life and all that he has said and done, however trivial, may be prayed in aid in determining what his intention was at any given moment of time.

In a memorable passage in *Agulian* v. *Cyganik*, Mummery LJ stated:

> The Court must look back at the whole of the deceased's life, at what he had done with his life, at what life had done to him and at what were his inferred intentions in order to decide whether he had acquired a domicile of choice in England by the date of his death. Soren Kierkegaard's aphorism that 'life must be lived forwards, but can only be understood backwards' resonates in the biographical data of domicile disputes.

Oral or written declarations on the part of the deceased are relevant but unlikely to be conclusive. The court should not rely on those statements unless corroborated by consistent actions (Purle J in *Kebbeh* v. *Farmer* [2015] EWHC 3827 (Ch)).

The fact that residence is precarious or illegal is relevant to the question of intention (but illegal presence does not prevent residence) (*Witkowska* v. *Kaminski* [2006] EWHC 1940 (Ch)).

One can acquire a domicile of choice without naturalisation. On the other hand, citizenship is not decisive (as in *Kebbeh* v. *Farmer*).

An intention to be buried in a particular place has in some cases been treated as an important factor, but in other cases has been discounted.

In *Sylvester* v. *Sylvester* (2012) (reported at [2014] WTLR 127) arrangements for social security assistance and the NHS were regarded as significant factors.

A very real practical consideration is the impact of cost. Both *Holliday* v. *Musa* [2012] EWCA Civ 1268 and *Agulian* v. *Cyganik* involved lengthy first instance hearings respectively, and both went on to appeal on this preliminary issue.

2.8 THE BRUSSELS IV 'BERMUDA TRIANGLE'

Under the European Succession Regulation (known as 'Brussels IV'), EU Member State residents now have a single set of rules which govern jurisdiction and applicable law in succession matters. The new rules look primarily to the deceased's place of habitual residence, but an individual may elect that his succession should be governed by the law of his nationality (at the time of making the election or at death), whether or not he is a national of a Member State.

Anyone (whatever their domicile), including UK subjects, with property in a Member State is able to elect out of the forced heirship regime that would otherwise apply by specifying in their will that the law of their nationality should apply.

There is a fascinating consequence for English nationals domiciled outside England and Wales in that they should be able to elect for English succession law to apply to their (non UK, Irish, Danish) EU assets without opting into the 1975 Act. The precondition of a 1975 Act claim is domicile in England and Wales. So an English national who dies domiciled in France will not be affected by the 1975 Act even if he elects for English law to govern his succession. The same applies to the estate of a French domiciliary represented entirely by English realty, which will be governed by English succession law but will not be affected by the 1975 Act. Even if the EU court with jurisdiction over the assets disagreed with this analysis, it is hard to see it accepting that it was appropriate for it to attempt to exercise its discretion on the basis of English case law and precedents.

2.9 TAX

Consideration should be given to the fiscal implications of arguing for or against a particular domicile. For example, a finding that the deceased was domiciled in England and Wales may lead to an inheritance tax liability on property which would otherwise have been accepted by HMRC as being excluded property for inheritance tax purposes. HMRC may also investigate the deceased's lifetime tax reporting on offshore income and gains.

CHAPTER 3

Categories of applicant

3.1 INTRODUCTION

The classes of persons who may apply for provision under the Inheritance (Provision for Family and Dependants) Act 1975 are listed in s.1(1) of the Act as follows:

(a)   the spouse or civil partner of the deceased;

(b)   a former spouse or former civil partner of the deceased, but not one who has formed a subsequent marriage or civil partnership;

(ba) any person (not being a person included in paragraph (a) or (b) above) to whom subsection (1A) or (1B) below applies;

(c)   a child of the deceased;

(d)   any person (not being a child of the deceased) who, in relation to any marriage or civil partnership to which the deceased was at any time a party, or otherwise in relation to any family in which the deceased at any time stood in the role of a parent, was treated by the deceased as a child of the family;

(e)   any person (not being a person included in the foregoing paragraphs of this subsection) who immediately before the death of the deceased was being maintained, either wholly or partly, by the deceased …

Section 1(1A) applies to a person if the deceased died on or after 1 January 1996 and:

during the whole of the period of two years ending immediately before the date when the deceased died, the person was living –

(a)   in the same household as the deceased, and

(b)   as the husband or wife of the deceased.

Section (1B) of the Act applies to a person if:

for the whole of the period of two years ending immediately before the date when the deceased died the person was living –

(a)   in the same household as the deceased, and

(b)   as the civil partner of the deceased.

The court has no jurisdiction to make provision for persons who do not fall within any of these classes. In every case, it is for the applicant to prove his or her standing to make a claim.

3.2 THE SURVIVING SPOUSE OR CIVIL PARTNER OF THE DECEASED

In order to qualify, the applicant must have been a party to a marriage that is recognised by the English courts. The individuals encompassed in this class now will include those who have married under the Marriages (Same Sex Couples) Act 2013, which came into force on 13 March 2014. The term spouse therefore covers the position of a same-sex spouse as well.

Section 1(1)(a) also includes civil (same sex) partners who have entered into a civil partnership pursuant to the Civil Partnership Act 2004 ('the 2004 Act'). Under s.1(1) of the 2004 Act, a civil partnership is defined as a relationship between two people of the same sex ('civil partners') formed when they register as civil partners of each other in accordance with the 2004 Act, Parts 2, 3 or 4. Dissolution and annulment both require an order of the court (2004 Act, ss.1(3) and 37).

Both spouses and civil partners are entitled to the enhanced level of reasonable financial provision, whether or not the same is for their maintenance, s.1(2)(a)(aa). There are provisions within the 1975 Act following the introduction of civil partnerships that mirror the position for spouses.

Since the introduction of the Marriages (Same Sex Couples) Act 2013, it has become possible for civil partners to convert their civil partnership to a marriage. This has been widely taken up and it is expected that the numbers of people embarking on civil partnerships will be limited. It is confined to same sex couples: see *Steinfield & Keiden* v. *Secretary of State for Education* [2016] EWHC 128 (Admin).

3.2.1 Date for qualification

The relevant date for assessment of whether an applicant falls within one of the classes of persons listed in s.1(1)(a) of the Act is the date of the deceased's death. If there has not been a decree absolute in the case of a marriage or a final dissolution order in the case of a civil partnership, the survivor will still qualify under s.1(1)(a).

Accordingly, if the applicant was the deceased's spouse at the date of his death but has remarried since the deceased's death, the remarriage will not affect the applicant's standing to make a claim. However, clearly, the fact of the remarriage will be a matter the court will take into account when deciding if the disposition of the deceased's estate effected by his will or the law relating to intestacy has made reasonable financial provision for the applicant and also when deciding how it should exercise its discretion to make provision for the applicant.

In most cases there will be no difficulty establishing whether an applicant was the surviving spouse of the deceased. It is good practice for a surviving spouse who seeks provision under the Act to exhibit a copy of the marriage certificate with the evidence in support of the claim and, in the majority of cases that will suffice as proof of standing.

However, in a minority of cases, an issue may arise as to whether there has been a marriage at all.

3.2.2 Non-marriage

There may be doubt as to whether the ceremony of marriage which was entered into by the deceased and the applicant was sufficient to amount to a marriage recognised by the law of England and Wales (see *Ghandhi* v. *Patel* [2002] 1 FLR 603 and *Gamal* v. *Al Maktoum* [2011] EWHC 3763 (Fam)). If the ceremony takes place in England and Wales, it will only amount to a marriage recognised by the law of England and Wales if it meets the requirements of the Marriage Act 1949. In *Ghandi* the couple underwent a Hindu marriage ceremony in a restaurant in this jurisdiction. The marriage did not comply with the formal requirements of the English Law. It fell into the category of a non-marriage, an event which may have marital qualities but which does not achieve the status of either a void or voidable marriage. The categorisation is vital, as if there was only a non-marriage then the claimant cannot have been a spouse under s.1(1)(a) and so would be unable to apply for reasonable financial provision unless he or she falls within one of the other categories of applicant in s.1.

Under the private international law of England and Wales, a marriage which takes place outside the jurisdiction will be recognised as a marriage so long as the ceremony met the formal requirements of a marriage under the law of the territory where it took place. If those formal requirements were met, the surviving spouse will fall within s.1(1)(a). If the validity of a foreign marriage is put in issue, the court is likely to require expert evidence from a suitably qualified lawyer in the relevant jurisdiction before being satisfied that a marriage took place. For more detailed guidance see *Dicey & Morris*, Chapter 17.

If neither the English or foreign marriage is entitled to recognition because it is a non-marriage then the surviving spouse is not able to bring proceedings under s.1(1)(a).

3.2.3 Void marriage

Section 25(4) of the Act provides as follows:

> For the purposes of this Act any reference to a spouse, wife or husband shall be treated as including a reference to a person who in good faith entered into a void marriage with the deceased unless either –
>
> (a) the marriage of the deceased and that person was dissolved or annulled during the lifetime of the deceased and the dissolution or annulment is recognised by the law of England and Wales, or
>
> (b) that person has during the lifetime of the deceased formed a subsequent marriage or civil partnership.

Section 25(4A) contains mirror provisions for civil partners, and provides that any reference to a civil partner shall include a person who, in good faith, entered into a void civil partnership with the deceased unless either the civil partnership between the deceased and that person was dissolved or annulled during the lifetime of the deceased in a manner recognised by the law of England and Wales or that person has, during the lifetime of the deceased, formed a subsequent civil partnership or marriage.

The concept of a 'void marriage' is recognised both by statute and by judicial authority as being something different from a non-marriage (see Marriage Act 1949, s.2; Matrimonial Causes Act 1973 (MCA 1973), s.11; *A-M* v. *A-M* [2001] 2 FLR 6; *Hudson* v. *Leigh* [2009] EWHC 1306 (Fam), approved by the Court of Appeal in *Sharbatly* v. *Shagroon* [2012] EWCA Civ 1407).

Section 11 of the MCA 1973 sets out the only grounds for a marriage being void as follows:

1. A marriage which is invalid under any of the provisions of the Marriage Acts 1949–86 (i.e. where the parties are within the prohibited degrees of relationship; where either party is under the age of 16 or the parties have intermarried in disregard of certain requirements as to the formation of marriage).
2. A marriage which takes place at a time when either party to it was already married or a civil partner.
3. A marriage entered into in a jurisdiction where polygamous marriage is permitted at a time where one or other of the parties is already married and where either party is domiciled in England and Wales. (But if neither of the parties to such a marriage is married, the fact that the marriage is potentially to be polygamous in the future and either of the parties to it is domiciled in England and Wales will not prevent it from being a valid marriage under the law of England and Wales.)

For the purposes of s.25(4) of the 1975 Act, an applicant will have entered into a void marriage in good faith if the applicant honestly believed that he or she was entering into a valid marriage at the time of entering into it (see *Gandhi* v. *Patel* (see **3.2.2**) at 629). In that case the court had to determine whether the applicant had an honest belief in the validity of the marriage. It was held that the applicant knew that the deceased was already married and therefore even if there had been reasons to find a void marriage, as opposed to a non-marriage, the applicant would not have entered the same in good faith, and therefore could not apply.

3.2.4 Polygamous marriages

All marriages that take place in England and Wales must be monogamous, and therefore polygamous marriages that take place in this jurisdiction are not valid. Further as set out at **3.2.3**, under MCA 1973, s.11 a polygamous marriage entered into abroad is void if either party was at the time domiciled in England and Wales. The rider to this is that, if at the point in time of the marriage there are no additional spouses, then that marriage can be recognised; as a consequence of which the first spouse could bring a claim under s.1(1)(a).

In the case of *Re Sehota* [1978] 1 WLR 1506, the parties had been married in India, and the marriage was recognised under Indian law. The deceased took a second wife and left her all his estate. After the marriage he had acquired a domicile of choice in England and Wales and, therefore, the English court had jurisdiction under the Act. The first wife was held to be entitled to apply as the wife (as one of two wives) of the deceased under s.1(1)(a).

In the *Official Solicitor* v. *Yemoh* [2010] EWHC 3727 (Ch), the issue was whether the several surviving spouses (married under the customary law of Ghana) qualified as widows of the deceased under the Administration of Estates Act 1925, s.46(1). They had been married in accordance with the law of the deceased's domicile. The deceased died intestate owning real property in this country. It was held that they did qualify as spouses and were entitled to share the statutory legacy.

3.2.5 Decree absolute

An applicant will qualify as a surviving spouse notwithstanding the fact that divorce or dissolution proceedings between the applicant and the deceased had commenced prior to the deceased's death, unless a decree absolute had actually been made prior to the death.

If no decree absolute or final dissolution order was made prior to the deceased's death, any ancillary relief order made prior to his death will have no direct effect (see *McMinn* v. *McMinn* [2003] 1 FLR 823). However, the terms of the order may be very relevant to the outcome of the 1975 Act claim. It may be possible for the terms of a consent order to be enforced as a contract against the deceased's estate, and this question should be considered before a claim is made under the Act.

If a party dies during the currency of financial remedy proceedings under MCA 1973, the suit abates and the survivor would have to bring proceedings under the 1975 Act: see the review of the case law in *Harb* v. *King Fahd Bin Abdul Aziz* [2005] EWCA Civ 1324.

If a decree of judicial separation was in force at the time of the deceased's death, then, subject to s.14 of the Act, the standard of reasonable financial provision made for the applicant will be the less generous standard which is available to applicants other than spouses (see s.1(2)(a) of the Act).

3.2.6 Section 14 discretion

Section 14(1) of the Act provides:

(1)   Where, within twelve months from the date on which a decree of divorce or nullity of marriage has been made absolute or a decree of judicial separation has been granted, a party to a marriage dies and –

(a)   an application for a financial provision order under section 23 of the Matrimonial Causes Act 1973 or a property adjustment order under section 24 of that Act has not been made by the other party to that marriage, or

(b)   such an application has been made but the proceedings thereon have not been determined at the time of death of the deceased, then, if an application for an order under section 2 of this Act is made by that other party, the court shall, notwithstanding anything in section 1 or section 3 of this Act, have power, if it thinks it just to do so, to treat that party for the purposes of that application as if the decree of divorce or nullity of marriage had not been made absolute or the decree of judicial separation had not been granted, as the case may be.

Similar provision is made for this period of grace for the former civil partner under s.14A of the Act. Section 14A gives the court a power to treat a person as a surviving civil partner of the deceased in circumstances where the deceased has died within 12 months of the making of a dissolution order, a nullity order, a separation order or a presumption of death order under Part 2, Chapter 2 of the 2004 Act in relation to their civil partnership, but their financial affairs had not been determined under the 2004 Act, Sched.5, Parts 1 or 2 prior to the deceased's death.

Thus, in cases where the financial affairs of the parties to the divorce or dissolution proceedings have not been determined in ancillary relief proceedings prior to the deceased's death, the court has a discretion, even after a decree absolute has been made, to treat the applicant as if he or she remained a spouse of the deceased for the purposes of the Act. Where there are divorce proceedings and one spouse has a valuable pension, it is sensible to delay the decree absolute pending the determination of the financial remedy proceedings.

3.3   FORMER SPOUSES AND FORMER CIVIL PARTNERS

A former spouse or civil partner of the deceased can make a claim for provision out of the estate of the deceased provided that, at the date of the deceased's death, he or she had not formed a subsequent marriage or civil partnership (1975 Act, s.1(1)(b)).

Section 25(1) of the Act defines 'former spouse' as a person whose marriage with the deceased was, during the lifetime of the deceased, either dissolved or annulled by decree of divorce granted under the law of the British Islands or dissolved or annulled under the law of any overseas territory which is recognised by the law of England and Wales. The same subsection defines 'former civil partner' as a person whose civil partnership with the deceased was, during the lifetime of the deceased, dissolved or annulled by an order made under the law of any part of the British Islands or in any overseas territory by a dissolution or annulment recognised by the law of England and Wales.

A former spouse or civil partner cannot make a claim if he or she has entered into a subsequent marriage or civil partnership by the time of the deceased's death. Section 25(5) of the Act makes clear that, for the purposes of s.1(1)(b), a subsequent marriage or civil partnership includes the formation of a marriage or civil partnership (as the case may be) which is either void or voidable. The distinction between a non-marriage and a void marriage has already been pointed out above. Sections 11 and 12 of the MCA 1973 set out the circumstances in which marriages celebrated after 31 July 1971 are void or voidable respectively. For the circumstances in which a civil partnership formed in England and Wales will be void, see s.49 of the 2004 Act.

In practice, in most cases, whether or not a particular person is a surviving former spouse or a former civil partner of the deceased within the meaning of s.1(1)(b) of the 1975 Act will be abundantly clear. However, in many cases, those persons will be unable to make a claim as a result of the family court having made an order during the deceased's lifetime under one or other of ss.15, 15ZA, 15A and 15B of the Act at the time the financial affairs of the parties to the marriage or civil partnership (as the case may be) were determined. If after the making of an order under s.15 there has been a resumption of cohabitation, the survivor of such a relationship may be able to apply under s.1(1)(ba): *Chekov* v. *Fryer* [2015] EWHC 1642 (Ch).

As mentioned above, in cases where the marriage has been determined in the 12 months leading up to the deceased's death without the financial affairs of the parties having been resolved, the court is able to treat the former spouse or civil partner as if he or she were a surviving spouse or civil partner (as the case may be) under one or other of ss.14 and 14A of the Act, thereby enabling the former spouse or civil partner to seek the more generous level of provision available to spouses or civil partners under the Act.

3.4 COHABITEES

If the deceased died on or after 1 January 1996, then a person who, during the whole of the period of two years ending immediately before the date when the deceased died, was living in the same household as the deceased as the husband or wife of the deceased, may make a claim under s.1(1)(ba) and s.1(1A).

In cases where the deceased died after 5 December 2005, a claim may also be made by a person who, during the whole of the period of two years ending immediately before the date when the deceased died, was living in the same household as the deceased as his or her civil partner in a same-sex relationship (1975 Act, s.1(1B)).

3.4.1 '... during the whole of the period of two years ending immediately before the death of the deceased ...'

In order to make a claim under s.1(1A) or (1B) of the Act, the applicant must have cohabited with the deceased for the whole of the period of two years ending immediately before the deceased's death. It is not necessary for the claimant to establish that his or her cohabitation with the deceased was lawful in this jurisdiction (see *Witkowska* v. *Kaminski* [2006] EWHC 1940 (Ch) at paras.44–51).

It is clear that absences of either of the parties resulting from hospital admissions or periods of respite care during the last two years of the deceased's life would not prevent this requirement being met (see *Re Watson* [1999] 1 FLR 878 at 882).

Moreover, if there is a temporary interruption in the cohabitation for other reasons during the two-year period leading up to the deceased's death, the applicant may still be able make a claim under the Act. In *Gully* v. *Dix* [2004] EWCA Civ 139 the Court of Appeal held that, when considering whether the requirement for two years' cohabitation has been met, the court is not obliged to confine itself to looking only at the two-year period leading up to the deceased's death but should also consider the preceding period to see what the established relationship between the parties was. If that relationship ended before or during the two-year period, then the test will not be satisfied. However, if the relationship was merely temporarily suspended, perhaps for a period of reflection about the future of a relationship going through a difficult time, then the applicant can satisfy the test. If there is clear evidence of the continuity of the relationship, even if there is some interruption in the cohabitation the claimant may still qualify; see the case of *Kaur* v. *Dhaliwal* [2014] EWHC 1991 (Ch).

However if the cohabitation is in its infancy and one party retains a further property, it will be necessary to demonstrate a full two years of living in the same household. In the case of *Kotke* v. *Saffrini* [2005] EWCA Civ 221, under the Fatal Accidents Act 1976, the survivor could not establish the requisite two years.

The retention of a requirement for a two-year cohabitation as a necessary qualification prior to securing a remedy under the Fatal Accidents Act 1976, s.1(3)(b) has been held not to be a breach of either Article 14 or 8 of the European Convention on Human Rights (ECHR): see *Swift* v. *Secretary of State for Justice* [2013] EWCA Civ 193. Therefore if the applicant falls short of the two-year cohabitation qualification under the 1975 Act, it will not be possible for him to challenge the requirement on the basis of a breach of ECHR.

3.4.2 '… living in the same household as the deceased …'

For the applicant to fall within s.1(1A) or (1B) of the 1975 Act, the applicant and the deceased must have been sharing the same 'household' during the relevant period. However, it involves both a physical connotation of a particular house (or houses – it is possible to have one household and two properties: see *Churchill* v. *Roach* [2002] EWHC 3230 (Ch)) as well as more abstract connotations of personal association. Living in the same household connotes more than physical presence satisfied by living under the same roof; it involves an evaluation of the parties' commitment to the relationship.

It is possible for two persons to be 'living in the same household' even if they are temporarily separated, provided that they are still held together by a particular tie (*Santos* v. *Santos* [1972] Fam 247 at 262–3; *Gully* v. *Dix* (see **3.4.1**)).

In *Churchill*, HHJ Norris QC pointed out that 'it is, of course, dangerous to try to define what "living in the same household" means'; however, he identified that cohabitation in the same household is likely to involve elements of permanence, frequency and intimacy of contact, mutual support, voluntary restraint upon personal freedom and community of resources.

3.4.3 '... living ... as the husband or wife of the deceased'

To qualify under s.1(1A) of the Act, the applicant must have been living with the deceased as his or her husband or wife. Although s.1(1A) treats this as a separate requirement from the requirement that the applicant have shared a household with the deceased, it was pointed out in *Re Watson* [1999] 1 FLR 878 (at 883) that it is very unlikely that a person could have lived with the deceased as his or her husband or wife without sharing the same household as the deceased and the two requirements will merge to a certain degree.

In the same case, Neuberger J cautioned against indulging in 'too much over-analysis' of this requirement. He held that the court should ask itself whether, in the opinion of a reasonable person with normal perceptions, it could be said that the two people in question were living together as husband and wife.

Similar wording contained in the Fatal Accidents Act 1976, s.1(3) was considered by the Court of Appeal in *Kotke* (see **3.4.1**). In that case the Court of Appeal held that the following are 'signposts' which tend to indicate that two persons are living together in the same household as husband and wife: whether the parties live under the same roof, illness, holidays and work and other periodical absences apart; whether there is stability; whether there is financial support; whether there is a sexual relationship.

However, the absence of any one of those signposts (other than, possibly, the first) is unlikely to be conclusive in any particular case. As Neuberger J pointed out in *Re Watson*, the court cannot ignore 'the multifarious nature of marital relationships'. In that case, the absence of a sexual relationship between the claimant and the deceased did not prevent the claimant from qualifying under s.1(1A) of the Act in circumstances where the claimant and the deceased had had a relationship for over 30 years, had lived alone together for the last 10 years, were closer to each other than any other person, made joint contributions to the household outgoings on an informal basis and where there were particular incidents at the commencement and end of the cohabitation which demonstrated the concern and affection which the deceased felt towards the claimant.

Similar phraseology is found in the Housing Act 1988, s.17(4), where if the claimant had lived as if the spouse of the deceased they may succeed to the assured tenancy. There was a comprehensive review of the case law relating to the concept of living together as husband and wife, in *Amicus Horizon* v. *Mabbott* [2012] EWCA Civ 895. In order to satisfy the description certain features will need to be established:

- The hallmarks of the relationship were essentially that there should be a degree of mutual interdependence, of the sharing of lives, of caring and love of commitment and support: *Fitzpatrick* v. *Sterling Housing Association Ltd* [2001] 1 AC 27, Lord Slynn.
- In *Nutting* v. *Southern Housing Group* [2004] EWHC 2982 (Ch) (a Housing Act case), Evans Lombe J adopted the recorder's approach which included answering the following questions:

(a) Have the parties set up home together?

(b) Is the relationship an emotional one of mutual lifetime commitment rather than simply one of convenience, friendship, companionship or the living together of lovers?

(c) Is the relationship one which has been presented to the outside world openly and unequivocally so that society considers it to be of permanent intent?

(d) Do the parties have a common life together, both domestically (in relation to the household) and externally (in relation to family and friends)?

Ward LJ in *Amicus* found the above indicia helpful, but having regard to the complexity of human relationships, the criteria may have to vary depending upon the facts. In the *Amicus* case both partners continued to claim independent state benefits, and there was evidence of the deceased's intention to retain her independence. The Court of Appeal agreed that the claimant had failed to demonstrate that the relationship was one of mutual lifetime commitment and was unequivocally displayed to the outside world.

It is clear that not every relationship where the parties live under the same roof for the majority of their time will equate to living together as husband and wife. It is more difficult to determine which set of facts will lead to a failure to fulfil the relevant criteria.

3.4.4 Same-sex cohabitees

It appears that s.1(1A) of the Act could be capable of applying to same-sex cohabitees (see *Saunders* v. *Garrett* [2005] WTLR 749). It has been held that Article 8 of the ECHR – the right to private and family life and home – is capable of being engaged by that subsection and, thus, that Article 14 of the Convention – which calls for an absence of discrimination in the exercise of Convention rights – may also be engaged. In circumstances where those rights are engaged, s.3 of the Human Rights Act 1998 requires the court to interpret s.1(1A) of the Act in a manner which complies with the Convention in so far as is possible (see *Ghaidan* v. *Godin-Mendoza* [2004] UKHL 30) and this would result in a construction which brings single sex cohabitees within the ambit of the subsection.

However, since the introduction of the Civil Partnership Act 2004, same-sex cohabitees who fell within the ambit of s.1(1A) of the 1975 Act are likely to apply under s.1(1B) of the Act instead. Section 1(1B) is concerned with applicants who were living with the deceased during the relevant two-year period and *who were living as if they were civil partners* during that period.

3.4.5 '… living … as the civil partner of the deceased'

Section 1(1B) of the Act requires the applicant to have been living as the civil partner of the deceased during the specified period.

However, in order to qualify as an applicant under s.1(1B) of the 1975 Act, the applicant must not only have been living as the deceased's civil partner, but must also have been *sharing the same household* as the deceased for a two-year period. As explained above, the authorities on s.1(1A) of the Act indicate that a shared household connotes an element of mutual support, of permanence, of frequency and intimacy of contact, of voluntary restraint upon personal freedom and of community of resources.

The indicia discussed above relating to living together as husband and wife involve clear open acknowledgment and public commitment to the relationship. This raises a difficult issue in respect of some same-sex relationships. It might be argued that by reason of society's attitude to same-sex relationships, the parties involved may have elected to treat the nature of their relationship with discretion.

In *Baynes* v. *Hedger* [2008] EWCA 1587 (Ch), an elderly female couple were in a relationship but had not lived in one household for many years and their respective declining health meant they were each only visitors in the other's house. Lewison J also concluded that the true nature of the relationship had not been disclosed or acknowledged to the outside world.

In *Ghaidan* v. *Godin-Mendoza*, Baroness Hale placed less emphasis on the necessity for open acknowledgment, when reviewing the central criteria stating as follows:

> Holding themselves out as married is one of those [a relevant factor], and if a heterosexual couple do so, it is likely that they will be held to be living together as such. But it is not a pre-requisite in the other private and public law contexts and I see no reason why it should be in this one. What matters most is the essential quality of the relationship, its marriage like intimacy, stability, and social and financial inter-dependence.

It may be possible to argue that if a party has elected to keep the nature of their same-sex relationship private for fear of discrimination, then the stated requirement for open acknowledgment should be relaxed. When examining the quality of the relationship it would still be necessary to be able to demonstrate long-term commitment, some romantic element, mutual support and financial inter-dependence.

3.5 CHILDREN

A child of the deceased is able to make a claim for provision from the deceased's estate. Section 25(1) of the 1975 Act defines a child as including an illegitimate child and a child *en ventre sa mere* at the date of the deceased's death.

There may be an initial question as to whether the applicant is a child of the deceased. The preferred course of the courts is to rely where possible upon scientific evidence as opposed to presumptions that developed before the availability of scientific testing. The established presumptions are:

- legitimacy;

- the registration of the birth documents; and
- a finding in other proceedings.

Pursuant to s.55A of the Family Law Act 1986, the court is able to make a declaration of parentage. There is a statutory regime developed under the Family Law Reform Act 1969, s.20 onwards, which provides for directions as to the use of scientific tests in respect of living subjects only. In *Spencer* v. *Anderson* [2016] EWHC 851 (Fam), it was held that the court had inherent jurisdiction to order the testing of pre-existing DNA samples of the deceased.

In the light of the rapid advances in relation to reproduction there can be complex issues arising as to parentage. The starting point has been that the child's parents are those that have provided the genetic material. For a detailed analysis of the situation under the HFEA 2008, see *Halsbury's Laws of England*, Volume 9 (para 92 onwards).

The child does not have to be a minor to apply, and their marital status does not affect their qualification. As to the approach in respect of an adult child's claim see the case of *Ilott* v. *Mitson* [2017] UKSC 17.

3.5.1 Adoption

An adopted child may only claim in respect of the estates of his adopted parents and not his natural parents (see Adoption Act 1976, s.39(2) and *Re Collins* [1990] Fam 56). Therefore if the child's birth parent dies after the date of the adoption their natural child will not be able to claim under s.1(1)(c).

There was a problem for the adopted minor child if their parent had died prior to their adoption and the children had inherited property, but the same was held on the statutory trusts and so contingent on their attaining 18. This has been addressed by the Inheritance and Trustees' Powers Act 2014, providing for the insertion of a new class under s.69(4) of the Adoption and Children Act 2002, in order to allow the child to retain the same.

3.6 PERSONS WHO IN THE CASE OF ANY MARRIAGE OR CIVIL PARTNERSHIP OF THE DECEASED WERE TREATED AS A CHILD OF THE FAMILY

This section deals with the position where the death occurs prior to 1 October 2014 and before the amendments under the Inheritance and Trustees' Powers Act 2014, came into force. For the position relating to deaths post 1 October 2014, see **3.8**.

Prior to the amendments, in order for the applicant to fall within s.1(1)(d) of the Act, the applicant must show that he was treated by the deceased as a child of the family in relation to a marriage or civil partnership between the deceased and another person. It follows that if the deceased has never been married or formed a civil partnership, the subsection cannot apply.

Again, it is important to note that adult applicants can fall within the ambit of s.1(1)(d) as well as minors.

3.6.1 Treated as a child of the family

Whether the applicant was treated as a child of the family in relation to a particular marriage or civil partnership of the deceased may not be easy to ascertain. The phrases 'child of the family' and 'treated ... as the child of the family' are not defined in the Act. Child of the family is a phrase adopted from the matrimonial sphere. Section 52 of the MCA 1973 defines a child of the family as follows (emphasis added):

> (b)   *any other child*, not being a child who is placed with those parties as foster parents by a local authority or voluntary organisation, *who has been treated by both of those parties as a child of their family*.

While applicants under s.1(1)(d) are often stepchildren of the deceased, any individual who had been treated as a child in relation to the marriage comprising the family unit can apply under s.1(1)(d). In *Re B (Child of the Family)* [1998] 1 FLR 347, a case under MCA 1973, a grandchild who had been brought up by his grandparents was held to fall within the definition.

The Act clearly contemplates applications under s.1(1)(d) by persons who were not maintained by the deceased (1975 Act, s.3(3) and *Re Leach (Deceased)* [1986] Ch 226 at 231).

To fall within the section, the treatment of the applicant 'as the child of the family' can have taken place at any time during the applicant's life and is not confined to his minority; see *Re Callaghan* [1985] FLR 116 at 120, approved in *Re Leach (Deceased)* at 236).

There must be or have been a substantial relationship between the deceased and the applicant. It should go beyond the cordial relationship that any step-parent could reasonably be expected to show a step-child (*Re Leach (Deceased)* at 235).

In *Roberts* v. *Fresco* [2017] EWHC 283 (Ch), the first claimant's stepmother died shortly after her father. The first claimant made a claim for provision from the estate of her late father, seeking an order under s.2(1)(f) varying what was alleged to have been a nuptial settlement of a property 'for the benefit of ...any person who was treated by the deceased as a child of the family in relation to that marriage'. The court found that there was a real prospect of the first claimant establishing that she was treated by her deceased father as a child of the family in relation to his second marriage as it was conceptually possible for the deceased to have treated her as his daughter in relation to both of his marriages. Whether or not this was a correct construction of s.3(1)(d) was not determined at trial as the case settled.

3.6.2 The treatment

The central question in any case is whether the deceased has, as wife or husband or civil partner under the relevant marriage or civil partnership, expressly or impliedly assumed the position of a parent towards the claimant, with the attendant responsibilities and privileges of that relationship (*Re Leach (Deceased)* at 237). Factors such as whether the applicant lived with the deceased as a minor child, whether the deceased made payments on behalf of the applicant when he or she was a minor child, whether the deceased exercised discipline over the applicant as a minor child, whether the deceased assumed the role of grandparent to an adult applicant's children, whether the deceased reposed confidence in the applicant as to his property and affairs, whether there was any dependency by the deceased upon the applicant for care during the deceased's later years, whether the deceased showed financial generosity towards the applicant and whether the deceased indicated an intention to confer testamentary benefit on the claimant are all of potential relevance (*Re Callaghan* at 121; *Re Leach (Deceased)* at 239).

3.7 PERSONS WHO IN RELATION TO ANY FAMILY IN WHICH THE DECEASED STOOD IN THE ROLE OF A PARENT

The Law Commission Report of 2011, *Intestacy and Family Provision* (Law Commission Report 331) concluded that the requirement of marriage or civil partnership before a child could be treated as a child of the family wrongly excluded claims by those who were treated as a child of the deceased alone or in the context of a cohabitation. Section 1(1)(d) has been amended by the Inheritance and Trustees' Powers Act 2014 so that where the relevant death is *after* 1 October 2014, a child of the family is:

> any person (not being a child of the deceased) who in relation to any marriage or civil partnership to which the deceased was at any time a party, or otherwise in relation to any family in which the deceased at any time stood in the role of a parent, was treated by the deceased as a child of the family.

It is expressly envisaged that the family may constitute only the deceased and the applicant. The previous case law as to the quality of the relationship *(Re Callaghan* at 121; *Re Leach (Deceased)* at 239) will be relevant in concluding whether the relationship was of sufficient substantive quality to qualify under the extended class. It will encompass situations where the parties were both adult at the time of the deceased standing in the role of a parent. It is important to remember that the applicant himself will be expected to have discharged some of the burdens of being a child. This may be illustrated by the provision of care for an extended period of time as 'the parent' declines in health. The Law Commission concluded that there may need to be litigation to establish the boundaries of this new class of applicant.

3.8 DEPENDANTS

Section 1(1)(e) of the 1975 Act permits any person (not being a person included in any of the other paragraphs of s.1(1)) who immediately before the death of the deceased was being maintained, either wholly or partly, by the deceased to make a claim under the Act.

Section 1(3) provides that, for the purpose of s.1(1)(e), a person shall be treated as having been maintained by the deceased either wholly or partly, as the case may be, if the deceased, otherwise than for valuable consideration, was making a substantial contribution in money or money's worth towards the reasonable needs of that person.

3.8.1 Death pre October 2014

Where an application is made under s.1(1)(e) and the death occurred prior to 1 October 2014, the court is directed to take into account the following under s.3(4) of the Act:

> the extent to which and the basis upon which the deceased assumed responsibility for the maintenance of the applicant, and to the length of time for which the deceased discharged that responsibility.

The courts construed this section as imposing a separate requirement so that, to fall within s.1(1)(e) the applicant had to show that the deceased had assumed responsibility for his maintenance: see *Jelley* v. *Iliffe* [1981] Fam 128. The court gave a wide construction to ss.1(1)(e) and 3(4) of the Act to avoid excluding otherwise meritorious applicants on the ground that they could not show the deceased had assumed responsibility for their maintenance. For example, in *Re B* [2000] Ch 662, the court held that a patient of the Court of Protection, who was mentally incapable of assuming responsibility for another person's maintenance, could nonetheless assume responsibility for that person's maintenance provided that person had indirectly benefited through payments made from the patient's estate with the authority of the Court of Protection.

In addition the applicant had to demonstrate that the provision being made by the deceased for them outweighed any contribution that they themselves were making. This 'balance sheet test' as applied in *Jelley* and other cases did not recognise the practical effect of mutual dependency situations.

3.8.2 Deaths post 1 October 2014

There have been two substantial amendments pursuant to the Law Commission *Intestacy and Family Provision Claims on Death* (Law Commission Report 331) recommendations, introduced by the Inheritance and Trustees' Powers Act 2014. The first amendment removes the requirement to demonstrate any assumption of responsibility as a pre-requisite to qualification. Therefore all the applicant now has to prove is the fact of maintenance, in order to establish eligibility to apply under s.1(1)(e). The question of whether the deceased assumed responsibility for the applicant's maintenance becomes a relevant consideration at the point at which the merits of the substantive claim fall to be considered.

The second area of reform relates to the balance sheet test, and removes the need to demonstrate that the deceased contributed more than the applicant did. The amended s.1(3) expands the description of dependent applicants as follows:

> For the purposes of subsection (1)(e) above, a person is to be treated as being maintained by the deceased (either wholly or partly, as the case may be) only if the deceased was making a substantial contribution in money or money's worth towards the reasonable needs of that person, other than a contribution made for full valuable consideration pursuant to an arrangement of a commercial nature.

Thus, as amended, where there has been a commercial arrangement between the applicant and the deceased (e.g. where a lodger was paying a full market rent), the applicant will not qualify. However, where there is an element of bounty, for example where the deceased accepted a below market rent from the applicant, the applicant may still qualify (see *Rees* v. *Newbury* [1998] 1 FLR 1041). A further example of a commercial arrangement which would prohibit qualification is the position of a carer who was paid to stay at the deceased's property.

3.8.3 '... immediately before the death of the deceased ...'

When deciding whether the applicant was being maintained immediately before the deceased's death, the court will not confine itself to considering the state of affairs in the instant before death. The court will consider whether, at the moment before death, there was a settled basis or arrangement of maintenance which subsisted at the date of the deceased's death, rather than focus on any particular fluctuation in the arrangement in the instant before death (*Re Beaumont (Deceased)* [1980] 1 Ch 444 at 451–2; *Jelley* v. *Iliffe* (see **3.8.1**) at 136, 141). The court will construe the term 'immediately' in a wide and purposive manner in circumstances where the deceased's normal pattern of provision was interrupted by ill-health.

3.8.4 '... was being maintained either wholly or partly by the deceased'

In order for an applicant to be regarded as having been maintained by the deceased, the deceased must have been making a substantial contribution (i.e. one that is evidently more than *de minimis*) in money or money's worth towards the reasonable needs of that person.

The court will consider the standard of living of the applicant in the relevant period prior to the deceased's death and ask itself whether the deceased was making a substantial contribution to the cost of meeting that standard of living.

There is no statutory definition of reasonable needs. The financial needs of the applicant are to be considered under s.3(1)(a) when evaluating the merits of the claim rather than eligibility. In *Negus* v. *Bahouse* [2008] EWCA Civ 1002, the Court of Appeal confirmed that the concept of financial needs for the maintenance class of applicant was flexible. The court's considerations will encompass the lifestyle of the particular claimant. While in that case the claimant qualified under s.1(1A), if the lifestyle of the applicant has been contributed to by the deceased then the standard of living may be relevant at the point of establishing standing for an applicant making a claim under s.1(1)(e). It will clearly be relevant in quantifying the level of reasonable financial provision.

Where needs are being considered in order to establish qualification one is looking at the reasonable needs of the party during the currency of the deceased's life and the deceased's contribution to the same. The deceased may have been contributing to any of the following expenditure:

(a)   provision for housing and/or the cost of running the same;
(b)   ability to defray house-keeping expenses;
(c)   provision for clothing;
(d)   provision for medical expenses; or
(e)   discretionary spending on items of entertainment, holidays, the level of which may depend upon an established standard of living.

The concept of reasonable needs will bear a close resemblance to the concept of maintenance. In *Ilott* v. *Mitson* [2017] UKSC 17, Lord Hughes expressly adopted the definition expounded in *Re Dennis* [1981] 2 AER 140 at 145 which was concentrated on the sums required to defray the cost of daily living.

Gifts of jewellery, without more by way of support for the necessities of life may not amount to a contribution to reasonable needs. For a restrictive interpretation of reasonable needs see the case of *McIntosh* v. *McIntosh* [2013] WTLR 1565, where the judge concluded that a modest contribution towards cigarettes, alcohol and petrol did not satisfy the test of needs within s.1(3). The issue of whether an application falls within s.1(1)(e) is likely to be very fact sensitive and a less parsimonious interpretation may be applied by a different tribunal.

CHAPTER 4

The general approach to claims

4.1 INTRODUCTION

For the practitioner one of the hardest tasks in advising clients as to the likely outcome of a claim under the Inheritance (Provision for Family and Dependants) Act 1975 is the uncertainty as to the award the court might make. That is the reason why so many of these cases do not go to trial and are resolved by some method of alternative dispute resolution (as to which see **Chapter 10**).

However, there is some guidance as to the approach the court ought to take in deciding whether a will or intestacy makes reasonable financial provision for the applicant and if not, what that provision ought to be, which at least ought to prevent a wrong turn being taken. The speech of Lord Hughes in the Supreme Court in *Ilott* v. *Mitson* [2017] UKSC 17 provides some broad guidelines, some of which perhaps move away from what has been the accepted orthodoxy.

4.2 THE TWO-STAGE APPROACH

The traditional way in which courts have approached claims under the 1975 Act is that once an applicant has demonstrated that they have standing to bring a claim (as to which see **Chapter 3**), the court conducts a two-stage process: first, the court asks whether the way in which the estate is disposed of under the will, or the intestacy rules, fails to make reasonable financial provision for the applicant ('the Threshold question'); secondly, if reasonable financial provision has not been made, whether any, and if so what, provision should be made for the applicant ('the Provision question') see: Oliver J in *Re Coventry* [1980] Ch 461 at 469. As Oliver J pointed out, this is required by the opening wording of s.3 the Act itself which reads:

> the court shall, in determining whether the disposition of the deceased's estate effected by his will or the law relating to intestacy, or the combination of his will and that law, is such as to make reasonable financial provision for the applicant and, if the court considers that reasonable financial provision has not been made, in determining whether and in what manner it shall exercise its powers under that section, have regard to the following matters.

In *Ilott* v. *Mitson*, on its first trip to the Court of Appeal, on the Threshold question the Court of Appeal said that the first question was a value judgment on the part of the court whereas the second was more akin to the exercise of discretion.

The failure by a judge to consider the two-stage test (pointed out to him by counsel while the judgment was in draft) led him to a conclusion which he then revised before handing down the judgment (see *Robinson* v. *Bird* [2003] EWCA Civ 1820). That case provides an example where the two-stage approach being overlooked resulted in error.

However, the two-stage approach received a rather less enthusiastic response from the Supreme Court in *Ilott* v. *Mitson*. That case was unusual in that the Threshold question had, during its tortuous appellate history, become detached from the Provision question which was the only issue before the Supreme Court (the Court of Appeal in 2011 having finally determined the Threshold question in Mrs Ilott's favour). Lord Hughes at para.23 cautioned against too rigid an adherence to the two-stage approach:

> It has become conventional to treat the consideration of a claim under the 1975 Act as a two-stage process, viz (1) has there been a failure to make reasonable financial provision and if so (2) what order ought to be made? That approach is founded to an extent on the terms of the Act, for it addresses the two questions successively in, first, section 1(1) and 1(2) and, second, section 2. In *In re Coventry* [1980] Ch 461, 487 Goff LJ referred to these as distinct questions, and indeed described the first as one of value judgment and the second as one of discretion. However, there is in most cases a very large degree of overlap between the two stages. Although section 2 does not in terms enjoin the court, if it has determined that the will or intestacy does not make reasonable financial provision for the claimant, to tailor its order to what is in all the circumstances reasonable, this is clearly the objective.

The section 3 factors (as to which see below) are enjoined at each stage of the process and so it is logical that the court is going to form a view as to the significance of each of those factors in a manner which overlaps. It is a mistake (not infrequently made) to assume that if a consideration of the section 3 factors leads to the conclusion that the will or intestacy does not make reasonable financial provision for the applicant, it is a mere matter of calculating what the applicant requires for his maintenance in order to answer the Provision question. That is clearly not the right approach. The section 3 factors, as Lord Hughes recognised, have to be taken into account at both stages and there may be significant factors which weigh against an applicant's needs being fulfilled.

It is also important that the court answers the right question at the Threshold stage. The question is not whether the testator has acted reasonably. As Lord Hughes put it in *Ilott* v. *Mitson* at para.17:

> there may not always be a significant difference in outcome between applying the correct test contained in the Act, and asking the wrong question whether the deceased acted reasonably. If the will does not make reasonable financial provision for the claimant, it may often be because the deceased acted unreasonably in failing to make it. For this

reason it is very easy to slip into the error of applying the wrong test. It is necessary for courts to be alert to the danger, because the two tests will by no means invariably arrive at the same answer.

He went on to set out examples of where a testator may have acted entirely reasonably in making the will he did because circumstances later changed dramatically; for example, as in *Re Hancock* [1998] 2 FLR 346 where the testator behaved entirely reasonably leaving land used by a family business to children involved in the business but after his death the increased development value of the land meant that looked at objectively his will did not make reasonable financial provision for his daughter. Lord Hughes also drew on examples where the actions of a testator might be unreasonable or even spiteful but where it could not be said that the will did not make reasonable financial provision for the applicant; for example, *Re Jennings* [1994] Ch 286 where a father left nothing to his son whom he had failed to support during his lifetime which might have been said to be unreasonable but the will did not fail to make reasonable provision for the son as he had no requirement for maintenance.

4.3 THE MEANING OF MAINTENANCE

In the case of every applicant apart from spouses and civil partners, the standard of provision is what is required for their maintenance. The term is not defined in the 1975 Act and the courts have shown marked reluctance to provide a comprehensive definition. The Court of Appeal in *Re Coventry* [1984] 1 Ch 461 stated that maintenance means more than mere subsistence but less than anything which might be required for the claimant's benefit or welfare. Goff LJ in that case cited with approval the Canadian case of *Re Duranceau* [1952] 3 DLR 714 at 720 where the emphasis was put on the applicant's '*station in life*' determining the standard of maintenance. That is a statement firmly rooted in 1952 but in essence it is the life which the applicant is in fact leading which is relevant to the standard of maintenance, not a lifestyle to which they might aspire, or to use the words in *Duranceau* of living 'neither luxuriously nor miserably, but decently and comfortably' in accordance with a standard of living determined by the applicant's particular circumstances.

The authorities also establish that maintenance 'connotes only payments which either directly or indirectly enable the Applicant in the future to discharge the costs of his daily living at whatever standard of living is appropriate to him' (see *Re Dennis* [1981] 2 All ER 140 at 145) while not preventing provision being made to purchase a property if that would defray the cost of day-to-day living, for example, by relieving the applicant of rental costs (as in *Re Callaghan* [1985] Fam 1).

In *Re Myers* [2004] EWHC 1944 (Fam), Munby J awarded a sum to meet the claimant's housing needs out of a very large estate but ordered it to be held on trust for the applicant for life. He said: 'the purpose of the Act is not to award legacies or to make capital provision for claimants, however deserving, but simply to make provision for their maintenance'.

What constitutes maintenance was at the heart of the appeal to the Supreme Court in *Ilott* v. *Mitson*. The Court of Appeal in determining the Provision question had awarded Mrs Ilott a lump sum with which to purchase her housing association property plus a sum to meet the costs of the purchase. As she was in receipt of housing benefit, the rent she saved was relatively insignificant.

Lord Hughes in considering what constituted maintenance agreed with the previous decisions set out above and his judgment provides very helpful guidance on the approach the court ought to take to maintenance. Any suggestion that anything which might benefit the claimant is maintenance has been roundly dismissed. In para.14, Lord Hughes said:

> The concept of maintenance is no doubt broad, but the distinction made by the differing paragraphs of section 1(2) shows that it cannot extend to any or every thing which it would be desirable for the claimant to have. It must import provision to meet the everyday expenses of living.

He accepted however that maintenance could take many forms and is not limited to subsistence level. He also made it clear that he was not suggesting that it has to take the form of periodical payments but that a capitalised sum could meet income needs and that the provision of housing could also be appropriate. That reflects the decided cases. For example in *Espinosa* v. *Bourke* [1999] 1 FLR 747 the court made an award which enabled the claimant to pay off business debts and in *Re Pearce (Deceased)* [1998] 2 FLR 705 a sum was awarded to enable the claimant to introduce capital into a business.

Lord Hughes gave his seal of approval to the approach adopted by Munby J in *Re Myers* of providing housing held on a life interest trust rather than by way of outright provision. There is no doubt this is going to cause some difficulty of a practical nature. While as a matter of principle Lord Hughes' approach is correct, it may, however, prove unpopular as parties (whether claimants or defendants) rarely want to be tied together by a life interest. There is often a great deal to be said for a clean break and it remains to be seen how this approach will work in practice.

4.4 THE SECTION 3 FACTORS

Section 3 of the 1975 Act sets out the factors which the court must take into account when assessing whether the will or intestacy has made reasonable financial provision for the applicant and then in deciding what provision to make. As stated above at each stage of the process the court has to have regard to the section 3 factors. While at first this gives some comfort that there is a structured approach to 1975 Act claims, the factors are so widely drawn (particularly s.3(1)(g) ('any other matter, including the conduct of the applicant or any other person, which in the circumstances of the case the court may consider relevant'), that the court can pretty much take anything into account.

There is little doubt that this can give rise to difficulty. As Black LJ said in *Ilott* v. *Mitson* [2011] EWCA Civ 346 at para.88 (in the Court of Appeal on the Threshold question):

> A dispassionate study of each of the matters set out in section 3(1) will not provide the answer to the question whether the will makes reasonable financial provision for the applicant, no matter how thorough and careful it is … section 3 provides no guidance about the relative importance to be attached to each of the relevant criteria. So between the dispassionate study and the answer to the first question lies the value judgment to which the authorities have referred. It seems to me that the jurisprudence reveals a struggle to articulate, for the benefit of the parties in the particular case and of practitioners, how that value judgment has been, or should be, made on a given set of facts.

There are general factors which apply to every category of applicant and then specific factors to which s.3 requires the court to have regard in relation to particular types of applicant. The general factors which are applicable to all cases will be looked at before setting out a summary of the specific matters which the court must take into account when faced with an application by a particular claimant which are dealt with elsewhere in this book in greater detail.

4.4.1   General factors: a summary

In deciding whether the will or intestacy of the deceased makes reasonable financial provision for the applicant and in assessing the quantum of the claim, the court must have regard to the following general matters (1975 Act, s.3):

(a)   the financial resources and financial needs which the applicant has or is likely to have in the foreseeable future;

(b)   the financial resources and financial needs which any other applicant for an order under section 2 of this Act has or is likely to have in the foreseeable future;

(c)   the financial resources and financial needs which any beneficiary of the estate of the deceased has or is likely to have in the foreseeable future;

(d)   any obligations and responsibilities which the deceased had towards any applicant for an order under the said section 2 or towards any beneficiary of the estate of the deceased;

(e)   the size and nature of the net estate of the deceased;

(f)   any physical or mental disability of any applicant for an order under the said section 2 or any beneficiary of the estate of the deceased;

(g)   any other matter, including the conduct of the applicant or any other person, which in the circumstances of the case the court may consider relevant.

4.4.2   The timing issue

In looking at these factors the court has to take into account the facts as known to the court at the date of the hearing (1975 Act, s.1(6)). A striking example of this principle can be found in *Re Hancock (Deceased)* [1998] 2 FLR 346, where by the date of the hearing a plot of land comprised in the estate had greatly increased in value. This emphasises the objective nature of the process in that the facts as might have been known by the deceased are irrelevant.

The timing issue took on a particular importance in *Ilott* v. *Mitson* because the Threshold issue and the Provision issue became detached. The trial took place in 2007 and the Threshold issue was determined on the facts applicable at that date. The Provision issue on the other hand was determined by the Court of Appeal on the basis of facts as they obtained in 2015 (although it admitted those facts informally without having any evidence on them). In the end the Supreme Court did not need to decide the issue and the comments of Lord Hughes are *obiter*.

Lord Hughes dealt with the matter by saying that, on an appeal, if the question is whether the trial judge made an error of principle the facts and evidence must be taken as they stood before him. If the appellate court had to remake the decision on the merits, as ordinarily it should not, any request to adduce further evidence would have to be judged by the principles set out in *Ladd* v. *Marshall* [1954] 1 WLR 1489. Those principles are that to admit new evidence on an appeal:

(a) it must be shown that the evidence could not with reasonable diligence have been obtained for use at the trial;

(b) the evidence must be such that, if given, it would probably have an important influence on the result of the case, though it need not be decisive; and

(c) the evidence must be such as presumably to be believed, or, in other words, it must be apparently credible, though it need not be incontrovertible.

It therefore seems that the appeal court will, if exercising its discretion afresh, do so on the facts before the trial judge unless these quite stringent conditions can be met, although evidence of up-to-date circumstances at the date of the appeal could never have been obtained at the date of trial; so some uncertainty still remains as to how the courts will approach this issue.

4.4.3 The financial needs and resources of the applicant

In many, if not all, cases this is the factor together with the size of the estate which attains the greatest importance. Financial resources include the earning capacity of the applicant (1975 Act, s.1(6)) and financial needs take into account financial obligations and responsibilities. The standard approach is to list the outgoings of the claimant including expenditure on items such as entertainment and holidays. If the applicant has dependants, then the expenditure on them can also be included. **Appendix B4** contains a suggested schedule which can be adapted depending on the circumstances of the client. If there is a serious challenge to the amount of outgoings set out then they may need to be backed up with documentary evidence such as bills and bank statements.

The applicant may also have a need for housing and it can be helpful to the court to provide particulars of suitable properties on the market either to rent or to buy.

As far as resources are concerned, these may include actual earnings and of course earning capacity has to be taken into account. Pensions and income from investments all have to be taken into account as well as any capital of which the claimant is in possession, and any entitlement which the claimant may have to any gifts under the will or on intestacy.

There are particular difficulties in relation to applicants who are in receipt of benefits. This was one of the difficulties which beset *Ilott* v. *Mitson*. If the benefits are means tested then an award of a capital sum over any applicable limit will mean that the applicant loses the benefits and may end up worse off than before the award was made. In the past the courts have rejected claims where an award from a small estate would only have the effect of relieving the state of providing benefits: see *Re E* [1966] 1 WLR 709. The Court of Appeal at the Provision stage in *Ilott* likened an applicant dependent on benefits to someone who was elderly or disabled. That analogy was firmly rejected by Lord Hughes in the Supreme Court. As he pointed out it cannot be right to treat someone in receipt of state benefits as having more needs which may well be the case where the applicant is disabled. The receipt of means-tested state benefits is an indication of the applicant's financial position and of course part of their resources. It has no other status.

4.4.4   The financial needs and resources of any other applicant

This is a factor which will only apply if there is more than one claim made for provision out of the estate under the Act and that does not occur frequently. In essence the court will need to weigh in the balance the financial position of each of the applicants in deciding whether the disposition of the deceased's estate makes reasonable financial provision and then in assessing the claim.

4.4.5   The financial needs and resources of beneficiaries

The financial position of the beneficiaries of the estate has to be weighed in the balance. Sometimes beneficiaries are reluctant to disclose information about their needs and resources, in which case the court can simply assume that they are comfortably off and the factor will not weigh against the claim. However, if beneficiaries give any evidence of their financial position they run the risk of having to make full disclosure of all documents on the subject and of being cross-examined on this area if the matter comes to trial.

In *Ilott* v. *Mitson* the issue arose as to the position of charities as beneficiaries. They do not of course have needs to plead in the true sense but the Court of Appeal had treated that as justifying a larger award to the applicant than might otherwise have been made. Lord Hughes firmly rejected that idea and emphasised that they were the chosen beneficiaries of the testatrix. That has wider implications where beneficiaries other than charities do not put their needs in issue. They are still the chosen beneficiaries of the testator and their position cannot simply be ignored.

4.4.6 The obligations of the deceased towards any applicants or beneficiaries

In some cases the obligations of the deceased towards an applicant or beneficiary may be obvious: for example, the obligation of the deceased to his spouse or civil partner; the obligation of a parent to a minor child. In other cases the matter may not be so clear cut.

Claims concerning adult children have given rise to problems in this area because there is no legal obligation on a parent to support an adult child. This issue, specific to adult children, is dealt with in more detail in **Chapter 6**.

4.4.7 The size and nature of the net estate

There is no doubt that the size and nature of the net estate is a crucial factor. In cases such as *Re Myers* [2004] EWHC 1944 (Fam) (claim by an adult daughter against her father's estate worth £8.million) the substantial nature of the estate clearly weighed in favour of the claimant. Where the estate is small, the court may be less willing to make an award in favour of an applicant to whom the deceased did not owe obligations. What is more, the size of the net estate will obviously have crucial ramifications as far as the size of any award is concerned. In the case of a spouse or civil partner, the size of the estate has to be taken into account in looking at the award which might have been made on a divorce or dissolution of the partnership.

The net estate is defined in s.25(1) of the Act as follows:

'net estate', in relation to a deceased person, means –

(a) all property of which the deceased had power to dispose by his will (otherwise than by virtue of a special power of appointment) less the amount of his funeral, testamentary and administration expenses, debts and liabilities, including any inheritance tax payable out of his estate on his death;

(b) any property in respect of which the deceased held a general power of appointment (not being a power exercisable by will) which has not been exercised;

(c) any sum of money or other property which is treated for the purposes of this Act as part of the net estate of the deceased by virtue of section 8(1) or (2) of this Act;

(d) any property which is treated for the purposes of this Act as part of the net estate of the deceased by virtue of an order made under section 9 of the Act;

(e) any sum of money or other property which is, by reason of a disposition or contract made by the deceased, ordered under section 10 or 11 of this Act to be provided for the purpose of the making of financial provision under this Act.

Therefore, the net estate comprises property which the deceased owned less liabilities of the estate including tax. There must also be taken into account property which he or she has nominated another should receive under s.8 of the Act. That section is fairly limited in extent and covers payments nominated under enactments. Benefits nominated within a private pension scheme were not within s.8(1) (see *Re Cairnes, sub nom Howard* v. *Cairnes* (1983) 4 FLR 225 and **Chapter 9**). Similarly, property owned jointly by the deceased with another which passes by survivorship can also be treated as part of the net estate if the appropriate application is made under s.9 of the Act (as amended in 2014). Cases where jointly owned property has been treated as part of the net estate include: *Kourkgy* v. *Lusher* (1983) 4 FLR 65; *Re Crawford (Deceased)* (1982) 4 FLR 273 (joint bank account); *Jessop* v. *Jessop* [1992] 2 FLR 591; *Powell* v. *Osborne* [1993] 1 FLR 1001 (property subject to a mortgage secured by an endowment policy); and *Dingmar* v. *Dingmar* [2006] EWCA Civ 942 albeit under s.9 in its original form before amendment in 2014; and see further **Chapter 9**. The net estate also includes property which is the subject of a court order under ss.10 and 11 of the Act (see again **Chapter 9**).

The nature of the net estate is also important. The estate may be large but illiquid and it is always of concern to the court how any award should be met. To take a not uncommon example: the net estate is largely tied up in the modest matrimonial home of the deceased which his widow of many years occupies. His adult children make a claim for provision. The court will be reluctant in such a case, whatever the circumstances, to make an order which will mean the house will need to be sold. Other difficult cases may arise where the bulk of the estate is tied up in shares in the family business which may be difficult to realise, or in a landed estate.

Particular problems may arise where there are unquantified liabilities of an estate. For example, the deceased's lifetime tax affairs may not be in order, and there could be a large claim from HMRC for tax and penalties. In such circumstances it may take some time before the court can ascertain the size and nature of the net estate. Similar problems can arise if there is litigation pending against the estate or disputes as to the ownership of assets in the estate. In general terms the court needs to have these matters resolved before it can make any award under the Act (see, for example, *King* v. *Dubrey* [2015] EWCA Civ 581 – a claim to a house by way of *donatio mortis causa*, with a claim under the 1975 Act in the alternative).

Information as to the net estate must be provided in a written statement by the personal representative to the action in accordance with CPR, rule 57.16 and the Practice Direction to CPR, Part 57, para.16 (see **Chapter 8**).

4.4.8 Mental or physical disability of any applicant or beneficiary

Mental and physical disability is not defined by the Act itself. Certainly the sort of mental incapacity which would lead to a claimant being a patient under the Mental Capacity Act 2005 would be included. Someone who suffered a disability which was a protected characteristic within the Equality Act 2010 would also be able to pray that in aid. It is questionable whether anything else would qualify. Certainly in *Robinson* v. *Bird* [2003] EWCA Civ 1820 where the claimant suffered from body dysmorphic syndrome necessitating plastic surgery the court did not treat this as a disability.

However, an illness falling short of a disability which prevented the claimant or beneficiary from working in the short or long term would be taken into account in assessing the needs and resources of the claimant or beneficiary.

4.4.9 Any other matter including conduct

This provision enables the court to take into account circumstances which do not otherwise fall within the other factors. Most frequently that will equate to conduct. It should be noted that it is the conduct of any person which the court can take into account and not just that of the applicant. It may be the conduct of the deceased which is relevant. Therefore, in *Marks* v. *Shafier* [2001] All ER (D) 193 the adult son of the deceased relied, albeit unsuccessfully on the facts, on the abusive conduct of the deceased towards him as a child as justifying the estrangement between them. In *Re Jennings* [1994] Ch 286 the Court of Appeal refused to place any weight on the conduct of a neglectful father where the conduct had occurred many years before and had no impact on the claimant's financial position at the date of the application. In general terms, great care has to be taken in relying too heavily or at all on conduct. Courts often find it unhelpful and distracting to trawl through the rights and wrongs of events which may have happened many years before and may find it hard to make findings in respect of matters when they cannot hear the deceased's side of the story.

In *Cunliffe* v. *Fielden* [2005] EWCA Civ 1508, for example, a great deal of time at trial was taken on the subject of the conduct of the widow who had been the deceased's housekeeper and married him shortly after going to work for him. Reliance on conduct proved unsuccessful.

However, the court will inevitably make findings of fact in respect of the relationship between the deceased and the claimant, even in cases where conduct is not the main plank of the defence to the claim by the estate and beneficiaries. Therefore, conduct and other related circumstances frequently do play a part in the court's decision. However, it is a rare case where the conduct of the claimant who is otherwise in need of maintenance from the estate will defeat the claim. In *Espinosa* v. *Bourke* [1999] 1 FLR 747 the court at first instance rejected a claim by an adult daughter because of her conduct towards her father. The Court of Appeal held that the conduct on her part did not outweigh her need for provision for her maintenance.

Conduct also clearly played a part in another claim by an adult child in *Re Myers* (above). In that case the daughter applicant was in her sixties and had suffered a difficult relationship with her deceased father. She was awarded provision and the court found that she had not behaved as badly to her father as he had seemed to believe.

Good behaviour on the part of the applicant can also strengthen a case. For example, in *Re Abram (Deceased)* [1996] 2 FLR 379 the court relied on the fact that a son had worked in the family business for little remuneration for years in the expectation that it would be left to him. In *Re Pearce (Deceased)* [1998] 2 FLR 705 a similar consideration was taken into account, namely that a son had done a great deal of work on the family farm in the expectation that it would be his one day.

In *Ilott* v. *Mitson* the two striking facts were the extremely straitened circumstances in which the applicant lived and her complete estrangement from her mother throughout the whole of her adult life, lasting for some 25 years. The Court of Appeal had rejected the estrangement as being a reason for the District Judge to limit the award to her and criticised him for not explaining how the award he had made had been limited, but Lord Hughes considered otherwise. He regarded conduct of this kind of considerable importance and went on to say:

> If, by contrast with the present case, the claimant were a child of the deceased who had remained exceptionally and confidentially close to her mother throughout, had supported and nurtured her in her old age at some cost in time and money to herself, and if she had been promised many times that she would be looked after in the will, it could not be said that the judge was required first to assess reasonable financial provision on the basis of some supposed norm of filial relationship, neither particularly close nor particularly distant, and then to lift the provision by an identified amount to recognise the special closeness between the two ladies. But without going through any such exercise, and yet adhering to the concept of maintenance, a judge ought in such circumstances to attach importance to the closeness of the relationship in arriving at his assessment of what reasonable financial provision requires.

Therefore a line has to be drawn between conduct which will have little impact on the outcome of a case and which may serve to inflame relations between the parties (and thus make settlement less likely) and matters such as lengthy estrangement which clearly is going to have an impact on the way in which the court approaches the case.

4.4.10 Factors specific to certain categories of applicant

These factors are simply summarised at this point and dealt with in more detail in **Chapter 6** which deals with specific categories of applicant.

- **Applications by spouses and civil partners.** The 1975 Act requires that these applicants be treated differently from other claimants. As stated above, in other cases it has to be shown that the provision is reasonable for the *maintenance* of the applicant. In the case of a spouse it is the more generous test of what is reasonable provision. In addition to the factors under s.3 of the Act which have to be taken into account, in respect of spouses the court has to consider:
  - the age of the applicant and the duration of the marriage;
  - the contribution made by the applicant to the welfare of the family of the deceased, including any contribution made by looking after the home or caring for the family;
  - the provision which the applicant might reasonably have expected to receive if on the day on which the deceased died the marriage, instead of being terminated by death, had been terminated by divorce but nothing requires the court to treat such provision as setting an upper or lower limit on the provision which may be made by an order under s.2.
- **Former spouses and civil partners.** In the case of an application by a former spouse or civil partner of the deceased, the age of the applicant and the duration of the marriage or partnership are particular factors to be taken into account and

the contribution made by the applicant to the welfare of the family of the deceased, including any contribution made by looking after the home or caring for the family.

- **Cohabitants.** In the case of an applicant whose application is made under s.1(1)(ba) of the 1975 Act as someone who has lived in the same household as the husband or wife or civil partner of the deceased for at least a two-year period, the court will look at the age of the applicant and the length of the period during which the applicant lived as the husband or wife or civil partner of the deceased and in the same household as the deceased, and the contribution made by the applicant to the welfare of the family of the deceased, including any contribution made by looking after the home or caring for the family.
- **Children.** The additional factor to which the court must have regard in relation to a child is to the manner in which the applicant was being or in which he might expect to be, educated or trained. This is a factor which in general will apply only to minor children, although a child who has reached his majority but is in full-time education can also rely upon it.
- **Child of the family.** The first special factor with regard to such an applicant is the manner in which the applicant was being or in which he might expect to be educated or trained, the same factor which applies in respect of a child. This will, of course, have more application in respect of an application by a minor child. However, as set out in **Chapter 3**, a person treated as a child of the family can already be an adult when they become a step-child. The further additional factors which the court must take into account are whether the deceased maintained the applicant and, if so, the length of time for which and basis on which the deceased did so, and the extent of the contribution made by way of maintenance; and whether and, if so, to what extent the deceased assumed responsibility for the maintenance of the applicant. The court also has to have regard to whether in assuming and discharging that responsibility, the deceased did so knowing that the applicant was not his own child.
- **Dependants.** In the case of a claim by a dependant, the court will additionally take into account the length of time for which and basis on which the deceased maintained the applicant, and the extent of the contribution made by way of maintenance and whether and, if so, to what extent the deceased assumed responsibility for the maintenance of the applicant.

4.5 ASSESSING AWARDS

Assessing the size of an award under the Act is one of the most difficult aspects of the jurisdiction. One of the problems is that each case will turn very much on its own facts and the result in one reported decision will rarely be helpful in ascertaining what the court is likely to do in another.

In cases where the test is what is reasonable for the maintenance of the applicant (the meaning of which is discussed above), a good starting point has to be the reasonable needs and resources of the applicant. Is there an income shortfall? Can that shortfall be satisfied by a lump sum award calculated by reference to a table? For this purpose the Duxbury tables are most frequently used, whereby a sum needed to produce a particular income for an applicant of that gender and age is shown on the basis that the capital will be reduced to nil by their expected date of death. All this needs to be looked at in light of the current and future expected earning capacity of the applicant.

The Duxbury Tables take their name from the case *Duxbury* v. *Duxbury* [1992] Fam 62n where the methodology was first employed by an accountant, for use in a financial remedy claim under MCA 1973. The task he was set was to determine the capital sum necessary to provide an income net of tax over the life expectancy of the applicant. The applicant is assumed to have resort to both the income and the capital of the fund, on the assumption that at the date of her expected demise the sum will have been spent. The three key assumptions made in the calculations are:

(a)   an average income yield of 3 per cent pa;
(b)   average capital growth of 3.75 per cent pa gross; and
(c)   average inflation of 3 per cent.

Arguably these are not sums which a cautious investor would achieve and of course life expectancy will not always be as predicted. The usefulness of Duxbury calculations for recipients with a life expectancy of less than about 15 years (women over about 76 and men over about 73) is questionable, with some recipients living more than twice longer than expected; and the shorter the expectancy the less likely it is that the average returns will return to those historically achievable over longer terms.

The capital sum suggested for the capitalisation of any income need is predicated on the basis that the recipient will also receive a full state pension which will increase in line with inflation. Therefore when the Duxbury tables refer to an income of £20,000 per annum, for example, that includes whatever the full state pension is at the time.

This has led to some question marks over whether there is a better alternative to Duxbury and some commentators have suggested the Ogden Tables which were developed for personal injury cases. However the point was argued before the court in *Re Myers* [2004] EWHC 1944 (Fam) without success and Duxbury calculations have received the seal of approval in *Cunliffe* v. *Fielden* (see **4.4.9**), *Lilleyman* v. *Lilleyman* [2012] EWHC 821 (Ch) and *Ilott* v. *Mitson* in the Supreme Court (para.15).

It is worth considering alternative ways of softening some of the disadvantages of Duxbury perhaps by asking for a capital cushion or, if there is a life interest trust of property set up, providing that the trustees should have power to advance capital.

The next question might be whether there is a housing need and how that might best be satisfied. Sometimes, in a strong case, it will be by the provision of a capital sum so that an applicant may purchase a house outright, but it is clear from the Supreme Court in *Ilott* v. *Mitson* that in most maintenance cases a life interest trust will be more appropriate (although it is doubtful that such trusts which bind the warring parties together will be very welcome in practice). In other cases, it will be the provision of more income so that rent can be paid. The payment of debts and the injection of capital into an existing business or the provision of capital to start one up might also be regarded as maintenance.

Although the reasonable needs and resources of an applicant provide a starting point, the inquiry will rarely stop there. The merits of the claim by the particular applicant have to be balanced against claims by other applicants and beneficiaries, particularly those to whom the deceased owed obligations. All this has to be looked at in the context of the size of the net estate which can be crucial in assessing the size of an award. Where the estate is small and the claims on it numerous, the court may well not be able to satisfy even the most basic needs of an applicant by an award. Where the estate is large, the court has more room for manoeuvre but a large estate should not encourage the court to go beyond what is required for the reasonable maintenance of an applicant nor to give more to a claimant whose claim is not particularly meritorious.

In respect of other cases of spouses, civil partners and former spouses and civil partners where death occurs within 12 months of the dissolution of the marriage or civil partnership and where the court exercises its discretion to treat them as spouses and civil partners (s.14 of the Act), the issue is what is a reasonable provision. As set out above, in those cases the court is required to cross-check the provision it is proposing to make against the relief which might have been made on divorce or the dissolution of the civil partnership. It is still important to look at the financial needs and resources of the claimant and the other factors which s.3 requires the court to consider. However, in a large estate, the court will not stop at what is required for the reasonable maintenance of the applicant but will usually be more generous. In the case of a modest estate, awarding the spouse or civil partner one half of the joint assets might not provide them with enough to satisfy their reasonable needs and there is no reason in such a case why the court should feel constrained to limit the award in such a way as the Act in its amended form acknowledges. As the courts have stressed, in a divorce there are two people to provide for, whereas there is only one surviving party to the marriage to provide for on death.

The best approach in each case is to go through the various factors under s.3 of the Act and see which way they point in terms of the award and then come to a conclusion about a range of possible awards which the court might possibly make.

4.6   DEATH OF THE APPLICANT OR POTENTIAL APPLICANT

It is well established that once an applicant dies, his personal representatives cannot bring a claim on his behalf; nor can they continue a claim which has been commenced. The authorities were recently reviewed by Mr Simon Monty QC in *Roberts* v. *Fresco* [2017] EWHC 283 (Ch) where he confirmed the previous decisions of Booth J in *Whytte* v. *Ticehurst* [1986] Fam 64 *and Re Bramwell (Deceased)* [1988] 2 FLR 263 where Sheldon J came to the same conclusion.

Section 1(1) of the Law Reform (Miscellaneous Provisions) Act 1934 abolished the common law rule that personal actions die with the person and provided that 'all causes of action subsisting against or vested in [the deceased] shall survive against, or, as the case may be, for the benefit of, his estate'. However the issue is whether a right to apply for provision under the 1975 Act is a cause of action or a mere hope or contingency. In the matrimonial jurisdiction there is clear Court of Appeal authority, that a claim under the MCA 1973 could not be brought after the death of the defendant, and that such a claim was not a 'cause of action' under the 1934 Act (although the second point was decided rather reluctantly by the Court of Appeal); see *Harb* v. *King Fahd Bin Abdul Aziz* [2005] EWCA Civ 1324.

Mr Monty QC held that a claim under the 1975 Act gave a personal right to bring a claim, but that right was not itself a cause of action but a hope or contingency which falls short of being a cause of action. It is only when the court carries out the exercise of looking at the section 3 factors that a cause of action arises. What is in the estate at the date of death of the applicant or potential applicant is not an enforceable right but the right to make a claim.

If an applicant dies after a claim has been made, a difficult question arises as to how the costs of the proceedings to the date of death ought to be dealt with. In theory the deceased applicant has lost the case. The authors' experience is that the claim is discontinued with each party bearing their own costs, but there appears to be no authority on the point.

CHAPTER 5

Surviving spouses and civil partners

5.1 LEVEL OF PROVISION

In this section we examine claims by applicants who qualify under s.1(1)(a) of the Inheritance (Provision for Family and Dependants) Act 1975 as the spouse or civil partner of the deceased. This class of applicant includes those in a same-sex marriage, pursuant to the Marriage (Same Sex Couples) Act 2013. Prior to the introduction of same-sex marriages, the Civil Partnership Act 2004 came into force for same-sex couples only. The guidance below therefore applies to both marriage and civil partnerships.

The level of provision for a spouse or civil partner is higher than that of any other class of applicant. What amounts to 'reasonable financial provision' for this class of applicant is defined in s.2(1) as follows:

> such financial provision as it would be reasonable in all the circumstances of the case for a husband or wife to receive, whether or not that is required for his or her maintenance.

The higher level of provision, over and above maintenance, is applicable where there is a subsisting marriage or civil partnership. There is a limited period of grace: where there has been a final decree dissolving the marriage or civil partnership, and the deceased dies within 12 months of the same, then the higher level of provision will still apply provided there has not been a concluded application for financial remedy orders either under MCA 1973 or the Civil Partnership Act 2004.

The right to make the claim is personal to the survivor and requires his own survival to the making of the order. The claim does not survive for the benefit of his estate: see *Roberts* v. *Fresco* [2017] EWHC 283 (Ch).

5.2 A SHORT HISTORY

There is a short history of the enhanced level of provision for surviving spouses given by Lord Hughes in *Ilott* v. *Mitson* [2017] UKSC 17 at para.13:

> Historically, when family provision was first introduced by the 1938 Act, all claims including those of surviving unseparated spouses, were thus limited [to maintenance].

That demonstrates the significance attached by the English law to testamentary freedom. The change to the test in the case of surviving unseparated spouses was made by the 1975 Act, following consultation and reports by the Law Commission: Law Com 52 (22 May 1973) and Law Com 61 (31 July 1974). The latter report made it clear that recommendation was designed not to introduce, even in the case of surviving present spouses, a general power to re-write the testator's will, but rather to bring provision for such spouses into line with the developing approach of the family court.

At that stage the family court had new extended powers under the MCA 1973 to make lump sum and property adjustment orders, in addition to maintenance provision. This provision recognised other factors such as the length of the marriage and the non-financial contributions to the family. Lord Hughes identified the purpose of the higher standard of provision under the 1975 Act as follows:

the mischief to which the change was directed was the risk of a surviving spouse finding herself in a worse position that if the marriage had ended by divorce rather than by death.

While it may seem insensitive to the surviving spouse to make reference to the ending of the marriage by divorce rather than death, the comparison provides a valuable safeguard for the widow or widower.

5.3 THE INHERITANCE (PROVISION FOR FAMILY AND DEPENDANTS) ACT 1975

The 1975 Act included within the section 3 considerations a series of special factors to be taken account of where the applicant was a spouse or civil partner. These included at s.3(2), a direction that the court should:

have regard to the provision which the applicant might reasonably have expected to receive if on the day on which the deceased died the marriage instead of being terminated by death, had been terminated by a decree of divorce.

This is known variously as the divorce fiction, divorce comparator or divorce cross-check. While the position on death, where there is only one surviving spouse, is fundamentally different to the circumstances that exist following a divorce and an application under MCA 1973 for a financial remedies order, it provides an important cross-check. This difference requires the court to undertake what has been described as mental gymnastics when considering the divorce fiction.

The application of the divorce fiction does not require a 'slavish and wholly artificial comprehensive enactment of the ancillary relief process'; see the case of *P v. G* [2004] EWHC 2944 (Fam). Thus the court will look at the assets that actually form part of the deceased's net estate at trial as opposed to what value his assets would have been given had the spouses divorced. The court will undertake a broad assessment of what the outcome might have been if the marriage had been determined by divorce.

While it is clear that the aim of the Law Commission in 1974 was to seek to guard against the surviving spouse securing less than a divorcing spouse, there was some judicial concern that the divorce fiction amounted to something of a straitjacket for the courts in respect of 1975 Act claims. Therefore the Law Commission Report (Law Commission Report 331): *Intestacy and Family Provision Claims on Death*, recommended that a rider be added to the divorce fiction. Pursuant to the Inheritance and Trustees' Powers Act 2014 an amendment was made to s.3(2), so that while regard should be had to the divorce fiction:

> nothing requires the court to treat such provision as setting an upper or lower limit on the provision which may be made by an order under section 2.

Despite this amendment the divorce fiction remains an important consideration, and can be the magnetic factor in a case. It is one consideration that provides some welcome guidance in an area of wide judicial value judgments and discretion.

The other special considerations that relate to spouses or civil partners are themselves borrowed from MCA 1973, s.25 and are set out in s.3(2) of the 1975 Act as follows:

(a)   the age of the applicant and the duration of the marriage or civil partnership;
(b)   the contribution made by the applicant to the welfare of the family of the deceased, including any contribution made by looking after the home for caring for the family.

While these special considerations appear confined to the period of the marriage, under the MCA 1973, the court there has regard to the period of time the parties have cohabited, prior to the marriage. This may well be of particular importance where there is a same-sex relationship of cohabitation which has developed into civil partnership or marriage once the legislation provided for this. See the case of *Lawrence* v. *Gallagher* [2012] EWCA Civ 394, for confirmation of the same principles applying to a civil partnership.

5.4 DEVELOPMENT OF THE MATRIMONIAL LAW PRINCIPLES

In order to evaluate the merits of a claim by a spouse or civil partner it is necessary to have regard to the developments in matrimonial law.

From the inception of MCA 1973 until the seminal case of *White* v. *White* [2001] 1 AC 596, the explicit aim of the provision post divorce had been the satisfaction of the economically weaker spouse's reasonable requirements, or needs: see *Preston* v. *Preston* [1982] Fam 17. The concept of these requirements was a flexible one reflecting in large part the resources of the parties and the standard of living to which they had been accustomed. The awards (usually to the wife), were made up of suitable housing and income provision. Where there was sufficient liquid capital there would be an award of a fund representing capitalised periodical payments, and in default, an ongoing periodical payments order. The capital fund was known as the

Duxbury fund, taken from the case of *Duxbury* v. *Duxbury* [1992] Fam 62. The methodology of calculating the value of the fund is explained in the publication *At a Glance* at Table 9 (*At a Glance: Essential Tables for Financial Remedies*, Family Law Bar Association, 2017). The central feature is that it is a fund to be drawn down against so upon the expiration of the recipient's life expectancy, the capital would be exhausted. The use of the Duxbury model meant that after a long marriage an elderly spouse would receive a modest award which was to be wholly spent upon her death. There was no expectation that the recipient spouse would be able to leave substantial sums, even to the children of the marriage. The Duxbury approach is explained further in **Chapter 4**.

Once the benchmark of satisfaction of the recipient's needs as described above had been achieved, then any surplus was retained by the partner in whose name the assets were.

Lord Nicholls in *White* identified this approach as being discriminatory between the husband and wife in their respective roles, whichever role, be it home-maker or bread-winner, the marital partners have adopted. The value of the non-financial role is found in the language of MCA 1973 at s.25(1)(f) as to the contributions made by the care of the family. Thus there should be no bias in favour of the money-earner at the expense of the home-maker.

As a consequence of this prohibition on discrimination Lord Nicholls held:

> a judge would always be well advised to check his tentative views against the yardstick of equality of division. As a general guide, equality should be departed from only if, and to the extent that there is good reason for doing so.

5.4.1 Post *White* developments

Following the cases of *Miller* v. *Miller; McFarlane* v. *McFarlane* [2006] UKHL 24 and *Charman* v. *Charman (No 4)* [2007] EWCA Civ 503, the yardstick of equal division by way of a cross-check came to be interpreted as a starting point, and there is now in practice a sharing principle, to the effect that there will be equal sharing, unless there is a good non-discriminatory reason for unequal division. The Court of Appeal in *Sharp* v. *Sharp* [2017] EWCA Civ 408 have recently warned that a blanket application of the equal sharing principle would be 'an impermissible judicial gloss on statute'. In conjunction with the annunciation of the sharing principle there has been the development and recognition of factors that result in a different division of the assets. The non-discriminatory reasons which justify an unequal division of the assets, are discussed below.

5.4.2 The three principles

The principles identified in *Miller*, informing the distribution of assets on divorce, are now clearly set as being: 'need (generously interpreted), compensation, and sharing'. Those three principles must be applied in the light of the size and nature of all the computed resources. Where there are two living parties, and often dependent children, the fact that resources are limited will impact upon the application of the principles, so that needs are the pre-eminent factor. In *Charman* it is made clear that where the application of the needs principle would amount to an award of property greater than the result produced under the sharing principle, then the needs principle is pre-eminent. Therefore satisfaction of needs supply a valid reason for the departure from the sharing principle. Often the tension created between limited available capital and needs is resolved under MCA 1973 by the payment of ongoing periodical payments to the less well off spouse. (For detailed guidance on the principles relating to needs see the publication by the Family Justice Council: *Guidance on 'Financial Needs' on Divorce*, June 2016, available at **www.gov.uk/ publications/guidance-on-financial-needs-on-divorce**.) Correspondingly where the application of the sharing principle would produce a result greater than that suggested by needs then the *White* revolution means that the sharing principle should prevail.

There is a fundamentally different position between the pre *White* position and the current correct application of the principles enunciated in *White*. The outcome of equal sharing is not, however, the universal answer in the search for a fair division of assets. Since *White* there has been significant development of principles in relation to the nature of the assets; it is therefore necessary to keep abreast of the evolution of this area of financial remedies under MCA 1973.

5.4.3   Non-matrimonial property

The introduction of the sharing principle has led to a close examination of the origin of the assets held by either party to the marriage. In the immediate aftermath of *White* it was held that while the sharing principle was said to apply to all the assets irrespective of origin, the origin of the assets did supply a valid reason for departure from equality.

There is no statutory definition of non-matrimonial property under the MCA 1973. In *White* the same is identified as being from a source external to the marriage, for example, by way of gift or inheritance. Another species of non-matrimonial property is that which has been generated by a spouse prior to the marriage, which is pre-acquired property. There may have been the development of post separation assets. All of the above can be distinguished from the marital assets, sometimes described as the marital acquest.

The central message of the appellate courts has been that the origin of the assets may be relevant, but that factor will have limited impact if the applicant's financial needs cannot be satisfied without recourse to that property. Further the court's attitude (from *Miller* v. *Miller* onwards) towards the matrimonial home has been to hold that the same will normally be classed as matrimonial property, even where contributions to its purchase have been from non-matrimonial property.

There have been a series of cases seeking to limit the sharing principle to matrimonial property, on the basis that while matrimonial property or marital acquest is the product of the couple's common endeavour, the non-matrimonial property is not. Fairness dictated that where possible the owner of the non-matrimonial property should keep it. Therefore the transfer of non-matrimonial property should not occur unless it is demonstrated that the transferee needs access to that property. In *Jones* v. *Jones* [2011] EWCA Civ 41, the Court of Appeal held that where there is a surplus of assets (after the satisfaction of needs), it was appropriate to adopt the following forensic process:

(a)   the identification of the matrimonial or non-matrimonial property;
(b)   the application of the equal-sharing principle to matrimonial property; and
(c)   an analysis of whether there was a need to have recourse to the non-matrimonial property, e.g. if the satisfaction of needs require the same.

Mostyn J, in *JL* v. *SL (No 2)* [2015] EWHC 360 (Fam), coined the following memorable phrase: 'the application to non-matrimonial property of the sharing principle (as opposed to the needs principle) remained as rare as a white leopard'.

It is vital to remember that an argument as to the origin of the assets is only likely to be of relevance where the parties have a significant surplus over their needs. In a smaller value case the assets will all be required to make provision for the respective parties' needs. This requirement to satisfy the parties' needs and the resulting necessity to access non-matrimonial property is clearly set out in the Privy Council case of *Scatliffe* v. *Scatliffe* [2016] UKPC 36.

What is also difficult is the forensic process itself. How does one attribute a precise value to an asset brought into a marriage many years ago? Is only the historic value relevant or rather should it be on the basis of some passive economic growth attributed to the capital? The extent of the difficulties can be seen in the case of *Jones,* where there is an honest recognition by the judiciary that there is an element of arbitrariness in attributing values to businesses brought into a marriage many years ago. Where the asset is represented by an inheritance, but the funds were used for family purposes it is difficult to untangle the family finances, and to surgically extract the same. On occasions in the matrimonial sphere the approach can appear rather more impressionistic than forensic, with there being a modest adjustment in the equal sharing principle to reflect the origin of the assets.

The duration of the marriage under MCA 1973 is highly relevant in a divorce context. In *Sharp* the couple were both economically active and the marriage was childless. The bulk of the wealth emanated from the wife's earnings. There had been a significant separation of finances during the marriage. Lord Justice MacFarlane held that on the correct reading of the majority of the court in *Miller* there was recognition that in short childless marriages of dual earners, with retention of separate finances, fairness may require the reduction from a full 50 per cent share or the exclusion of some unilateral property from the 50 per cent calculation. This follows the judgment of Baroness Hale in *Miller* where she acknowledges as a valid reason for departure the existence of business assets generated solely by the husband during a short marriage, described as unilateral assets. Therefore post *Sharp* there can be a valid non-discriminatory reason for departure from equal sharing in a short dual career marriage even if the funds were accrued during the currency of the marriage by the efforts of one party. Although in the case of a claim under the Act the fact that a marriage was short will be a less critical factor than it would be in the case of a divorce, it is still an important factor which can point against equality of division (see *Cunliffe* v. *Fielden* at para.30).

It should be noted that there was a marked reticence by the House of Lords in *Miller* to expand the definition of non-matrimonial property to include unilateral assets as a species of non-matrimonial property. It is only in a minority of the short marriage cases that *Sharp* will apply.

Where a marriage is of long duration there is more likely to have been some mingling of the non-matrimonial assets; this fact may cause the asset to become a matrimonial asset. The joint reliance on the same can substantially diminish the weight to be accorded to the origin of the asset.

The problem under MCA 1973, is that it is largely the 'big money' cases that made their way to the appeal courts. The reality is that for the vast majority of financial remedy cases the satisfaction of needs will absorb all the parties' assets and there will be no surplus to distribute. The origin of the assets will be of minimal relevance in such circumstances.

5.4.4 Nuptial agreements

There is a formal method of acknowledging the practical separation of finances during a marriage and this is by the adoption of a pre or post nuptial agreement. The parties cannot contract out of the right to make an application to the court (see *Hyman* v. *Hyman* [1929] AC 601); however, the presence of a properly negotiated agreement will be highly relevant. In *Granatino* v. *Radmacher* [2010] UKSC 42 a continental couple's nuptial agreement was reviewed by the Supreme Court. It was held that the wife (a wealthy heiress) only had to make provision for housing for her husband and very limited financial provision as a consequence of their nuptial agreement. A pre-nuptial contract would only be upheld if each party had made full disclosure of their resources, were in receipt of legal advice and had time to reflect prior to voluntarily entering into the same. Such an agreement will have the effect of displacing the sharing principle and even depressing the level of the needs of the recipient party, see *WW* v. *HW* [2015] EWHC 1844 (Fam).

The Law Commission in their Report: *Matrimonial Property Needs and Agreements* (Law Commission Report 343) recommended that while such agreements should no longer be void, there should be a limitation on the same so that the needs of the economically weaker party should still be met. However, in the absence of legislation, the case law from the Supreme Court and below recognises and confers a greater degree of autonomy to spouses. Where there is a formal agreement, entered into with legal advice, the same can circumscribe the extent to which one spouse can recover from the other in the event of a marital breakdown.

Therefore if a nuptial agreement has been entered into where the claim is under the 1975 Act, the court would have regard to the terms of the same when applying the divorce fiction. Further the agreement would, under s.3(1)(g) of the 1975 Act, be a relevant piece of conduct to be taken account of by the court.

On exceedingly rare occasions it has been argued that the contribution of one of the spouses should be recognised as special in the sense of extraordinary, and so justify a departure from equal sharing. Thus far the reported cases have been in relation to the generation of large financial wealth, and the court has been loath to endorse a departure; see *Work* v. *Gray* [2017] EWHC Civ 270.

5.4.5 Periodical payments

Under the MCA 1973, a central issue is whether the economically weaker spouse requires ongoing periodical payments for the future. The justification for ongoing support is the needs of the recipient spouse: see *SS* v. *NS* [2014] EWHC 112 (Fam). The needs may well have been generated as a result of decisions taken during the marriage, for example, a career break to care for children.

On very rare occasions, where a high earning spouse has forfeited a well-paid career to provide support for the family, the principle of compensation may come into play. This may be reflected in an enhanced level of periodical payments beyond the satisfaction of budgeted needs: see *H* v. *H* [2014] EWHC 760 (Fam).

There is no statutory definition of needs, and their quantification in each case involves a consideration of all the statutory criteria in MCA 1973, s.25(2). The recent case law has adopted the expression 'need (generously interpreted)', in circumstances where there is a reasonable level of resources available to the parties. The court is directed by s.25(2)(c) to consider the standard of living enjoyed prior to the breakdown of the marriage. Therefore the appropriate level of periodical payments will be variable having regard to the amount of financial income enjoyed by the parties and their spending patterns during the marriage.

There is a statutory provision in MCA 1973, s.25A(2) which enjoins the court to consider a clean break, where the recipient spouse is able to adjust without undue hardship to their financial dependence. The duration and level of ongoing periodical payments has been the subject of a review by the Law Commission in its 2014 report, *Matrimonial Property, Needs and Agreements* (Law Commission Report 343).

This statutory directive to achieve a termination of financial dependence, where possible at the end of a marriage, is confined to the MCA 1973. There is no such statutory imperative under the 1975 Act, and the absence of the directive to move to financial independence represents a fundamental difference between the two jurisdictions. This is just one example of the mental gymnastics required in order to apply the divorce fiction.

Under the Act the court will be considering long term provision from the estate. However, the deceased's earning stream will normally have ceased. The court will therefore be concentrating on satisfying the survivor's need for income from the assets that have fallen into the estate. Note that in certain circumstances a pension may have been released to the surviving spouse, and some spouses may have an earning capacity.

5.5 THE APPLICATION OF THE DIVORCE CROSS-CHECK

The above review of the recent developments under MCA 1973, means that decisions in respect of claims made by surviving spouses under the Act before *White* should be treated with circumspection. Although it is interesting to note that in *Re Besterman* [1984] Ch 458, the court determining a widow's family provision claim was clear that the premise for the higher level of provision in the Act for surviving spouses was to ensure that the surviving spouse received a share of the family assets and that, accordingly, provision by way of an annuity only (representing, as it did, capitalised maintenance) was wholly insufficient.

5.5.1 The process

As we have seen the process of the divorce cross-check does not require a 'meticulous quasi divorce application' to be embarked upon by a court determining a claim under the Act. The applicant spouse has to bring into play their own assets, so that the court can in the first instance compute the total assets owned by the couple. Thereafter the divorce cross-check does involve arriving at a general overview as to the range of award that the applicant might have secured had there been a divorce. Under s.3(5) of the Act the court has to have regard to the facts as they are known to the court at the date of hearing. This statutory directive means having regard to assets that have fallen in as a consequence of death, e.g. pensions and life policies. These assets may well have swollen the size of the estate, and would not be available upon a divorce. The overview conducted by the court under the Act should be on the basis of the assets as they are found to be post death, together with their up to date valuation: see *P* v. *G, P and P* [2004] EWHC 2944 (Fam).

The process of arriving at an overview of the divorce cross-check should involve the following steps:

- Compute all the assets either in the estate or owned by the survivor.
- Consider the duration of the marriage.
- Examine the nature of the assets and their origin.
- Consider the standard of living of the parties.
- Consider any income stream of the survivor.

5.5.2   The weight to be given to the divorce cross-check

There is no hierarchy contained in the application of the section 3 factors. However, the special considerations in respect of an application by a spouse or civil partner are important considerations and on occasions will provide the magnetic factor that influences the level of provision made for the spouse. The divorce cross-check does not in isolation provide an automatic answer to claim under the Act and all the remaining s.3 factors fall to be considered.

Wall LJ in *Cunliffe* v. *Fielden* identifies the very different task the court is engaged upon under the 1975 Act:

> a deceased spouse who leaves a widow is entitled to bequeath his estate to whomsoever he pleases; his only statutory obligation is to make reasonable financial provision for his widow. In such a case depending upon the value of the estate, the concept of equality may bear little relation to such provision.

The Inheritance and Trustees' Powers Act 2014 has amended s.3(2) so as to add the following rider:

> but nothing requires the court to treat such provision as setting an upper or lower limit on the provision which may be made by an order under section 2.

However, the continued rationale for the divorce cross-check is made clear by Lord Hughes in the Supreme Court decision of *Ilott*. The creation of the higher level of provision for the surviving spouse was to ensure something akin to a level playing field with the position of a divorcing spouse. It is therefore suggested that there remains a cogent argument in many cases that the divorce cross-check does provide guidance as to the lower limit of what would amount to reasonable financial provision.

5.6   EXAMPLES OF THE APPLICATION OF THE DIVORCE CROSS-CHECK

There is a fundamental difference between the two jurisdictions: on divorce the assets are to be divided between the two spouses in order to satisfy their needs whereas on death provision is to be made for only one spouse under the Act. Black J observed in *P* v. *G, P and P* [2004] EWHC 2944 (Fam) that this difference not infrequently results in greater provision being made under the Act and would have been made on divorce.

However, the court is enjoined to consider the beneficiaries of the deceased's estate under s.3(1)(c), and whether the deceased owed them any competing obligation under s.3(1)(d), so the consideration of the Act is not confined to the circumstances of the couple, and under the 1975 Act the court will have to have regard to both the beneficiaries' circumstances and whether the deceased owed them any obligation. This will be in the context of the weight to be accorded to the deceased's testamentary wishes. *Ilott* is a reminder of the importance of the deceased having chosen his beneficiaries, and even if they do not have needs their position cannot simply be ignored.

5.6.1 Small estates

It is where the estate is small that it might easily be demonstrated that the rigid application of the divorce fiction often would fall short of making reasonable financial provision for the surviving spouse. The difference between the potential outcome of MCA 1973 and the actual outcome of a claim under the Act can be demonstrated by the case of *Iqbal* v. *Ahmed* [2011] EWCA Civ 900 where there was a lengthy (22 years) second marriage. The widow had no earning capacity and was occupying a modest property purchased by the deceased prior to his marriage. The first instance tribunal awarded her a 50 per cent share in the property and a full life interest in the remaining 50 per cent. The deceased's beneficiary under his will was a son from his first marriage who was comfortably off. The Court of Appeal dismissed the son's appeal holding that the widow's need to remain in the matrimonial home was the pre-eminent consideration that overrode any consideration of the origin of the asset. Furthermore in order to have a modicum of financial security in the future she required outright ownership of at least 50 per cent. The widow would, however, only have the use of the remaining 50 per cent while she needed it during her lifetime. Thus the widow's needs required her to have access to the deceased's share of the matrimonial home, but did not justify an outright transfer of the same.

5.6.2 Life interest

In most instances the deceased's overriding obligation will have been to make reasonable financial provision for the surviving spouse. However, where the sharing principle in the divorce fiction has been applied and found wanting in relation to the survivor's needs, some limitation may be placed upon the ownership or use of the asset by the surviving spouse. In *Iqbal* the tension between the widow's needs and the deceased's testamentary wishes was solved by granting the widow only a life interest in the remaining half share of the matrimonial home, with the child of the first marriage as the remainderman. *Ilott* emphasises the continued relevance of the testator's wishes when arriving at what amounts to reasonable financial provision. If, after the application of the sharing principle, the needs of the survivor can be met by the provision of a life interest, the court may utilise this type of provision.

5.6.3 Duration of the marriage

Where there has been a long marriage, as in the case of the 37-year marriage in *McNulty* v. *McNulty* [2002] EWHC 123 (Ch), the court will be concerned that the survivor enjoys financial security for the remainder of their lives, and this may require in excess of the result suggested by the divorce cross-check. The total value of the family assets amounted to just under £600,000, the award to the spouse left her with total assets of £365,000 owned outright, or 60 per cent of the assets.

5.6.4 Large estate and lengthy marriage

A generous award was received by the surviving spouse in the case of *P* v. *G P and P*. The estate was valued at £4.5–£5 million. The marriage was a second marriage of 22 years' duration. The beneficiaries were the deceased's children, two of whom by a former marriage. The parties had enjoyed a high standard of living with an income of £300,000 gross pa. The widow had been left the benefit of a very valuable pension, paying her £90,000 pa net, but only a life interest in the marital home. The children sought to argue that the capital value of the pension should be ascribed to the widow's share of any assets. However the nature of the pension was only to provide an income stream and not realisable capital. Therefore Black J declined to treat 50 per cent of the pension fund value as a payment on account to the widow in lieu of liquid assets. The widow retained the whole of pension assets. An additional award of £2 million was made equating to approximately 40 per cent of the liquid assets, excluding the pension. This was a generous award and were the case heard now, there would be greater argument as to the origin of the assets. The widow was able to demonstrate a very high standard of living over the length of the marriage, and Black J concluded that she should be entitled to financial security for the duration of her life time.

The estranged family's finances were still linked by reason of the pension funds investments in the deceased's businesses, which were still operating. The widow sought an order under the Act to ensure that her pension funds were utilised in the purchase of an annuity. The power to direct this in respect of certain personal pension schemes is to be found in s.2(1)(f) which confers power to make an order;

> varying any ante-nuptial or post-nuptial settlement … made on the parties to the marriage to which the deceased was one of the parties, the variation being for the benefit of the surviving party to that marriage..

The central question was whether the pension scheme could be characterised as a nuptial settlement. There is a similar power under s.24(1)(c) of the MCA 1973. The wide construction of the same is to be found in the House of Lord's case of *Brooks* v. *Brooks* [1996] AC 375. In *Brooks* Lord Nicholls held:

> The section is concerned with a settlement 'made on the parties to the marriage'. So, broadly stated, the disposition must be one which makes some form of continuing provision for both or either of the parties to a marriage.

In *Brooks* the husband's pension included the ability for the husband to elect to give up a portion of his pension so as to provide for a pension (from his death) to his wife or other dependants. Lord Nicholls concluded that the ability to make provision for the spouse in this way constituted a post nuptial settlement. For further detail as to the width of this power to enable an order to be made against assets that would not otherwise fall within the definition of the net estate at s.25, see **Chapter 9**.

5.6.5 Standard of living

Where the estate is large, it is the more likely that the application of the sharing principle, when applying the divorce cross-check, will provide sufficient capital outright in order to make reasonable financial provision for the surviving spouse.

This was found to be the position in the case of *Wooldridge* v. *Wooldridge* [2016] Fam Law 451. The deceased's marriage had lasted 11 years. He had been a successful businessman during much of his adult life. The estate comprised a family home worth £4 million by the date of trial, which passed to the widow under the will. The remaining estate assets were valued at £6.8 million. The beneficiaries were the deceased's children. The adult child by his previous relationship was heavily involved in the running of the family business run from a valuable polo estate and the younger son was still a child. The widow had secured a further £1.95 million under a fatal accident arising out of her husband's death and, at the time of the trial, had assets of £10.5 million. It was acknowledged that she had received more than she would have been entitled to by an application of the sharing principle under the divorce cross-check. Her claim was brought on the basis of her needs calculated against the background of a 'super rich' standard of living. However, the judge found there to be a significant degree of forensic exaggeration by the wife in relation to the historic standard of living. The cost of the pleaded needs exceeded the family's declared income by a substantial margin. The widow's investments of £5 million would have provided her with a Duxbury type income stream of £210,000 pa. The judge concluded that the widow's needs were more than satisfied by this provision and her claim failed. The mere fact that the deceased no longer has needs which themselves fall to be satisfied does not mean that the survivor can aspire to a significantly higher standard of living than that enjoyed during the currency of the marriage. Nor does the absence of the surviving spouse give the court a general power to re-write the deceased's will.

5.6.7 Large estate; short marriage and needs

Where there is a large estate and a surviving spouse of a short marriage, an application of the divorce fiction will involve a close consideration of the origin of the assets. There will often be non-matrimonial property. The needs of the surviving spouse will be central to application of the divorce cross-check. The application of the divorce fiction post *White* was considered under the 1975 Act by the Court of Appeal in the case of *Cunliffe* v. *Fielden*. This was a short second marriage of only one year's duration. The deceased's assets, valued at £1.4 million, were all acquired prior to the marriage. The brevity of the marriage and the origin of the assets were valid arguments against an equal division of the assets. Therefore the case focused upon the widow's needs, as opposed to her potential entitlement to share in the assets. Lord Justice Wall referred to the distinction between a marriage ended by death and one ended by divorce (at para.30) in a manner which suggests that the court hearing a claim under the Act may take a more generous view of the surviving spouse's needs on the ground that, unlike the case on divorce, he or she had a legitimate expectation that the marriage would continue.

The fact that there is no statutory directive under the 1975 Act as to the transition to independence (in contrast to MCA 1973) offers an explanation for the difference in approach to provision. Under MCA 1973 after a short marriage (such as that in *Cunliffe* v. *Fielden*) the matrimonial court would be seeking to impose an early termination of financial dependence and order a clean break, capitalising periodical payments for an adjustment period only. The court hearing a claim under the Act is not directed to take such an approach.

The widow in *Fielden* was only 48 years old, with limited earning capacity. The bulk of her £600,000 award related to capitalisation of her reasonable needs to run until the expiration of her life expectancy using the Duxbury Tables. Given the brevity of the marriage, it was concluded that her reasonable needs should be calculated at a markedly lower level than she fleetingly enjoyed, in the marriage. This involved the move to a more modest home. In addition the calculation of her reasonable needs in discharging her daily cost of living was reduced. However, her life expectancy gave rise to a large multiplier, to apply to the annual figure or multiplicand. The appeal in *Fielden* was heard prior to the House of Lords decision in *Miller* under MCA 1973, and in the early days of the developing case law on non-matrimonial property and, when viewed in the light of the law as it has developed since *Miller*, it can be regarded as a generous award.

5.6.8 Large estate and short marriage

In the case of *Lilleyman* v. *Lilleyman* [2012] EWHC 821 (Ch), Briggs J provided clear guidance as to the relevance of the divorce fiction and the presence of non-matrimonial property. The estate was in the region of £6 million. The bulk of this value was tied up in a family business that the deceased had developed entirely prior to his second marriage, and in which his sons by his first marriage worked. The deceased and applicant's cohabitation or marriage totalled less than four years' duration. The judge sought to analyse the principles from the MCA 1973 cases in respect of non-matrimonial property, in the following terms:

1. It is necessary to prove that property is non-matrimonial in origin.
2. A matrimonial home will usually be regarded as matrimonial property.
3. Property acquired during the marriage, other than by inheritance or gift, is usually matrimonial property.
4. Non-matrimonial property may change its nature if it is committed to long-term family use.
5. Where there is a business brought into the marriage by one party, its value at the inception of the marriage will be non-matrimonial, but the increase in

value by reason of activity (as opposed to passive economic growth) may be part of the fruits of the marital partnership.

6. Where there is a pre-existing family business it may be positively unfair to have recourse to it for the purposes of equal sharing, particularly if to do so may strip it of much of its value.

In *Lilleyman* there was limited matrimonial property, comprising domestic properties that the spouses had contributed to and purchased during the currency of the relationship. There had been a modest increase in the value of the business, since the marriage. The judge attributed only 50 per cent of the growth to the deceased's activity in the business, and therefore delineated that increase as matrimonial property as opposed to that which represented passive economic growth only. Post the *Sharp* decision above it can be argued that in such a short marriage any increase in value in the non-matrimonial asset, should not be added to the computation of the marital acquest. The origin of the assets led the tribunal to conclude that the sharing principle did not apply to the vast majority of the value of the deceased's estate.

The matrimonial assets were calculated at just over £1.475 million, and therefore the application of the equal sharing principle would have yielded an award on divorce of £737,000. The widow had assets in her own name to the approximate value of £300,000. The award under the Act was a transfer of value of £500,000. This represented equal sharing of the matrimonial property in respect of the divorce cross-check.

The judge evaluated the impact of the equal sharing principle against provision fashioned solely with regard to the widow's needs, and concluded that her needs were more than satisfied by the application of the sharing principle to the limited matrimonial pot.

The deceased's desire to ensure that the next generation received the bulk of his business assets was to be respected, and while there was not a legal obligation under s.3(1)(d) the fact of the sons' involvement gave rise to some level of a moral obligation.

5.6.9   Conduct

For conduct to be taken account of pursuant to MCA 1973, s.25, it has to be of such an extreme nature that it would be inequitable for the court to ignore it when considering the distribution of finances following divorce. A substantial dissipation of assets or violent assault may be deemed to be of sufficient severity.

It appears that the court is more willing to consider conduct under s.3(1)(g) in the context of a claim under the 1975 Act than it is under s.25 of MCA 1973 and conduct will be taken into account provided it is relevant. In *Ilott* the court concluded that the estrangement between the deceased and her only child could amount to relevant conduct. However, it must be borne in mind that the purpose of the Act is not to reward or punish parties for good or bad conduct and the degree to which conduct will be considered relevant is likely to be limited. The court is unlikely to be prepared to consider a detailed account of the spouses' conduct during the marriage and there are costs implications of filing evidence that provides such an account. Financial misconduct was held to be relevant in the case of *Baron* v. *Woodhead* [2008] EWHC 810 (Ch). Although there may not have been reprehensible conduct involved, the very fact of a long term *de facto* separation between the parties prior to the death of the deceased will be a relevant factor.

5.6.10 Long term separation

On occasions the parties have separated and failed to embark upon proceedings to achieve a formal dissolution of the marriage or civil partnership. Under MCA 1973 there is no limitation period within which financial remedy proceedings have to be brought: see *Wyatt* v. *Vince* [2015] UKSC 14. There the proceedings were brought 18 years after decree absolute. The fact of the delay and the substantial post-separation assets accrued by the husband meant that any award should be limited to a very modest contribution to the wife's needs. In that case had the claim been against the husband's estate the fact of the decree absolute would have reduced the former wife's status to that of an applicant under s.1(1)(b) of the Act as a former spouse, but the delay would also count against her.

The attitude of the court under the Act to a claim by a surviving spouse or civil partner following a long separation without financial dependence is relatively hostile. In the case of *Hope* v. *Knight* [2010] EWHC 3443 (Ch), there had been no proceedings to dissolve the marriage but after a 20-year separation and an absence of financial dependence the court dismissed the widow's claim.

CHAPTER 6

Provision for applicants on the maintenance standard

6.1 INTRODUCTION

We have looked at who qualifies as an applicant under the Inheritance (Provision for Family and Dependants) Act 1975 (**Chapter 3**) and the general approach to claims under the Act (**Chapter 4**). This chapter looks in more detail at the specific factors a court must take into account both in deciding whether the will or intestacy has made reasonable financial provision for the applicant and in deciding what order to make, as well as some problems which can arise in relation to specific categories of applicant where the standard of provision is reasonable financial provision for their maintenance.

What is meant by maintenance is dealt with in **Chapter 4** as are the factors which the court is directed to take into account in every case.

6.2 COHABITANTS

Whether or not someone qualifies as a cohabitant is dealt with in **Chapter 3**. Cohabitation can take many forms: the relationship may be a relatively casual one where the parties are not totally committed to one another (see: *Cattle* v. *Evans* [2011] EWHC 945 (Ch) where the relationship was off and on) or it may be as close to a marriage as it is possible to be (e.g. *Lewis* v. *Warner* [2016] EWHC 1787 (Ch) where the couple had lived together for 20 years). It often comes as something of a shock to cohabitees who have perhaps been in a relationship for many years which closely resembles a marriage to find that provision for them is limited to what is required for their maintenance. The far more generous approach the Act provides for spouses and civil partners (see **Chapter 5**) does not apply to cohabitees, however long their relationship may have lasted.

As well as taking into account the general s.3 factors (dealt with in **Chapter 4**) the court must have regard to age of the applicant and the length of the period during which the applicant lived as the husband or wife or civil partner of the deceased and in the same household as the deceased and the contribution made by the applicant to the welfare of the family of the deceased, including any contribution made by looking after the home or caring for the family.

The length of the cohabitation is important and may have an impact on how easy it is for the applicant to maintain their standard of living in the future. The age of the applicant is also important. It will have an impact on future earning potential but also the need for provision for care or a special type of accommodation. For example in *Re Watson* [1999] 1 FLR 878, Neuberger J awarded the elderly applicant with health problems a sum to meet her income needs and the balance of the purchase money needed to buy a bungalow which was more suitable for her needs than the accommodation she was occupying.

If cohabitation for at least two years can be demonstrated, it is not an essential requirement to show that the applicant has been dependent on the deceased but of course that will still be a relevant factor. The theme running through many of the cases is the attempt by the court to replicate the standard of living enjoyed by the applicant while the deceased was alive, but with an eye to the future, particularly if the applicant is elderly. In other words the court is attempting to alleviate hardship which may result after the death but in doing so it is restricted to what is required for the applicant's maintenance. In *Swetenham* v. *Walkley* [2014] WTLR 845 an award was made where the deceased had not provided financial support to the applicant who was 80, but he had provided emotional and other support and his death had resulted in her having to move to a care home.

As set out in **Chapter 4**, the guidance of the Supreme Court in *Ilott* v. *Mitson* [2017] UKSC 17 reinforces the point that maintenance involves the defraying of day-to-day living costs and does not extend to granting capital to the applicant.

Consistent with this approach (albeit that the case was decided a few days before the Supreme Court handed down judgment in *Ilott*) is the case of *Re Martin (Deceased)* [2017] EWHC 491 (Ch) where on appeal the judge changed an award which gave the deceased's half share in the home they shared to the applicant to confer on her only a life interest. The defendant to the application was the deceased's wife with whom he had not lived for 20 years but who inherited everything under his will.

Prior to *Ilott*, there were cases where the courts have been quite generous to cohabitants, for example: *Musa* v. *Holliday* [2012] EWCA Civ 1268, where after a six-year cohabitation which produced a child, the court ordered the transfer of shares in a business in which the applicant worked and the outright transfer of the house in which she and her child lived and the Court of Appeal considered that this was within the range of decisions the judge could make.

In *Negus* v. *Bahouse* [2008] EWCA 1002 the Court of Appeal refused permission to appeal in a case where the applicant had lived with the deceased for seven years in some luxury. She was awarded the property in which they had lived outright plus a capital sum to provide for her future needs of £240,000. The Court of Appeal held that the court was entitled to take into account the luxurious life she had led with the deceased.

As with other cases where maintenance is the standard of provision, claims often divide into what the applicant needs for housing, income and possibly the payment of debts. Usually, if the court decides that that the age of the applicant and the length of the cohabitation justify the applicant's income needs being met for the rest of their life (which may be justified in the case of a long cohabitation and an applicant who has little earning capacity or who is elderly) a Duxbury sum may be appropriate as a way of meeting that income need. Although the court clearly has power to order maintenance payments, they are rarely seen in practice. Usually both parties wish to have any income provision by way of lump sum to provide a clean break and to avoid the winding up of the estate being delayed for long periods.

As far as housing needs are concerned, courts have varied in the past as to whether outright provision is appropriate (e.g. *Negus* v. *Bahouse* and *Musa* v. *Holliday*) or whether a life interest is more appropriate (e.g. *Cattle* v. *Evans*; *Re Martin (Deceased)*). There is no reason, of course, why a sum in respect of rent could not be awarded although it is likely the court would capitalise it.

Applicants are often keen not to have a life interest in a property as it ties warring parties together and issues as to maintenance of the property can be difficult to resolve (something recognised in *Webster* v. *Webster* [2008] EWHC 31 (Ch), where there was an outright transfer of the house in which they had lived free of mortgage, but no provision for income). This is particularly the case with cohabitees where perhaps they have lived in a property for many years which is in the name of the deceased or where they are entitled only to a share in it.

It is not clear how the decision in *Ilott* will affect claims by cohabitees. In principle the comments of Lord Hughes, who favoured life interest trusts in general as being the appropriate way of providing housing where the standard of provision was maintenance, were not limited to claims by adult children. Having said that, a long term cohabitee, who perhaps owns half the property already and cannot buy out the estate's interest, might have an argument for outright provision of the other share, particularly if it could be said that the proceeds of the whole property might be needed to fund future care in old age.

An interesting recent case but which is subject to appeal (a second appeal) is *Lewis* v. *Warner* [2016] EWHC 1787 (Ch), where the applicant, a gentleman of 91, had lived with the deceased for 20 years in a property in her name. He had assets more than sufficient to support himself but he wanted to stay in the property which had been his home for so long. The judge at first instance gave him an option to purchase the property at full market value. The appeal against that decision was dismissed, the court holding that maintenance could exceptionally encompass an arrangement for full consideration. What the applicant required for his maintenance was not financial provision as usually understood but the provision of a particular roof over his head. Whatever happens on appeal, this is an unusual case and unlikely to be followed frequently.

6.3 MINOR CHILDREN

Claims by minor children (and those who have reached majority but who are still dependent and in full time education) are very different from those by adult children which are dealt with below. In general terms the obligation of a parent to a minor or dependent child will be a strong and compelling factor in favour of provision being made. The additional factor in s.3 specific to children is the manner in which the applicant was being or in which he might expect to be educated or trained. Again, as with other applicants, provision is pinned to the standard of living to which the child was accustomed. The specific factor focuses on whether the child was likely to receive a private education and whether that child might be expected to go to university.

There are few decided cases on the appropriate provision for minor children. This is largely because most cases are compromised. The claim of the minor child is invariably strong and the only question is the quantum of that claim. An exception to this might be where the surviving parent is wealthy enough that the death of the parent makes little difference to the maintenance of the child. Some aspects of the claim for maintenance are easy: school fees, child care costs and outgoings which can be specifically linked to the child. Other costs can be more problematic: for example housing and the cost of maintaining a property. If there is a claim as well by the surviving parent of the child, the court will need to consider how far the child's maintenance will be covered by provision made for that parent, whether by way of housing or income provision.

Clearly an important issue is the extent to which the child was maintained by the deceased during the deceased's lifetime. However, that ought not to be a determinative factor. If the deceased did not fulfil his or her obligations to support the child during his or her lifetime, that ought not to count against an otherwise meritorious claim.

Some guidance might be derived from the cases under s.15 of and Sched.1 to the Children Act 1989. Some care must be taken because the provisions of that legislation are different from the 1975 Act and are not pinned to a concept of maintenance but the amount parents should provide for the benefit of the child. However, in general, the approach of the court (as set out by the Court of Appeal in *Re P (a Child)* [2003] EWCA Civ 837) may provide some guidance. In that case Bodey J provided the following guidelines (at para.76):

i)   The welfare of the child while a minor, although not paramount, is naturally a very relevant consideration . . .

ii)   Considerations as to the length and nature of the parents' relationship and whether or not the child was planned are generally of little if any relevance, since the child's needs and dependency are the same regardless ...

iii)   One of the '... financial needs of the child ...' (to which by paragraph 4(1)(c) the court must pay regard) is for him or her to be cared for by a mother who is in a position, both financially and generally, to provide that caring. So it is well established that a child's need for a carer enables account to be taken of the caring parent's needs ...

iv)   '... the child is entitled to be brought up in circumstances which bear some sort of relationship with the parent's current resources and standard of living ...' – per Hale J in *J* v. *C (Child: Financial Provision)* [[1999] 1 FLR 152] ...

v)   However, as this latter concept lends itself to demands going potentially far wider than those reasonably necessary to enable the mother properly to support the child, '... [the Court] has to guard against unreasonable claims made on the child's behalf but with the disguised element of providing for the mother's benefit rather than for the child ...': *J* v. *C (Child: Financial Provision)* (above).

vi)   In cases where the father's resources permit and the mother lacks significant resources of her own, she will generally need suitable accommodation for herself and the child, settled for the duration of the child's minority with reversion to the father; a capital allowance for setting up the home and for a car; and income provision (with the expense of the child's education being taken care of, generally, by the father direct with the school).

vii) Such income provision is reviewable from time to time, according to the changing circumstances of the parties and of the child.

viii) The overall result achieved by orders under Schedule 1 should be fair, just and reasonable taking into account all the circumstances.

If there is already an order in place under Sched.1 to the Children Act 1989 that might provide some guidance as to the level of provision for the child. There would seem to be no reason in principle in a case where such an order was not in place why the court could not derive some guidance from the approach of the courts in Children Act cases, for example in the provision of housing until the child is independent. An allowance for the surviving parent to live on is perhaps more controversial in a case where the focus is what is required for the child's mainte-nance, but it may be that providing an income for the surviving parent to stay at home rather than paying for child care costs makes sense in the circumstances of the case.

There can be particular concerns about children with disabilities where their future is uncertain. Medical evidence or in the case of learning disabilities the evidence of educational psychologists may be required for the court to assess how long the child might require maintenance from the estate.

There may also have to be speculation about tertiary education – particularly if the child is still very young.

As with other maintenance applicants, the court may be reluctant to award maintenance payments as this delays the winding up of the estate; although in the case of a child where a great deal of speculation may be required as to their future needs it may seem a sensible solution to the problem.

6.4   ADULT CHILDREN

Claims by adult children undoubtedly cause particular problems. In the 1938 Act only (1) sons under the age of 21; (2) unmarried daughters regardless of age; and (3) sons or daughters who 'by reason of some mental or physical disability' were incapable of maintaining themselves could make an application under the Act. The

Law Commission regarded this as outmoded and although they considered placing some restrictions on who could apply, in the end opted to include all adult children on the basis that the courts would be able to work out the deserving from the undeserving.

However, it has proved difficult. In the case of other applicants where the maintenance standard is the relevant standard, the task of the court at the provision stage is often to attempt to replicate a standard of living: to make up for the impact that the death has had on the applicant. This is particularly apparent in the case of a minor child being supported by the deceased or a cohabitee whose life is inevitably going to be affected by the death of his or her partner (as to which see above).

In the case of adult children who have been financially independent of their parents for many years, the death of a parent is unlikely to make a great deal of difference to their ability to maintain themselves. Notwithstanding that, there is often a feeling that parents should leave money to their children and for many adult children an expectation that this will happen.

Many of the cases involving adult children turn on the issue of whether or not the deceased had an obligation to that child. In *Re Coventry (Deceased), Coventry* v. *Coventry* [1980] Ch 461, it was held that an adult son capable of earning his own living had to demonstrate some additional factor such as a moral obligation on the part of the deceased to make provision for him before his claim could succeed. That decision led to an argument in *Re Hancock (Deceased)* [1998] 2 FLR 346 that in all cases of a claim by an adult child, some sort of obligation had to be shown. The Court of Appeal rejected that argument and held that all the factors set out in s.3 of the Act had to be weighed in the balance; that was the approach which that court adopted in *Espinosa* v. *Bourke* [1999] 1 FLR 747. In that case Butler-Sloss LJ stated:

> subsection 1(1)(d) refers to 'any obligations and responsibilities'. Plainly those obligations and responsibilities extend beyond legal obligations and that is why, in my view, the word moral has been used to underline and explain that the deceased's obligation and responsibilities are not to be narrowly construed as legal obligations but to be taken into account in a broad sense of obligation and responsibility.

It is therefore clear that this subsection does not refer only to legal obligations which the deceased had to any claimant. Indeed, some of the successful adult children cases provide some excellent examples of where the court has found an obligation which the deceased owed to the claimant which goes beyond any legal obligation. For example, see *Goodchild* v. *Goodchild* [1996] 1 WLR 694 (a son in necessitous circumstances who had been promised provision and whose mother had left her estate to his father on that basis); *Re Abram (Deceased)* [1996] 2 FLR 379 (a son who had worked in the family business for little remuneration for years in the expectation it would be left to him); *Re Pearce (Deceased)* [1998] 2 FLR 705 (a son who had done a great deal of work on the family farm in the expectation it would be his one day); *Re Hancock (Deceased)* (a daughter in necessitous circumstances where the estate was large and promises had been made by the deceased to his wife that he would benefit her); and *Espinosa* v. *Bourke* (a daughter who had cared for her father and had been promised provision and had no means of earning her own living).

It is clear that the failure of the deceased to meet obligations which he had to a child many years before his death will not create an obligation which will weigh in favour of an adult applicant. In *Re Jennings* [1994] Ch 286 the Court of Appeal rejected the claim by a well-off adult claimant whose father had failed to maintain him as a child or indeed to play any role in his life. The Court of Appeal held that obligations and responsibilities could not include obligations in the past.

While it is clear that a moral obligation is not a prerequisite to a claim by an adult child succeeding, the concept was approved by the Supreme Court in *Ilott* v. *Mitson* where Lord Hughes said that:

> Oliver J's reference to moral claim must be understood as explained by the Court of Appeal in both *In re Coventry* itself and subsequently in *In re Hancock*, where the judge had held that there was no moral claim on the part of the claimant daughter. There is no requirement for a moral claim as a sine qua non for all applications under the 1975 Act, and Oliver J did not impose one. He meant no more, but no less, than that in the case of a claimant adult son well capable of living independently, something more than the qualifying relationship is needed to found a claim, and that in the case before him the additional something could only be a moral claim. That will be true of a number of cases. Clearly, the presence or absence of a moral claim will often be at the centre of the decision under the 1975 Act.

Ilott was a case with striking facts: the deceased and her daughter had been estranged for the whole of the daughter's adult life as she had left home to live with her boyfriend of whom her mother disapproved at 17. The case might have been an easier one had Mrs Ilott not been heavily reliant on state benefits to support her. It was clear that there was a legitimate range of awards which might have been made with which it would not have been open to an appellate court to interfere and that rejection of the claim altogether would have been justified.

If an adult child is actually being maintained by a parent whether by the provision of a roof over their head or financially, then it may be easier to assess an award by reference to that. In other cases where the adult child has been financially independent (even if not well off) the task of the court is much more difficult. However, the court has to guard against a redistribution of the estate to do what it perceives to be fair. Instead it has to stick firmly to what it considers to be required for the applicant's maintenance.

Re Myers [2004] EWHC 1944 (Fam) (a case which Lord Hughes approved in *Ilott*) contains a helpful illustration of this principle in the judgment of Munby J (as he then was) in a claim by an adult daughter. In that case the net estate was extremely substantial (c. £8.3 million) and it was common ground that the claimant had a housing need. The estate was clearly large enough to purchase a property for the applicant outright and thereby meet her housing need, and the court considered that £275,000 would be an appropriately valued property (expressly applying the dictum in *Re Coventry*). Despite this, the property was not purchased for the applicant outright but settled on her for life. This was because, as Munby J correctly stated:

> the purpose of the Act is not to award legacies or to make capital provision for claimants, however deserving, but simply to make provision for their maintenance.

6.5   APPLICANTS TREATED AS A CHILD

Interesting issues arise as to who can apply under this head and this is dealt with in **Chapter 3**. However, once an applicant has established that he or she was a person (not being a child of the deceased) who in relation to any marriage or civil partnership to which the deceased was at any time a party, or otherwise in relation to any family in which the deceased at any time stood in the role of a parent, was treated by the deceased as a child of the family, then the authors would suggest that the same considerations come into play as with applicants who are children both minor and adult.

The further additional factors which the court must take into account are whether the deceased maintained the applicant and, if so, the length of time for which and basis on which the deceased did so, and the extent of the contribution made by way of maintenance; and whether and, if so, to what extent the deceased assumed responsibility for the maintenance of the applicant. The court also has to have regard to whether in assuming and discharging that responsibility, the deceased did so knowing that the applicant was not his own child.

Those additional factors are really relevant to claims by minor children. The leading reported cases have involved adult applicants and they seem to have been treated little differently from natural adult children. In *Re Callaghan* [1985] Fam 1, a stepson who had a very close relationship with the deceased was awarded £15,000 so that he could purchase his council house free of mortgage. In *Re Leach* [1986] Ch 226, a stepdaughter was awarded half the modest estate to discharge debts and produce an income for her in retirement. Neither of these awards appears to have been affected by the applicant being a stepchild rather than the natural child of the deceased.

6.6   FORMER SPOUSES AND CIVIL PARTNERS

In the case of an application by a former spouse or civil partner of the deceased (not treated as a spouse or civil partner where the divorce or dissolution has taken place within 12 months of death), the age of the applicant and the duration of the marriage or partnership are particular factors to be taken into account and the contribution made by the applicant to the welfare of the family of the deceased, including any contribution made by looking after the home or caring for the family.

It has been held that exceptional circumstances must be shown before provision will be made for a former spouse (see *Re Fullard (Deceased)* [1982] Fam 42 and *Barass* v. *Harding* [2001] 1 FLR 138); particularly in the case where there has been a clean break; and that principle will apply even where there is an intestacy and the estate of the deceased will go *bona vacantia* (see *Cameron* v. *Treasury Solicitor* [1996] 2 FLR 716).

However, where there is a maintenance order in place (not secured after death) and the applicant is left without means of support, the court may make an order: *Re Farrow* [1987] 1 FLR 205.

Cases are rare because it has become common practice for an order under s.15 of the 1975 Act to be sought excluding claims by former spouses and civil partners once the financial claims have been settled.

6.7 DEPENDANTS

Since the introduction of cohabitees as a category of applicant in 1995, applications by dependants have decreased. The requirements for qualification in this category are set out in **Chapter 3** and were changed in 2014.

In such claims the court will take into account in addition to the s.3 factors the length of time for which and basis on which the deceased maintained the applicant, and the extent of the contribution made by way of maintenance and whether and, if so, to what extent the deceased assumed responsibility for the maintenance of the applicant. Amendments were made to the 1975 Act by the Inheritance and Trustee Powers Act 2014 to make it clear that it is not a threshold requirement that the deceased assumed responsibility for the maintenance of the applicant. However, it is still a factor which the court will take into account. The absence of any responsibility to maintain led to the rejection of a claim in *Baynes* v. *Hedger* [2009] WTLR 740 where an aunt had made soft loans to her goddaughter to bail her out of financial difficulties but had not assumed responsibility to maintain her.

The level at which the applicant has been maintained during his lifetime is clearly very important to such claims although all the s.3 factors have to be taken into account. The assessment of such claims is going to depend in most cases on replicating a standard of living for the applicant to prevent him from suffering hardship because the support he received from the deceased has terminated.

CHAPTER 7

Anti-avoidance provisions

7.1   INTRODUCTION

Sections 10 to 13 of the Inheritance (Provision for Family and Dependants) Act 1975 contain provisions which enable the court to set aside or inhibit transactions entered into by the deceased with a view to defeating a claim for provision out of his estate under the Act.

The sections apply to transactions entered into by the deceased after the commencement of the Act (1 April 1976).

7.2   DISPOSITIONS INTENDED TO DEFEAT APPLICATIONS FOR FINANCIAL PROVISION

Section 10 of the Act provides as follows:

(1)   Where an application is made to the court for an order under section 2 of this Act, the applicant may, in the proceedings on that application, apply to the court for an order under subsection (2) below.

(2)   Where on an application under subsection (1) above the court is satisfied –

(a)   that, less than six years before the date of the death of the deceased, the deceased with the intention of defeating an application for financial provision under this Act made a disposition, and

(b)   that full valuable consideration for that disposition was not given by the person to whom or for the benefit of whom the disposition was made (in this section referred to as 'the donee') or by any other person, and

(c)   that the exercise of the powers conferred by this section would facilitate the making of financial provision for the applicant under this Act,

then, subject to the provisions of this section and sections 12 and 13 of this Act, the court may order the donee (whether or not at the date of the order he holds any interest in the property disposed of to him or for his benefit by the deceased) to provide, for the purpose of the making of that financial provision, such sum of money or other property as may be specified in the order.

7.3 PRELIMINARY POINTS ON SECTION 10

An application under s.10 of the Act can only be made where the applicant has applied for an order making financial provision under s.2 of the Act. However, provided an application for an order under s.2 has been made within the time limit specified in s.4 (or outside that time limit with the permission of the court), a s.10 application can be made at any time before the application for an order under s.2 has been finally determined.

The court can only make an order under s.10 if such an order will 'facilitate the making of financial provision' for the claimant under s.2. Section 2(1)(a)–(e) list various forms of order which the court can make in relation to the deceased's 'net estate' so as to make provision for the claimant. Section 25(1) of the Act includes in the definition of the 'net estate' any sum of money or other property which is ordered to be provided under s.10. Thus, if the deceased left no property in his estate by reason of having made a disposition within the ambit of s.10, it would still be open to the claimant to apply for an order under s.2 together with an order under s.10 of the Act.

Although the court can only make an order under s.2 if it concludes that the dispositions of the deceased's estate (as opposed to his 'net estate') on death were not such as to make reasonable provision for the claimant, it is possible for a claimant who has received the entirety of the deceased's estate under his will or under the intestacy provisions to seek relief under s.10. This is because the court may still conclude that the dispositions of the deceased's estate did not in fact make reasonable provision for the claimant in the light of the size and nature of the 'net estate' which, by virtue of s.15, will include money or property ordered to be provided under s.10 (see *Dellal* v. *Dellal* [2015] EWHC 907 (Fam)).

Unlike MCA 1973, s.37, s.10 does not confer a power on the court to set aside a transaction; relief under s.10 takes the form of an order against the 'donee' to pay a sum of money or provide property. This and other differences between s.37 and s.10 are discussed in *AC* v. *DC* [2012] EWHC 2032 (Fam).

An order can be made under s.10 against the 'donee' whether or not he still retains any interest in the property which was disposed of to him or for his benefit by the deceased. However, if the relevant disposition was a payment of money, the donee's potential liability is limited to the sum of money paid to him by the deceased (after any inheritance tax paid by him is deducted) and if the relevant disposition was a transfer of property, the donee's liability is limited to the value of that property at the date of death of the deceased (again, after deduction of the relevant inheritance tax). If the donee has transferred the property to a third party, the donee's liability will be limited to the value of that property at the date of that disposal.

The section does not give rise to a proprietary remedy; the applicant cannot trace the property disposed of by the deceased into the hands of the ultimate owner. Thus, any liability which the donee owes pursuant to an order made under s.10 would not take priority over other liabilities in his bankruptcy. Section 10(5) does, however, enable both a donee who is subject to an application under s.10 and the applicant to seek a similar order against any person to whom the donee disposed of the property in question for less than full valuable consideration.

Section 12(3) of the Act enables the court, when making an order under s.10 (or s.11), to make such consequential directions as it thinks fit for giving effect to that order or securing a 'fair adjustment for the rights of the persons affected thereby'. Section 12(4) provides that the court's power to make orders under s.10 (and s.11) against a donee are exercisable in like manner against the personal representative of the donee. However, the subsection provides protection for a personal representative of a donee who distributes without notice of a s.10 (or s.11) claim.

7.4   THE DISPOSITION

For the court's s.10 powers to come into play, there must have been a disposition within the ambit of the section. Any dispositions made by will, *donatio mortis causa*, nomination within s.8 of the 1975 Act or any exercise of a special power of appointment are expressly excluded from its ambit. Otherwise, s.10(7) defines disposition widely so as to include 'any payment of money (including the payment of a premium under a policy of life assurance) and any conveyance, assurance, appointment or gift of property of any description, whether made by an instrument or otherwise'.

In *Newlon Housing Trust* v. *Alsulaimen* [1999] 1 AC 313 the House of Lords held that service of a notice to quit in respect of a periodic tenancy was not a 'disposition of property' for the purposes of MCA 1973, s.37. Lord Hoffmann held that it was essential to a disposition of property in that context that there was property of which the disponor disposes and which could be restored by exercise of the court's powers under s.37 whereas service of a notice to quit had caused the property in question, the periodic tenancy, to cease to exist. Although the court does not have power to set aside a transaction under s.10, and s.10(2) expressly provides that an order can be made whether or not the donee holds any interest in the property disposed of to him at the date of the order, s 10(4) does appear to contemplate that the property disposed will exist and have some value at the date of death of the deceased. Accordingly, it is thought likely that service of notice to quit by the deceased would not be treated as a disposition for the purposes of s.10. Similarly, it is thought that an exercise by the deceased of a power to exclude the claimant as a beneficiary of a nuptial settlement would not be regarded as a disposition for the purposes of s.10 (see *Mubarak* v. *Mubarik* [2007] EWHC 220 (Fam) at paras.71–76) even if the power exercised was not a special power of appointment expressly excluded from the ambit of the section by s.10(7)(b).

On the face of it a claim made under s.10 against a defendant which does not identify any disposition made by the deceased to that defendant within the six-year period ending on the deceased's death would not have a real prospect of success and, as such, would be vulnerable to an application for summary dismissal. However, depending on the circumstances of the case, the court may be prepared to adjourn an application for summary judgment by the defendant until the claimant has been provided with disclosure under CPR rule 31.12 of documents that he could have obtained in an application for pre-action disclosure under CPR rule 31.16 (although the court is likely to require an explanation as to why no application under CPR rule 31.16 was made).

Unlike s.11 or MCA 1973, s.37 which can apply to transactions whenever they are made, s.10 is subject to a rigid time limit and only transactions made within six years of the deceased's death fall within the section.

Section 10 only captures dispositions made by the deceased. In *Kemmis* v. *Kemmis* [1988] 2 FLR 223 the Court of Appeal held that a disposition made 'by the other party to the proceedings' for the purposes of MCA 1973, s.37 included a disposition made by a company which the court found to be a nominee or bare trustee of the husband. It is thought that the court would find that a disposition made by a nominee or bare trustee of the deceased falls within s.10 (to the extent that it is not a disposition captured by the provisions applicable to trustees in s.13). However, a disposition made by a company that is owned and controlled by the deceased but not his nominee or bare trustee will only fall within s.10 if the company's separate legal personality is being abused for the purpose of some relevant wrongdoing so that the court is able to pierce the corporate veil (see *Petrodel* v. *Prest* [2013] UKSC 34). It is possible that the interposition of a company in a transaction made initially by the deceased for the purposes of avoiding a claim under s.2 would be sufficient wrongdoing for these purposes.

The disposition must have been made for less than 'full valuable consideration'. Section 25(2) of the Act makes clear that 'valuable consideration' does not include marriage or a promise of marriage. It is assumed that 'full' consideration means consideration of a value equal to the market value of the asset disposed of. However, it is unclear whether 'full' consideration should mean something in addition to market value in the case of a special purchaser.

7.5 THE INTENTION

For an application under s.10 to succeed, the claimant must show that, on the balance of probabilities, the deceased made the disposition with the intention, though not necessarily the sole intention, of preventing an order for financial provision being made under the Act, or reducing the amount of provision which may have been granted (see s.12(1) of the Act).

There is no statutory presumption to assist the claimant with this task (cf. MCA 1973, s.37(5) and s.12(2) of the Act) and, without doubt, establishing the requisite intention on the part of the deceased will be the most difficult hurdle which the claimant will face when seeking to make an application under s.10.

Perhaps this evidential difficulty explains why there are few reported decisions concerning applications under s.10 of the Act. Some guidance as to the likely approach of the court can be gathered from authorities on other similar statutory provisions, such as MCA 1973, s.37 (court's power to set aside dispositions made with the intention of defeating claims for financial relief under that Act) or s.423 of the Insolvency Act 1986 (court's power to set aside transactions at an undervalue made for the purpose of defeating creditors).

In *Kemmis* v. *Kemmis* (at 241), the Court of Appeal held, in the context of an appeal concerning MCA 1973, s.37, that, in circumstances where the statutory presumption in s.37(5) did not apply, the applicant must establish intention in a subjective sense; that is, by reference to the state of mind of the deceased rather than the natural consequences of his acts alone. The approach of the court considering a s.10 claim (where no presumption arises) will be similar. The claimant is not, however, required to show that the intention in question was the dominant intention of the party making the disposition, only that the intention concerned played a substantial part in his intentions as a whole (see *Kemmis* at 246).

It appears that the claimant need not show that the deceased had in mind the act itself: a general desire to protect his asset from the claimant after his death will suffice (see e.g. *Dawkins* v. *Judd* [1986] 2 FLR 360; *Re Kennedy (Deceased), sub nom: Kennedy* v. *the Official Solicitor* (unreported, 22 May 1980, Shoreditch CC)).

Moreover, as was pointed out in *Kemmis* (at 241), in any case where the court is asked to determine whether a person had a particular intention, the court will usually be thrown back on inference and, when drawing inferences in the context of an application under s.10, it will be proper for the court to take into account the natural consequences of the deceased's act; although those consequences should not, of themselves, be sufficient to establish the necessary intention.

In some cases the deceased's contemporaneous declarations will (provided they are disclosed – on this subject please refer to the discussion on privilege in **Chapter 11**) make the claimant's task of establishing the requisite intention relatively straightforward (as was the case in *Dawkins* v. *Judd* and in *Hanbury* v. *Hanbury* [1999] 2 FLR 255). However, in the majority of cases there will be very little material, beyond the natural consequences of the act in question, available to the claimant and establishing the requisite intention will be highly problematical.

7.6   FACTORS THE COURT WILL TAKE INTO ACCOUNT

In contrast to the court's powers under MCA 1973, s.37, s.10 of the 1975 Act enables the court to make an order against the donee even if the donee provided valuable consideration (provided that the consideration which he or any other party provided was not 'full'), acted in good faith and received the property in question with no notice of the deceased's intention to defeat a claim under the Act.

However, the court's powers under s.10 are discretionary and s.10(6) directs the court to take into account the circumstances in which the disposition was made and any valuable consideration given for it as well as the relationship of the donee to the deceased, the conduct and financial resources of the donee and all the other circumstances of the case when determining whether and in what manner to exercise its powers under s.10. It is considered most unlikely that the court would choose to exercise its powers under s.10 so as to make an order against a person who provided consideration which was close to the full value of the property concerned and who acted in good faith.

7.7 CONTRACTS TO LEAVE PROPERTY BY WILL

Section 11 of the Act provides:

(1)   Where an application is made to a court for an order under section 2 of this Act, the applicant may, in the proceedings on that application, apply to the court for an order under this section.

(2)   Where on an application under subsection (1) above the court is satisfied –

(a)   the deceased made a contract by which he agreed to leave by his will a sum of money or other property to any person or by which he agreed that a sum of money or other property would be paid or transferred to any person out of his estate, and

(b)   that the deceased made that contract with the intention of defeating an application for financial provision under this Act, and

(c)   that when the contract was made full valuable consideration for that contract was not given or promised by the person with whom or for the benefit of whom the contract was made (in this section referred to as 'the donee') or by any other person, and

(d)   that the exercise of the powers under this section would facilitate the making of financial provision for an applicant under this Act, then, subject to the provisions of this section and sections 12 and 13 of this Act, the court may make any one or more of the following orders ...

7.8 PRELIMINARY POINTS ON SECTION 11

The preliminary points made in relation to s.10 above also apply to s.11 of the 1975 Act. An application for an order under s.11 can only be made if it is coupled with an application for an order under s.2; it can be made at any time within existing proceedings for an order under s.2; the court may only exercise its s.11 powers to facilitate making provision under s.2 and, if the s.11 powers are exercised, they do not give rise to a tracing remedy. In addition to making an order that the donee or his personal representative repay any money or property paid or transferred to him pursuant to a contract within the ambit of the section, the court can, under s.11(2)(ii) make an order preventing the deceased's personal representatives from giving effect to the contract in question.

Section 11(3) limits the scope of the s.11 powers so that they may only be exercised to the extent that the property transferred or money paid pursuant to the relevant contract exceeds the value of the consideration given.

7.9 CONTRACTS WITHIN THE AMBIT OF THE SECTION

In order for an agreement by the deceased to leave money or property by will or to dispose of money or property in his estate to fall within the ambit of the section, that agreement must be a 'contract' made by the deceased.

The agreement will not amount to a contract unless the essential characteristics of a contract, including offer and acceptance, are present (see e.g. *Irani* v. *Irani* [2006] EWHC 1811 (Ch)). Moreover, the agreement will only amount to a binding contract if it was either made under seal or supported by consideration, i.e. something of value in the eye of the law (see *Thomas* v. *Thomas* (1842) 2 QB 851) passing from the other contracting party to the deceased (see *Schaeffer* v. *Schuhmann* [1972] AC 572; *Maddison* v. *Alderson* (1882–3) LR 8 App Cas 467). Gratuitous promises or assurances made by the deceased, even those which induce detrimental reliance on the part of the promisee which may be enforceable in equity under the doctrine of proprietary estoppel, will not fall within the ambit of s.11. (Although, somewhat incongruously, the other contracting party is referred to in s.11 as 'the donee'.) Moreover, the agreement must comply with any relevant formality requirements (see e.g. *Irani* v. *Irani* above).

Any contract of the nature specified in s.11(2)(a) may fall within the ambit of s.11 provided that it was made after the commencement of the Act itself.

7.10 THE REQUISITE INTENTION

To be within the ambit of the section, the contract must have been made with the intention of defeating an application for financial provision under the Act. The approach of the court on this issue is likely to be similar to s.10 save in one respect. Section 12(2) of the Act provides that:

> Where an application is made under section 11 of this Act with respect to any contract made by the deceased and no valuable consideration was given or promised by any person for that contract then … it shall be presumed, unless the contrary is shown, that the deceased made that contract with the intention of defeating an application for financial provision under this Act.

In most cases where the deceased agreed to leave property by will or to dispose of his estate in a particular way for no valuable consideration, the agreement will have been gratuitous and, accordingly, will not amount to a contract at all and will be outside the ambit of s.11 altogether. However, there may be rare cases where the deceased made an agreement under seal or an agreement for nominal consideration or an agreement for inadequate consideration, all of which could amount to contracts within the ambit of s.11, but where the presumption in s.12(2) would apply.

7.11   FACTORS THE COURT WILL TAKE INTO ACCOUNT

Just as is the case with its power under s.10 of the Act, the court's power under s.11 is discretionary. Section 11(4) directs the court to take into account the circumstances in which the contract was made, the relationship, if any, of the donee to the deceased, the conduct and financial resources of the donee and all the other circumstances of the case when determining whether, and to what extent, to exercise its powers.

7.12   TRUSTEES

Section 13 of the Act contains special provisions which apply in the case of any application made under either s.10 or s.11 in respect of a disposition or contract made between the deceased and a trustee, or the donee and a trustee. In such a case, the order made by the court against the donee must be limited to the aggregate value of the money or property transferred (or property representing that property) in the hands of the trustee at the time the order is made. Moreover, a trustee is not to be made liable to account on the basis that he has distributed without taking account of the possibility of a claim under s.10 or s.11 (see s.13(2) of the Act).

The fact that the claimant's remedy under ss.10 and 11 against a trustee is limited to the value of the property in the hands of the trustee at the time the order is made means that the claimant could be severely prejudiced by distributions made by the trustee before his s.10 or s.11 claim is determined. Presumably, if an application has been made under s.10 or s.11 against a trustee and that trustee is put on notice of the application but refuses to provide an undertaking not to make any distributions of the relevant property pending determination of the claim, it would be possible for the claimant to seek injunctive relief so as to restrain the trustee from making such distributions.

CHAPTER 8

Procedure

8.1 PRE-ACTION STEPS

There is no CPR pre-action protocol specifically for claims under the Inheritance (Provision for Family and Dependants) Act 1975. Therefore the general Pre-Action Conduct and Protocols Practice Direction applies (CPR Section C1-001). The Association of Contentious Trust and Probate Specialists (ACTAPS) has also produced Practice Guidance for the Resolution of Probate and Trust Disputes ('the ACTAPS Code'), including claims under the 1975 Act. The ACTAPS Code can be found at **Appendix C2**. A draft Letter of Claim can be found at **Appendix B1**.

The pre-action protocol requires a claimant to send a Letter of Claim to all defendants (see below at **8.7.2**). The letter should address the relevant sections of the Act, in particular:

(a)   his or her status as an eligible applicant under s.1; and

(b)   why the claimant has not received 'reasonable financial provision', addressing each of the s.3 factors so far as possible in answering that question. It is important that the claimant states his or her present and future financial needs and resources, and provides corroborating documents where possible.

A claim under the Act may be an alternative remedy to be pursued in the event that a primary claim fails; examples are a claim against the validity of a will, and a remedy based upon proprietary estoppel. It is tempting in such circumstances to put off consideration of the details of the claim under the Act pending the resolution of the principal claim. Such an approach is short-sighted, particularly if, as it should be, the aim is to settle the case. It may well be that the result of the claimant losing his primary claim would be that his claim under the Act is enhanced.

As with all claims, there is a risk as to costs if the claimant has failed to engage in any meaningful pre-action steps. Early dialogue between the parties to a claim will often lead to settlement without the necessity to issue proceedings (see **Chapter 9**).

A common problem encountered in claims under the Act is the misplaced zeal of personal representatives who adopt the role of guardians of the status quo and seek to 'protect' the estate from the claim. This in turn can lead to the exclusion of the beneficiaries from negotiations, when their consent is essential to any compromise or settlement. See **Chapter 12** for information about the role of personal representatives in proceedings brought under the Act.

8.2   CAVEAT AND NOTICE OF GRANT

The claimant should not enter a caveat where the only relief sought is provision under the Act. The purpose of a caveat is to prevent the issue of a grant where there is a substantive case against it. Caveats are used for disputes over the validity of the will or who should apply for the grant (the Non-Contentious Probate Rules 1987, SI 1987/2024, rule 44). By contrast, a claim under the Act is predicated on validity of the testamentary documents (or an intestacy). An unnecessary caveat issued by a claimant under the Act will often cause irritation to defendants that is ultimately counter-productive to resolution of the claim.

In *Parnall* v. *Hurst* [2003] WTLR 997 the claimant's solicitors were heavily criticised:

> To enter a caveat where the caveator's intention is to make a claim under the Inheritance Act is wholly wrong… because ex hypothesi the validity of the will is admitted.

There used to be some uncertainty whether a claimant could bring a claim pre-grant. The Inheritance and Trustees' Powers Act 2014 expressly amended s.4 to make clear that 'nothing prevents the making of an application before [a grant of] representation is first taken out'.

It is often in a claimant's interests for there to be a grant (or some progress towards a grant) before issuing the claim. Without a grant it may be difficult to ascertain the size and nature of the net estate (s.3(1)(e)). A grant also resolves any doubt over the identity of the personal representatives.

Given that the six-month time limit (see **8.4**) runs from the date of grant, it is good practice to issue a standing search under the Non-Contentious Probate Rules 1987, rule 43 so that the claimant has notice of a grant once it is made. Notice will be given of any grant made up to 12 months before and six months after the date of application. Application is made to the probate manager at the Principal Registry, or to any district or sub-registry, on payment of a fee, and must be renewed every six months.

8.3   WHERE TO ISSUE PROCEEDINGS

The High Court and the county court both have jurisdiction to hear claims under the Act, regardless of the size of the deceased's estate or the size and nature of the claimant's claim. The county court's unlimited jurisdiction is conferred by the County Courts Act 1984, s.25 (as amended by the High Court and County Courts Jurisdiction Order 1991, SI 1991/724). The Order suggests that claims of more than £50,000 should be tried in the High Court (Article 7(4) of the Order) but in practice, claims with values far in excess of that which have been issued in the High Court are either being heard by a master or being transferred to the county court (including, surprisingly, *Wooldridge* v. *Wooldridge* [2016] Fam Law 451, the biggest money widow claim reported to date).

In the High Court, proceedings under the Act may be commenced in or transferred to either the Chancery Division (now referred to as the Business and Property Courts, Property, Trusts and Probate List (ChD)) or the Family Division (CPR rule 57.15). There is no simple answer to the question of which is more appropriate. On the one hand, a spousal claim that relies heavily on the 'deemed divorce' provision in s.3(2) of the 1975 Act may fare better in the Family Division than in the chancery. On the other hand, the chancery will be the appropriate venue if there are 'chancery' issues in play, such as tax, trusts or company law. There may also be other claims in the proceedings (e.g. construction of the will, proprietary estoppel, beneficial interest claims) that will dictate the choice of the chancery.

8.4   WHEN TO ISSUE PROCEEDINGS

The simple rule is that a claim under the Act should be issued within six months of the grant of representation. Section 4 of the Act provides as follows:

> An application for an order under section 2 of the Act shall not, except with permission of the court, be made after the end of the period of six months from the date on which representation with respect to the estate of the deceased is first taken out (but nothing prevents the making of an application before such representation is first taken out).

It is thought that time does not include the day the grant of representation is issued, so that, if a grant is taken out on 27 April, proceedings must be issued at the latest on 27 October. Brooke LJ computed time in that way at para.6 of *Hannigan* v. *Hannigan* [2000] 2 FCR 650, CA. The view is also supported by *Trow* v. *Ind Coope (West Midlands)* [1967] 2 QB 899, a case concerning the computation of a period of time by reference to a date '*beginning with* …'. However there is some authority for the contrary view that the six-month period includes the day on which the grant of representation issued. Caution therefore suggests that a claim should not be issued at the last minute.

8.4.1   What type of grant?

There used to be some uncertainty over whether a limited grant will start time running under s.4 of the Act.

Section 4 refers to the date upon which representation is 'first taken out'. Section 23 was amended by the Inheritance and Trustee Powers Act 2014 so it excludes limited grants. The new s.23 provides:

Determination of date on which representation was first taken out

(1)   The following are to be left out of account when considering for the purposes of this Act when representation with respect to the estate of a deceased person was first taken out –

    (a)   a grant limited to settled land or to trust property,

    (b)   any other grant that does not permit any of the estate to be distributed,

    (c)   a grant limited to real estate or to personal estate, unless a grant limited to the remainder of the estate has previously been made or is made at the same time,

    (d)   a grant, or its equivalent, made outside the United Kingdom (but see subsection (2) below).

(2)   A grant sealed under section 2 of the Colonial Probates Act 1892 counts as a grant made in the United Kingdom for the purposes of this section, but is to be taken as dated on the date of sealing.

Section 23(1)(b) covers, for example, a grant *ad colligenda bona* which allows management of the estate to prevent loss where there is otherwise no one authorised to administer it. Another example is a grant *ad litem* which is limited to bringing or defending a claim. Those grants do not permit distribution of the estate to beneficiaries.

8.4.2   Late claims

Section 4 of the Act permits late claims to be brought with the permission of the court. The Act contains no guidance about the court's exercise of its discretion in permitting a late application.

Assistance can be obtained from *Re Salmon (Deceased)* [1981] Ch 167 which offers a non-exhaustive list of guidelines.

1.   The court's discretion is unfettered and must be exercised judicially, in accordance with what is right and proper;

2.   The onus is on the claimant to show sufficient grounds for not applying the time bar. The claimant must make out a substantive case for it being just and proper for the court to exercise its discretion;

3.   It is material to consider whether the claimant has acted promptly;

4.   It is material whether or not negotiations were begun within the time limit;

5.   It is material whether the estate has been distributed before the claim was notified to the defendants; and

6.   It is material whether dismissal would leave the claimant without recourse to anyone.

Since *Re Salmon (Deceased)*, courts have tended also to consider the substantive merits of the claimant's claim as a factor to be taken into account. In *McNulty* v. *McNulty* [2002] EWHC 123 (Ch) the strong merits of the claim were a decisive reason for granting the claimant permission to apply out of time three and a half years late. It was also highly significant that there had been no distribution of the estate and no prejudice to the beneficiaries.

In *Berger* v. *Berger* [2013] EWCA Civ 1305, a spouse was not granted permission to make a claim under the Act six years after the expiry of the time limit. The Court of Appeal held that the claimant had an arguable case and the estate had not been fully distributed; residue was therefore large enough to fund any provision that might have been made for a widow. Conversely, the fact that the spouse's central complaint of insufficient income was apparent from the early days. Her claim was not triggered by some extraneous event, or an action by the defendants.

It may be difficult to justify a late claim against an estate where the claimant has an obvious remedy against professional advisers. Yet there are clear disadvantages to a professional negligence claim which may make it unsuitable. Damages for 'loss of a chance' to bring a claim under the Act may be discounted to reflect the inherent risk of litigation. Moreover, a remedy in damages will not give the claimant the variety of orders available to him as an applicant for an order under s.2 of the Act.

Applicants seeking permission to make a claim after the expiry of the six-month limit must ensure their applications are supported by evidence that will address:

(a) the chronology of the delay and, in particular, the date upon which the claimant became aware of the availability of a remedy under the Act and all the steps taken since that date, including consultation with solicitors and counsel, notice of the claim to the defendants and any negotiations;

(b) the merits of the claim. If (as is most likely) the application for permission under s.4 of the Act is included in the claim form with the claim for provision under s.2 of the Act, the evidence served with the claim form should include all the evidence in support of the substantive claim. Any temptation to foreshorten the evidence for the substantive claim in anticipation of an opportunity to serve further evidence once permission has been granted should be resisted; and

(c) why a professional negligence claim will either provide an inadequate remedy or is inappropriate, or otherwise unavailable.

8.5 STARTING A CLAIM

The procedure to adopt in making a claim under the Act is governed by CPR rules 57.14–57.16 and the Practice Direction to CPR Part 57.

A claim under the Act should be brought under Part 8 (CPR rule 57.16). If an additional claim is brought by the claimant, it can be included in the Part 8 claim form and addressed in the claimant's evidence. The only exception is where the alternative claim is a contentious probate claim, which necessitates the Part 7 procedure (CPR rule 57.3). In such a case the claims should be issued separately and directions for the cases to be heard together can be made subsequently.

As with all Part 8 claims, the claim form should be in Practice Form N208 and include:

(a)   a statement that CPR Part 8 applies to the claim;

(b)   a reference to any enactment under which the claim is being brought (thus, a claim form issued for provision under the Act should include a statement 'This claim is bought under the Inheritance (Provision for Family and Dependants) Act 1975' and the heading should include the words 'In the matter of the Inheritance (Provision for Family and Dependants) Act 1975');

(c)   a statement of the remedy sought and the legal basis for that remedy; and

(d)   if either the claimant or any of the defendants sue or are being sued in a representative capacity, a description of that representative capacity. In a claim under the Act, the only obvious application of this requirement is in the description of the deceased's personal representatives as such.

CPR rule 57.16(3A) states that where no grant has been obtained the written evidence must explain the reasons why it has not been possible for a grant to be obtained. That appears to be an unnecessary gloss on the amended s.4 of the Act.

The Part 8 procedure is modified for claims under the Act by CPR rule 57.16(3)–(5):

1.   The claimant is required to exhibit to the witness statement filed in support of the claim:

(a) a copy of the grant of representation of the deceased's estate (whether of probate or of letters of administration); and

(b) any testamentary document in respect of which the grant of representation was made.

But see above as to the position if there is no grant at the time the claim is issued.

2.   A defendant has 21 days after service of the claim form to file and serve an acknowledgement of service and the written evidence upon which he intends to rely (CPR rule 57.16(4)). The parties may agree to extend time for the defendant to file and serve the written evidence up to 14 days after the defendant files his acknowledgement of service (para.7.5 of the Practice Direction to CPR Part 8). There are further modifications for responses to a claim form served out of the jurisdiction (CPR rule 57.16(4A)).

3.   A defendant who is a personal representative may file an acknowledgement of service stating that he will not take any part in the proceedings but will abide and be bound by the outcome of the proceedings (para.15 of the Practice Direction to CPR Part 57). A defendant who is a personal representative must file and serve in evidence the information required by para.16 of the Practice Direction to CPR Part 57, as set out in **8.8.1**. A claimant may serve further evidence in reply within 14 days of the defendant's evidence (see CPR rule 8.5(5)). The parties can agree to extend time for the claimant to file evidence

in reply by no more than 28 days after service of the defendant's evidence on the claimant (para.7.5 of the Practice Direction to CPR Part 8).

8.6 WHAT TO INCLUDE IN THE CLAIM FORM

8.6.1 Details of claim

The claim form need do no more than:

(a) identify the deceased by name and specify the date of death, stating the date that a grant of representation was taken out and identifying a will or intestacy as appropriate;

(b) identify the claimant and state that he applies under s.1 of the Act (placing the claimant within the relevant subsection);

(c) state the grounds for the application being that the disposition of the deceased's estate fails to make reasonable financial provision for the claimant;

(d) state that the claimant seeks provision from the deceased's estate under s.2 of the Act (there is no necessity to say precisely what provision is sought);

(e) identify the defendants and state whether they are the deceased's personal representatives or the beneficiaries of the deceased's estate (or both) and/or defendants for the purpose of an application under ss.8, 9, 10 and 11 of the Act (see further below);

(f) make applications under other sections of the Act:

   (i) s.4, for permission to apply out of time;

   (ii) s.5, for interim relief;

   (iii) s.8, to treat nominated property and property the subject of a *donatio mortis causa* as property available to satisfy a claim for provision from the deceased's estate;

   (iv) s.9, to treat the deceased's jointly owned property passing by survivorship as property available to satisfy a claim for provision from the deceased's estate;

   (v) ss.10 and 11, to treat property the subject of a transaction intended to defeat the Act as property available to satisfy a claim for provision from the deceased's estate; and

(g) make provision for the costs of the application.

8.6.2 Interim relief

An application for interim relief under s.5 need not be made on issue of the claim form, but there is no reason not to include it if the evidence is available and the benefit is apparent. In an appropriate case, an interim application will tend to concentrate the minds of the defendants and make them realise both the seriousness of the claim and the practical consequences of having to satisfy it.

8.6.3   Relief under ss. 8, 9, 10 and 11

Section 9 deals with property owned by the deceased as a joint tenant (which therefore passed by survivorship). Prior to the Inheritance and Trustees' Powers Act 2014 the court did not have a discretion to allow a claim under s.9 to be brought out of time (even if the permission was granted to bring the main claim out of time). Therefore claims under s.9 had to be brought within the six-month time limit. That stipulation has now fallen away for deaths after 1 October 2014. Claims under s.9 can be sought in the Part 8 claim form or at a later stage. For example, it may be that a claimant only realised the necessity of s.9 when evidence concerning the assets in the estate is filed by the personal representative. The s.9 application will be subject to the usual principles applying to late claims (see **8.4.2**).

If the defendant to a claim under ss.8, 9, 10 or 11 is otherwise not a party to the claim, the claimant will need to apply to have him added under CPR Part 19. Such a person may well succeed in opposing an application to amend and add him as a party if there has been significant delay.

8.7   PARTIES AND CONFLICTS OF INTEREST

8.7.1   Claimants

The general rule in litigation is that all claimants must have identical interests and must act through one solicitor. In claims under the Act the general rule still applies, but with some modification allowing claimants to be separately represented.

Paragraph 17(1) of the Practice Direction to CPR Part 57 provides that, where there is a conflict of interest between two or more claimants who are making a claim jointly, any claimant may choose to be represented by separate solicitors or counsel, or may appear in person. If the claimants fail to take appropriate action in the face of a conflict, the court may do so. Paragraph 17(2) of the Practice Direction to CPR Part 57 provides that where the court considers such a conflict has arisen it may adjourn the application until the conflicted parties have separate representation.

The issue of conflicts will arise most frequently where a widow/widower or surviving cohabitee sues jointly with her or his children. There is often a real difficulty for such litigants to accept that their interests are not aligned. Yet they frequently will not be aligned because the one claim may reduce the other. It is essential that the parties are warned of this at the earliest stage so they can seek separate representation.

8.7.2　Defendants

There is no rule specifying who should be made defendants to a claim under the Act. The deceased's personal representatives should be joined.

In general the residuary beneficiaries should be joined as they will usually have a substantial interest in the estate. If there are many residuary beneficiaries, they can be represented by just one of their number using a representation order under CPR rule 19.7(2)(d). This may only be used for beneficiaries with the same interest. If the residuary estate is held on discretionary trusts, it is usually sufficient to join the trustees without joining any member of the discretionary class.

Some thought should be given to whether other beneficiaries should be joined. For example, beneficiaries of small pecuniary legacies, particularly in a large estate, are unlikely to want to defend a claim and may well find that their legacies are left untouched in any event. Notice of the claim under CPR rule 19.8A(2) may be sufficient. If not already on notice, parties served with notice of a judgment will be bound by the judgment unless they apply within 28 days to set it aside (CPR rule 19.8A(8)). Orders under CPR rule 19 can be dealt with at the first directions hearing (see **8.9**).

A claimant may state that he will not claim against particular legacies. This would not prevent the court from considering how to satisfy a claim. Nor would it necessarily stop other defendant beneficiaries seeking to persuade the court to ring-fence their interests and look elsewhere in the estate for funds to pay the claimant. But in practice it can be a useful means to limit the number of defendants and keep costs down.

Other defendants who may be neither beneficiaries nor personal representatives are those affected by applications under ss.8, 9, 10 and 11 of the Act. They must be joined.

8.7.3　Children and protected parties

Just as joint claimants must consider whether there may be a conflict between them, so too must defendants where questions arise concerning who should act as the litigation friend of a child or a protected party under CPR Part 21. Unfortunately parents of minor children are often appointed litigation friend for their offspring when there is a serious risk that the interests of the child and parent may conflict. The same may apply to a litigation friend for a party who lacks capacity under the Mental Capacity Act 2005 and is a protected party within CPR rule 21.1(2)(d). Section 2 of the 2005 Act defines lack of capacity in the following way:

> For the purposes of this Act, a person lacks capacity in relation to a matter if at the material time he is unable to make a decision for himself in relation to the matter because of an impairment of, or a disturbance in the functioning of, the mind or brain.

Capacity is time and issue specific (see *Masterman-Lister* v. *Brutton & Co* [2002] EWCA Civ 1889) and therefore the question is whether the person is capable of understanding (with legal assistance) the proceedings.

CPR rule 21.4(3) requires that a person who is to act as a litigation friend can fairly and competently conduct proceedings on behalf of the child or patient and has no interest adverse to that of the child or patient. The court has power under CPR rule 21.7 to terminate the appointment of a litigation friend if that person does not satisfy those requirements.

8.8　EVIDENCE

8.8.1　Personal representatives

The Practice Direction to CPR Part 57 at para.16 deals with the evidence to be filed by the personal representatives. As far as possible this evidence must include full details of the deceased's net estate and the persons or classes of persons beneficially interested in the estate (including their names and addresses, the value of their interests and whether any beneficiary is a child or protected party).

Personal representatives should also give evidence of 'any fact that might affect the exercise of the court's powers' (para.16(4)). Personal representatives who are neither claimants nor beneficiaries should remain neutral and avoid comment on the merits of the case. They should also avoid other contentious but arguably irrelevant issues, such as the deceased's reasons for making a will in the terms he did.

8.8.2　Claimants

A claimant should address the following issues in the witness statement served with the claim form:

1.　The deceased's death; the disposition of the estate by will or intestacy; the claimant's benefit under either; the identity of the personal representatives; and the date of the grant of representation to the personal representatives (if any). A copy of the death certificate, the will (if there is one) and the grant of representation should be exhibited.

2.　The status of the claimant as an applicant under s.1(1) of the Act. The formal relationship (if any) between the deceased and the claimant should be described and the relevant documentary evidence exhibited. The informal relationship (if any) between claimant and the deceased should also be described: for example, how the claimant and the deceased lived together as if married, how the claimant was treated as a child of the family or how the claimant was maintained by the deceased. This part of the evidence should address issues of responsibility and obligation (s.3(1)(d) of the Act) and any other relevant matter (s.3(1)(g)) as well as the age of the claimant, the duration of the marriage/civil partnership, and the claimant's contribution to the welfare of the deceased's family.

3. The claimant's present net income and expenditure, identifying the source of any income. Expenditure should be presented clearly and by reference to corresponding income periods. It should be possible to tell at a glance whether the claimant is living within his income. It is important to be comprehensive in the survey of expenditure and to include apparently inessential and non-recurrent items (e.g. building repairs, car maintenance, gifts and holidays). However, the claimant should avoid artificially inflating his income needs in an obvious manner. To do so incurs various risks: (i) to costs; (ii) to his credibility; and (iii) to the possibility that the court attacks the entire schedule including legitimate expenditure.

4. The claimant's future income and expenditure. Depending upon the age of a claimant, it is important to look ahead to any likely alteration in a claimant's circumstances, for example promotion, redundancy or retirement, or ability to work if not currently in work.

5. The claimant's present and future capital resources including savings, house (net of any mortgage), investments, car, pension rights and any other valuable capital assets. Again, the evidence should address any likely depletion (or increase) expected to affect these assets.

The claimant's evidence should avoid irrelevant observations on the deceased's conduct. It should be borne in mind that the rationale behind the Act is to provide financial provision to applicants who satisfy the statutory requirement that the disposition of the deceased's estate fails to make reasonable financial provision for them. This is an objective test. The purpose of the Act is not to make reparation for any perceived wrongful conduct on the part of the deceased. The inclusion of irrelevant evidence tends to make it difficult for the parties to focus on the real merits of a claim and reach a negotiated settlement.

8.8.3 Defendants

There are no rules governing evidence from defendants who are not personal representatives. They may wish to adduce evidence of their own present and future financial needs and resources, but they are not obliged to do so. In the absence of any evidence concerning a beneficiary's financial position the court will not take their needs into account. In general, defendants are well advised to avoid comment on the claimant's conduct. The court is unlikely to take this into account and, as above, it tends to aggravate matters and make reaching a settlement harder.

8.9 DIRECTIONS

Part 8 claims are allocated to the multi-track, and case management directions are covered by CPR Part 29. Part 8 claims do not automatically fall within the costs case management regime but the court may order them to do so. It is normal for the court to fix a case management hearing at which the following will be considered:

(a)   disclosure and inspection;
(b)   expert evidence;
(c)   further evidence of fact;
(d)   stay for alternative dispute resolution;
(e)   directions for trial;
(f)   further case management; and
(g)   other matters, including joinder of parties, representation of interested parties, other claims.

Most of the relevant documents should have been exhibited to the evidence served by the parties. If not, it may be necessary to obtain an order for standard disclosure and inspection. This is likely to relate to evidence concerning the claimant's financial needs and resources and/or assets in the estate.

In most cases valuations of assets in the estate (or sometimes those belonging to the claimant) should be agreed by the parties. Shares in a private company or land with development opportunities may prove difficult. In practice, both sides often adduce their own evidence without the need for a court direction. Only if there is significant disagreement should the parties seek an order for expert evidence. Usually the court will direct that valuation evidence be provided by a single joint expert in accordance with CPR rule 35.7.

The court will consider evidence of the parties' circumstances at trial (as opposed to the situation at the date of death or the date of issue of the claim) (1975 Act, s.3(5)). For that reason it is usually appropriate for the parties to be directed to file further evidence shortly before trial.

It is common for a stay of proceedings to be ordered to enable parties to seek a settlement or compromise by alternative dispute resolution (see **Chapter 10**).

The court will consider whether to order the trial of a preliminary issue (e.g. whether the deceased died domiciled in England and Wales; whether the claim should be permitted out of time under s.4; or what assets are comprised in the estate). It will also give directions as to place, length and date of trial, the filing and exchange of skeleton arguments and the trial timetable. Further case management may be ordered in an appropriate case.

Finally, the court should consider whether all necessary parties have been joined, whether any representation order is needed for unborn or unascertained persons (CPR rule 19.7) or for members of a class of beneficiaries (CPR rule 19.6), and whether notice of the proceedings should be served on any non-party under CPR rule 19.8A.

The cost management provisions of the CPR (including costs management conferences) do not apply to Part 8 Claims unless the court so orders (CPR rule 3.12(1A)). The authors' view is that this would happen rarely. For example, the court may undertake costs management where (relative to most 1975 Act claims) the value of the claim is high and the witness evidence is substantial.

8.10 HEARINGS

The general rule is that hearings are public (CPR rule 39.2(1)). There is provision for a claim to be heard in private if it involves confidential information or is necessary to protect the interests of any child or protected party (CPR rule 39.2) but the power is rarely used in 1975 Act claims. The Practice Direction to CPR Part 39 also provides that transcripts of hearings in private will not be provided to non-parties unless permitted by the court.

High Court masters and district judges in the county court both have jurisdiction to try claims under the Act (see CPR rule 2.4 and Practice Direction B to CPR Part 2). The previous limit to the jurisdiction of a master or district judge to approve compromises of claims has been removed.

Although a Part 8 claim, as with other contentious litigation, evidence from witnesses is given orally. The general rule is that a witness's statement will stand as his or her evidence-in-chief although the evidence given in the statement may be amplified, and further evidence given concerning matters that have arisen since statements were filed and served (CPR rule 32.5). Witnesses may be subject to cross-examination on their evidence (CPR rule 32.11).

8.11 LODGING ORDER

Section 19(3) of the Act stipulates that if the court makes an order under the Act, the original grant (together with a sealed copy of the order) must be sent to the Principal Registry of the Family Division for a memorandum of the order to be endorsed on or permanently annexed to the grant (see also CPR Practice Direction 57, para.18.2).

8.12 APPEALS

Appeals from the decision of a district judge or master will be to a circuit judge or High Court judge respectively. Appeals from a circuit judge are to a High Court judge, and those from the High Court judge are to the Court of Appeal (para.3.5 of Practice Direction 52A).

There is no right of appeal from a decision in an application under the Act: a would-be appellant requires permission to appeal. An application for permission may be made to the tribunal that heard the case at first instance, or from the appeal court in an appeal notice (CPR rule 52.3(2)). A litigant is well advised to seek permission from the lower court by oral application at the conclusion of the proceedings. This involves no additional cost to either party and leaves a further opportunity to apply for permission if the application is refused.

If it is necessary to apply by notice for permission to appeal, the application must be made within 21 days from the date of the decision of the lower court, unless the lower court directs otherwise (CPR rule 52.1(2)(b)).

An appeal will succeed only where the decision of the lower court was wrong or unjust because of a serious procedural or other irregularity in the proceedings of the lower court (CPR rule 52.21(3)). The following warning appears in *Ilott* v. *Mitson* [2017] UKSC 17 at para.24:

> Whether best described as a value judgment or as a discretion (and the former is preferable), both stages of the process are highly individual in every case. The order made by the judge ought to be upset only if he has erred in principle or in law. An appellate court will be very slow to interfere and should never do so simply on the grounds that its judge(s) would have been inclined, if sitting at first instance, to have reached a different conclusion. The well-known observations of Lord Hoffmann in *Piglowska v Piglowski* [1999] 1 WLR 1360 esp. at pp 1373–1374 are directly in point. It is to 'kill the parties with kindness' to permit marginal appeals in cases which are essentially individual value judgments such as those under the 1975 Act should be.

An appeal is a review of a decision and not a re-hearing. Only in exceptional circumstances will oral evidence or new evidence be admitted.

8.13   COSTS

The general principle under CPR rule 44.4(2) is that costs follow the event. It should not be assumed that the parties' costs of litigation will be awarded from the estate, especially where the estate is small.

A successful claimant who has not engaged with any pre-action correspondence and/or has refused any meaningful alternative dispute resolution may well be penalised in costs (*Lilleyman* v. *Lilleyman* [2012] EWHC 1056 (Ch)). The court will be obliged to apply the costs consequences of any Part 36 offer, although it may disallow some of those costs (*Lilleyman* v. *Lilleyman*). Non-Part 36 offers will of course be relevant.

A personal representative will expect to recover his costs from the estate on an indemnity basis to the extent they are not recovered from any other party. However, if a personal representative has acted inappropriately in the proceedings (e.g. by actively opposing the claimant's claim) he may be denied the usual indemnity.

CHAPTER 9

Orders which the court can make

9.1 THE NET ESTATE

Before addressing how the court may order provision to be made for a successful applicant, it is necessary to consider from what assets such provision will be made. Section 2 of the Inheritance (Provision for Family and Dependants) Act 1975 envisages awards being made from the deceased's 'net estate'. 'Net estate' is defined in s.25(1) of the Act as follows:

(a) all property of which the deceased had power to dispose by his will (otherwise than by virtue of a special power of appointment) less the amount of his funeral, testamentary and administration expenses, debts and liabilities, including any capital transfer tax payable out of his estate on his death;

(b) any property in respect of which the deceased held a general power of appointment (not being a power exercisable by will) which has not been exercised;

(c) any sum of money or other property which is treated for the purposes of this Act as part of the net estate of the deceased by virtue of section 8(1) or (2) of this Act;

(d) any property which is treated for the purposes of this Act as part of the net estate of the deceased by virtue of an order made under section 9 of the Act;

(e) any sum of money or other property which is, by reason of a disposition or contract made by the deceased, ordered under section 10 or 11 of this Act to be provided for the purposes of the making of financial provision under this Act.

9.1.1 Generally

This part of the chapter will consider the definition of the 'net estate' generally and will look in particular at nominations and joint property, which are the subject of the definition in s.25(c) and (d). Dispositions and contracts under ss.10 and 11 of the Act (s.25(1), definition of 'net estate', subsection (e)) are dealt with in **Chapter 7**.

The definition of 'net estate' in s.25(1)(a) of the Act will catch the entire estate of most deceased persons. The definition in (a) is of all property which the deceased 'had power to dispose of by his will'. Two points should be noted. The first is that it makes no difference that the deceased may have died wholly or partially intestate: he *had power* to leave his property by will, and (a) encompasses all the property he could have disposed of had he exercised that power. The second point is that an estate may include property payable to a deceased's personal representatives that

91

was not the deceased's property to dispose of in his lifetime. It may be thought such property could not in practice have been disposed of by a will. For example, personal representatives may be paid money under policies of life assurance written on the life of the deceased or they may receive moneys under the terms of the deceased's pension policy. These sums do fall within the s.25(1) definition of 'net estate' in (a). The reason is that this property could be disposed of by the deceased under a gift of residue or even as a specific gift, notwithstanding the property only falls into the deceased's estate on death.

The qualification within the s.25(1) definition of 'net estate' in (a) 'otherwise than by special power of appointment' is intended to deal with the self-evident proposition that property which may be disposed of by the deceased by will in exercise of a special power of appointment is not property that the deceased owned or could have owned beneficially in his lifetime. In contrast, property in (b) is property that the deceased could have appointed to himself during his lifetime and which otherwise vests in a third party on the death of the deceased in default of the exercise of the general power of appointment. Such property will remain to be treated as part of the deceased's net estate for the purposes of the Act.

The 'net estate' will include:

- foreign property if it passes under an English grant. This will not include foreign immovable property;
- the deceased's share in property held for him and others as tenants in common, including his share in partnership property.

The 'net estate' will not include:

- benefits payable under pension schemes and insurance policies that are not payable to the personal representatives and do not fall within s.8(1) of the Act;
- foreign property that the deceased could not dispose of by will.

The treatment of foreign property, whether as an asset in the 'net estate' or as property passing to the applicant or a beneficiary of the estate, must be investigated by parties to a claim since the ownership and disposition of such assets will be relevant even if they do not fall into the 'net estate' (*Bheekun* v. *Williams* [1999] 2 FLR 229).

In deciding whether to make provision for an applicant and what order to make, the court will consider (amongst other factors listed in s.3 of the Act) 'the size and nature of the net estate'. This consideration will take place at the date of trial and will deal with the property in the net estate in its then current form (s.3(5) and *Dingmar* v. *Dingmar* [2006] EWCA Civ 942, paras.55 and 56). It is important to recognise that s.2(1) of the Act enables the court to make orders specifically related to property in the net estate so that, for example, the court may order the transfer of particular property to the applicant (s.2(1)(c)) rather than simply the periodical or lump sum payment of money (s.2(1)(a) and (b)).

9.1.2 Nominations and property received as *donatio mortis causa*

Section 8(1) of the Act provides that any sum of money or other property nominated by the deceased in someone's favour 'in accordance with the provisions of any enactment' will be treated as part of the net estate 'to the extent of the value thereof at the date of the death of the deceased' after the deduction of any inheritance tax payable in respect of it. It is a requirement that the nomination is in force at the date of death and is made in accordance with the provisions of 'any enactment'. This type of nomination generally encompasses nominations made in respect of sums (whose size is limited by statute) held in accounts subject to the Friendly Societies Act 1974, ss.66 and 67 and the Industrial and Provident Societies Act 1965, ss.23 and 24.

In most cases a nomination falling within s.8(1) will be a nomination made by the deceased under an occupational pension scheme. Section 8(1) will apply if the scheme is founded on an enactment and the employee has a power to nominate. Private sector schemes will generally not have been established by Act of Parliament so the section will not apply (see *Re Cairnes, sub nom Howard* v. *Cairnes* (1983) 4 FLR 225). Similarly, any public sector scheme established by statutory instrument rather than Act of Parliament will fall outside the section. Section 8(1) does not apply where pension benefits are payable automatically under the scheme rules to a specific individual (e.g. a surviving spouse) nor where the trustees of the scheme have a discretion to decide who is to be paid. Benefits payable to the deceased's personal representative are within the s.25 definition of 'net estate' under (a) in any event.

Section 8(2) provides that where a deceased has made a gift as a *donatio mortis causa* the sum of money or other property the subject of the gift will be treated as an asset in the net estate for the purposes of the Act, subject to the deduction of inheritance tax payable on it, to the extent of the value of the gift at the date of the deceased's death. To make an effective *donatio mortis causa* the subject matter of the gift or something representing must have been delivered by the deceased to the donee in contemplation of imminent death in terms that make the gift absolute and irrevocable only on death (see *King* v. *Dubrey* [2015] EWCA Civ 581). Accordingly, the circumstances in which s.8(2) is engaged are very uncommon.

Section 8(3) provides that the amount of inheritance tax to be deducted for the purposes of s.8 should not exceed the amount of tax actually borne by the person nominated by the deceased or who has received money or property as a *donatio mortis causa*.

It is clear from the terms of s.25 and s.8 that money or property which was the subject of a statutory nomination in force at the deceased's death or of a *donatio mortis causa*, after deduction of inheritance tax, will be treated as part of the deceased's net estate for the purposes of the Act without the need for the court to so order. The position is different in relation to property held by the deceased on a joint tenancy which falls within the ambit of s.9(1) of the Act (see **9.1.3**).

9.1.3 Joint property

Section 9 of the Act contains a provision that can be of use to an applicant who seeks provision in circumstances where the deceased's estate is small and property which the deceased held on a joint tenancy has passed by survivorship. Often an application under s.9 will concern a matrimonial home or a property shared by cohabitees.

Section 9 provides that where a deceased person was a beneficial joint tenant of property that has passed to the survivor or survivors on his death, then, if an application is made for an order under s.2 of the Act, the court can order that the deceased's severable share in that property can be treated as part of the deceased's net estate for the purposes of facilitating the making of provision for the claimant 'to such extent as appears to the court to be just in all the circumstances of the case'.

Unlike property falling within s.8, the deceased's severable share will only be treated as part of his net estate for the purposes of the Act if and to the extent that this is necessary to make provision for the applicant. Thus the court is unlikely to make an application under s.9 in circumstances where the property which is already within the net estate is of sufficient value to make reasonable provision for the applicant unless that property is illiquid or has some other characteristic that makes it unsuitable as a source of provision for the applicant.

Prior to 1 October 2014 an application for an order under s.9 could only be made by an applicant who had issued a claim for relief under under s.2 within six months of the date of the grant of representation with respect to the estate being taken out. This meant that no relief could be sought under s.9 in cases where the applicant had had to seek an extension of time to make his claim under s.4 of the Act. Moreover, although there was no express provision requiring a s.9 application to be made within the six-month time limit, in *Dingmar* v. *Dingmar* Lloyd LJ stated (at para.23) that a s.9 application also had to be made within six months of the grant of representation.

As a result of amendments to s.9 of the Act made by para.2 of Sched.2 to the Inheritance and Trustees' Powers Act 2014, an application for an order under s.9 may now be made whenever a claim has been made for an order under s.2 of the Act regardless of when that claim was made.

Any property can be the subject of a beneficial joint tenancy and s.9 expressly applies to the deceased's severable share in 'any property'. In *Powell* v. *Osborne* [1993] 1 FLR 1001, the court held that the benefit of an endowment policy or a life policy assigned for the benefit of a mortgagee or otherwise intended to discharge a mortgage on joint property on the death of a joint tenant will be taken into account so that any debt secured on the property is set off and the deceased's severable share treated as if free of the burden of the debt.

Prior to the amendments which came into effect on 1 October 2014, s.9(1) provided that the court could treat the deceased's severable share in the relevant property 'at the value thereof immediately before his death' as part of the deceased's net estate to that extent that it appeared to it to be just. It had been assumed that this reference in the s.9(1) to the 'value immediately before' the deceased's death was intended to exclude any increase in the value of the severable share between the deceased's death and the trial of the claim from the ambit of s.9. However, in *Dingmar* v. *Dingmar* (see **9.1.1**) the majority of the Court of Appeal held that there was no such cap on the value of the severable share that could be treated as part of the deceased's net estate under that section and the court had power to treat the monetary value of the deceased's severable share in the relevant property as at the date of trial as part of his net estate under s.9 as if he had effected a severance immediately prior to his death.

The decision of the majority in *Dingmar* v. *Dingmar* (which overturned the decision at first instance on this point) was regarded by some commentators as surprising as it appeared to give no meaning to the words 'at the value immediately before his death' in s. 9(1) as it was then enacted. However, amendments to s.9 introduced by paras.7(2)(b) and 7(3) of Sched.2 to the 2014 Act have put the matter beyond doubt. Paragraph 7(2)(b) removed the words 'the value immediately before his death' from s.9(1) and para.7(3) added a new s.9(1A) which provides as follows:

> Where an order is made under subsection (1) the value of the deceased's severable share of the property concerned is taken for the purposes of this Act to be the value that the share would have had at the date of the hearing of the application for an order under section 2 had the share been severed immediately before the deceased's death, unless the court orders that the share is to be valued at a different date.

As a result it is clear that court may, if it appears to it to be just to do so in all the circumstances of the case, treat the market value of the deceased's severable share at trial as part of his net estate as if he had severed the joint tenancy immediately prior to his death.

The deceased's severable share in property he held on a joint tenancy is included as part of his estate for inheritance tax purposes at its value immediately prior to his death (Inheritance Tax Act 1984, s.4). The survivor or survivors are liable for the inheritance tax attributable to that share as the persons in whom the property vests beneficially on the deceased's death (s.200(1)(c)). The deceased's personal representatives are also liable for such tax (Inheritance Tax Act 1984, s.200(1)(a)).

Section 9(2) of the Act provides that, in determining the extent to which the deceased's severable share is to be treated as part of the net estate for the purposes of making provision under s.2 of the Act, the court 'shall have regard to' inheritance tax payable in respect of that severable share. In contrast to the provisions in s.8, the court's powers under s.9 are not limited to the value of the severable share net of inheritance tax paid by any particular person. The inheritance tax consequences of an order under s.9 are discussed more fully in **9.5**.

9.2 THE COURT'S POWERS: SECTION 2 OF THE 1975 ACT

9.2.1 Periodical payments

Section 2(1)(a) of the Act provides that the court may make an order for periodical payments to the applicant in a sum and for the period specified in the order. This enables both a start and an end date to be specified in the order. Section 2(2) and (3) make further provision for the mechanics of an order for periodical payments and reflect the likely difficulties inherent in ongoing provision to an applicant by way of periodical payments from an estate. In deciding how to fund an order for periodical payments (and, indeed, whether to make such an order at all) the court will have in mind the size and nature of the net estate. If, for example, the estate includes a share in a family business now vested in beneficiaries, this may be the source of periodical payments but care will be needed to ensure that the payments are secure and that they can be maintained at the requisite level.

Section 2(2)(a)–(c) of the Act provide alternative forms of order for periodical payments and give the court a general power to make such order for periodical payments from the whole or some part or other of the net estate as it thinks fit. Under s.2(3) the court may order the setting aside or appropriation of a part of the net estate (but no larger part than is sufficient at the date of the order) to produce by its income the amount required for the periodical payments. The restriction on the size of the part of the estate that may be set aside or appropriated requires the court to take account of future rates of return on investment. In practice, this means that the court will need to be referred to capitalisation tables or annuity costs in order to gauge the appropriate size of the sum to be set aside or appropriated. (See **9.4** for the provisions in the Act for the variation of periodical payment awards.)

9.2.2 Lump sum payments

Section 2(1)(b) of the Act covers by far the most common type of award that is made under the Act: a lump sum payment. The attraction of such an award is its finality but therein lies one of its shortcomings: there is no provision for a subsequent variation of a lump sum so it is important to factor in contingencies such as inflation and likely alterations in the applicant's circumstances, for example deteriorating health, redundancy, retirement (see *Re Besterman* [1984] Ch 458 at 476).

The court may order a lump sum to be paid by instalments under s.7(1) of the Act. If an order is made for a lump sum to be paid by instalments the payee, the personal representatives or the trustees of the fund from which the lump sum is to be paid may apply under s.7(2) for an order to vary the number of instalments, the date on which the instalments are payable or the amount payable on each instalment. Such an application cannot seek a variation of the quantum of the total lump sum to be paid (in contrast to periodical payments under s.2(1)(a) which may be varied in quantum and terminated altogether under s.6).

9.2.3 Transfer of property in the estate

Under s.2(1)(c) of the Act the court may order the transfer of a particular property in the net estate to an applicant. This may, for example, be the matrimonial home, or a share of it. The transfer of a particular property to an applicant may be made subject to a charge (ordered in exercise of the court's powers under s.2(4)) for the payment of legacies to beneficiaries of the estate. By this means the court has the flexibility to preserve an asset of particular value or utility to the applicant while at the same time making appropriate provision for other applicants or beneficiaries of the estate. It also avoids the trouble and expense that may be involved in settling the same property on trust for the applicant for life under s.2(1)(d) (*Churchill* v. *Roach* [2003] WTLR 779).

9.2.4 Settlement of property

Section 2(1)(d) of the Act allows the court to order the settlement of specific property 'comprised in' the net estate 'for the benefit of the applicant'. Although the order must be for the benefit of the applicant, the order need not be for his exclusive benefit and, indeed, it is hard to conceive of a settlement involving limited (rather than absolute) interests in property that would not also be for the benefit of persons other than the applicant. A settlement may be required for a minor child, for example, because of the difficulties of such an applicant holding property before the age of 18. The particular requirements of individual applicants need to be considered carefully both in making an order under this subsection and in drafting the terms of any settlement. Do state benefits need to be protected? If so, a discretionary trust may be appropriate, or a limited entitlement to income only with a discretion to advance capital. Is there a risk of bankruptcy or will an award otherwise be for the benefit of the applicant's creditors rather than the applicant himself? If so, property can be settled on a protective trust under the Trustee Act 1925, s.33.

As happened in the following two cases referred to, a court may order a settlement of a house for the occupation of the applicant. The terms of such a trust must make adequate provision for the maintenance and insurance of such property (and any substitute), clearly stating who is liable to pay and the consequences of failing to do so. In *Re Krubert (Deceased)* [1997] Ch 97 at first instance the judge ordered the matrimonial home to be transferred to the applicant absolutely. On appeal the applicant was given an absolute interest in the estate *apart* from the matrimonial home which was settled on trust for her for life. On appeal in *Harrington* v. *Gill* [1983] 4 FLR 265 the applicant (who had lived with the deceased as his wife for six years) was awarded a life interest in the deceased's house in addition to the lump sum and income awarded to her at first instance. Such an approach has been approved by the Supreme Court in *Ilott* v. *Mitson* [2017] UKSC 17 where provision on the maintenance standard was awarded in respect of housing

Rather than paying a lump sum to an applicant, a court may order the acquisition of specific property using assets in the estate. The acquired property may then be transferred to the applicant or to trustees to be held on the terms of a settlement (1975 Act, s.2(1)(e)). This is a cumbersome formula that seems of limited value if the acquired property is to be transferred immediately to the applicant absolutely. It is possible that the cost of acquisition may be sufficiently obscure to merit an order in this form rather than a lump sum payment under s.2(1)(b) of the Act. The provision makes more sense in the context of a transfer to trustees to hold for the benefit of the applicant and others which will be necessary where, for example, the applicant is a child or where the court is awarding a limited interest in a dwelling house that needs to be purchased.

9.2.5 Variation of ante-nuptial and post-nuptial settlements and ante- and post-civil partnership settlements

Section 2(1)(f) enables the court to vary any 'ante-nuptial or post-nuptial settlement … made on the parties to a marriage to which the deceased was one of the parties' for the benefit of the surviving spouse or any child of that marriage or 'any person who was treated by the deceased as a child of the family in relation to that marriage'. It is at least arguable that the latter expression includes a person who was a child of one of the parties to the deceased's marriage by a previous marriage (see *Roberts* v. *Fresco* [2017] EWHC 283 (Ch) paras.63–64).

Section 2(1)(g) contains a similar power for the court to vary 'any settlement' made 'on the civil partners' during the subsistence of a civil partnership or 'in anticipation of the formation of a civil partnership by the deceased'.

The power conferred on the court by s.2(1)(f) of the Act is similar to that conferred on the court in connection with divorce proceedings under MCA 1973, s.24(1)(c) and 'nuptial settlement' will be construed in the same way in both contexts.

The expression 'nuptial settlement' has been given a wide meaning for the purposes of s.24(1)(c) of the 1973 Act. It has been held that 'settlement' is not limited to an express trust created by deed but will extend to any form of disposition (or arrangement) which makes some form of continuing provision for either or both of the parties to the marriage. For example, a life assurance policy that makes provision for both parties to a marriage (or civil partnership) may be a nuptial settlement.

It was established in *Brooks* v. *Brooks* [1996] AC 375 that a pension scheme could be varied as a post-nuptial settlement under s.24(1)(c) of the 1973 Act. That provision has since been amended specifically to exclude pension schemes from its ambit but a pension scheme will still fall within the ambit of s.2(1)(f) by virtue of the reasoning in *Brooks*.

To qualify as a nuptial settlement the arrangement does have to have some sort of nuptial flavour: in other words it needs to have been a settlement made on the deceased or upon his spouse in the character of husband or wife or upon both as spouses with reference to his, her or their married state (*Prinsep* v. *Prinsep* [1929] P 225 at 232). In *Brooks* Lord Nichols held that the expressions 'post nuptial' and 'ante nuptial' settlements embrace all settlements 'in respect of the particular marriage, whether made before or after the marriage'.

Thus a settlement created before the marriage at a time when the marriage was not within the contemplation of the settlor cannot be nuptial. Similarly, a settlement made before the deceased became a civil partner can only fall within s.2(1)(g) if it is made 'in anticipation of the formation of the partnership'.

It is generally easier to establish that a settlement has a 'nuptial' character if it was made during the course of the deceased's marriage, particularly if it was made by the deceased or his spouse. However, it is suggested that, as a settlement will not be nuptial unless it was made on the deceased or his spouse in the character of husband or wife, not all settlements made on the deceased or his spouse during the course of the deceased's marriage will be nuptial. For example, property may have been settled on the deceased in his character as the person who holds or will hold a particular title as opposed to his character as husband and without reference to his married state.

Section 2(1)(g)(i) captures settlements made during the subsistence of a civil partnership or in anticipation of the formation of a civil partnership 'on the civil partners'. It seems likely that the court will interpret the words 'on the civil partners' as importing a requirement that the settlement be made on one or both of the civil partners in that character with reference to their civil partnership (see *Prinsep* above).

Arden LJ in *Charalambous* v. *Charalambous* [2004] EWCA Civ 1030 expressed the view (*obiter*) that, to be a nuptial settlement within s 24(1)(c) of the 1973 Act, the settlement had to be nuptial when it was made. However, there is first instance authority suggesting that a settlement that it is not nuptial when it is made can brought within s.24(1)(c) ('nuptialised') by an exercise of trustees' dispositive powers for the benefit of one or other of the spouses or, perhaps, by an alteration in the identity of the trustees (see, for example, *Quan* v. *Bray* [2014] EWHC 3340 (Fam); *Joy* v. *Marancho* [2015] EWHC 2507 (Fam)). There is disagreement at first instance as to whether the marriage of a person who is an existing beneficiary of a non-nuptial settlement can of itself cause that settlement to be nuptialised (compare the view of Sir Peter Singer in *Joy* with that of Coleridge J in *Quan*); it is suggested that the better view is that it cannot. In *Quan*, the Court of Appeal declined to decide whether a settlement that was non-nuptial at inception could be nuptialised if there was in fact a flow of benefits to one of the parties to the marriage during the course of the marriage as it was unnecessary for them to decide the point to determine the wife's appeal (see [2017] EWCA Civ 405 at para.69).

It seems that a settlement that is nuptial when it is made may also lose its nuptial quality. In *Charalambous* Thorpe LJ expressed the view (*obiter*) that a settlement that was nuptial when it was made could lose its nuptial character if the husband and wife were excluded as beneficiaries but whether or not this was the case would depend on the motive for the exclusion of the spouse(s).

It has been held in the context of s. 24(1)(c) that property owned by the trustees of what would otherwise be a non-nuptial settlement can be subject to its own nuptial settlement. For example if trustees of a non-nuptial settlement have made a house available to the deceased and his wife to occupy, the right to occupy that house, or, possibly the house itself, might be subject to a separate nuptial settlement. It seems likely that the court would adopt a similar approach when considering if a property in the trust fund of a settlement that is outside the ambit of s.2(1)(f) or (g) of the Act is itself subject to a separate settlement within the ambit of one of those sections.

In circumstances where the court does exercise its power to vary a nuptial settlement the court will not usually make an order that defeats the beneficiaries' rights without conferring some compensating benefit on them (see *Hashem* v. *Shayif* [2008] EWHC 2380 (Fam) at para 290). However, the court's approach may be different if the claim is made by a surviving spouse and the trust assets were built up by the efforts of one or both of the spouses during the marriage (see the approach of the court under s.24(1)(c) in, *BJ* v. *MJ (Financial Remedy: Overseas Trust* [2011] EWHC 2708 (Fam)).

The court will not make a variation order under MCA 1973, s.24(1)(c) against offshore trustees if it believes that the order will not be enforced by the jurisdiction exercising control over those trustees (see *Hamlin* v. *Hamlin* [1986] Fam 11; *BJ* v. *MJ*) and it is unlikely that a court would make a variation order under s.2 against offshore trustees that could not be enforced in the trustees' home jurisdiction. However, it has been held that the court can enforce an order made under s.24(1)(c) directly against assets held by such trustees or even by companies (offshore or onshore) held by those trustees (see, for example, *Hope* v. *Krecji* [2012] EWHC 1780 (Fam)).

9.3 INTERIM ORDERS

In an applicant has sought an order under s.2 of the Act, then the court has power, under s.5 of the Act, to order that 'there shall be paid to the applicant out of the net estate of the deceased such sum or sums … at such intervals as the court thinks reasonable' until such date as the court may specify, which must not be later than the date on which the court either makes an order under s.2 or decides not to exercise its powers under s.2.

The court will only make an order for interim provision under s.5 if the applicant is able to satisfy the court that:

- he is in immediate need of financial assistance;
- it is not yet possible to determine what order, if any, should be made under s.2; and
- there is property in the deceased's net estate that is or can be made available to meet the applicant's needs.

An order under s.5 can take the form of a single sum or periodical payments. The court can direct that a property in the estate be appropriated for the purpose of making periodic payments but there is no power for the court to direct the transfer of a particular property to the applicant as interim provision. There is no express power for the court to make a property in the estate available for occupation by the applicant by way of interim provision; however, it is arguable that the court has such a power under s.5(2) (although see *Smith* v. *Smith* [2011] EWHC 2133 (Ch) at para.20).

The court is able to make any interim provision under s.5 'subject to such conditions and restrictions' as it thinks fit to impose. So, for example, the court may make it a condition of an order for periodical payments that the applicant continue to reside at a certain property. An order under s.5 is often expressly stated to be made on account of the provision that may be ordered under s.2 at the final hearing.

The applicant must produce convincing evidence that he is in immediate need of financial assistance. This is because if a court makes an order under s.5 it will be pre-empting the final decision at trial. Statements made by the applicant in his witness statement that are not backed up by documentary evidence are unlikely to suffice (see *Smith* v. *Smith* at paras.27 and 30). Although applications under s.5 are usually dealt with on the basis of written evidence, in an appropriate case the court can direct cross-examination of the applicant.

In addition to establishing an immediate need for financial assistance, an applicant for an order under s.5 will also need to produce evidence relevant to the factors listed in s.3 of the Act. Section 5(3) states that the court shall have regard to s.3 factors 'so far as the urgency of the case permits'. An applicant seeking interim provision is not obliged to prove his claim for relief under s.2 as if at trial; however, for his application to succeed he will need to show his claim for relief under s.2 has a real prospect of success.

If there is no property in the net estate available from which interim provision can be made the application under s.5 will not succeed. However, this does not mean that the court will only make an interim order for provision if the estate is comprised of cash or other liquid assets. Section 5(1)(b) refers to property that is 'or can be' made available to meet the needs of the applicant. Also, the court's powers under s.2(4) apply to orders under s.5 so that the court may make 'such consequential and supplemental provisions as the court thinks necessary or expedient for the purpose of giving effect to the order'. The court's powers under s.2(4) appear to be wide enough to order a sale of an asset to provide liquid funds for an interim payment or interim periodical payments.

An application may be included in the claim form, with evidence in the witness statement filed in support. Otherwise an application would be made by interim application under CPR Part 23, with evidence in support. Applications under s.5 may be renewed and interim orders may be varied. There is no express provision within s.5 for the repayment of an interim award in the event that the applicant is ultimately unsuccessful; indeed the terms of s.5(1) expressly recognise the possibility of the court declining to make an order under s.2 at the final hearing.

Under MCA 1973, s.22 the court has a power to order either party to the marriage to make periodical payments to the other pending the determination of the suit. This section was amended with effect from 1 April 2013 so as to expressly prohibit the court from ordering a party to the marriage to pay the other party any amount in respect of his or her legal costs of the proceedings and, at the same time, new provisions enabling the court to make provision for the parties' legal costs were included in the 1973 Act. Prior to the amendment of that section it was established that there was power for the court to include an allowance for legal costs as part of an order for maintenance pending suit but only in circumstances where the applicant could demonstrate the he could not reasonably procure legal advice and representation by any other means. In such circumstances the court might make a costs allowance but ultimately this was a matter for the court's discretion after weighing up other relevant factors (see *A* v. *A (Maintenance Pending Suit: Provision for Legal Fees)* [2001] 1 FLR 377; *Moses-Taiga* v. *Taiga* [2005] EWCA Civ 1013 at para.25; *TL* v. *ML* [2005] EWHC 2860 (Fam) at paras.126 to 129; *Currey* v. *Currey* [2006] EWCA Civ 1338 at paras.14 to 21).

There is no express prohibition in s.5 which would prevent the court from including an allowance for costs in any order for interim provision under s.5 and, although there is no reported case on the point, the court is likely to include such a costs allowance as part of an award for interim provision under s.5 provided the applicant is able to satisfy the court that he cannot reasonably procure legal advice and representation by other means and that there is property in the estate available to meet that allowance and provided there are no equally powerful factors that would persuade the court against making such an allowance in the exercise of its discretion.

Personal representatives are protected in paying any sum directed by the court under an order under s.5 from 'any liability by reason of that estate not being sufficient to make the payment' except that the protection is lost if the personal representative has 'reasonable cause to know that the estate is not sufficient'. If he has such reasonable cause and makes the distribution he will be liable to the estate's creditors and beneficiaries, notwithstanding the order of the court. For this reason it is important that personal representatives are respondents to any application for an interim award under s.5 and that they actively participate in the application at least to the extent of providing the court with up-to-date evidence of the size and nature of the net estate.

9.4   CONSEQUENTIAL AND SUPPLEMENTAL ORDERS AND VARIATIONS

Section 2(4) of the Act provides that the court in making an order under that section may make:

> such consequential and supplemental provisions as the court thinks necessary or expedient for the purposes of giving effect to the order or for the purposes of securing that the order operates fairly as between one beneficiary of the estate of the deceased and another
> …

It is by this means that the court is able to consider the needs and resources of the beneficiaries of an estate, as it is required to do under s.3(1)(c), and to ensure that the overall disposition of the deceased's net estate, allowing for the order in favour of the applicant, operates fairly and practically.

This power is sufficiently wide to enable the court to settle the estate on new trusts which benefit persons other than the applicant (see *Hanbury* v. *Hanbury* [1999] 2 FLR 255) and enables a court to vary the dispositions of the estate so that they are more tax efficient. If the order under s.2(4) is properly within the jurisdiction of the court the fact that it was sought with the motive of achieving a better tax position is usually irrelevant; however, where the effect of an order under s.2(4) is to confer a substantial advantage on the parties to the claim at the expense of the revenue the court must be satisfied that the order is not only within its jurisdiction but one which can properly be made. In such cases the court will not usually be prepared to make the order simply on the basis of the parties' consent but will require at least some evidence that grounds for seeking the order sought are made out (see *Re Goodchild, decd* [1997] 1 WLR 1216 at 1229B, 1331D–G).

Section 6 of the Act enables the court to vary or discharge an order made under s.2(1)(a) (periodical payments order) on application by any of the following persons: other eligible applicants for provision under the Act; the deceased's personal representatives; the trustees of any property from which periodical payments are being made; and beneficiaries of the deceased's estate. Note that other eligible applicants may apply even though they did not make an application within time in the first instance. A 'beneficiary' as defined in s.25 includes the donee of property subject to s.8 of the Act but not the surviving joint tenant of property subject to s.9 of the Act. An application under s.6 may be made more than once by the same (or different) applicants. The discharge of an order for periodical payments will be final but the court does have power to 'suspend' the operation of an order so that it may be reactivated on later application. If an order was made under s.2(1)(a) in favour of an applicant, then on application to vary that original order the court may make a 'new' order for periodical payments in favour of a different s.1 applicant.

Section 6 orders can only be made in respect of the property referred to in s.6(6), defined as 'relevant property', which is the property from which periodical payments are being or have been made. In the latter case, where periodical payments have ceased on the occurrence of a specific event (unless the specified event was remarriage or the formation of a new civil partnership) or a limited period has expired, s.6(3) requires the application to be made within six months of the date the payments ceased.

Under s.6 of the Act, the court may order discharge or suspension, variation of the amount up or down, a lump sum payment to the applicant or a transfer of the property from which the periodical payments are being made. It cannot make any of the orders that it had power to make under s.2(1)(d), (e) and (f) nor ss.9, 10 and 11 of the Act (see s.6(9)). In practice, there will be little flexibility to make meaningful variations other than those that seek to discharge the order and dispose of the capital from which the periodical payments are made. In making an order the court will have regard to all the circumstances of the case, including any change concerning matters it had regard to when the original order was made.

9.5 TAX IMPLICATIONS OF ORDERS

Section 19 of the Act provides:

> Where an order is made under section 2 of this Act then for all purposes, including the purposes of the enactments relating to inheritance tax, the will or the law relating to intestacy, or both the will and the law relating to intestacy, as the case may be, shall have effect and be deemed to have had effect as from the deceased's death subject to the provisions of the order.

The provisions made in the order are therefore treated as if they had appeared in the will or on intestacy. This may have an impact on the inheritance tax and capital gains tax position. This in turn may have a specific impact on the net estate and s.2(3A) (added by way of amendment to the Act in 2014) provides that in assessing for the purposes of an order under s.2 the extent (if any) to which the net estate is reduced by any debts or liabilities (including any inheritance tax paid or payable out of the estate), the court may assume that the order has already been made. So, if, for example, an award to a spouse reduces the amount of inheritance tax payable, that will be taken into account when looking at the value of the net estate.

Inheritance tax is charged on death as if, immediately before his death, the deceased had made a transfer of value and the value transferred by it had been equal to the value of his estate immediately before his death (s.4(1) of the Inheritance Tax Act 1984). Exemptions are provided for certain gifts including those to spouses (s.18 of the Inheritance Tax Act 1984) and charities (s.23). Therefore it can be seen that an order which makes an award to a spouse or which redirects assets away from charity will have an impact on the way in which inheritance tax is charged on the estate.

The Inheritance Tax Act makes specific provision for orders made under the Act in s.146. In essence that section follows the terms of s.19 of the Act so that the award is read back into the will or the devolution of the estate on intestacy.

Section 146(2) of the Inheritance Tax Act makes specific provision in relation to orders setting aside dispositions under s.10 (as to which see **Chapter 7**). In essence, any lifetime tax can be claimed back provided a claim is made within four years and tax is charged on death as if the lifetime transfer had not been made.

As we have seen above, where money or property is treated as part of the deceased's estate automatically under s.8, it is after deduction of inheritance tax paid by the person who received that property by nomination or *donatio mortis causa*. Section 146(4)(a) makes clear that any adjustment to the inheritance tax paid which arises by virtue of s.19(1) of the Act or s.146(1) of the Inheritance Tax Act shall not affect the tax deducted under s.8(3) and any repayment of that tax by reason of the operation of s.19(1) or s.146(1) shall be made to the personal representatives and not that person. So, for example, if a person who is not exempt from inheritance tax receives £100 as a *donatio mortis causa* in respect of which he has paid £40 inheritance tax, £60 will be treated as part of the net estate under s.8(2) and if that £60 then passes to an exempt beneficiary under an order made under s.2 the tax repaid will be paid to the personal representatives and not the donee.

Section 146(4)(b) contains a similar provision in respect of 'the amount of tax to which the court is to have regard under section 9(2) of the Act'. Thus if immediately before the deceased's death he held a property worth £200 on a joint tenancy with his son and, on his death, the son paid £40 inheritance tax in respect of his father's share that passed to him by survivorship, the court would have regard to the tax paid by the son when deciding if and to what extent it should make an order under s.9(1) in respect of the father's severable share. If it did make a s.9 order in respect of the whole or any part of that share so as to make provision for the deceased's spouse under s.2 of the Act, the resultant inheritance tax saving (arising by virtue of s.19(1) of the Act) would be paid to the personal representatives not to the son. Although in theory s.146(4) could operate unfairly against a non-exempt joint tenant by leaving him with neither the severable share nor the tax he had paid in respect of it, it is unlikely that the court would be persuaded to make an order under s.9 that had this effect.

Section 146(6) deals with settled property and provides:

> anything which is done in compliance with an order under the 1975 Act or occurs on the coming into force of such an order, and which would (apart from this subsection) constitute an occasion on which tax is chargeable under any provision, other than section 79, of Chapter III of Part III of this Act, shall not constitute such an occasion; and where an order under the 1975 Act provides for property to be settled or for the variation of a settlement, and (apart from this subsection) tax would be charged under section 52(1) above on the coming into force of the order, section 52(1) shall not apply.

Section 52 of the Inheritance Tax Act 1984 provides that where an interest in possession comes to an end during the life of a beneficiary, that beneficiary will be treated as if he had made a transfer of value equal to the value of the property in which his interest subsisted. Therefore, if, for example, the court made an order varying a settlement and it involved the termination of an interest in possession, no charge would arise under s.52 by virtue of s.146. If, however, the court order creates an interest in possession in favour of an applicant, it is thought that s.146(6) will not relieve the later termination of that interest (HMRC expresses this view in its manual at IHTM35208). The section can be useful in compromising claims where there is a subsisting life interest under the will (as to which see **Chapter 10**).

Section 146(8) applies the above provision to Tomlin orders provided that any of the terms in the Schedule of the order are terms which could have been included in an order under s.2 or s.10 of the 1975 Act. The impact of tax on compromises of claims under the Act is dealt with in more detail in **Chapter 10**.

For capital gains tax purposes, an order under s.2 of the Act (as opposed to a Tomlin order as to which see **Chapter 10**) will be treated as retrospective. On death s.62 of the Taxation of Chargeable Gains Act 1992 provides a scheme whereby the personal representatives are deemed to acquire the assets of which the deceased was competent to dispose at market value (with no disposal by the deceased) and any legatee acquires that asset from the personal representative at the market value at the date of death. Therefore those in receipt of awards under the Act will be treated as legatees acquiring those assets at the market value at the date of death.

9.6   RESTRICTION PROHIBITING APPLICATION

If there have been financial remedy proceedings under either the MCA 1973 or the Civil Partnership Act 2004, the ability of the survivor to apply to the court may have been dismissed. The relevant provisions are found at s.15 and s.15ZA of the Act. When dealing with financial matters the court can if it considers it just to do so, order that the survivor shall not be entitled to apply for relief under s.2 of the 1975 Act. Where there has been a full clean break and there are no ongoing periodical payments the matrimonial court will make such orders. If, however, there is a continued financial dependency for joint lives, then it is unlikely that any order under s.15 will be made.

On occasions divorced spouses may reconcile and thereafter cohabit. In the case of *Chekov* v. *Fryer* [2015] EWHC 1642 (Ch), the parties' financial arrangements as spouses had been concluded under the MCA 1973. The order included a dismissal under s.15. The applicant sought to apply as a cohabitee, under s.1(1(ba) and contended that s.15 did not apply to her where she qualified as a different class of applicant. The Master concluded that she was entitled to apply.

9.7   RETAINING THE HIGHER LEVEL OF PROVISION

Where there has been either a decree absolute, a judicial separation or a dissolution order, the fomer spouses or former civil partners no longer qualify under s.1(2)(a) or (aa) for the higher standard of provision for spouses. However the survivors may not have been able to secure financial remedy relief under either the MCA 1973 or the Civil Partnership Act 2004 in the time frame after decree absolute. To mitigate this potential hardship the family provision court has a discretion under ss.14 and 14A for a period limited to 12 months after the decree or dissolution order to treat the survivor as if he were still the spouse or civil partner.

In limited circumstances it is possible to secure the delay of the making of the decree absolute until after the financial remedy proceedings, see *Thakkar* v. *Thakkar* [2016] EWHC 2488 (Fam).

9.8 SECURED PERIODICAL PAYMENTS

Where there is an order for periodical payments made under the MCA 1973 or Civil Partnership Act 2004, there is power for the court to make these payments secured or charged upon an asset to ensure payment. This happens only on very rare occasions. There is also the ability to provide that the secured periodical payments order can continue beyond the death of the payer and his personal representatives will be bound by the order.

Sections 31(6) and 36 of the MCA 1973 give the court power to vary the orders post death on either the application of the payee or the personal representative. This jurisdiction does overlap with the family provision jurisdiction under the Act. If an applicant does make an application for an order under s.2 of the Act the court shall have power to vary or discharge the secured periodical payments order, pursuant to s.16 of the 1975 Act, and the variation of s.16 will be considered alongside the application for an order under s.2.

The retention of the matrimonial jurisdiction to vary or discharge secured periodical payments will be relevant where there has been an order under s.15 which prohibits an application under the Act.

9.9 MAINTENANCE AGREEMENTS

A similiar power is contained at s.17 in respect of a maintenance agreement. It is defined in MCA 1973, s.34(2) as being an agreement (whether or not in writing) governing the rights and liabilities towards each other in respect of payments or the disposition of property. For s.17 to apply the agreement must have provided for the payments to have continued after the death of the deceased.

9.10 APPLICATION UNDER MCA 1973

In the event that an application is made under MCA 1973, s.31(6) or s.36 to vary a secured periodical payment or a maintenance agreement, s.18 of the Act provides that the court can treat the application as accompanied by an application under s.2. However, it can only do so where there is not a s.15 bar in place.

In practice one does not come across ss.17 to 18 of the 1975 Act. It is rare to find a secured periodical payment which would survive the payer's death. Further maintenance agreements are not common as most separating parties take steps to dissolve their marriages or civil partnerships and thereafter secure final court orders in respect of their finances.

CHAPTER 10

Compromise

10.1 INTRODUCTION

The vast majority of claims under the Inheritance (Provision for Family and Dependants) Act 1975 are compromised. The focus in civil litigation since the introduction of the Civil Procedure Rules 1998 (CPR) has been on alternative dispute resolution (ADR) and mediation has become widespread. ADR is particularly appropriate for claims of this kind where often the only issue between the parties is the amount of an award which can be negotiated but where following a bereavement emotions can be running high.

There are undoubted advantages in compromising rather than fighting a case. The first is that a bitterly fought contested claim often between members of the family will go nowhere towards healing family rifts. It also means that the settlement can be structured in a tax efficient manner which can make a compromise extremely attractive if, for example, it is possible to fund provision for a widow partially out of saved inheritance tax. Furthermore, this jurisdiction can be notoriously unpredictable and therefore the certainty of a negotiated settlement can be preferable to leaving the matter in the hands of the judge.

There are various ways in which a claim can be compromised. Sometimes it is possible to settle the claim before proceedings are issued by use of a Deed of Variation. If that is entered into within two years of the date of death it may have certain tax advantages as set out below. That is not always the most tax efficient way of proceeding and sometimes cases have to be settled by way of a court order. The circumstances in which this is the case and the form of that order are dealt with below.

Particular problems can arise where there are parties to the claim or beneficiaries who lack capacity or are children. The particular problems which can arise in such cases are dealt with below (see **10.5**).

There may also be cases where the estate is held wholly or partly on discretionary trusts and it is the trustees of those trusts who, far from being able to take the neutral stance which executors can take, have to defend an action and decide on what basis to compromise it. There has been doubt expressed as to whether personal representatives have power under the Trustee Act 1925, s.15 (which provides that trustees can compromise any claim made in respect of the estate) to compromise claims under the 1975 Act. Certainly, as a matter of good practice, in normal circumstances, personal representatives would not compromise a claim without consulting with and obtaining the consent of all adult beneficiaries who have capacity. The position is different for trustees of a discretionary trust and it is clear that they have power under the Trustee Act 1925, s.15 to compromise the claim. However, like all trustees, they can seek the directions of the court under its inherent jurisdiction (in accordance with the procedure set out in CPR Part 64) to sanction a compromise into which they wish to enter which will then afford them protection against any complaint by the beneficiaries. Such an application should be brought by a separate CPR Part 8 claim outside the proceedings of the 1975 Act with the beneficiaries (or representatives of them joined).

10.2 ALTERNATIVE DISPUTE RESOLUTION

10.2.1 Mediation

While negotiations take place round a table and in correspondence and many cases are settled that way (including by use of Part 36 offers as to which see **8.13**) mediation has become extremely popular in this area. Mediation is a facilitated negotiation with an experienced mediator who tries to broker a compromise between the parties. In this jurisdiction mediation is a voluntary process although there is robust judicial encouragement during the case management process to promote it, including providing for a stay in the proceedings so that mediation can take place (see *Halsey* v. *Milton Keynes General NHS Trust* [2004] EWCA Civ 576). There are also potential costs consequences for unreasonable refusal to mediate even for a party who ultimately succeeds. In *PGF II SA* v. *OMFS Co 1 Ltd* [2013] EWCA Civ 1288 the Court of Appeal reviewed the authorities on unreasonable refusal to mediate and confirmed the approach of the Court of Appeal in *Halsey* v. *Milton Keynes General NHS Trust* as follows:

1. The court should not compel parties to mediate even were it within its power to do so. Nonetheless the court may need to encourage the parties to embark on ADR in appropriate cases, and that encouragement may be robust.
2. The court's power to have regard to the parties' conduct when deciding whether to depart from the general rule that the unsuccessful party should pay the successful party's costs includes power to deprive the successful party of some or all of its costs on the grounds of its unreasonable refusal to agree to ADR.
3. For that purpose the burden is on the unsuccessful party to show that the successful party's refusal is unreasonable. There is no presumption in favour of ADR.

The Court of Appeal in *PGF II SA* v. *OMFS Co 1 Ltd* supplemented those points with the following non-exhaustive considerations:

- the nature of the dispute;
- the merits of the case;
- the extent to which other settlement methods have been attempted;
- whether the costs of the ADR would be disproportionately high;
- whether any delay in setting up and attending the ADR would have been prejudicial;
- whether the ADR had any reasonable prospect of success.

As was stressed by the Court of Appeal in *PGF II*, how the court should approach its task as part of a balancing act and of course as in all matters of costs the court has a wide discretion. However, what the Court of Appeal also made clear was that constructive engagement with the process of mediation was required of a party.

In a 1975 Act claim, mediation has a very high chance of success, particularly as the litigation is often not about whether there is a claim at all (as with other types of dispute) but how much that claim is worth. Refusing to mediate in a 1975 Act claim is likely to attract the opprobrium of the court when the question of costs arises.

Choosing the time at which to mediate can be difficult. Mediating too early can be a waste of time if the parties feel they do not have enough information, particularly about needs and resources or the size of the net estate. However, that must be balanced against settling a dispute at an early stage where there may be tax advantages and before the parties' positions become too entrenched, not least because of costs being run up.

The parties and the mediator enter into a mediation agreement which provides for the terms on which the mediation will take place and that agreement usually expressly provides that what happens in the mediation is confidential to the parties and the mediator (see *Farm Assist (in liquidation)* v. *The Secretary of State for the Environment, Food and Rural Affairs (No. 2)* [2009] EWHC 1102 (TCC)). That confidentiality is important and will only be overridden if the interests of justice require it.

Further, negotiations in a mediation are without prejudice which means that they cannot be referred to in proceedings if the negotiations break down, see: *Unilever plc* v. *The Proctor & Gamble Co.* [2000] 1 WLR 2436 where Robert Walker LJ also usefully summarised some of the exceptions to this rule. One of those exceptions is where a party has been guilty of unambiguous impropriety (see *Ferster* v. *Ferster* [2016] EWCA Civ 717 which concerned threats amounting to blackmail in a post mediation offer). It is also open to the parties (but not the mediator) to waive the privilege (*Farm Assist (No. 2)*).

10.2.2 Financial dispute resolution

It has long been the practice of the family courts to hold financial dispute resolution (FDR) hearings which are hearings held before a District Judge or High Court Judge in private on a relatively informal basis where the parties can make limited representations and the court can, through giving indications as to the type of order it might make, encourage the parties towards settlement (see Part 9 of the Family Procedure Rules 2010). The judge who deals with the FDR hearing will be different from the judge who hears the trial if negotiations prove unsuccessful. The judge acts both as facilitator and evaluator in order to promote settlement between the parties.

In 1975 Act claims brought in the Family Division, although the CPR apply, it has long been the practice for the court at the case management conference to order an FDR-style hearing, even in cases where the parties have tried mediation. Everything which takes place at such a hearing is without prejudice.

Following the Chancery Modernisation Review conducted by Briggs LJ, FDR hearings were introduced into the Chancery Division and the rules applying to them can be found in para.18.16 onwards of the Chancery Guide 2016. The court will not direct an FDR hearing unless all parties agree to it. Like FDR hearings in the Family Division the role of the judge is both to facilitate and evaluate and FDR hearings are both non-binding and without prejudice.

The FDR hearing is an important and extremely useful tool in the ADR armoury. The indication of a judge who regularly hears such cases may break the deadlock between the parties. For example, it can often be difficult for defendants to accept that the court can override the wishes of the deceased and hearing a judge indicate what provision might be made can help to manage their expectations. Similar difficulties can be encountered with claimants limited to the maintenance standard of provision who find it hard to accept that the award made to them will be confined to what they need rather than what they perceive to be fair.

10.2.3 Early neutral evaluation

This form of ADR is also judge led and will only occur with the agreement of the parties. It provides for a judge (who might be a part-time judge) to provide the parties with a non-binding view as to the merits of the claim or a particular part of it, although the parties can agree the opinion should be binding. As with an FDR hearing the process is without prejudice and it may or may not involve a hearing. The practice is set out from para.18.7 onwards of the Chancery Guide 2016. In a 1975 Act claim the more dynamic process of an FDR hearing may better suit settling the question of quantum. However, in 1975 Act cases where there are preliminary issues, for example, as to the assets comprised in the estate or the construction of the will, early neutral evaluation may have a role to play.

10.3 COMPROMISE WITHOUT PROCEEDINGS

Leaving aside cases which involve children and protected parties, a claim under the Act can be settled at any time out of court. However, the decision as to whether there needs to be a court order or not will usually be driven by tax considerations.

The effect of the Inheritance Tax Act 1984, s.146 (as set out below) is to read the terms of any order back to the disposition on death so that any award will be treated for inheritance tax purposes as if it devolved under the terms of the will or intestacy. That reading back includes terms contained in a schedule to any Tomlin order. Therefore, if a claim is brought in an estate where the beneficiaries are exempt, i.e. spouses, civil partners or charities, there is a real incentive for parties to negotiate a compromise before proceedings are issued so that the benefit of the inheritance tax exemption is not forfeited and the terms are not retrospective. Comfort can be taken, if negotiations are still ongoing but the six-month deadline imminent, from cases such as *Re Salmon (Deceased)* [1981] Ch 167 (see **Chapter 8**) which indicate strongly that the court will not deny permission to issue out of time if negotiations are in progress. Nevertheless, it would be sensible for exempt defendants to confirm well in advance of the expiration of the six-month deadline that they will not object to an application to issue out of time to allow discussions to proceed.

If, however, it is wished to ensure that the effect of any agreed terms are retrospective for tax, a deed of variation which alters the dispositions made by the will or on the intestacy of the deceased has certain favourable tax consequences if made within two years of the date of death. For the purposes of inheritance tax, the variation is treated as if the deceased had made a will in those terms (Inheritance Tax Act 1984, s.142(1)) and the estate will be charged to tax accordingly. Therefore, for parties giving up interests in the estate in order to make provision, they will not be treated as making any sort of transfer of value for inheritance tax. It is important if advantage is to be taken of this section that the deed of variation states that s.142 is intended to apply to it.

There is a similar provision in respect of capital gains tax contained in the Taxation of Chargeable Gains Act 1992, s.62(6) which provides that a variation does not constitute a disposal for the purposes of capital gains tax. That is important because frequently a beneficiary will be giving up rights in the estate or to property in order to satisfy a claim. Secondly, the variation is treated for the purposes of s.62 (which specifies the capital gains tax treatment on death) as if the variation had been made by the deceased. There are subtle but nevertheless important differences between this and the provision in the Inheritance Tax Act 1984, s.142. Section 142 makes the deed of variation effective for all inheritance tax purposes whereas the Taxation of Chargeable Gains Act 1992, s.62 makes it retrospective only for the provisions relating to death.

This may be of importance if, for example, the deed of variation sets up a trust. For inheritance tax purposes the settlor will be the deceased. However, for capital gains tax purposes, it will be the person who is giving up assets to create that trust who will be regarded as the settlor (see *Marshall (Inspector of Taxes)* v. *Kerr* [1994] STC 638).

What is more, the fiction that the deed is retrospective does not extend to anything other than inheritance and capital gains tax. The provisions of the deed are not as a matter of general law retrospective; neither are they retrospective for income tax purposes. So if a settlement is created the person providing the funds for that settlement will be the settlor, and if there is income payable to a beneficiary prior to the deed being entered into that beneficiary will be entitled to the income (subject to the deed providing to the contrary) and will be liable to income tax on it.

Sometimes concern is expressed that the compromise of the proceedings amounts to external consideration for the variation which disqualifies the deed from falling within s.142, by reason of s.142(3). HMRC does not take the point in respect of the compromise of proceedings under the 1975 Act and, as a matter of practice, numerous claims are dealt with in this way without the need for proceedings being brought.

There are certain procedural requirements which have to be complied with as far as the deed of variation is concerned. There is, in fact, no requirement that the variation be effected by deed (although that is how it is usually done) and all that is needed is an instrument in writing. The personal representatives need only be parties, strictly speaking, if the variation results in more tax being paid, but it is usual to join them and since they are necessary parties to any claim under the 1975 Act, it would be unusual not to do so. The other parties should include any beneficiary whose entitlement is affected and, of course, the claimant if not a beneficiary. Since August 2002 every instrument must contain a statement of intent to the following effect:

> The parties to this variation intend that the provisions of section 142(1) Inheritance Tax Act 1984 and section 62(6) Taxation of Chargeable Gains Act 1992 shall apply.

It is important to get the deed of variation right first time round. There can be no second variation purporting to re-direct the same property (*Russell* v. *Inland Revenue Commissioners* [1988] STC 195) although if evidence is available the court will rectify the deed (*Lake* v. *Lake* [1989] STC 865).

Compromise of a claim in this way is only possible if the claimant and all the affected beneficiaries are of full age and capacity. If there are beneficiaries who are under the age of 18 or lack capacity and whose entitlement under the will is affected then there has to be an application to the court for approval in the ways suggested below, or the court can approve the deed of variation on behalf of the children or patients under its jurisdiction under the Variation of Trusts Act 1958. This is dealt with in more detail below.

A deed under s.142 may be unnecessary in cases where the potential claimant is a beneficiary under a discretionary trust set up by the will. Section 144 of the Inheritance Tax Act 1984 provides that an appointment out of a discretionary trust within two years of the date of death is treated as if the will had provided for the property to be held as specified in the appointment. Further, it is not treated as a chargeable event for inheritance tax purposes.

10.4   ORDERS OF THE COURT

If proceedings are already underway the obvious way forward is to seek an order of the court. In other cases, the two-year period may have expired and so the retrospective tax effects of a deed of variation may no longer be available and an order under the Act might be the answer.

Section 19 of the Act provides:

> Where an order is made under section 2 of this Act then for all purposes, including the purposes of the enactments relating to inheritance tax, the will or the law relating to intestacy, or both the will and the law relating to intestacy, as the case may be, shall have effect and be deemed to have had effect as from the deceased's death subject to the provisions of the order.

The provisions made in the order are therefore treated as if they had appeared in the will or on intestacy. This may have an impact on the inheritance tax position and will affect the income and capital gains tax position.

That is the case in respect of orders made under the Act. However, the most usual way of settling cases of this kind is by way of a Tomlin order – that is, an order which stays the proceedings save for the purpose of carrying the agreed terms into effect. Those terms are contained in a schedule to the order and are in effect a contract between the parties. Except where the order has to be approved on behalf of children or others lacking capacity, the court is unconcerned as to the nature of those terms. A Tomlin order has the distinct advantage that the parties can include in the scheduled terms a compromise of any matters which might be between them and not just those relating to the proceedings under the Act. However, such an order is, arguably, not an order made under s.2 of the Act as required by s.19.

There is no problem with a Tomlin order as far as inheritance tax is concerned because the Inheritance Tax Act 1984, s.146(8) provides that where an order is made staying or dismissing proceedings under the 1975 Act on terms set out in or scheduled to the order, the section (which makes orders retrospective for inheritance tax purposes) shall have effect as if any of those terms which could have been included in an order under s.2 or s.10 of the 1975 Act were provisions of such an order. Therefore, insofar as the terms in the schedule to the Tomlin order relate to provision for the applicant, they will be effective for inheritance tax purposes as if they were dispositions made by the deceased by his will or on his intestacy.

Unfortunately, the position is not so straightforward as far as capital gains tax is concerned. This can be important because some beneficiaries may be giving up interests under the estate to satisfy a claim and these would constitute a disposal for capital gains tax purposes if not read back into the dispositions on death. If the terms are scheduled to a Tomlin order and the court is not required to approve them on behalf of a child or protected party (as to which see below), then the order will not be regarded as retrospective for capital gains tax. If it is made within two years and there is a statement of intention to the effect that the Taxation of Chargeable Gains Act 1992, s.62(6) applies, then the retrospective effect will be available. However, if the order is made more than two years after death and there could be a capital gains tax disposal by a beneficiary, a Tomlin order should not be used. There is always a particular concern that a beneficiary might be regarded not as disposing of any particular asset but of his interest in the unadministered estate and the base cost for that would be nil, although in practice HMRC appears not to take the point.

The answer is for the parties to ask the court to make an order under s.2 of the Act rather than to have a Tomlin order. This will mean that there will usually have to be a short hearing to persuade the court that the compromise which has been reached is such that the court could make an order to that effect under s.2 of the Act.

10.5   CHILDREN AND PROTECTED PARTIES

As set out above (see **10.1**), it is not possible to settle a claim under the Act out of court where there is a patient or child involved. CPR rule 21.1(2) defines a child as a person under 18 and a protected party as someone who lacks capacity, or an intended party, who lacks capacity to conduct the proceedings. Lack of capacity within this context means lack of capacity within the meaning of the Mental Capacity Act 2005. Section 2 of that Act defines lack of capacity in the following way:

(1)   For the purposes of this Act, a person lacks capacity in relation to a matter if at the material time he is unable to make a decision for himself in relation to the matter because of an impairment of, or a disturbance in the functioning of, the mind or brain.

Capacity is time and issue specific (see *Masterman-Lister* v. *Brutton & Co* [2002] EWCA Civ 1889) and therefore the question is whether the person is capable of understanding (with legal assistance) the proceedings and the settlement which is being proposed.

There are a number of ways in which a claim under the Act can be settled where there are children and protected parties involved:

1. Deed of variation approved on behalf of the child or protected party by the court or the Court of Protection under the Variation of Trusts Act 1958 as being for their benefit.
2. Application to the court using the procedure under CPR rule 21.10(2) for the approval of the compromise on behalf of the child or protected party.
3. Order made in proceedings under the Act and approved by the court.

10.5.1   Deed of variation

In the case of a deed of variation to which all parties who have capacity have consented, and where one of the parties lacks capacity, application should be made to the Court of Protection for its approval under the Mental Capacity Act 2005 which is a cheaper and easier procedure than a full-blown application under the

Variation of Trusts Act 1958. If there is a person who lacks capacity and someone else on whose behalf the approval of the court is sought (for example someone in a class of beneficiaries not yet born), then the Court of Protection should be asked to give its approval on behalf of that person first and then an application can be made as set out below to the Chancery Division of the High Court.

In a case where a child is involved, the application is to the Chancery Division of the High Court under the Variation of Trusts Act 1958 and the procedure can be found in the CPR Part 64 and the Practice Directions to those rules and para.29.22 onwards of the Chancery Guide 2016. That practice can be summarised as follows:

1. A Part 8 claim is brought supported by written evidence which exhibits the proposed deed of variation (referred to in this jurisdiction as the arrangement).
2. Minor children need separate representation and the litigation friend appointed on their behalf needs to file evidence exhibiting the opinion of the lawyer representing the children that it is for their benefit including the instructions to that lawyer.
3. Applications are referred in the first instance to a Chancery Master who may deal with the application himself or herself.

As set out above, if there are children and persons lacking capacity, then the Court of Protection rules whether it is for the benefit of the protected party prior to an application being made to the court for approval on behalf of the children or unborns. In all cases the court will only approve the arrangement if it is satisfied that the application is for the benefit of the child or protected party. In doing that the court will, of course, take into account the fact that a claim under the 1975 Act is being compromised. As set out above, the practice requires an opinion from counsel or other suitably qualified lawyer on behalf of the child, unborns or protected party which sets out why the proposed variation is for their benefit.

10.5.2 Application under CPR rule 21.10(2)

This procedure enables an application to be made to the court before proceedings are issued solely for the purpose of the court approving the compromise on behalf of the child or protected party. The application is made by way of a Part 8 claim supported by a statement of the litigation friend appointed specifically for the purpose of this application which sets out the following information: the age and occupation (if any) of the child or protected party and the litigation friend's approval of the settlement or compromise. The statement must exhibit an opinion of counsel or solicitor for the child or protected party and, if not clear from that opinion, the instructions which gave rise to it which set out the benefit of the compromise to the child or protected party. The latter requirement is stated by the rules not to apply to clear cases but it is unlikely that a claim under the 1975 Act would ever fall within that category. Such applications are usually heard by a Master or District Judge unless there is something particularly complex about the matter.

10.5.3 Order in the proceedings

In cases where there are proceedings underway, the obvious course will be to have a consent order in the proceedings themselves. In other cases there may be good reason for starting proceedings in order to settle them and have the court approve the settlement within the proceedings. That is often the course taken where more than two years have passed since the date of death of the deceased and it is not possible to take advantage of the provisions of s.142 of the Inheritance Tax Act 1984 and s.62(6) of the Taxation of Chargeable Gains Act 1992. This is because, as explained above at **10.4**, orders under the 1975 Act have retrospective effect for all purposes (see s.19 of the Act). However, the position is not so straightforward where a Tomlin-type order is used (as to which see **10.4**). In such a case the court needs to approve the order on behalf of the child or protected party and will almost always require an opinion from counsel or the solicitor acting to the effect that the terms proposed are for their benefit.

As set out above, a Tomlin order will be regarded as retrospective for inheritance tax purposes. However, for capital gains tax purposes, it will generally not be regarded as such. The position is different where the court has to approve the Tomlin order on behalf of a child or protected party. In those circumstances, provided that the court directs the personal representatives to carry the terms of the scheduled compromise into effect, rather than simply giving them liberty to enter into the compromise, HMRC regards the Tomlin order as retrospective for capital gains tax purposes.

If the child is the claimant then thought needs to be given as to whether the sum agreed by way of provision should be paid into court or held on private trusts. It is probably right to say that if the award is substantial a private trust is more flexible as applications do not have to be made to court whenever the child needs money. On the other hand, if the award is modest the court may not be keen on the fund having to bear the expense of trust administration. Having said that, if members of the family are prepared to act free of charge, it can still be worth considering.

Sometimes the child will be a defendant – perhaps entitled on intestacy to a fund on attaining 18. When compromising a claim the parties often wish to take the opportunity to postpone the date on which the children will obtain capital from 18 to, say, 21 or 25. It is at best doubtful whether the court has jurisdiction to do this as part of an order made under the Act, bearing in mind that in general the court does not have power to settle the property of a child. In any event, as a matter of practice, capital which is to vest in defendant children at 18 is frequently postponed to a later date. The Finance Act 2006 introduced changes to the way in which trusts for children, usually framed as accumulation and maintenance trusts within s.71 of the Inheritance Tax Act 1984, are taxed and this is a further consideration to bear in mind if asking a court to approve an order which involves the postponement of capital.

The Finance Act 2006 abolished the special treatment which accumulation and maintenance trusts received. Instead, the treatment was initially limited to trusts for bereaved minors as set out in the new s.71A of the Inheritance Tax Act 1984. These are trusts established by will of a parent of the child in question where the child obtains capital at 18. These trusts will apply to wills which are varied either by a Deed of Variation under s.142 of the Inheritance Tax Act 1984 which has been approved by the court as set out above, or a consent order under the 1975 Act which has retrospective effect for tax purposes in respect of deaths after 22 March 2000. At a very late stage the government introduced s.71D of the 1984 Act which provides that trusts will obtain special tax treatment if set up by the will of a deceased parent where capital and income vest in the child not later than the age of 25.

The tax implications of such trusts are as follows. While the beneficiary is under the age of 18, there are no anniversary or exit charges. Once the beneficiary attains 18 the special charging regime (laid down in s.71F) applies, namely that inheritance tax becomes payable until the capital vests at a maximum rate of 4.2 per cent on the value of the property. Therefore, while trusts where children do not attain a vested interest in capital until they are 25 are less attractive than they used to be from a tax perspective, the taxation treatment is not disastrous and the sense in keeping capital away from an immature beneficiary at 18 may well outweigh any tax disadvantages.

As far as protected parties are concerned, it may make a great deal of sense for trusts to be used in respect of any agreed provision for them. Disabled trusts under the Inheritance Tax Act 1984, s.89 have always been regarded as rather inflexible but the definition of those trusts has been widened by the Finance Act 2006 which has introduced s.89B. Frequently, the way in which claims on behalf of protected parties are settled is for a discretionary trust to be established in the protected party's favour which will not affect the social security benefits to which they may be entitled and which provide inherent flexibility. The Finance Act 2006 has not made any changes to the way in which those trusts are taxed.

10.6   TAX CONSIDERATIONS: USE OF THE SPOUSE AND CIVIL PARTNERSHIP EXEMPTION

One of the advantages of settling a claim under the Act rather than taking the matter to court is that the consent order can be structured in such a way as to save inheritance tax where there is a spouse or a civil partner involved. In particular, the use of short-term life interests to obtain the spouse/civil partner exemption where in fact the property will eventually go elsewhere is a very tax efficient way of proceeding. If the court is being asked to approve the order then the comments of the Court of Appeal in *Goodchild* v. *Goodchild* [1997] 1 WLR 1216 at 1231, where artificial arrangements to save tax were being criticised robustly, should be taken into account. However, particularly where provision is being made for a widow/ widower or civil partner the courts are generally sympathetic to orders which are structured to mitigate tax.

Thought should therefore be given to conferring on a spouse or civil partner a short-term life interest in a fund which is intended ultimately to go, say, to children.

The life interest should last for longer than two years from the date of death if the Inheritance Tax Act 1984, s.142 is being relied upon. This is because s.142(4) provides that an interest in possession which lasts for less than two years from the date of death is treated as if it had not existed, which would mean the spouse/civil partner exemption would be lost. The aim is to attract spouse/civil partner relief for the estate over and above the nil rate band for inheritance tax.

While the same considerations do not apply if the Inheritance Tax Act 1984, s.146 is being relied upon rather than s.142, as a matter of practice, HMRC looks at any life interest less than five years with a degree of suspicion but it seems to be generally accepted that this method will work. It is a method which is proposed in *Foster's Inheritance Tax* (Richard Wallington (ed.), looseleaf, LexisNexis) where the editors conclude that the Ramsay doctrine (which applies to tax avoidance schemes) cannot apply in these circumstances. There is a reality about the short-term life interest given to the spouse or civil partner: he or she reaps the benefit of the income from the fund in which he or she has an interest for the short period when it subsists and that can make a great deal of sense when, for example, a widow has actually been living in a property which it is agreed she will have to vacate. Moreover, when the short-term life interest comes to an end, there will be a potentially exempt transfer on the part of the spouse/civil partner which could result in inheritance tax having to be paid if they do not survive for seven years. It is usual to insure against this eventuality.

While the Finance Act 2006 changed the way in which life interests under trusts were taxed in general, there is an exception as far as immediate post-death interests in possession are concerned. Such interests will be taxed in the same way as an interest in possession trust established prior to the changes made in 2006 (see s.49(1A)(iii) of the Inheritance Tax Act 1984). Such a trust can only be established by a will or by a deed of variation (including a deed of variation being utilised to compromise a claim under the 1975 Act as to which see **10.5.1**) or order under the 1975 Act (where proceedings have been already issued or the two-year period for a deed of variation has elapsed) which varies the provisions of the will or those on intestacy. The existence of powers of appointment or advancement will not prevent an interest in possession qualifying as an immediate post-death interest in possession. It does not have to be in favour of a spouse or civil partner but the exception is crucially important in this context to the compromise of claims where interest in possession trusts in favour of a surviving spouse or civil partner are established in order to take advantage of the spouse/civil partner exemption.

Considerable care does have to be taken when the immediate post-death interest in possession is terminated. The termination of the immediate post-death interest in possession during the lifetime of the surviving spouse/civil partner will only be a potentially exempt transfer if the trust comes to an end (subject to a few limited exceptions). If the surviving spouse's/civil partner's interest is followed, say, by a life interest in favour of another beneficiary, that will be taxed as a relevant property settlement and the termination of the immediate post-death interest in possession will be immediately chargeable to inheritance tax.

The other point to note is that any termination of a surviving spouse's/civil partner's interest will be treated as a gift for the purposes of the gift with reservation rules (see Finance Act 1986, s.102ZA introduced by the Finance Act 2006). It is therefore important that the immediate post-death interest in possession is not followed, say, by a discretionary trust under which the surviving spouse/civil partner is a beneficiary. Otherwise, on the death of the surviving spouse/civil partner the property in the trust will be treated as part of his estate for inheritance tax purposes.

There is a particular tax advantage if there is already a life interest contained in a will for the benefit of a widow/widower/surviving civil partner (referred to hereafter as the widow). Take for example a case where the whole of the estate is left on life interest trusts for a widow with remainder to adult children. The widow wants an absolute entitlement to capital and she and the children wish to divide the estate between them. It looks at first sight as if any order will be retrospective and the spouse exemption will be lost in respect of half of the estate. A short-term life interest could be created over the children's half but on its termination there would be a potentially exempt transfer (assuming no subsequent trusts). At this point s.146(6) of the Inheritance Tax Act 1984 comes into play. It provides:

> Anything which is done in compliance with an order under the 1975 Act or occurs on the coming into force of such an order, and which would (apart from this subsection) constitute an occasion on which tax is chargeable under any provision, other than section 79, of Chapter III of Part III of this Act, shall not constitute such an occasion; and where an order under the 1975 Act provides for property to be settled or for the variation of a settlement, and (apart from this subsection) tax would be charged under section 52(1) above on the coming into force of the order, section 52(1) shall not apply.

An order of the Court (including it would seem one made by way of Tomlin and falling within s.146(8)) which varies the settlement e.g. by termination of the life interest would normally be chargeable under s.51(1) of the 1984 Act. However, it seems that section 146(6) relieves that charge. Therefore the interest in possession in favour of the widow can be terminated without there being any inheritance tax charge although considerable care needs to be taken in the drafting of any order.

10.7 CHARITIES

Care has to be taken where charities are beneficiaries of the estate and a claim for provision is being made. For inheritance tax purposes, a gift to charity is exempt and therefore the retrospective effect of any deed of variation or order compromising a claim might result in more inheritance tax being payable rather than less. Clearly, if the claim is made by another exempt beneficiary, such as a spouse or civil partner, then no difficulty arises. Similarly, the nil rate band for inheritance tax might be available and any claim settled within that band.

The important trap to watch for is that an instrument which falls within the Inheritance Tax Act 1984, s.142 and any order compromising proceedings (and thus falling within the 1984 Act, s.146(1)) will be read back into the will or the intestacy. Therefore, the charity exemption can be lost if the compromise is settled in this way and the payment to the claimant will be treated as chargeable and tax paid on it accordingly if the nil rate band is exceeded.

One solution to the problem (if it is possible) is to settle the claim without proceedings being issued. This may involve the charity in agreeing not to take a point on the six-month time limit (although there is some risk to the claimant in such a course as the court could, in theory, refuse to extend time; however, that would be most unlikely to happen in practice). Care still needs to be taken. Section 29A of the Inheritance Tax Act 1984 provides that if, in settlement of a claim against the deceased's estate, a charity effects a disposition of property not derived from the transfer (that is, from the estate), then the result would be much the same as if s.146 had applied. In other words, any payment by the charity to compromise the claim needs to be made by the charity out of funds it receives from the estate.

There is a further argument under Inheritance Tax Act 1984, s.23(5) that property passing to the claimant in settlement of the claim is not property of charities or held on trust for charitable purposes only. One argument against this is that if s.23(5) is used in this way to restrict the charity tax relief then this would render s.29A meaningless.

A charity may wish to involve the Charity Commissioners in any compromise. The Charity Commission's consent is not required to any compromise of a claim under the 1975 Act, but if the charity is in significant doubt about the propriety of settling or compromising the claim, the Commission can be asked to sanction it, or to provide advice to the charity, under ss.105 and 110 respectively of the Charities Act 2011. An application for such consent or advice is very unusual and the Charity Commission guide CC38 (**www.gov.uk/government/uploads/system/uploads/ attachment_data/file/544792/CC38.pdf**) does not suggest obtaining Charity Commission approval but does say: 'To properly carry out their duty of care, trustees should make a fully informed decision, taking specialist advice from a suitably qualified person.'

In the context of a genuine claim under the 1975 Act, all of the above is accepted practice and, in the authors' view, is thus unlikely to fall within the compass of recently introduced anti-avoidance legislation such as the General Anti-Abuse Rule.

CHAPTER 11

Will drafting and the will file

11.1 LIABILITY OF THE WILL DRAFTSMAN IN RESPECT OF CLAIMS UNDER THE 1975 ACT

It is a common complaint of (unsuccessful) defendants to a 1975 Act claim that their loss i.e. the award under the Act plus costs must be attributable to the will draftsman's failure to advise the testator appropriately. From that would flow a *White* v. *Jones* type of claim. There is also a potential claim by the personal representatives for any unrecovered costs incurred in the litigation.

There is to date no judicial authority imposing a duty on a will draftsman to give advice on the potential for claims under the Act, although it is clearly regarded as good practice to do so. The authors of *Risk Negligence in Wills, Estates and Trusts* (M. Frost, P. Reed and M. Baxter, 2nd edn, Oxford University Press, 2014) note that asking if the client requires advice is a 'win/win situation for the will-preparer – a refusal can reduce the potential for a claim against the will-preparer (if properly recorded) while requiring the advice can produce additional work'.

Whether there is any loss must be in doubt.

If a claim has gone to trial and succeeded, it follows that the judge regarded the will as failing to make reasonable provision and therefore the award really reflects what ought to have been included in the will. There is no loss caused by the draftsman. As to costs, it follows that the judge regarded the defendant(s) as having failed to concede when they ought.

Conceivably it might be argued that had the deceased been advised, he would have implemented legitimate avoidance provisions that successfully escaped the ambit of s.10 (see **Chapter 6**). However, limitation issues will restrict the number of estates in which such circumstances might conceivably arise, and the authors suggest that evidential difficulties will render such a claim highly unlikely.

It is possible that the court orders costs be paid from the estate rather than that they follow the event (i.e. loser pays). In those circumstances personal representatives may be able to recover those costs although the authors are not aware of any precedent.

11.2 STATEMENT OF REASONS FOR EXCLUDING A BENEFICIARY

The court can take into account the reasons of the testator for leaving someone out of his will.

However, although the court can take such a statement into account, the jurisdiction is an objective one. The subjective view of the testator that he has made reasonable provision for a potential claimant may not objectively be a good reason for the lack of provision. The fact that the deceased in *Ilott* v. *Mitson* [2017] UKSC 17 wrote a letter explaining why she was cutting her daughter out of the will did not prevent an award being made.

If the testator is determined to leave someone out of their will who could have a claim, then a statement in the body of the will itself or in a letter accompanying it, which explains why a potential claimant has been excluded, might have some limited effect.

Caution needs to be exercised. In *Singer* v. *Isaac* [2001] WTLR 1045, Master Bowles described memoranda as 'manifestly prepared with the benefit of legal advice' and 'self-serving documents, being self-justificatory of the deceased's conduct'. The existence of such documents can be seen by a jaundiced court as recognition that, subject to the explanation or reasons put forward, reasonable financial provision has not been made. In *Nahajec* v. *Fowle* [2017] EW Misc 11 (CC) inconsistencies with the evidence undermined any weight attributable to the testator's side letter to the executor.

A testator, determined to thwart potential claims, is well advised to ensure that reasons given in a side letter are sustainable, and to keep reviewing on a regular basis any side letter. *Singer* v. *Isaac* suggests that home-made letters may possibly be regarded as more convincing. That leads onto questions of whether solicitors should retain file notes of discussions with a testator recording reasons given for excluding beneficiaries or whether those file notes are best destroyed.

11.3 AGREEMENTS TO EXCLUDE THE 1975 ACT

Other than ss.15, 15A and 15ZA barring claims under the Act as a term of an order on divorce, nullity or judicial separation, there is no way to directly oust the court's jurisdiction. However, the Supreme Court in *Radmacher* v. *Granatino* [2010] UKSC 42 in the context of a divorce stated that:

> The Court should give effect to a nuptial agreement that is freely entered into by each party with a full appreciation of its implications unless in the circumstances prevailing it would not be fair to hold the parties to their agreement.

Thus while nuptial agreements are not enforced under statute in England and Wales, the Supreme Court has confirmed that where an agreement has been freely negotiated with legal advice and there are no vitiating factors present, it would be wrong simply to disregard it. Rather it is the court's duty to step in to alleviate any unfairness, and to ensure that the applicant party is not left in a predicament of real need.

The Law Commission in *Matrimonial Property, Needs and Agreements* (Law Commission Report 343) decided against recommending that qualifying nuptial agreements should be able to exclude a claim under the 1975 Act. However, a well-drafted agreement that provides for the survivor's needs may influence any 1975 Act claim. It will certainly be a section 3(1)(g) factor the court may take into account.

11.4   NON-DISPUTATION CLAUSES

Some testators try to avoid any dispute over their will by using a non-disputation clause. For example, if a beneficiary contests the will he will lose his interest under it. Again such a clause cannot oust the court's jurisdiction under the Act.

In *Nathan* v. *Leonard* [2002] EWHC 1701 (Ch) the court held that such a clause of very wide ambit in a home-made codicil would have been valid (had it not been void for uncertainty). It had provided that all beneficiaries would lose their interests if any challenge was made to the will, even those innocent of the challenge. The judge was influenced by the fact that such a condition does not prevent an application being made. If the claimant has a meritorious case the fact that the condition operates to deprive him of any benefit under the will counts in favour of the claim, not against it. Thus, where there was a clear failure to make proper provision for someone, it would always be open to them to decide to make a claim under the Act and lose their provision under the will.

On the other hand, if the claim is more questionable, the condition may have the effect of deterring the applicant from bringing the claim. This opens the door to the possibility of using a non-disputation clause in a will to try to discourage such a claim.

11.5   ADVICE CONCERNING ANTI-AVOIDANCE

Once advised about the potential impact of the Act, a testator may wish to try to avoid its impact by disposing of property during his lifetime. Such tactics may not work. As set out in **Chapter 6**, the court has power under s.10 of the Act to set aside dispositions made for less than full valuable consideration less than six years before the death with the intention of defeating an application under the Act. Such applications are rare because of the difficulty of establishing the requisite intention, but a solicitor's attendance note has sometimes provided the necessary proof.

A contract made by the deceased to leave property by will to a third party with the intention of defeating an application under the Act can also be set aside under s.11 of the Act. These provisions are dealt with in more detail in **Chapter 6** but the draftsman should alert any testator to these anti-avoidance provisions in appropriate cases.

11.6   DISCLOSURE OF WILL FILE POST-DEATH

Claimants frequently anticipate that the will file contains information that may be pertinent to their claim. Notes or correspondence may reveal the testator's reasoning (the testator is, of course, no longer able to cast light on that process).

The Law Society's *Guidance on File Retention: Wills and Probate* directs solicitors to retain a copy of revoked wills on the basis that it is possible that 'where an Inheritance (Provision for Family and Dependants) Act 1975 claim is made an earlier revoked will may be produced as evidence of a settled or disturbed pattern of behaviour or thought by the testator'. However, because the assessment of reasonable provision is objective, the relevance of revoked wills to 1975 Act claims is limited.

How should firms holding will files respond to requests to inspect the original will file and/or for copies of previous wills? Similarly, what stance should personal representatives adopt?

Legal professional privilege provides that solicitor–client communications for the purpose of obtaining legal advice are protected from disclosure.

It appears that the relevance of privilege and will files has not been addressed by the court in any reported claim under the Act. That may well be because (other than for applications under s.10 of the Act) the deceased's reasons are, strictly speaking, not relevant to the objective assessment of whether or not reasonable financial provision has been made, and because as a matter of practice, personal representatives agree to disclose.

Privilege survives the death of the testator and vests in the testator's personal representatives and successors in title (see: *Bullivant* v. *Attorney-General of Victoria* [1901] AC 196). *Halsbury's Laws of England* (4th edn Reissue, Vol.17(2) at para.291, LexisNexis) states that 'privilege belongs equally to all who derive title under the testator, whether personal representatives [or] beneficiaries'.

The ACTAPS Code makes clear that copies of all wills, drafts, written instructions and so forth should be disclosed (see **Appendix C2**). The ACTAPS Code is specifically intended to apply to claims under the Act. This appears to be predicated on the basis that a claim under the Act is analogous to a contentious probate action and the reasoning in the Court of Appeal decision in *Larke* v. *Nugus* [2000] WTLR 1033 applies to claims under the Act. In *Larke* v. *Nugus* the solicitor draftsman was heavily criticised for failing to provide information about the drafting of a contested will.

There is however a significant difference between a contentious probate action (where *Larke* v. *Nugus* undoubtedly does apply to solicitor draftsmen) and a claim under the Act. In a contentious probate action the identity of the personal representative is yet to be established whereas with a claim under the Act a grant is generally already in place.

As any privilege belongs to the personal representatives, firms holding the original will file should seek the permission of the personal representatives before disclosing any documents covered by privilege. (In New Zealand it has been held that earlier wills of the testator are not privileged (*Re Moore* [1965] NZLR 895 – see *Tyler's Family Provision* (R. D. Oughton, 3rd edn, Butterworths, 1998, at p.363)).)

Personal representatives are defendants to any claim under the Act. The Practice Direction to CPR Part 57 states that the written evidence filed by a personal representative must state any facts which might affect the exercise of the court's powers under the Act.

That provision does not mention privileged information. Statutory provisions have to state expressly that they are overriding legal professional privilege if they are to have that effect. It is therefore the personal representatives' choice whether or not they waive privilege in respect of the will file.

In a probate claim, where the considerations are somewhat different, the personal representatives' duty is to those who benefit from the estate and they should bear in mind the words of Lord Rodger in *Three Rivers D.C.* v. *Bank of England* [2005] 1 AC 610 at 656, when rejecting the Court of Appeal's assertion that there was no good reason for privilege to attach to the presentation of a will: 'Divulging the provisions during the testator's lifetime or disclosing the reasons for them after the testator's death could often cause incalculable harm and misery.'

Tyler's Family Provision at p.363 suggests that failure to allow professional privilege to be claimed on a claim under the Act might lead to capricious results, for example, if a former spouse were allowed to see otherwise privileged communications passing between the deceased and his lawyers in matrimonial proceedings. However, there is no suggestion in *Larke* v. *Nugus* that the waiver of privilege extends to any documents other than those relating to the preparation of wills.

A waiver of privilege must be exercised carefully in order to avoid unintended collateral waiver, which occurs where waiver of privilege in respect of one document is held to extend to all documents relating to the same transaction. Waiver should be for documents relating to the preparation of the will and only those documents.

It appears that personal representatives face alternatives. The first is to confirm whether or not they hold, or have control of, any will file for the deceased and to seek agreement to disclosure from those with a beneficial interest who are defending the claim brought under the Act. If that agreement is withheld they can put the onus for an application for pre-action disclosure onto the claimant, making clear that the personal representatives will be neutral and that those objecting must bear the cost risks of opposing disclosure.

The second alternative is that personal representatives should disclose to all parties. A well-founded claim brought under the Act is not a claim against the estate but to an entitlement to benefit from the estate. Asserting privilege over testamentary documents is arguably inconsistent with the personal representatives' neutral role, with the overriding objective of the CPR, and with the Practice Direction to CPR Part 57.

The authors' view is that the first alternative is the safer because personal representatives do not have an obligation to disclose privileged material. They hold that privilege for the benefit of those who are beneficiaries (and unless and until an order is made, the claimant is not a beneficiary). To disclose it without the beneficiaries' approval may give rise to the risk of a breach of duty claim.

There is a risk such an approach provokes judicial irritation with the personal representatives, and so it is worth spelling out very clearly to the objecting beneficiary the probable costs consequence of non-disclosure. Presumably, in a situation where one beneficiary objects and the other does not, costs consequences should be visited on the former.

At the very least, if personal representatives have good reason to encourage progress and non-disclosure of the file is causing blockage, to give some protection from criticism they will wish to be satisfied that there is some merit to any purported claim and may for that purpose require to see a draft witness statement.

Cases such as *Westendorp* v. *Warwick* [2006] EWHC 915 (Ch) (non-disclosure of medical evidence in a will validity action) suggest that courts may well draw adverse inferences from any refusal by defendants to waive privilege (but for the reasons given, the beneficiaries should take responsibility).

CHAPTER 12

Role of the personal representative/trustee

12.1 PERSONAL REPRESENTATIVES – NEUTRALITY

Personal representatives must be joined as defendants and file evidence (see **Chapter 8**).

However, personal representatives who adopt a partisan approach to claims under the Act do so at personal risk as to costs. That is because a personal representative's duty is to collect in, administer and preserve the estate for the benefit of those entitled to it. A claim under the Inheritance (Provision for Family and Dependants) Act 1975 is not, and should not be treated as, a claim against or 'hostile' to the estate: it does not seek to diminish the assets available for distribution but only to establish the claim of someone who seeks to be treated as a beneficiary.

It is for the beneficiaries to explore settlement with the claimant. There may be circumstances in which personal representatives are ideally placed to play 'honest broker'. But they do so at some risk if they incur any cost without agreement (from whoever will end up bearing that cost).

It is doubtful whether personal representatives have power under the Trustee Act 1925, s.15 (which provides that trustees can compromise any claim made in respect of the estate) to compromise claims under the 1975 Act.

12.2 PERSONAL REPRESENTATIVES – CONFLICT OF INTEREST

What if the personal representative is also the claimant or one of the beneficiaries adversely affected?

There is no reason why a personal representative cannot make or defend a claim and continue to act as a personal representative. Accordingly, there is no need to renounce the right to a grant. To do so is likely to increase costs and cause delay while an eligible alternative is appointed.

A claimant or defendant beneficiary who is also a personal representative must comply with the requirements of CPR rule 57.16 (see **8.8.1**) concerning evidence but then go on to include any evidence that he considers relevant to his claim (or defence). An alternative approach is to file two statements but that seems likely to be cumbersome.

Where the same firm is representing the personal representative in that capacity and as claimant or adversely affected beneficiary, it is important to ensure that files are run separately and costs are properly attributed, whether (i) to the personal representative in fulfilling his or her obligations in the administration, (ii) to the (the authors suggest) very limited costs of fulfilling the personal representative's obligations in the claim, and (iii) to the active pursuit of a claim or defence (the bulk of the litigation costs).

12.3 PERSONAL REPRESENTATIVES – DISTRIBUTIONS

Section 20 of the Act absolves personal representatives of liability to any successful claimant where the claim was issued after the end of the six months from the first grant of representation.

That protection appears to endure, even if the personal representative is on notice that an application is being made outside that six-month period.

The recommended practice is for personal representatives to wait for ten months from the grant of representation on the basis that a claimant may have issued but not served.

Ten months is arrived at by adding the four months for service of the claim allowed by CPR rule 7.5(1) to the six months provided for under s.20 of the Act.

12.4 TRUSTEES AS DEFENDANTS

Where the estate is held on trust, the personal representatives are often also named as trustees.

Whereas in their personal representative capacity they are neutral, in their capacity as trustees they are likely to face the task of actively defending the 1975 Act claim. It is also clear that trustees have power under the Trustee Act 1925, s.15 to compromise a claim.

They therefore face the classic dilemma for trustees. Inactivity may leave them vulnerable to a breach of trust claim. Conversely, failure to prevent a successful claim (and incurring the claimant's adverse costs) and/or compromising without beneficiary approval may leave them vulnerable to a breach of trust claim.

It is usually sensible for trustees to consult with beneficiaries about the response to a claim and/or about any proposed compromise. However, unless the beneficiaries are able to approve a course of action, and/or if the trustees are concerned about the risk of criticism from the beneficiaries, it may well be necessary for them to seek the directions of the court under the *Beddoe* jurisdiction (in accordance with the procedure set out in CPR Part 64).

Such an application should be brought by a separate CPR Part 8 claim outside the 1975 Act proceedings with the beneficiaries (or representatives of them joined).

Consideration needs to be given to the economics, particularly in small estates.

Statutory extracts

Administration of Estates Act 1925, Part IV

[1925 c.23]

PART IV DISTRIBUTION OF RESIDUARY ESTATE

45 Abolition of descent to heir, curtesy, dower and escheat

(1) With regard to the real estate and personal inheritance of every person dying after the commencement of this Act, there shall be abolished –

    (a) All existing modes rules and canons of descent, and of devolution by special occupancy or otherwise, of real estate, or of a personal inheritance, whether operating by the general law or by the custom of gavelkind or borough english or by any other custom of any county, locality, or manor, or otherwise howsoever; and

    (b) Tenancy by the curtesy and every other estate and interest of a husband in real estate as to which his wife dies intestate, whether arising under the general law or by custom or otherwise; and

    (c) Dower and freebench and every other estate and interest of a wife in real estate as to which her husband dies intestate, whether arising under the general law or by custom or otherwise: Provided that where a right (if any) to freebench or other like right has attached before the commencement of this Act which cannot be barred by a testamentary or other disposition made by the husband, such right shall, unless released, remain in force as an equitable interest; and

    (d) Escheat to the Crown or the Duchy of Lancaster or the Duke of Cornwall or to a mesne lord for want of heirs.

(2) Nothing in this section affects the descent or devolution of an entailed interest.

46 Succession to real and personal estate on intestacy

(1) The residuary estate of an intestate shall be distributed in the manner or be held on the trusts mentioned in this section, namely –

    (i) If the intestate leaves a spouse or civil partner, then in accordance with the following table:

TABLE

(1) If the intestate leaves no issue:	the residuary estate shall be held in trust for the surviving spouse or civil partner absolutely.
(2) If the intestate leaves issue:	(A) the surviving spouse or civil partner shall take the personal chattels absolutely;

TABLE

(B) the residuary estate of the intestate (other than the personal chattels) shall stand charged with the payment of a fixed net sum, free of death duties and costs, to the surviving spouse or civil partner, together with simple interest on it from the date of the death at the rate provided for by subsection (1A) until paid or appropriated; and

(C) subject to providing for the sum and interest referred to in paragraph (B), the residuary estate (other than the personal chattels) shall be held –

(a) as to one half, in trust for the surviving spouse or civil partner absolutely, and

(b) as to the other half, on the statutory trusts for the issue of the intestate.

The amount of the fixed net sum referred to in paragraph (B) of case (2) of this Table is to be determined in accordance with Schedule 1A.

The fixed net sums referred to in paragraphs (2) and (3) of this Table shall be of the amounts provided by or under section 1 of the Family Provision Act 1966.

(ii) If the intestate leaves issue but no spouse or civil partner, the residuary estate of the intestate shall be held on the statutory trusts for the issue of the intestate;

(iii) If the intestate leaves no spouse or civil partner and no issue but both parents, then . . . the residuary estate of the intestate shall be held in trust for the father and mother in equal shares absolutely;

(iv) If the intestate leaves no spouse or civil partner and no issue but one parent, then . . . the residuary estate of the intestate shall be held in trust for the surviving father or mother absolutely;

(v) If the intestate leaves no spouse or civil partner and no issue and no parent, then . . . the residuary estate of the intestate shall be held in trust for the following persons living at the death of the intestate, and in the following order and manner, namely –

First, on the statutory trusts for the brothers and sisters of the whole blood of the intestate; but if no person takes an absolutely vested interest under such trusts, then

Secondly, on the statutory trusts for the brothers and sisters of the half blood of the intestate; but if no person takes an absolutely vested interest under such trusts; then

Thirdly, for the grandparents of the intestate and, if more than one survive the intestate, in equal shares; but if there is no member of this class; then

Fourthly, on the statutory trusts for the uncles and aunts of the intestate (being brothers or sisters of the whole blood of a parent of the intestate); but if no person takes an absolutely vested interest under such trusts; then

Fifthly, on the statutory trusts for the uncles and aunts of the intestate (being brothers or sisters of the half blood of a parent of the intestate); . . .

(vi) In default of any person taking an absolute interest under the foregoing provisions, the residuary estate of the intestate shall belong to the Crown or to the Duchy of Lancaster or to the Duke of Cornwall for the time being, as the case may be, as bona vacantia, and in lieu of any right to escheat.

The Crown or the said Duchy or the said Duke may (without prejudice to the powers reserved by section nine of the Civil List Act, 1910, or any other powers), out of the whole or any part of the property devolving on them respectively, provide, in accordance with the existing practice, for dependants, whether kindred or not, of the intestate, and other persons for whom the intestate might reasonably have been expected to make provision.

(1A) The interest rate referred to in paragraph (B) of case (2) of the Table in subsection (1)(i) is the Bank of England rate that had effect at the end of the day on which the intestate died.

(2) A husband and wife shall for all purposes of distribution or division under the foregoing provisions of this section be treated as two persons.

(2A) Where the intestate's spouse or civil partner survived the intestate but died before the end of the period of 28 days beginning with the day on which the intestate died, this section shall have effect as respects the intestate as if the spouse or civil partner had not survived the intestate.

(3) [*Repealed*]

(4) The interest payable on the fixed net sum payable to a surviving spouse or civil partner shall be primarily payable out of income.

(5) In subsection (1A) 'Bank of England rate' means –

    (a) the rate announced by the Monetary Policy Committee of the Bank of England as the official bank rate, or

    (b) where an order under section 19 of the Bank of England Act 1998 (reserve powers) is in force, any equivalent rate determined by the Treasury under that section.

(6) The Lord Chancellor may by order made by statutory instrument amend the definition of 'Bank of England rate' in subsection (5) (but this subsection does not affect the generality of subsection (7)(b)).

(7) The Lord Chancellor may by order made by statutory instrument –

    (a) amend subsection (1A) so as to substitute a different interest rate (however specified or identified) for the interest rate for the time being provided for by that subsection;

    (b) make any amendments of, or repeals in, this section that may be consequential on or incidental to any amendment made by virtue of paragraph (a).

(8) A statutory instrument containing an order under subsection (6) is subject to annulment pursuant to a resolution of either House of Parliament.

(9) A statutory instrument containing an order under subsection (7) may not be made unless a draft of the instrument has been laid before and approved by a resolution of each House of Parliament.

46A   Disclaimer or forfeiture on intestacy

(1) This section applies where a person –

    (a) is entitled in accordance with section 46 to an interest in the residuary estate of an intestate but disclaims it, or

    (b) would have been so entitled had the person not been precluded by the forfeiture rule from acquiring it.

(2) The person is to be treated for the purposes of this Part as having died immediately before the intestate.

(3) But in a case within subsection (1)(b), subsection (2) does not affect the power conferred by section 2 of the Forfeiture Act 1982 (power of court to modify the forfeiture rule).

(4) In this section 'forfeiture rule' has the same meaning as in the Forfeiture Act 1982.

47   Statutory trusts in favour of issue and other classes of relatives of intestate

(1) Where under this Part of this Act the residuary estate of an intestate, or any part thereof,

is directed to be held on the statutory trusts for the issue of the intestate, the same shall be held upon the following trusts, namely –

(i)   In trust, in equal shares if more than one, for all or any the children or child of the intestate, living at the death of the intestate, who attain the age of eighteen years or marry under that age or form a civil partnership under that age, and for all or any of the issue living at the death of the intestate who attain the age of eighteen years or marry, or form a civil partnership, under that age of any child of the intestate who predeceases the intestate, such issue to take through all degrees, according to their stocks, in equal shares if more than one, the share which their parent would have taken if living at the death of the intestate, and so that (subject to section 46A) no issue shall take whose parent is living at the death of the intestate and so capable of taking;

(ii)   The statutory power of advancement, and the statutory provisions which relate to maintenance and accumulation of surplus income, shall apply, but when an infant marries, or forms a civil partnership, such infant shall be entitled to give valid receipts for the income of the infant's share or interest;

(iii)   [*Repealed*]

(iv)   The personal representatives may permit any infant contingently interested to have the use and enjoyment of any personal chattels in such manner and subject to such conditions (if any) as the personal representatives may consider reasonable, and without being liable to account for any consequential loss.

(2)   If the trusts in favour of the issue of the intestate fail by reason of no child or other issue attaining an absolutely vested interest –

(a)   the residuary estate of the intestate and the income thereof and all statutory accumulations, if any, of the income thereof, or so much thereof as may not have been paid or applied under any power affecting the same, shall go, devolve and be held under the provisions of this Part of this Act as if the intestate had died without leaving issue living at the death of the intestate;

(b)   references in this Part of this Act to the intestate 'leaving no issue' shall be construed as 'leaving no issue who attain an absolutely vested interest';

(c)   references in this Part of this Act to the intestate 'leaving issue' or 'leaving a child or other issue' shall be construed as 'leaving issue who attain an absolutely vested interest.'

(3)   Where under this Part of this Act the residuary estate of an intestate or any part thereof is directed to be held on the statutory trusts for any class of relatives of the intestate, other than issue of the intestate, the same shall be held on trusts corresponding to the statutory trusts for the issue of the intestate (other than the provision for bringing any money or property into account) as if such trusts (other than as aforesaid) were repeated with the substitution of references to the members or member of that class for references to the children or child of the intestate.

(4)   References in paragraph(i) of subsection(1) of the last foregoing section to the intestate leaving, or not leaving, a member of the class consisting of brothers or sisters of the whole blood of the intestate and issue of brothers or sisters of the whole blood of the intestate shall be construed as references to the intestate leaving, or not leaving, a member of that class who attains an absolutely vested interest.

(4A) Subsections (2) and (4) are subject to section 46A.

(4B) Subsections (4C) and (4D) apply if a beneficiary under the statutory trusts –

(a)   fails to attain an absolutely vested interest because the beneficiary dies without having reached 18 and without having married or formed a civil partnership, and

(b)   dies leaving issue.

(4C) The beneficiary is to be treated for the purposes of this Part as having died immediately before the intestate.

(4D) The residuary estate (together with the income from it and any statutory accumulations of income from it) or so much of it as has not been paid or applied under a power affecting it is to devolve accordingly.

(5) [*Repealed*]

47A Right of surviving spouse to have own life interest redeemed

[*Repealed*]

48 Powers of personal representative in respect of interests of surviving spouse

(1) [*Repealed*]

(2) The personal representatives may raise –

(a) the fixed net sum or any part thereof and the interest thereon payable to the surviving spouse or civil partner of the intestate on the security of the whole or any part of the residuary estate of the intestate (other than the personal chattels), so far as that estate may be sufficient for the purpose or the said sum and interest may not have been satisfied by an appropriation under the statutory power available in that behalf;

(b) [*Repealed*]

and the amount, if any, properly required for the payment of the costs of the transaction.

49 Application to cases of partial intestacy

(1) Where any person dies leaving a will effectively disposing of part of his property, this Part of this Act shall have effect as respects the part of his property not so disposed of subject to the provisions contained in the will and subject to the following modifications –

(a) [*Repealed*]

(b) The personal representative shall, subject to his rights and powers for the purposes of administration, be a trustee for the persons entitled under this Part of this Act in respect of the part of the estate not expressly disposed of unless it appears by the will that the personal representative is intended to take such part beneficially.

(2) [*Repealed*]

(3) [*Repealed*]

(4) [*Repealed*]

50 Construction of documents

(1) References to any Statutes of Distribution in an instrument inter vivos made or in a will coming into operation after the commencement of this Act, shall be construed as references to this Part of this Act; and references in such an instrument or will to statutory next of kin shall be construed, unless the context otherwise requires, as referring to the persons who would take beneficially on an intestacy under the foregoing provisions of this Part of this Act.

(2) Trusts declared in an instrument inter vivos made, or in a will coming into operation, before the commencement of this Act by reference to the Statutes of Distribution, shall, unless the contrary thereby appears, be construed as referring to the enactments (other

than the Intestates' Estates Act, 1890) relating to the distribution of effects of intestates which were in force immediately before the commencement of this Act.

(3) In subsection (1) of this section the reference to this Part of this Act, or the foregoing provisions of this Part of this Act, shall in relation to an instrument inter vivos made, or a will or codicil coming into operation, after the coming into force of section 18 of the Family Law Reform Act 1987 (but not in relation to instruments inter vivos made or wills or codicils coming into operation earlier) be construed as including references to that section.

51 Savings

(1) Nothing in this Part of this Act affects the right of any person to take beneficially, by purchase, as heir either general or special.

(2) The foregoing provisions of this Part of this Act do not apply to any beneficial interest in real estate (not including chattels real) to which a person of unsound mind or defective living and of full age at the commencement of this Act, and unable, by reason of his incapacity, to make a will, who thereafter dies intestate in respect of such interest without having recovered his testamentary capacity, was entitled at his death, and any such beneficial interest (not being an interest ceasing on his death), shall, without prejudice to any will of the deceased, devolve in accordance with the general law in force before the commencement of this Act applicable to freehold land, and that law shall, notwithstanding any repeal, apply to the case.

For the purposes of this subsection, a person of unsound mind or defective who dies intestate as respects any beneficial interest in real estate shall not be deemed to have recovered his testamentary capacity unless his . . . receiver has been discharged.

(3) Where an infant dies after the commencement of this Act without having been married or having formed a civil partnership, and without issue, and independently of this subsection he would, at his death, have been equitably entitled under a trust or settlement (including a will) to a vested estate in fee simple or absolute interest in free hold land, or in any property . . . to devolve therewith or as freehold land, such infant shall be deemed to have had a life interest, and the trust or settlement shall be construed accordingly.

(4) [*Repealed*]

52 Interpretation of Part IV

In this Part of this Act 'real and personal estate' means every beneficial interest (including rights of entry and reverter) of the intestate in real and personal estate which (otherwise than in right of a power of appointment or of the testamentary power conferred by statute to dispose of entailed interests) he could, if of full age and capacity, have disposed of by his will and references (however expressed) to any relationship between two persons shall be construed in accordance with section 1 of the Family Law Reform Act 1987.

Matrimonial Causes Act 1973 (extracts)

[1973 c.18]

PART I   DIVORCE, NULLITY AND OTHER MATRIMONIAL SUITS

…

Nullity

11   Grounds on which a marriage is void

A marriage celebrated after 31st July 1971, other than a marriage to which section 12A applies, shall be void on the following grounds only, that is to say –

(a)   that it is not a valid marriage under the provisions of the Marriage Acts 1949 to 1986 (that is to say where –

    (i)   the parties are within the prohibited degrees of relationship;

    (ii)   either party is under the age of sixteen; or

    (iii)   the parties have intermarried in disregard of certain requirements as to the formation of marriage);

(b)   that at the time of the marriage either party was already lawfully married or a civil partner;

(c)   [*Repealed*]

(d)   in the case of a polygamous marriage entered into outside England and Wales, that either party was at the time of the marriage domiciled in England and Wales.

For the purposes of paragraph (d) of this subsection a marriage is not polygamous if at its inception neither party has any spouse additional to the other.

12   Grounds on which a marriage is voidable

(1)   A marriage celebrated after 31st July 1971, other than a marriage to which section 12A applies, shall be voidable on the following grounds only, that is to say –

    (a)   that the marriage has not been consummated owing to the incapacity of either party to consummate it;

    (b)   that the marriage has not been consummated owing to the wilful refusal of the respondent to consummate it;

    (c)   that either party to the marriage did not validly consent to it, whether in consequence of duress, mistake, unsoundness of mind or otherwise;

    (d)   that at the time of the marriage either party, though capable of giving a valid consent, was suffering (whether continuously or intermittently) from mental disorder within the meaning of the Mental Health Act 1983 of such a kind or to such an extent as to be unfitted for marriage;

(e) that at the time of the marriage the respondent was suffering from venereal disease in a communicable form;

(f) that at the time of the marriage the respondent was pregnant by some person other than the petitioner;

(g) that an interim gender recognition certificate under the Gender Recognition Act 2004 has, after the time of the marriage, been issued to either party to the marriage;

(h) that the respondent is a person whose gender at the time of the marriage had become the acquired gender under the Gender Recognition Act 2004.

(2) Paragraphs (a) and (b) of subsection (1) do not apply to the marriage of a same sex couple.

12A Ground on which a marriage converted from a civil partnership is void or voidable

(1) This section applies to a marriage which has been converted, or is purported to have been converted, from a civil partnership under section 9 of the 2013 Act and regulations made under that section.

(2) A marriage which results from the purported conversion of a void civil partnership is void.

(3) A marriage which results from the conversion of a civil partnership is voidable if any of paragraphs (c) to (h) of section 12(1) applied at the date from which the marriage is treated as having subsisted in accordance with section 9(6) of the 2013 Act.

(4) In this section, the '2013 Act' means the Marriage (Same Sex Couples) Act 2013.

…

PART II   FINANCIAL RELIEF FOR PARTIES TO MARRIAGE AND CHILDREN OF FAMILY

Financial provision and property adjustment orders

21   Financial provision and property adjustment orders

(1) The financial provision orders for the purposes of this Act are the orders for periodical or lump sum provision available (subject to the provisions of this Act) under section 23 below for the purpose of adjusting the financial position of the parties to a marriage and any children of the family in connection with proceedings for divorce, nullity of marriage or judicial separation and under section 27(6) below on proof of neglect by one party to a marriage to provide, or to make a proper contribution towards, reasonable maintenance for the other or a child of the family, that is to say –

(a) any order for periodical payments in favour of a party to a marriage under section 23(1)(a) or 27(6)(a) or in favour of a child of the family under section 23(1)(d), (2) or (4) or 27(6)(d);

(b) any order for secured periodical payments in favour of a party to a marriage under section 23(1)(b) or 27(6)(b) or in favour of a child of the family under section 23(1)(e), (2) or (4) or 27(6)(e); and

(c) any order for lump sum provision in favour of a party to a marriage under section 23(1)(c) or 27(6)(c) or in favour of a child of the family under section 23(1)(f), (2) or (4) or 27(6)(f);

and references in this Act (except in paragraphs 17(1) and 23 of Schedule 1 below) to periodical payments orders, secured periodical payments orders, and orders for the payment of a lump sum are references to all or some of the financial provision orders requiring the sort of financial provision in question according as the context of each reference may require.

(2) The property adjustment orders for the purposes of this Act are the orders dealing with property rights available (subject to the provisions of this Act) under section 24 below for the purpose of adjusting the financial position of the parties to a marriage and any children of the family on or after the grant of a decree of divorce, nullity of marriage or judicial separation, that is to say –

(a) any order under subsection (1)(a) of that section for a transfer of property;

(b) any order under subsection (1)(b) of that section for a settlement of property; and

(c) any order under subsection (1)(c) or (d) of that section for a variation of settlement.

21A   Pension sharing orders

(1) For the purposes of this Act, a pension sharing order is an order which –

(a) provides that one party's –

(i) shareable rights under a specified pension arrangement, or

(ii) shareable state scheme rights,

be subject to pension sharing for the benefit of the other party, and

(b) specifies the percentage value to be transferred.

(2) In subsection (1) above –

(a) the reference to shareable rights under a pension arrangement is to rights in relation to which pension sharing is available under Chapter I of Part IV of the Welfare Reform and Pensions Act 1999, or under corresponding Northern Ireland legislation,

(b) the reference to shareable state scheme rights is to rights in relation to which pension sharing is available under Chapter II of Part IV of the Welfare Reform and Pensions Act 1999, or under corresponding Northern Ireland legislation, and

(c) 'party' means a party to a marriage.

21B   Pension compensation sharing orders

(1) For the purposes of this Act, a pension compensation sharing order is an order which –

(a) provides that one party's shareable rights to PPF compensation that derive from rights under a specified pension scheme are to be subject to pension compensation sharing for the benefit of the other party, and

(b) specifies the percentage value to be transferred.

(2) In subsection (1) –

(a) the reference to shareable rights to PPF compensation is to rights in relation to which pension compensation sharing is available under Chapter 1 of Part 3 of the Pensions Act 2008 or under corresponding Northern Ireland legislation;

(b) 'party' means a party to a marriage;

(c) 'specified' means specified in the order.

21C   Pension compensation: interpretation

In this Part –

'PPF compensation' means compensation payable under the pension compensation provisions;

'the pension compensation provisions' means –

(a) Chapter 3 of Part 2 of the Pensions Act 2004 (pension protection) and any regulations or order made under it,

(b) Chapter 1 of Part 3 of the Pensions Act 2008 (pension compensation on divorce etc) and any regulations or order made under it, and

(c) any provision corresponding to the provisions mentioned in paragraph (a) or (b) in force in Northern Ireland.

Ancillary relief in connection with divorce proceedings, etc.

22 Maintenance pending suit

(1) On a petition for divorce, nullity of marriage or judicial separation, the court may make an order for maintenance pending suit, that is to say, an order requiring either party to the marriage to make to the other such periodical payments for his or her maintenance and for such term, being a term beginning not earlier than the date of the presentation of the petition and ending with the date of the determination of the suit, as the court thinks reasonable.

(2) An order under this section may not require a party to a marriage to pay to the other party any amount in respect of legal services for the purposes of the proceedings.

(3) In subsection (2) 'legal services' has the same meaning as in section 22ZA.

…

23 Financial provision orders in connection with divorce proceedings, etc.

(1) On granting a decree of divorce, a decree of nullity of marriage or a decree of judicial separation or at any time thereafter (whether, in the case of a decree of divorce or of nullity of marriage, before or after the decree is made absolute), the court may make any one or more of the following orders, that is to say –

(a) an order that either party to the marriage shall make to the other such periodical payments, for such term, as may be specified in the order;

(b) an order that either party to the marriage shall secure to the other to the satisfaction of the court such periodical payments, for such term, as may be so specified;

(c) an order that either party to the marriage shall pay to the other such lump sum or sums as may be so specified;

(d) an order that a party to the marriage shall make to such person as may be specified in the order for the benefit of a child of the family, or to such a child, such periodical payments, for such term, as may be so specified;

(e) an order that a party to the marriage shall secure to such person as may be so specified for the benefit of such a child, or to such a child, to the satisfaction of the court, such periodical payments, for such term, as may be so specified;

(f) an order that a party to the marriage shall pay to such person as may be so specified for the benefit of such a child, or to such a child, such lump sum as may be so specified;

subject, however, in the case of an order under paragraph (d), (e) or (f) above, to the restrictions imposed by section 29(1) and (3) below on the making of financial provision orders in favour of children who have attained the age of eighteen.

(2) The court may also, subject to those restrictions, make any one or more of the orders mentioned in subsection (1)(d), (e) and (f) above –

    (a)   in any proceedings for divorce, nullity of marriage or judicial separation, before granting a decree; and

    (b)   where any such proceedings are dismissed after the beginning of the trial, either forthwith or within a reasonable period after the dismissal.

(3)   Without prejudice to the generality of subsection (1)(c) or (f) above –

    (a)   an order under this section that a party to a marriage shall pay a lump sum to the other party may be made for the purpose of enabling that other party to meet any liabilities or expenses reasonably incurred by him or her in maintaining himself or herself or any child of the family before making an application for an order under this section in his or her favour;

    (b)   an order under this section for the payment of a lump sum to or for the benefit of a child of the family may be made for the purpose of enabling any liabilities or expenses reasonably incurred by or for the benefit of that child before the making of an application for an order under this section in his favour to be met; and

    (c)   an order under this section for the payment of a lump sum may provide for the payment of that sum by instalments of such amount as may be specified in the order and may require the payment of the instalments to be secured to the satisfaction of the court.

(4)   The power of the court under subsection (1) or (2)(a) above to make an order in favour of a child of the family shall be exercisable from time to time; and where the court makes an order in favour of a child under subsection (2)(b) above, it may from time to time, subject to the restrictions mentioned in subsection (1) above, make a further order in his favour of any of the kinds mentioned in subsection (1)(d), (e) or (f) above.

(5)   Without prejudice to the power to give a direction under section 30 below for the settlement of an instrument by conveyancing counsel, where an order is made under subsection (1)(a), (b) or (c) above on or after granting a decree of divorce or nullity of marriage, neither the order nor any settlement made in pursuance of the order shall take effect unless the decree has been made absolute.

(6)   Where the court –

    (a)   makes an order under this section for the payment of a lump sum; and

    (b)   directs –

        (i)   that payment of that sum or any part of it shall be deferred; or

        (ii) that that sum or any part of it shall be paid by instalments,

the court may order that the amount deferred or the instalments shall carry interest at such rate as may be specified by the order from such date, not earlier than the date of the order, as may be so specified, until the date when payment of it is due.

24   Property adjustment orders in connection with divorce proceedings, etc.

(1)   On granting a decree of divorce, a decree of nullity of marriage or a decree of judicial separation or at any time thereafter (whether, in the case of a decree of divorce or of nullity of marriage, before or after the decree is made absolute), the court may make any one or more of the following orders, that is to say –

    (a)   an order that a party to the marriage shall transfer to the other party, to any child of the family or to such person as may be specified in the order for the benefit of such a child such property as may be so specified, being property to which the first-mentioned party is entitled, either in possession or reversion;

    (b)   an order that a settlement of such property as may be so specified, being property to which a party to the marriage is so entitled, be made to the satisfaction of the court for the benefit of the other party to the marriage and of the children of the family or either or any of them;

(c) an order varying for the benefit of the parties to the marriage and of the children of the family or either or any of them any ante-nuptial or post-nuptial settlement (including such a settlement made by will or codicil) made on the parties to the marriage, other than one in the form of a pension arrangement (within the meaning of section 25D below);

(d) an order extinguishing or reducing the interest of either of the parties to the marriage under any such settlement, other than one in the form of a pension arrangement (within the meaning of section 25D below);

subject, however, in the case of an order under paragraph (a) above, to the restrictions imposed by section 29(1) and (3) below on the making of orders for a transfer of property in favour of children who have attained the age of eighteen.

(2) The court may make an order under subsection (1)(c) above notwithstanding that there are no children of the family.

(3) Without prejudice to the power to give a direction under section 30 below for the settlement of an instrument by conveyancing counsel, where an order is made under this section on or after granting a decree of divorce or nullity of marriage, neither the order nor any settlement made in pursuance of the order shall take effect unless the decree has been made absolute.

24A   Orders for sale of property

(1) Where the court makes an order under section 22ZA or makes under section 23 or 24 of this Act a secured periodical payments order, an order for the payment of a lump sum or a property adjustment order, then, on making that order or at any time thereafter, the court may make a further order for the sale of such property as may be specified in the order, being property in which or in the proceeds of sale of which either or both of the parties to the marriage has or have a beneficial interest, either in possession or reversion.

(2) Any order made under subsection (1) above may contain such consequential or supplementary provisions as the court thinks fit and, without prejudice to the generality of the foregoing provision, may include –

(a) provision requiring the making of a payment out of the proceeds of sale of the property to which the order relates, and

(b) provision requiring any such property to be offered for sale to a person, or class of persons, specified in the order.

(3) Where an order is made under subsection (1) above on or after the grant of a decree of divorce or nullity of marriage, the order shall not take effect unless the decree has been made absolute.

(4) Where an order is made under subsection (1) above, the court may direct that the order, or such provision thereof as the court may specify, shall not take effect until the occurrence of an event specified by the court or the expiration of a period so specified.

(5) Where an order under subsection (1) above contains a provision requiring the proceeds of sale of the property to which the order relates to be used to secure periodical payments to a party to the marriage, the order shall cease to have effect on the death or re-marriage of, or formation of a civil partnership by, that person.

(6) Where a party to a marriage has a beneficial interest in any property, or in the proceeds of sale thereof, and some other person who is not a party to the marriage also has a beneficial interest in that property or in the proceeds of sale thereof, then, before deciding whether to make an order under this section in relation to that property, it shall be the duty of the court to give that other person an opportunity to make representations

with respect to the order; and any representations made by that other person shall be included among the circumstances to which the court is required to have regard under section 25(1) below.

24B   Pension sharing orders in connection with divorce proceedings etc.

(1)   On granting a decree of divorce or a decree of nullity of marriage or at any time thereafter (whether before or after the decree is made absolute), the court may, on an application made under this section, make one or more pension sharing orders in relation to the marriage.

(2)   A pension sharing order under this section is not to take effect unless the decree on or after which it is made has been made absolute.

(3)   A pension sharing order under this section may not be made in relation to a pension arrangement which –

   (a)   is the subject of a pension sharing order in relation to the marriage, or
   (b)   has been the subject of pension sharing between the parties to the marriage.

(4)   A pension sharing order under this section may not be made in relation to shareable state scheme rights if –

   (a)   such rights are the subject of a pension sharing order in relation to the marriage, or
   (b)   such rights have been the subject of pension sharing between the parties to the marriage.

(5)   A pension sharing order under this section may not be made in relation to the rights of a person under a pension arrangement if there is in force a requirement imposed by virtue of section 25B or 25C below which relates to benefits or future benefits to which he is entitled under the pension arrangement.

24C   Pension sharing orders: duty to stay

(1)   No pension sharing order may be made so as to take effect before the end of such period after the making of the order as may be prescribed by regulations made by the Lord Chancellor.

(2)   The power to make regulations under this section shall be exercisable by statutory instrument which shall be subject to annulment in pursuance of a resolution of either House of Parliament.

24D   Pension sharing orders: apportionment of charges

If a pension sharing order relates to rights under a pension arrangement, the court may include in the order provision about the apportionment between the parties of any charge under section 41 of the Welfare Reform and Pensions Act 1999 (charges in respect of pension sharing costs), or under corresponding Northern Ireland legislation.

24E   Pension compensation sharing orders in connection with divorce proceedings

(1)   On granting a decree of divorce or a decree of nullity of marriage or at any time thereafter (whether before or after the decree is made absolute), the court may, on an application made under this section, make a pension compensation sharing order in relation to the marriage.

(2)   A pension compensation sharing order under this section is not to take effect unless the decree on or after which it is made has been made absolute.

(3) A pension compensation sharing order under this section may not be made in relation to rights to PPF compensation that –

    (a)   are the subject of pension attachment,

    (b)   derive from rights under a pension scheme that were the subject of pension sharing between the parties to the marriage,

    (c)   are the subject of pension compensation attachment, or

    (d)   are or have been the subject of pension compensation sharing between the parties to the marriage.

(4) For the purposes of subsection (3)(a), rights to PPF compensation 'are the subject of pension attachment' if any of the following three conditions is met.

(5) The first condition is that –

    (a)   the rights derive from rights under a pension scheme in relation to which an order was made under section 23 imposing a requirement by virtue of section 25B(4), and

    (b)   that order, as modified under section 25E(3), remains in force.

(6) The second condition is that –

    (a)   the rights derive from rights under a pension scheme in relation to which an order was made under section 23 imposing a requirement by virtue of section 25B(7), and

    (b)   that order –

        (i)   has been complied with, or

        (ii)   has not been complied with and, as modified under section 25E(5), remains in force.

(7) The third condition is that –

    (a)   the rights derive from rights under a pension scheme in relation to which an order was made under section 23 imposing a requirement by virtue of section 25C, and

    (b)   that order remains in force.

(8) For the purposes of subsection (3)(b), rights under a pension scheme 'were the subject of pension sharing between the parties to the marriage' if the rights were at any time the subject of a pension sharing order in relation to the marriage or a previous marriage between the same parties.

(9) For the purposes of subsection (3)(c), rights to PPF compensation 'are the subject of pension compensation attachment' if there is in force a requirement imposed by virtue of section 25F relating to them.

(10) For the purposes of subsection (3)(d), rights to PPF compensation 'are or have been the subject of pension compensation sharing between the parties to the marriage' if they are or have ever been the subject of a pension compensation sharing order in relation to the marriage or a previous marriage between the same parties.

24F   Pension compensation sharing orders: duty to stay

(1) No pension compensation sharing order may be made so as to take effect before the end of such period after the making of the order as may be prescribed by regulations made by the Lord Chancellor.

(2) The power to make regulations under this section shall be exercisable by statutory instrument which shall be subject to annulment in pursuance of a resolution of either House of Parliament.

24G Pension compensation sharing orders: apportionment of charges

The court may include in a pension compensation sharing order provision about the apportionment between the parties of any charge under section 117 of the Pensions Act 2008 (charges in respect of pension compensation sharing costs), or under corresponding Northern Ireland legislation.

25 Matters to which court is to have regard in deciding how to exercise its powers under ss. 23, 24, 24A, 24B and 24E

(1) It shall be the duty of the court in deciding whether to exercise its powers under section 23, 24, 24A, 24B or 24E above and, if so, in what manner, to have regard to all the circumstances of the case, first consideration being given to the welfare while a minor of any child of the family who has not attained the age of eighteen.

(2) As regards the exercise of the powers of the court under section 23(1)(a), (b) or (c), 24, 24A, 24B or 24E above in relation to a party to the marriage, the court shall in particular have regard to the following matters –

    (a) the income, earning capacity, property and other financial resources which each of the parties to the marriage has or is likely to have in the foreseeable future, including in the case of earning capacity any increase in that capacity which it would in the opinion of the court be reasonable to expect a party to the marriage to take steps to acquire;

    (b) the financial needs, obligations and responsibilities which each of the parties to the marriage has or is likely to have in the foreseeable future;

    (c) the standard of living enjoyed by the family before the breakdown of the marriage;

    (d) the age of each party to the marriage and the duration of the marriage;

    (e) any physical or mental disability of either of the parties to the marriage;

    (f) the contributions which each of the parties has made or is likely in the foreseeable future to make to the welfare of the family, including any contribution by looking after the home or caring for the family;

    (g) the conduct of each of the parties, if that conduct is such that it would in the opinion of the court be inequitable to disregard it;

    (h) in the case of proceedings for divorce or nullity of marriage, the value to each of the parties to the marriage of any benefit . . . which, by reason of the dissolution or annulment of the marriage, that party will lose the chance of acquiring.

(3) As regards the exercise of the powers of the court under section 23(1)(d) or , (e) or (f), (2) (4), 24 or 24A above in relation to a child of the family, the court shall in particular have regard to the following matters –

    (a) the financial needs of the child;

    (b) the income, earning capacity (if any), property and other financial resources of the child;

    (c) any physical or mental disability of the child;

    (d) the manner in which he was being and in which the parties to the marriage expected him to be educated or trained;

    (e) the considerations mentioned in relation to the parties to the marriage in paragraphs (a), (b), (c) and (e) of subsection (2) above.

(4) As regards the exercise of the powers of the court under section 23(1)(d), (e) or (f), (2) or (4), 24 or 24A above against a party to a marriage in favour of a child of the family who is not the child of that party, the court shall also have regard –

    (a) to whether that party assumed any responsibility for the child's maintenance, and, if so, to the extent to which, and the basis upon which, that party assumed such responsibility and to the length of time for which that party discharged such responsibility;

(b) to whether in assuming and discharging such responsibility that party did so knowing that the child was not his or her own;

(c) to the liability of any other person to maintain the child.

25A Exercise of court's powers in favour of party to marriage on decree of divorce or nullity of marriage

(1) Where on or after the grant of a decree of divorce or nullity of marriage the court decides to exercise its powers under section 23(1)(a), (b) or (c), 24, 24A, 24B or 24E above in favour of a party to the marriage, it shall be the duty of the court to consider whether it would be appropriate so to exercise those powers that the financial obligations of each party towards the other will be terminated as soon after the grant of the decree as the court considers just and reasonable.

(2) Where the court decides in such a case to make a periodical payments or secured periodical payments order in favour of a party to the marriage, the court shall in particular consider whether it would be appropriate to require those payments to be made or secured only for such term as would in the opinion of the court be sufficient to enable the party in whose favour the order is made to adjust without undue hardship to the termination of his or her financial dependence on the other party.

(3) Where on or after the grant of a decree of divorce or nullity of marriage an application is made by a party to the marriage for a periodical payments or secured periodical payments order in his or her favour, then, if the court considers that no continuing obligation should be imposed on either party to make or secure periodical payments in favour of the other, the court may dismiss the application with a direction that the applicant shall not be entitled to make any further application in relation to that marriage for an order under section 23(1)(a) or (b) above.

25B Pensions

(1) The matters to which the court is to have regard under section 25(2) above include –

(a) in the case of paragraph (a) , any benefits under a pension arrangement which a party to the marriage has or is likely to have, and

(b) in the case of paragraph (h) , any benefits under a pension arrangement which, by reason of the dissolution or annulment of the marriage, a party to the marriage will lose the chance of acquiring,

and, accordingly, in relation to benefits under a pension arrangement, section 25(2)(a) above shall have effect as if 'in the foreseeable future' were omitted.

. . .

(3) The following provisions apply where, having regard to any benefits under a pension arrangement, the court determines to make an order under section 23 above.

(4) To the extent to which the order is made having regard to any benefits under a pension arrangement, the order may require the person responsible for the pension arrangement in question, if at any time any payment in respect of any benefits under the arrangement becomes due to the party with pension rights, to make a payment for the benefit of the other party.

(5) The order must express the amount of any payment required to be made by virtue of subsection (4) above as a percentage of the payment which becomes due to the party with pension rights.

(6) Any such payment by the person responsible for the arrangement –

(a)   shall discharge so much of his liability to the party with pension rights as corresponds to the amount of the payment, and

(b)   shall be treated for all purposes as a payment made by the party with pension rights in or towards the discharge of his liability under the order.

(7)   Where the party with pension rights has a right of commutation under the arrangement, the order may require him to exercise it to any extent; and this section applies to any payment due in consequence of commutation in pursuance of the order as it applies to other payments in respect of benefits under the arrangement.

(7A) The power conferred by subsection (7) above may not be exercised for the purpose of commuting a benefit payable to the party with pension rights to a benefit payable to the other party.

(7B) The power conferred by subsection (4) or (7) above may not be exercised in relation to a pension arrangement which –

(a)   is the subject of a pension sharing order in relation to the marriage, or

(b)   has been the subject of pension sharing between the parties to the marriage.

(7C) In subsection (1) above, references to benefits under a pension arrangement include any benefits by way of pension, whether under a pension arrangement or not.

25C   Pensions: lump sums

(1)   The power of the court under section 23 above to order a party to a marriage to pay a lump sum to the other party includes, where the benefits which the party with pension rights has or is likely to have under a pension arrangement include any lump sum payable in respect of his death, power to make any of the following provision by the order.

(2)   The court may –

(a)   if the person responsible for the pension arrangement in question has power to determine the person to whom the sum, or any part of it, is to be paid, require him to pay the whole or part of that sum, when it becomes due, to the other party,

(b)   if the party with pension rights has power to nominate the person to whom the sum, or any part of it, is to be paid, require the party with pension rights to nominate the other party in respect of the whole or part of that sum,

(c)   in any other case, require the person responsible for the pension arrangement in question to pay the whole or part of that sum, when it becomes due, for the benefit of the other party instead of to the person to whom, apart from the order, it would be paid.

(3)   Any payment by the person responsible for the arrangement under an order made under section 23 above by virtue of this section shall discharge so much of his liability in respect of the party with pension rights as corresponds to the amount of the payment.

(4)   The powers conferred by this section may not be exercised in relation to a pension arrangement which –

(a) is the subject of a pension sharing order in relation to the marriage, or

(b) has been the subject of pension sharing between the parties to the marriage.

25D   Pensions: supplementary

(1)   Where –

(a)   an order made under section 23 above by virtue of section 25B or 25C above imposes any requirement on the person responsible for a pension arrangement ('the first arrangement') and the party with pension rights acquires rights under another pension arrangement ('the new arrangement') which are derived (directly or indirectly) from the whole of his rights under the first arrangement, and

(b)   the person responsible for the new arrangement has been given notice in accordance with regulations made by the Lord Chancellor,

the order shall have effect as if it had been made instead in respect of the person responsible for the new arrangement.

(2)   The Lord Chancellor may by regulations –

(a)   in relation to any provision of sections 25B or 25C above which authorises the court making an order under section 23 above to require the person responsible for a pension arrangement to make a payment for the benefit of the other party, make provision as to the person to whom, and the terms on which, the payment is to be made,

(ab) make, in relation to payment under a mistaken belief as to the continuation in force of a provision included by virtue of section 25B or 25C above in an order under section 23 above, provision about the rights or liabilities of the payer, the payee or the person to whom the payment was due,

(b)   require notices to be given in respect of changes of circumstances relevant to such orders which include provision made by virtue of sections 25B and 25C above,

(ba) make provision for the person responsible for a pension arrangement to be discharged in prescribed circumstances from a requirement imposed by virtue of section 25B or 25C above,

. . .

(e)   make provision about calculation and verification in relation to the valuation of –

(i)   benefits under a pension arrangement, or
(ii)   shareable state scheme rights,

for the purposes of the court's functions in connection with the exercise of any of its powers under this Part of this Act.

. . .

(2A) Regulations under subsection (2)(e) above may include –

(a)   provision for calculation or verification in accordance with guidance from time to time prepared by a prescribed person, and

(b)   provision by reference to regulations under section 30 or 49(4) of the Welfare Reform and Pensions Act 1999.

(2B) Regulations under subsection (2) above may make different provision for different cases.

(2C) Power to make regulations under this section shall be exercisable by statutory instrument which shall be subject to annulment in pursuance of a resolution of either House of Parliament.

(3)   In this section and sections 25B and 25C above –

'occupational pension scheme' has the same meaning as in the Pension Schemes Act 1993;

'the party with pension rights' means the party to the marriage who has or is likely to have benefits under a pension arrangement and 'the other party' means the other party to the marriage;

'pension arrangement' means –

(a)   an occupational pension scheme,
(b)   a personal pension scheme,
(c)   a retirement annuity contract,

150

(d)   an annuity or insurance policy purchased, or transferred, for the purpose of giving effect to rights under an occupational pension scheme or a personal pension scheme, and

(e)   an annuity purchased, or entered into, for the purpose of discharging liability in respect of a pension credit under section 29(1)(b) of the Welfare Reform and Pensions Act 1999 or under corresponding Northern Ireland legislation;

'personal pension scheme' has the same meaning as in the Pension Schemes Act 1993;

'prescribed' means prescribed by regulations;

'retirement annuity contract' means a contract or scheme approved under Chapter III of Part XIV of the Income and Corporation Taxes Act 1988;

'shareable state scheme rights' has the same meaning as in section 21A(1) above; and

'trustees or managers', in relation to an occupational pension scheme or a personal pension scheme, means –

    (a)   in the case of a scheme established under a trust, the trustees of the scheme, and

    (b)   in any other case, the managers of the scheme.

(4)   In this section and sections 25B and 25C above, references to the person responsible for a pension arrangement are –

(a)   in the case of an occupational pension scheme or a personal pension scheme, to the trustees or managers of the scheme,

(b)   in the case of a retirement annuity contract or an annuity falling within paragraph (d) or (e) of the definition of 'pension arrangement' above, the provider of the annuity, and

(c)   in the case of an insurance policy falling within paragraph (d) of the definition of that expression, the insurer.

25E   The Pension Protection Fund

(1)   The matters to which the court is to have regard under section 25(2) include –

(a)   in the case of paragraph (a), any PPF compensation to which a party to the marriage is or is likely to be entitled, and

(b)   in the case of paragraph (h), any PPF compensation which, by reason of the dissolution or annulment of the marriage, a party to the marriage will lose the chance of acquiring entitlement to,

and, accordingly, in relation to PPF compensation, section 25(2)(a) shall have effect as if 'in the foreseeable future' were omitted.

(2)   Subsection (3) applies in relation to an order under section 23 so far as it includes provision made by virtue of section 25B(4) which –

(a)   imposed requirements on the trustees or managers of an occupational pension scheme for which the Board has assumed responsibility in accordance with Chapter 3 of Part 2 of the Pensions Act 2004 (pension protection) or any provision in force in Northern Ireland corresponding to that Chapter, and

(b)   was made before the trustees or managers of the scheme received the transfer notice in relation to the scheme.

(3)   The order is to have effect from the time when the trustees or managers of the scheme receive the transfer notice –

(a)   as if, except in prescribed descriptions of case –

(i) references in the order to the trustees or managers of the scheme were references to the Board, and

(ii) references in the order to any pension or lump sum to which the party with pension rights is or may become entitled under the scheme were references to any PPF compensation to which that person is or may become entitled in respect of the pension or lump sum, and

(b) subject to such other modifications as may be prescribed.

(4) Subsection (5) applies to an order under section 23 if –

(a) it includes provision made by virtue of section 25B(7) which requires the party with pension rights to exercise his right of commutation under an occupational pension scheme to any extent, and

(b) before the requirement is complied with the Board has assumed responsibility for the scheme as mentioned in subsection (2)(a).

(5) From the time the trustees or managers of the scheme receive the transfer notice, the order is to have effect with such modifications as may be prescribed.

(6) Regulations may modify section 25C as it applies in relation to an occupational pension scheme at any time when there is an assessment period in relation to the scheme.

(7) Where the court makes a pension sharing order in respect of a person's shareable rights under an occupational pension scheme, or an order which includes provision made by virtue of section 25B(4) or (7) in relation to such a scheme, the Board subsequently assuming responsibility for the scheme as mentioned in subsection (2)(a) does not affect –

(a) the powers of the court under section 31 to vary or discharge the order or to suspend or revive any provision of it, or

(b) on an appeal, the powers of the appeal court to affirm, reinstate, set aside or vary the order.

(8) Regulations may make such consequential modifications of any provision of, or made by virtue of, this Part as appear to the Lord Chancellor necessary or expedient to give effect to the provisions of this section.

(9) In this section–

'assessment period' means an assessment period within the meaning of Part 2 of the Pensions Act 2004 (pension protection) (see sections 132 and 159 of that Act) or an equivalent period under any provision in force in Northern Ireland corresponding to that Part;

'the Board' means the Board of the Pension Protection Fund;

'occupational pension scheme' has the same meaning as in the Pension Schemes Act 1993;

'prescribed' means prescribed by regulations;

. . .

'regulations' means regulations made by the Lord Chancellor;

'shareable rights' are rights in relation to which pension sharing is available under Chapter 1 of Part 4 of the Welfare Reform and Pensions Act 1999 or any provision in force in Northern Ireland corresponding to that Chapter;

'transfer notice' has the same meaning as in section 160 of the Pensions Act 2004 or any corresponding provision in force in Northern Ireland.

(10) Any power to make regulations under this section is exercisable by statutory instrument, which shall be subject to annulment in pursuance of a resolution of either House of Parliament.

25F   Attachment of pension compensation

(1)   This section applies where, having regard to any PPF compensation to which a party to the marriage is or is likely to be entitled, the court determines to make an order under section 23.

(2)   To the extent to which the order is made having regard to such compensation, the order may require the Board of the Pension Protection Fund, if at any time any payment in respect of PPF compensation becomes due to the party with compensation rights, to make a payment for the benefit of the other party.

(3)   The order must express the amount of any payment required to be made by virtue of subsection (2) as a percentage of the payment which becomes due to the party with compensation rights.

(4)   Any such payment by the Board of the Pension Protection Fund –

(a)   shall discharge so much of its liability to the party with compensation rights as corresponds to the amount of the payment, and

(b)   shall be treated for all purposes as a payment made by the party with compensation rights in or towards the discharge of that party's liability under the order.

(5)   Where the party with compensation rights has a right to commute any PPF compensation, the order may require that party to exercise it to any extent; and this section applies to any payment due in consequence of commutation in pursuance of the order as it applies to other payments in respect of PPF compensation.

(6)   The power conferred by subsection (5) may not be exercised for the purpose of commuting compensation payable to the party with compensation rights to compensation payable to the other party.

(7)   The power conferred by subsection (2) or (5) may not be exercised in relation to rights to PPF compensation that –

(a)   derive from rights under a pension scheme that were at any time the subject of a pension sharing order in relation to the marriage, or a previous marriage between the same parties, or

(b)   are or have ever been the subject of a pension compensation sharing order in relation to the marriage or a previous marriage between the same parties.

25G   Pension compensation: supplementary

(1)   The Lord Chancellor may by regulations –

(a)   make provision, in relation to any provision of section 25F which authorises the court making an order under section 23 to require the Board of the Pension Protection Fund to make a payment for the benefit of the other party, as to the person to whom, and the terms on which, the payment is to be made;

(b)   make provision, in relation to payment under a mistaken belief as to the continuation in force of a provision included by virtue of section 25F in an order under section 23, about the rights or liabilities of the payer, the payee or the person to whom the payment was due;

(c)   require notices to be given in respect of changes of circumstances relevant to orders under section 23 which include provision made by virtue of section 25F;

(d)   make provision for the Board of the Pension Protection Fund to be discharged in prescribed circumstances from a requirement imposed by virtue of section 25F;

(e)   make provision about calculation and verification in relation to the valuation of PPF compensation for the purposes of the court's functions in connection with the exercise of any of its powers under this Part.

(2)   Regulations under subsection (1)(e) may include –

(a) provision for calculation or verification in accordance with guidance from time to time prepared by a prescribed person;

(b) provision by reference to regulations under section 112 of the Pensions Act 2008.

(3) Regulations under subsection (1) may make different provision for different cases.

(4) The power to make regulations under subsection (1) is exercisable by statutory instrument which shall be subject to annulment in pursuance of a resolution of either House of Parliament.

(5) In this section and section 25F –

'the party with compensation rights' means the party to the marriage who is or is likely to be entitled to PPF compensation, and 'the other party' means the other party to the marriage;

'prescribed' means prescribed by regulations.

...

Variation, discharge and enforcement of certain orders, etc.

31 Variation, discharge, etc., of certain orders for financial relief

(1) Where the court has made an order to which this section applies, then, subject to the provisions of this section and of section 28(1A) above, the court shall have power to vary or discharge the order or to suspend any provision thereof temporarily and to revive the operation of any provision so suspended.

(2) This section applies to the following orders, that is to say –

(a) any order for maintenance pending suit and any interim order for maintenance;

(b) any periodical payments order;

(c) any secured periodical payments order;

(d) any order made by virtue of section 23(3)(c) or 27(7)(b) above (provision for payment of a lump sum by instalments);

(dd) any deferred order made by virtue of section 23(1)(c) (lump sums) which includes provision made by virtue of –

(i) section 25B(4), . . .

(ii) section 25C, or

(iii) section 25F(2),

(provision in respect of pension rights or pension compensation rights)

(e) any order for a settlement of property under section 24(1)(b) or for a variation of settlement under section 24(1)(c) or (d) above, being an order made on or after the grant of a decree of judicial separation.

(f) any order made under section 24A(1) above for the sale of property

(fa) a pension sharing order under section 24B which is made at a time when no divorce order has been made, and no separation order is in force, in relation to the marriage;

(g) a pension sharing order under section 24BB above, or a pension compensation sharing order under section 24E above, which is made at a time before the decree has been made absolute.

(2A) Where the court has made an order referred to in subsection (2)(a), (b) or (c) above, then, subject to the provisions of this section, the court shall have power to remit the payment of any arrears due under the order or of any part thereof.

(2B) Where the court has made an order referred to in subsection (2)(dd)(ii) above, this section shall cease to apply to the order on the death of either of the parties to the marriage

(3)   The powers exercisable by the court under this section in relation to an order shall be exercisable also in relation to any instrument executed in pursuance of the order.

(4)   The court shall not exercise the powers conferred by this section in relation to an order for a settlement under section 24(1)(b) or for a variation of settlement under section 24(1)(c) or (d) above except on an application made in proceedings –

(a)   for the rescission of the decree of judicial separation by reference to which the order was made, or

(b)   for the dissolution of the marriage in question.

(4A) In relation to an order which falls within paragraph (de), (ea), (fa) or (g) of subsection (2) above ('the subsection (2) order') –

(a)   the powers conferred by this section may be exercised –

(i)   only on an application made before the subsection (2) order has or, but for paragraph (b) below, would have taken effect; and

(ii)   only if, at the time when the application is made, the decree has not been made absolute; and

(b)   an application made in accordance with paragraph (a) above prevents the subsection (2) order from taking effect before the application has been dealt with.

(4B) No variation of a pension sharing order, or a pension compensation sharing order, under section 24BB above shall be made so as to take effect before the decree is made absolute.

(4C) The variation of a pension sharing order, or a pension compensation sharing order, prevents the order taking effect before the end of such period after the making of the variation as may be prescribed by regulations made by the Lord Chancellor.

(5)   Subject to subsections (7A) to (7G) below and without prejudice to any power exercisable by virtue of subsection (2)(d), (dd), (e) or (g) above or otherwise than by virtue of this section no property adjustment order or pension sharing order or pension compensation sharing order shall be made on an application for the variation of a periodical payments or secured periodical payments order made (whether in favour of a party to a marriage or in favour of a child of the family) under section 23 above, and no order for the payment of a lump sum shall be made on an application for the variation of a periodical payments or secured periodical payments order in favour of a party to a marriage (whether made under section 23 or under section 27 above).

(6)   Where the person liable to make payments under a secured periodical payments order has died, an application under this section relating to that order (and to any order made under section 24A(1) above which requires the proceeds of sale of property to be used for securing those payments) may be made by the person entitled to payments under the periodical payments order or by the personal representatives of the deceased person, but no such application shall, except with the permission of the court, be made after the end of the period of six months from the date on which representation in regard to the estate of that person is first taken out.

(7)   In exercising the powers conferred by this section the court shall have regard to all the circumstances of the case, first consideration being given to the welfare while a minor of any child of the family who has not attained the age of eighteen, and the circumstances of the case shall include any change in any of the matters to which the court was required to have regard when making the order to which the application relates, and –

(a)   in the case of a periodical payments or secured periodical payments order made on or after the grant of a decree of divorce or nullity of marriage, the court shall consider whether in all the circumstances and after having regard to any such change it would be appropriate to vary the order so that payments under the order

155

are required to be made or secured only for such further period as will in the opinion of the court be sufficient (in the light of any proposed exercise by the court, where the marriage has been dissolved, of its powers under subsection (7B) below) to enable the party in whose favour the order was made to adjust without undue hardship to the termination of those payments;

(b) in a case where the party against whom the order was made has died, the circumstances of the case shall also include the changed circumstances resulting from his or her death.

(7A) Subsection (7B) below applies where, after the dissolution of a marriage, the court –

(a) discharges a periodical payments order or secured periodical payments order made in favour of a party to the marriage; or

(b) varies such an order so that payments under the order are required to be made or secured only for such further period as is determined by the court.

(7B) The court has power, in addition to any power it has apart from this subsection, to make supplemental provision consisting of any of –

(a) an order for the payment of a lump sum in favour of a party to the marriage;

(b) one or more property adjustment orders in favour of a party to the marriage;

(ba) one or more pension sharing orders;

(bb) a pension compensation sharing order;

(c) a direction that the party in whose favour the original order discharged or varied was made is not entitled to make any further application for –

(i) a periodical payments or secured periodical payments order, or

(ii) an extension of the period to which the original order is limited by any variation made by the court.

(7C) An order for the payment of a lump sum made under subsection (7B) above may –

(a) provide for the payment of that sum by instalments of such amount as may be specified in the order; and

(b) require the payment of the instalments to be secured to the satisfaction of the court.

(7D) Section 23(6) above applies where the court makes an order for the payment of a lump sum under subsection (7B) above as it applies where the court makes such an order under section 23 above.

(7E) If under subsection (7B) above the court makes more than one property adjustment order in favour of the same party to the marriage, each of those orders must fall within a different paragraph of section 21(2) above.

(7F) Sections 24A and 30 above apply where the court makes a property adjustment order under subsection (7B) above as they apply where it makes such an order under section 24 above.

(7FA) Section 24B(3) above applies where the court makes a pension sharing order under subsection (7B) above as it applies where the court makes such an order under section 24B above.

(7G) Section 24BA(5) to (7) above apply in relation to a pension sharing order under subsection (7B) above as they apply in relation to a pension sharing order under section 24B above.

(7H) Subsections (3) to (10) of section 24E above apply in relation to a pension compensation sharing order under subsection (7B) above as they apply in relation to a pension compensation sharing order under that section.

(8) The personal representatives of a deceased person against whom a secured periodical payments order was made shall not be liable for having distributed any part of the estate

of the deceased after the expiration of the period of six months referred to in subsection (6) above on the ground that they ought to have taken into account the possibility that the court might permit an application under this section to be made after that period by the person entitled to payments under the order; but this subsection shall not prejudice any power to recover any part of the estate so distributed arising by virtue of the making of an order in pursuance of this section.

(9) The following are to be left out of account when considering for the purposes of subsection (6) above when representation was first taken out –

    (a) a grant limited to settled land or to trust property,

    (b) any other grant that does not permit any of the estate to be distributed,

    (c) a grant limited to real estate or to personal estate, unless a grant limited to the remainder of the estate has previously been made or is made at the same time,

    (d) a grant, or its equivalent, made outside the United Kingdom (but see subsection (9A) below).

(9A) A grant sealed under section 2 of the Colonial Probates Act 1892 counts as a grant made in the United Kingdom for the purposes of subsection (9) above, but is to be taken as dated on the date of sealing.

(10) Where the court, in exercise of its powers under this section, decides to vary or discharge a periodical payments or secured periodical payments order, then, subject to section 28(1) and (2) above, the court shall have power to direct that the variation or discharge shall not take effect until the expiration of such period as may be specified in the order.

(11) Where –

    (a) a periodical payments or secured periodical payments order in favour of more than one child ('the order') is in force;

    (b) the order requires payments specified in it to be made to or for the benefit of more than one child without apportioning those payments between them;

    (c) a maintenance calculation ('the calculation') is made with respect to one or more, but not all, of the children with respect to whom those payments are to be made; and

    (d) an application is made, before the end of the period of 6 months beginning with the date on which the assessment was made, for the variation or discharge of the order,

the court may, in exercise of its powers under this section to vary or discharge the order, direct that the variation or discharge shall take effect from the date on which the calculation took effect or any later date.

(12) Where –

    (a) an order ('the child order') of a kind prescribed for the purposes of section 10(1) of the Child Support Act 1991 is affected by a maintenance calculation;

    (b) on the date on which the child order became so affected there was in force a periodical payments or secured periodical payments order ('the spousal order') in favour of a party to a marriage having the care of the child in whose favour the child order was made; and

    (c) an application is made, before the end of the period of 6 months beginning with the date on which the maintenance calculation was made, for the spousal order to be varied or discharged,

the court may, in exercise of its powers under this section to vary or discharge the spousal order, direct that the variation or discharge shall take effect from the date on which the child order became so affected or any later date.

(13) For the purposes of subsection (12) above, an order is affected if it ceases to have effect or is modified by or under section 10 of the Child Support Act 1991.

(14) Subsections (11) and (12) above are without prejudice to any other power of the court to direct that the variation of discharge of an order under this section shall take effect from a date earlier than that on which the order for variation or discharge was made.

(15) The power to make regulations under subsection (4C) above shall be exercisable by statutory instrument which shall be subject to annulment in pursuance of a resolution of either House of Parliament.

31B Discharge of pension sharing orders on making of separation order

Where, after the making of a pension sharing order under section 24B above, in relation to a marriage, a separation order is made in relation to the marriage, the pension sharing order is discharged.

...

Maintenance agreements

34 Validity of maintenance agreements

(1) If a maintenance agreement includes a provision purporting to restrict any right to apply to a court for an order containing financial arrangements, then –

(a) that provision shall be void; but

(b) any other financial arrangements contained in the agreement shall not thereby be rendered void or unenforceable and shall, unless they are void or unenforceable for any other reason (and subject to sections 35 and 36 below), be binding on the parties to the agreement.

(2) In this section and in section 35 below –

'maintenance agreement' means any agreement in writing made, whether before or after the commencement of this Act, between the parties to a marriage, being –

(a) an agreement containing financial arrangements, whether made during the continuance or after the dissolution or annulment of the marriage; or

(b) a separation agreement which contains no financial arrangements in a case where no other agreement in writing between the same parties contains such arrangements;

'financial arrangements' means provisions governing the rights and liabilities towards one another when living separately of the parties to a marriage (including a marriage which has been dissolved or annulled) in respect of the making or securing of payments or the disposition or use of any property, including such rights and liabilities with respect to the maintenance or education of any child, whether or not a child of the family.

35 Alteration of agreements by court during lives of parties

(1) Where a maintenance agreement is for the time being subsisting and each of the parties to the agreement is for the time being either domiciled or resident in England and Wales, then, subject to subsections (1A) and (3) below, either party may apply to the court for an order under this section.

(1A) If an application or part of an application relates to a matter where jurisdiction falls to be determined by reference to the jurisdictional requirements of the Maintenance Regulation and Schedule 6 to the Civil Jurisdiction and Judgments (Maintenance) Regulations 2011 –

(a)   the requirement as to domicile or residence in subsection (1) does not apply to the application or that part of it, but

(b)   the court may not entertain the application or that part of it unless it has jurisdiction to do so by virtue of that Regulation and that Schedule.

(2)   If the court is satisfied either –

(a)   that by reason of a change in the circumstances in the light of which any financial arrangements contained in the agreement were made or, as the case may be, financial arrangements were omitted from it (including a change foreseen by the parties when making the agreement), the agreement should be altered so as to make different, or, as the case may be, so as to contain, financial arrangements, or

(b)   that the agreement does not contain proper financial arrangements with respect to any child of the family,

then subject to subsections (4) and (5) below, the court may by order make such alterations in the agreement –

(i)   by varying or revoking any financial arrangements contained in it, or

(ii)   by inserting in it financial arrangements for the benefit of one of the parties to the agreement or of a child of the family,

as may appear to the court to be just having regard to all the circumstances, including, if relevant, the matters mentioned in section 25(4) above; and the agreement shall have effect thereafter as if any alteration made by the order had been made by agreement between the parties and for valuable consideration.

(3)   [*Repealed*]

(4)   Where the court decides to alter, by order under this section, an agreement by inserting provision for the making or securing by one of the parties to the agreement of periodical payments for the maintenance of the other party or by increasing the rate of the periodical payments which the agreement provides shall be made by one of the parties for the maintenance of the other, the term for which the payments or, as the case may be, the additional payments attributable to the increase are to be made under the agreement as altered by the order shall be such term as the court may specify, subject to the following limits, that is to say –

(a)   where the payments will not be secured, the term shall be so defined as not to extend beyond the death of either of the parties to the agreement or the remarriage of, or formation of a civil partnership by, the party to whom the payments are to be made;

(b)   where the payments will be secured, the term shall be so defined as not to extend beyond the death or remarriage of, or formation of a civil partnership by, that party.

(5)   Where the court decides to alter, by order under this section, an agreement by inserting provision for the making or securing by one of the parties to the agreement of periodical payments for the maintenance of a child of the family or by increasing the rate of the periodical payments which the agreement provides shall be made or secured by one of the parties for the maintenance of such a child, then, in deciding the term for which under the agreement as altered by the order the payments, or as the case may be, the additional payments attributable to the increase are to be made or secured for the benefit of the child, the court shall apply the provisions of section 29(2) and (3) above as to age

limits as if the order in question were a periodical payments or secured periodical payments order in favour of the child.

(6) For the avoidance of doubt it is hereby declared that nothing in this section or in section 34 above affects any power of a court before which any proceedings between the parties to a maintenance agreement are brought under any other enactment (including a provision of this Act) to make an order containing financial arrangements or any right of either party to apply for such an order in such proceedings.

36 Alteration of agreements by court after death of one party

(1) Where a maintenance agreement within the meaning of section 34 above provides for the continuation of payments under the agreement after the death of one of the parties and that party dies domiciled in England and Wales, the surviving party or the personal representatives of the deceased party may, subject to subsections (2) and (3) below, apply to the court for an order under section 35 above.

(2) An application under this section shall not, except with the permission of the court, be made after the end of the period of six months from the date on which representation in regard to the estate of the deceased is first taken out.

(3) [Repealed]

(4) If a maintenance agreement is altered by the court on an application made in pursuance of subsection (1) above, the like consequences shall ensue as if the alteration had been made immediately before the death by agreement between the parties and for valuable consideration.

(5) The provisions of this section shall not render the personal representatives of the deceased liable for having distributed any part of the estate of the deceased after the expiration of the period of six months referred to in subsection (2) above on the ground that they ought to have taken into account the possibility that the court might permit an application by virtue of this section to be made by the surviving party after that period; but this subsection shall not prejudice any power to recover any part of the estate so distributed arising by virtue of the making of an order in pursuance of this section.

(6) Section 31(9) above shall apply for the purposes of subsection (2) above as it applies for the purposes of subsection (6) of section 31.

(7) [Repealed]

Miscellaneous and supplemental

37 Avoidance of transactions intended to prevent or reduce financial relief

(1) For the purposes of this section 'financial relief' means relief under any of the provisions of sections 22, 23, 24, 24B, 27, 31 (except subsection (6)) and 35 above, and any reference in this section to defeating a person's claim for financial relief is a reference to preventing financial relief from being granted to that person, or to that person for the benefit of a child of the family, or reducing the amount of any financial relief which might be so granted, or frustrating or impeding the enforcement of any order which might be or has been made at his instance under any of those provisions.

(2) Where proceedings for financial relief are brought by one person against another, the court may, on the application of the first-mentioned person –

(a) if it is satisfied that the other party to the proceedings is, with the intention of defeating the claim for financial relief, about to make any disposition or to transfer out of the jurisdiction or otherwise deal with any property, make such order as it thinks fit for restraining the other party from so doing or otherwise for protecting the claim;

(b)   if it is satisfied that the other party has, with that intention, made a reviewable disposition and that if the disposition were set aside financial relief or different financial relief would be granted to the applicant, make an order setting aside the disposition;

(c)   if it is satisfied, in a case where an order has been obtained under any of the provisions mentioned in subsection (1) above by the applicant against the other party, that the other party has, with that intention, made a reviewable disposition, make an order setting aside the disposition;

and an application for the purposes of paragraph (b) above shall be made in the proceedings for the financial relief in question.

(3)   Where the court makes an order under subsection (2)(b) or (c) above setting aside a disposition it shall give such consequential directions as it thinks fit for giving effect to the order (including directions requiring the making of any payments or the disposal of any property).

(4)   Any disposition made by the other party to the proceedings for financial relief in question (whether before or after the commencement of those proceedings) as is reviewable disposition for the purposes of subsection (2)(b) and (c) above unless it was made for valuable consideration (other than marriage) to a person who, at the time of the disposition, acted in relation to it in good faith and without notice of any intention on the part of the other party to defeat the applicant's claim for financial relief.

(5)   Where an application is made under this section with respect to a disposition which took place less than three years before the date of the application or with respect to a disposition or other dealing with property which is about to take place and the court is satisfied –

(a)   in a case falling within subsection (2)(a) or (b) above, that the disposition or other dealing would (apart from this section) have the consequence, or

(b)   in a case falling within subsection (2)(c) above, that the disposition has had the consequence,

of defeating the applicant's claim for financial relief, it shall be presumed, unless the contrary is shown, that the person who disposed of or is about to dispose of or deal with the property did so or, as the case may be, is about to do so, with the intention of defeating the applicant's claim for financial relief.

(6)   In this section 'disposition' does not include any provision contained in a will or codicil but, with that exception, includes any conveyance, assurance or gift of property of any description, whether made by an instrument or otherwise.

(7)   This section does not apply to a disposition made before 1st January 1968.

…

Inheritance (Provision for Family and Dependants) Act 1975

[1975 c.63]

An Act to make fresh provision for empowering the court to make orders for the making out of the estate of a deceased person of provision for the spouse, former spouse, child, child of the family or dependant of that person; and for matters connected therewith.

[12 November 1975]

BE IT ENACTED by the Queen's most Excellent Majesty, by and with the advice and consent of the Lords Spiritual and Temporal, and Commons, in this present Parliament assembled, and by the authority of the same, as follows:

1 Application for financial provision from deceased's estate

(1) Where after the commencement of this Act a person dies domiciled in England and Wales and is survived by any of the following persons –

   (a) the spouse or civil partner of the deceased;
   (b) a former spouse or former civil partner of the deceased, but not one who has formed a subsequent marriage or civil partnership;
   (ba) any person (not being a person included in paragraph (a) or (b) above) to whom subsection (1A) or (1B) below applies;
   (c) a child of the deceased;
   (d) any person (not being a child of the deceased) who in relation to any marriage or civil partnership to which the deceased was at any time a party, or otherwise in relation to any family in which the deceased at any time stood in the role of a parent, was treated by the deceased as a child of the family;
   (e) any person (not being a person included in the foregoing paragraphs of this subsection) who immediately before the death of the deceased was being maintained, either wholly or partly, by the deceased;

that person may apply to the court for an order under section 2 of this Act on the ground that the disposition of the deceased's estate effected by his will or the law relating to intestacy, or the combination of his will and that law, is not such as to make reasonable financial provision for the applicant.

(1A) This subsection applies to a person if the deceased died on or after 1st January 1996 and, during the whole of the period of two years ending immediately before the date when the deceased died, the person was living –

   (a) in the same household as the deceased, and
   (b) as the husband or wife of the deceased.

(1B) This subsection applies to a person if for the whole of the period of two years ending immediately before the date when the deceased died the person was living –

    (a)   in the same household as the deceased, and

    (b)   as the civil partner of the deceased.

(2)   In this Act 'reasonable financial provision' –

    (a)   in the case of an application made by virtue of subsection (1)(a) above by the husband or wife of the deceased (except where the marriage with the deceased was the subject of a decree of judicial separation and at the date of death the decree was in force and the separation was continuing), means such financial provision as it would be reasonable in all the circumstances of the case for a husband or wife to receive, whether or not that provision is required for his or her maintenance;

    (aa)   in the case of an application made by virtue of subsection (1)(a) above by the civil partner of the deceased (except where, at the date of death, a separation order under Chapter 2 of Part 2 of the Civil Partnership Act 2004 was in force in relation to the civil partnership and the separation was continuing), means such financial provision as it would be reasonable in all the circumstances of the case for a civil partner to receive, whether or not that provision is required for his or her maintenance;

    (b)   in the case of any other application made by virtue of subsection (1) above, means such financial provision as it would be reasonable in all the circumstances of the case for the applicant to receive for his maintenance.

(2A) The reference in subsection (1)(d) above to a family in which the deceased stood in the role of a parent includes a family of which the deceased was the only member (apart from the applicant).

(3)   For the purposes of subsection (1)(e) above, a person is to be treated as being maintained by the deceased (either wholly or partly, as the case may be) only if the deceased was making a substantial contribution in money or money's worth towards the reasonable needs of that person, other than a contribution made for full valuable consideration pursuant to an arrangement of a commercial nature.

2   Powers of court to make orders

(1)   Subject to the provisions of this Act, where an application is made for an order under this section, the court may, if it is satisfied that the disposition of the deceased's estate effected by his will or the law relating to intestacy, or the combination of his will and that law, is not such as to make reasonable financial provision for the applicant, make any one or more of the following orders –

    (a)   an order for the making to the applicant out of the net estate of the deceased of such periodical payments and for such term as may be specified in the order;

    (b)   an order for the payment to the applicant out of that estate of a lump sum of such amount as may be so specified;

    (c)   an order for the transfer to the applicant of such property comprised in that estate as may be so specified;

    (d)   an order for the settlement for the benefit of the applicant of such property comprised in that estate as may be so specified;

    (e)   an order for the acquisition out of property comprised in that estate of such property as may be so specified and for the transfer of the property so acquired to the applicant or for the settlement thereof for his benefit;

    (f)   an order varying any ante-nuptial or post-nuptial settlement (including such a settlement made by will) made on the parties to a marriage to which the deceased was one of the parties, the variation being for the benefit of the surviving party to that marriage, or any child of that marriage, or any person who was treated by the deceased as a child of the family in relation to that marriage;

(g)   an order varying any settlement made–

    (i)   during the subsistence of a civil partnership formed by the deceased, or

    (ii)   in anticipation of the formation of a civil partnership by the deceased,

on the civil partners (including such a settlement made by will), the variation being for the benefit of the surviving civil partner, or any child of both the civil partners, or any person who was treated by the deceased as a child of the family in relation to that civil partnership;

(h)   an order varying for the applicant's benefit the trusts on which the deceased's estate is held (whether arising under the will, or the law relating to intestacy, or both).

(2)   An order under subsection (1)(a) above providing for the making out of the net estate of the deceased of periodical payments may provide for –

    (a)   payments of such amount as may be specified in the order,

    (b)   payments equal to the whole of the income of the net estate or of such portion thereof as may be so specified,

    (c)   payments equal to the whole of the income of such part of the net estate as the court may direct to be set aside or appropriated for the making out of the income thereof of payments under this section,

or may provide for the amount of the payments or any of them to be determined in any other way the court thinks fit.

(3)   Where an order under subsection (1)(a) above provides for the making of payments of an amount specified in the order, the order may direct that such part of the net estate as may be so specified shall be set aside or appropriated for the making out of the income thereof of those payments; but no larger part of the net estate shall be so set aside or appropriated than is sufficient, at the date of the order, to produce by the income thereof the amount required for the making of those payments.

(3A)   In assessing for the purposes of an order under this section the extent (if any) to which the net estate is reduced by any debts or liabilities (including any inheritance tax paid or payable out of the estate), the court may assume that the order has already been made.

(4)   An order under this section may contain such consequential and supplemental provisions as the court thinks necessary or expedient for the purpose of giving effect to the order or for the purpose of securing that the order operates fairly as between one beneficiary of the estate of the deceased and another and may, in particular, but without prejudice to the generality of this subsection –

    (a)   order any person who holds any property which forms part of the net estate of the deceased to make such payment or transfer such property as may be specified in the order;

    (b)   vary the disposition of the deceased's estate effected by the will or the law relating to intestacy, or by both the will and the law relating to intestacy, in such manner as the court thinks fair and reasonable having regard to the provisions of the order and all the circumstances of the case;

    (c)   confer on the trustees of any property which is the subject of an order under this section such powers as appear to the court to be necessary or expedient.

3   Matters to which court is to have regard in exercising powers under s.2

(1)   Where an application is made for an order under section 2 of this Act, the court shall, in

determining whether the disposition of the deceased's estate effected by his will or the law relating to intestacy, or the combination of his will and that law, is such as to make reasonable financial provision for the applicant and, if the court considers that reasonable financial provision has not been made, in determining whether and in what manner it shall exercise its powers under that section, have regard to the following matters, that is to say –

(a) the financial resources and financial needs which the applicant has or is likely to have in the foreseeable future;
(b) the financial resources and financial needs which any other applicant for an order under section 2 of this Act has or is likely to have in the foreseeable future;
(c) the financial resources and financial needs which any beneficiary of the estate of the deceased has or is likely to have in the foreseeable future;
(d) any obligations and responsibilities which the deceased had towards any applicant for an order under the said section 2 or towards any beneficiary of the estate of the deceased;
(e) the size and nature of the net estate of the deceased;
(f) any physical or mental disability of any applicant for an order under the said section 2 or any beneficiary of the estate of the deceased;
(g) any other matter, including the conduct of the applicant or any other person, which in the circumstances of the case the court may consider relevant.

(2) This subsection applies, without prejudice to the generality of paragraph (g) of subsection (1) above, where an application for an order under section 2 of this Act is made by virtue of section 1(1)(a) or (b) of this Act.

The court shall, in addition to the matters specifically mentioned in paragraphs (a) to (f) of that subsection, have regard to –

(a) the age of the applicant and the duration of the marriage or civil partnership;
(b) the contribution made by the applicant to the welfare of the family of the deceased, including any contribution made by looking after the home or caring for the family.

In the case of an application by the wife or husband of the deceased, the court shall also, unless at the date of death a decree of judicial separation was in force and the separation was continuing, have regard to the provision which the applicant might reasonably have expected to receive if on the day on which the deceased died the marriage, instead of being terminated by death, had been terminated by a degree of divorce; but nothing requires the court to treat such provision as setting an upper or lower limit on the provision which may be made by an order under section 2.

In the case of an application by the civil partner of the deceased, the court shall also, unless at the date of the death a separation order under Chapter 2 of Part 2 of the Civil Partnership Act 2004 was in force and the separation was continuing, have regard to the provision which the applicant might reasonably have expected to receive if on the day on which the deceased died the civil partnership, instead of being terminated by death, had been terminated by a dissolution order; but nothing requires the court to treat such provision as setting an upper or lower limit on the provision which may be made by an order under section 2.

(2A) Without prejudice to the generality of paragraph (g) of subsection (1) above, where an application for an order under section 2 of this Act is made by virtue of section 1(1)(ba) of this Act, the court shall, in addition to the matters specifically mentioned in paragraphs (a) to (f) of that subsection, have regard to –

(a) the age of the applicant and the length of the period during which the applicant lived as the husband or wife or civil partner of the deceased and in the same household as the deceased;

(b) the contribution made by the applicant to the welfare of the family of the deceased, including any contribution made by looking after the home or caring for the family.

(3) Without prejudice to the generality of paragraph (g) of subsection (1) above, where an application for an order under section 2 of this Act is made by virtue of section 1(1)(c) or 1(1)(d) of this Act, the court shall, in addition to the matters specifically mentioned in paragraphs (a) to (f) of that subsection, have regard to the manner in which the applicant was being or in which he might expect to be educated or trained, and where the application is made by virtue of section 1(1)(d) the court shall also have regard –

(a) to whether the deceased maintained the applicant and, if so, to the length of time for which and basis on which the deceased did so, and to the extent of the contribution made by way of maintenance;

(aa) to whether and, if so, to what extent the deceased assumed responsibility for the maintenance of the applicant;

(b) to whether in maintaining or assuming responsibility for maintaining the applicant the deceased did so knowing that the applicant was not his own child;

(c) to the liability of any other person to maintain the applicant.

(4) Without prejudice to the generality of paragraph (g) of subsection (1) above, where an application for an order under section 2 of this Act is made by virtue of section 1(1)(e) of this Act, the court shall, in addition to the matters specifically mentioned in paragraphs (a) to (f) of that subsection, have regard –

(a) to the length of time for which and basis on which the deceased maintained the applicant, and to the extent of the contribution made by way of maintenance;

(b) to whether and, if so, to what extent the deceased assumed responsibility for the maintenance of the applicant.

(5) In considering the matters to which the court is required to have regard under this section, the court shall take into account the facts as known to the court at the date of the hearing.

(6) In considering the financial resources of any person for the purposes of this section the court shall take into account his earning capacity and in considering the financial needs of any person for the purposes of this section the court shall take into account his financial obligations and responsibilities.

4 Time-limit for applications

An application for an order under section 2 of this Act shall not, except with the permission of the court, be made after the end of the period of six months from the date on which representation with respect to the estate of the deceased is first taken out (but nothing prevents the making of an application before such representation is first taken out).

5 Interim orders

(1) Where on an application for an order under section 2 of this Act it appears to the court –

(a) that the applicant is in immediate need of financial assistance, but it is not yet possible to determine what order (if any) should be made under that section; and

(b) that property forming part of the net estate of the deceased is or can be made available to meet the need of the applicant;

the court may order that, subject to such conditions or restrictions, if any, as the court may impose and to any further order of the court, there shall be paid to the applicant out of the net estate of the deceased such sum or sums and (if more than one) at such intervals as the court thinks reasonable; and the court may order that, subject to the provisions of this Act, such payments are to be made until such date as the court may specify, not being later than the date on which the court either makes an order under the said section 2 or decides not to exercise its powers under that section.

(2) Subsections (2), (3) and (4) of section 2 of this Act shall apply in relation to an order under this section as they apply in relation to an order under that section.

(3) In determining what order, if any, should be made under this section the court shall, so far as the urgency of the case admits, have regard to the same matters as those to which the court is required to have regard under section 3 of this Act.

(4) An order made under section 2 of this Act may provide that any sum paid to the applicant by virtue of this section shall be treated to such an extent and in such manner as may be provided by that order as having been paid on account of any payment provided for by that order.

6 Variation, discharge etc. of orders for periodical payments

(1) Subject to the provisions of this Act, where the court has made an order under section 2(1)(a) of this Act (in this section referred to as 'the original order') for the making of periodical payments to any person (in this section referred to as 'the original recipient'), the court, on an application under this section, shall have power by order to vary or discharge the original order or to suspend any provision of it temporarily and to revive the operation of any provision so suspended.

(2) Without prejudice to the generality of subsection (1) above, an order made on an application for the variation of the original order may –

   (a) provide for the making out of any relevant property of such periodical payments and for such term as may be specified in the order to any person who has applied, or would but for section 4 of this Act be entitled to apply, for an order under section 2 of this Act (whether or not, in the case of any application, an order was made in favour of the applicant);

   (b) provide for the payment out of any relevant property of a lump sum of such amount as may be so specified to the original recipient or to any such person as is mentioned in paragraph (a) above;

   (c) provide for the transfer of the relevant property, or such part thereof as may be so specified, to the original recipient or to any such person as is so mentioned.

(3) Where the original order provides that any periodical payments payable thereunder to the original recipient are to cease on the occurrence of an event specified in the order (other than the formation of a subsequent marriage or civil partnership by a former spouse or former civil partner) or on the expiration of a period so specified, then, if, before the end of the period of six months from the date of the occurrence of that event or of the expiration of that period, an application is made for an order under this section, the court shall have power to make any order which it would have had power to make if the application had been made before the date (whether in favour of the original recipient or any such person as is mentioned in subsection (2)(a) above and whether having effect from that date or from such later date as the court may specify).

(4) Any reference in this section to the original order shall include a reference to an order made under this section and any reference in this section to the original recipient shall include a reference to any person to whom periodical payments are required to be made by virtue of an order under this section.

(5)   An application under this section may be made by any of the following persons, that is to say –

    (a)   any person who by virtue of section 1(1) of this Act has applied, or would but for section 4 of this Act be entitled to apply, for an order under section 2 of this Act,

    (b)   the personal representatives of the deceased,

    (c)   the trustees of any relevant property, and

    (d)   any beneficiary of the estate of the deceased.

(6)   An order under this section may only affect –

    (a)   property the income of which is at the date of the order applicable wholly or in part for the making of periodical payments to any person who has applied for an order under this Act, or

    (b)   in the case of an application under subsection (3) above in respect of payments which have ceased to be payable on the occurrence of an event or the expiration of a period, property the income of which was so applicable immediately before the occurrence of that event or the expiration of that period, as the case may be,

and any such property as is mentioned in paragraph (a) or (b) above is in subsections (2) and (5) above referred to as 'relevant property'.

(7)   In exercising the powers conferred by this section the court shall have regard to all the circumstances of the case, including any change in any of the matters to which the court was required to have regard when making the order to which the application relates.

(8)   Where the court makes an order under this section, it may give such consequential directions as it thinks necessary or expedient having regard to the provisions of the order.

(9)   No such order as is mentioned in sections 2(1)(d), (e) or (f), 9, 10 or 11 of this Act shall be made on an application under this section.

(10) For the avoidance of doubt it is hereby declared that, in relation to an order which provides for the making of periodical payments which are to cease on the occurrence of an event specified in the order (other than the formation of a subsequent marriage or civil partnership by a former spouse or former civil partner) or on the expiration of a period so specified, the power to vary an order includes power to provide for the making of periodical payments after the expiration that period or the occurrence of that event.

7   Payment of lump sums by instalments

(1)   An order under section 2(1)(b) or 6(2)(b) of this Act for the payment of a lump sum may provide for the payment of that sum by instalments of such amount as may be specified in the order.

(2)   Where an order is made by virtue of subsection (1) above, the court shall have power, on an application made by the person to whom the lump sum is payable, by the personal representatives of the deceased or by the trustees of the property out of which the lump sum is payable, to vary that order by varying the number of instalments payable, the amount of any instalment and the date on which any instalment becomes payable.

Property available for financial provision

8   Property treated as part of 'net estate'

(1)   Where a deceased person has in accordance with the provisions of any enactment nominated any person to receive any sum of money or other property on his death and that nomination is in force at the time of his death, that sum of money, after deducting therefrom any capital transfer tax payable in respect thereof, or that other property, to

the extent of the value thereof at the date of the death of the deceased after deducting therefrom any capital transfer tax so payable, shall be treated for the purposes of this Act as part of the net estate of the deceased; but this subsection shall not render any person liable for having paid that sum or transferred that other property to the person named in the nomination in accordance with the directions given in the nomination.

(2) Where any sum of money or other property is received by any person as a donatio mortis causa made by a deceased person, that sum of money, after deducting therefrom any capital transfer tax payable thereon, or that other property, to the extent of the value thereof at the date of the death of the deceased after deducting therefrom any capital transfer tax so payable, shall be treated for the purposes of this Act as part of the net estate of the deceased; but this subsection shall not render any person liable for having paid that sum or transferred that other property in order to give effect to that donatio mortis causa.

(3) The amount of capital transfer tax to be deducted for the purposes of this section shall not exceed the amount of that tax which has been borne by the person nominated by the deceased or, as the case may be, the person who has received a sum of money or other property as a donatio mortis causa.

9 Property held on a joint tenancy

(1) Where a deceased person was immediately before his death beneficially entitled to a joint tenancy of any property, then, if an application is made for an order under section 2 of this Act, the court for the purpose of facilitating the making of financial provision for the applicant under this Act may order that the deceased's severable share of that property shall, to such extent as appears to the court to be just in all the circumstances of the case, be treated for the purposes of this Act as part of the net estate of the deceased.

(1A) Where an order is made under subsection (1) the value of the deceased's severable share of the property concerned is taken for the purposes of this Act to be the value that the share would have had at the date of the hearing of the application for an order under section 2 had the share been severed immediately before the deceased's death, unless the court orders that the share is to be valued at a different date.

(2) In determining the extent to which any severable share is to be treated as part of the net estate of the deceased by virtue of an order under subsection (1) above, the court shall have regard to any capital transfer tax payable in respect of that severable share.

(3) Where an order is made under subsection (1) above, the provisions of this section shall not render any person liable for anything done by him before the order was made.

(4) For the avoidance of doubt it is hereby declared that for the purposes of this section there may be a joint tenancy of a chose in action.

Powers of court in relation to transactions intended to defeat applications for financial provision

10 Dispositions intended to defeat applications for financial provision

(1) Where an application is made to the court for an order under section 2 of this Act, the applicant may, in the proceedings on that application, apply to the court for an order under subsection (2) below.

(2) Where on an application under subsection (1) above the court is satisfied –

(a) that, less than six years before the date of the death of the deceased, the deceased with the intention of defeating an application for financial provision under this Act made a disposition, and

(b) that full valuable consideration for that disposition was not given by the person to whom or for the benefit of whom the disposition was made (in this section referred to as 'the donee') or by any other person, and

(c) that the exercise of the powers conferred by this section would facilitate the making of financial provision for the applicant under this Act,

then, subject to the provisions of this section and of sections 12 and 13 of this Act, the court may order the donee (whether or not at the date of the order he holds any interest in the property disposed of to him or for his benefit by the deceased) to provide, for the purpose of the making of that financial provision, such sum of money or other property as may be specified in the order.

(3) Where an order is made under subsection (2) above as respects any disposition made by the deceased which consisted of the payment of money to or for the benefit of the donee, the amount of any sum of money or the value of any property ordered to be provided under that subsection shall not exceed the amount of the payment made by the deceased after deducting therefrom any capital transfer tax borne by the donee in respect of that payment.

(4) Where an order is made under subsection (2) above as respects any disposition made by the deceased which consisted of the transfer of property (other than a sum of money) to or for the benefit of the donee, the amount of any sum of money or the value of any property ordered to be provided under that subsection shall not exceed the value at the date of the death of the deceased of the property disposed of by him to or for the benefit of the donee (or if that property has been disposed of by the person to whom it was transferred by the deceased, the value at the date of that disposal thereof) after deducting therefrom any capital transfer tax borne by the donee in respect of the transfer of that property by the deceased.

(5) Where an application (in this subsection referred to as 'the original application') is made for an order under subsection (2) above in relation to any disposition, then, if on an application under this subsection by the donee or by any applicant for an order under section 2 of this Act the court is satisfied –

(a) that, less than six years before the date of the death of the deceased, the deceased with the intention of defeating an application for financial provision under this Act made a disposition other than the disposition which is the subject of the original application, and

(b) that full valuable consideration for that other disposition was not given by the person to whom or for the benefit of whom that other disposition was made or by any other person,

the court may exercise in relation to the person to whom or for the benefit of whom that other disposition was made the powers which the court would have had under subsection (2) above if the original application had been made in respect of that other disposition and the court had been satisfied as to the matters set out in paragraphs (a), (b) and (c) of that subsection; and where any application is made under this subsection, any reference in this section (except in subsection (2)(b) to the donee shall include a reference to the person to whom or for the benefit of whom that other disposition was made.

(6) In determining whether and in what manner to exercise its powers under this section, the court shall have regard to the circumstances in which any disposition was made and any valuable consideration which was given therefor, the relationship, if any, of the donee to the deceased, the conduct and financial resources of the donee and all the other circumstances of the case.

(7) In this section 'disposition' does not include –

(a) any provision in a will, any such nomination as is mentioned in section 8(1) of this Act or any donatio mortis causa, or (b)　any appointment of property made, otherwise than by will, in the exercise of a special power of appointment,

but, subject to these exceptions, includes any payment of money (including the payment of a premium under a policy of assurance) and any conveyance, assurance, appointment or gift of property of any description, whether made by an instrument or otherwise.

(8)　The provisions of this section do not apply to any disposition made before the commencement of this Act.

11　Contracts to leave property by will

(1)　Where an application is made to a court for an order under section 2 of this Act, the applicant may, in the proceedings on that application, apply to the court for an order under this section.

(2)　Where on an application under subsection (1) above the court is satisfied –

(a)　that the deceased made a contract by which he agreed to leave by his will a sum of money or other property to any person or by which he agreed that a sum of money or other property would be paid or transferred to any person out of his estate, and

(b)　that the deceased made that contract with the intention of defeating an application for financial provision under this Act, and

(c)　that when the contract was made full valuable consideration for that contract was not given or promised by the person with whom or for the benefit of whom the contract was made (in this section referred to as 'the donee') or by any other person, and

(d)　that the exercise of the powers conferred by this section would facilitate the making of financial provision for the applicant under this Act,

then, subject to the provisions of this section and of sections 12 and 13 of this Act, the court may make any one or more of the following orders, that is to say –

(i)　if any money has been paid or any other property has been transferred to or for the benefit of the donee in accordance with the contract, an order directing the donee to provide, for the purpose of the making of that financial provision, such sum of money or other property as may be specified in the order;

(ii)　if the money or all the money has not been paid or the property or all the property has not been transferred in accordance with the contract, an order directing the personal representatives not to make any payment or transfer any property, or not to make any further payment or transfer any further property, as the case may be, in accordance therewith or directing the personal representatives only to make such payment or transfer such property as may be specified in the order.

(3)　Notwithstanding anything in subsection (2) above, the court may exercise its powers thereunder in relation to any contract made by the deceased only to the extent that the court considers that the amount of any sum of money paid or to be paid or the value of any property transferred or to be transferred in accordance with the contract exceeds the value of any valuable consideration given or to be given for that contract, and for this purpose the court shall have regard to the value of property at the date of the hearing.

(4)　In determining whether and in what manner to exercise its powers under this section, the court shall have regard to the circumstances in which the contract was made, the relationship, if any, of the donee to the deceased, the conduct and financial resources of the donee and all the other circumstances of the case.

(5)　Where an order has been made under subsection (2) above in relation to any contract, the rights of any person to enforce that contract or to recover damages or to obtain other relief for the breach thereof shall be subject to any adjustment made by the court under section 12(3) of this Act and shall survive to such extent only as is consistent with giving effect to the terms of that order.

(6) The provisions of this section do not apply to a contract made before the commencement of this Act.

12 Provisions supplementary to ss.10 and 11

(1) Where the exercise of any of the powers conferred by section 10 or 11 of this Act is conditional on the court being satisfied that a disposition or contract was made by a deceased person with the intention of defeating an application for financial provision under this Act, that condition shall be fulfilled if the court is of the opinion that, on a balance of probabilities, the intention of the deceased (though not necessarily his sole intention) in making the disposition or contract was to prevent an order for financial provision being made under this Act or to reduce the amount of the provision which might otherwise be granted by an order thereunder.

(2) Where an application is made under section 11 of this Act with respect to any contract made by the deceased and no valuable consideration was given or promised by any person for that contract then, notwithstanding anything in subsection (1) above, it shall be presumed, unless the contrary is shown, that the deceased made that contract with the intention of defeating an application for financial provision under this Act.

(3) Where the court makes an order under section 10 or 11 of this Act it may give such consequential directions as it thinks fit (including directions requiring the making of any payment or the transfer of any property) for giving effect to the order or for securing a fair adjustment of the rights of the persons affected thereby.

(4) Any power conferred on the court by the said section 10 or 11 to order the donee, in relation to any disposition or contract, to provide any sum of money or other property shall be exercisable in like manner in relation to the personal representative of the donee, and –

(a) any reference in section 10(4) to the disposal of property by the donee shall include a reference to disposal by the personal representative of the donee, and

(b) any reference in section 10(5) to an application by the donee under that subsection shall include a reference to an application by the personal representative of the donee;

but the court shall not have power under the said section 10 or 11 to make an order in respect of any property forming part of the estate of the donee which has been distributed by the personal representative; and the personal representative shall not be liable for having distributed any such property before he has notice of the making of an application under the said section 10 or 11 on the ground that he ought to have taken into account the possibility that such an application would be made.

13 Provisions as to trustees in relation to ss.10 and 11

(1) Where an application is made for –

(a) an order under section 10 of this Act in respect of a disposition made by the deceased to any person as a trustee, or

(b) an order under section 11 of this Act in respect of any payment made or property transferred, in accordance with a contract made by the deceased, to any person as a trustee, the powers of the court under the said section 10 or 11 to order that trustee to provide a sum of money or other property shall be subject to the following limitation (in addition, in a case of an application under section 10, to any provision regarding the deduction of capital transfer tax) namely, that the amount of any sum of money or the value of any property ordered to be provided –

(i) in the case of an application in respect of a disposition which consisted of the payment of money or an application in respect of the payment of money in accordance with a contract, shall not exceed the aggregate of so much of that money as is at the date of the order in the hands of the trustee and the value at that date of any property which represents that money or is derived therefrom and is at that date in the hands of the trustee;

(ii) in the case of an application in respect of a disposition which consisted of the transfer of property (other than a sum of money) or an application in respect of the transfer of property (other than a sum of money) in accordance with a contract, shall not exceed the aggregate of the value at the date of the order of so much of that property as is at that date in the hands of the trustee and the value at that date of any property which represents the first-mentioned property or is derived therefrom and is at that date in the hands of the trustee.

(2) Where any such application is made in respect of a disposition made to any person as a trustee or in respect of any payment made or property transferred in pursuance of a contract to any person as a trustee, the trustee shall not be liable for having distributed any money or other property on the ground that he ought to have taken into account the possibility that such an application would be made.

(3) Where any such application is made in respect of a disposition made to any person as a trustee or in respect of any payment made or property transferred in accordance with a contract to any person as a trustee, any reference in the said section 10 or 11 to the donee shall be construed as including a reference to the trustee or trustees for the time being of the trust in question and any reference in subsection (1) or (2) above to a trustee shall be construed in the same way.

Special provisions relating to cases of divorce, separation etc.

14 Provision as to cases where no financial relief was granted in divorce proceedings etc.

(1) Where, within twelve months from the date on which a decree of divorce or nullity of marriage has been made absolute or a decree of judicial separation has been granted, a party to the marriage dies and –

(a) an application for a financial provision order under section 23 of the Matrimonial Causes Act 1973 or a property adjustment order under section 24 of that Act has not been made by the other party to that marriage, or

(b) such an application has been made but the proceedings thereon have not been determined at the time of the death of the deceased,

then, if an application for an order under section 2 of this Act is made by that other party, the court shall, notwithstanding anything in section 1 or section 3 of this Act, have power, if it thinks it just to do so, to treat that party for the purposes of that application as if the decree of divorce or nullity of marriage had not been made absolute or the decree of judicial separation had not been granted, as the case may be.

(2) This section shall not apply in relation to a decree of judicial separation unless at the date of the death of the deceased the decree was in force and the separation was continuing.

14A Provision as to cases where no financial relief was granted in proceedings for the dissolution etc. of a civil partnership

(1) Subsection (2) below applies where –

    (a) a dissolution order, nullity order, separation order or presumption of death order has been made under Chapter 2 of Part 2 of the Civil Partnership Act 2004 in relation to a civil partnership,

    (b) one of the civil partners dies within twelve months from the date on which the order is made, and

    (c) either –

        (i) an application for a financial provision order under Part 1 of Schedule 5 to that Act or a property adjustment order under Part 2 of that Schedule has not been made by the other civil partner, or

        (ii) such an application has been made but the proceedings on the application have not been determined at the time of the death of the deceased.

(2) If an application for an order under section 2 of this Act is made by the surviving civil partner, the court shall, notwithstanding anything in section 1 or section 3 of this Act, have power, if it thinks it just to do so, to treat the surviving civil partner as if the order mentioned in subsection (1)(a) above had not been made.

(3) This section shall not apply in relation to a separation order unless at the date of the death of the deceased the separation order was in force and the separation was continuing.

15 Restriction imposed in divorce proceedings etc. on application under this Act

(1) On the grant of a decree of divorce, a decree of nullity of marriage or a decree of judicial separation or at any time thereafter the court, if it considers it just to do so, may, on the application of either party to the marriage, order that the other party to the marriage shall not on the death of the applicant be entitled to apply for an order under section 2 of this Act.

In this subsection 'the court' means the High Court or the family court.

(2) In the case of a decree of divorce or nullity of marriage an order may be made under subsection (1) above before or after the decree is made absolute, but if it is made before the decree is made absolute it shall not take effect unless the decree is made absolute.

(3) Where an order made under subsection (1) above on the grant of a decree of divorce or nullity of marriage has come into force with respect to a party to a marriage, then, on the death of the other party to that marriage, the court shall not entertain any application for an order under section 2 of this Act made by the first-mentioned party.

(4) Where an order made under subsection (1) above on the grant of a decree of judicial separation has come into force with respect to any party to a marriage, then, if the other party to that marriage dies while the decree is in force and the separation is continuing, the court shall not entertain any application for an order under section 2 of this Act made by the first-mentioned party.

15ZA Restriction imposed in proceedings for the dissolution etc. of a civil partnership on application under this Act

(1) On making a dissolution order, nullity order, separation order or presumption of death order under Chapter 2 of Part 2 of the Civil Partnership Act 2004, or at any time after making such an order, the court, if it considers it just to do so, may, on the application of either of the civil partners, order that the other civil partner shall not on the death of the applicant be entitled to apply for an order under section 2 of this Act.

(2) In subsection (1) above 'the court' means the High Court or the family court.

(3) In the case of a dissolution order, nullity order or presumption of death order ('the main order') an order may be made under subsection (1) above before (as well as after) the main order is made final, but if made before the main order is made final it shall not take effect unless the main order is made final.

(4) Where an order under subsection (1) above made in connection with a dissolution order, nullity order or presumption of death order has come into force with respect to a civil partner, then, on the death of the other civil partner, the court shall not entertain any application for an order under section 2 of this Act made by the surviving civil partner.

(5) Where an order under subsection (1) above made in connection with a separation order has come into force with respect to a civil partner, then, if the other civil partner dies while the separation order is in force and the separation is continuing, the court shall not entertain any application for an order under section 2 of this Act made by the surviving civil partner.

15A Restriction imposed in proceedings under Matrimonial and Family Proceedings Act 1984 on application under this Act

(1) On making an order under section 17 of the Matrimonial and Family Proceedings Act 1984 (orders for financial provision and property adjustment following overseas divorces, etc.) the court, if it considers it just to do so, may, on the application of either party to the marriage, order that the other party to the marriage shall not on the death of the applicant be entitled to apply for an order under section 2 of this Act.

In this subsection 'the court' means the High Court or the family court.

(2) Where an order under subsection (1) above has been made with respect to a party to a marriage which has been dissolved or annulled, then, on the death of the other party to that marriage, the court shall not entertain an application under section 2 of this Act made by the first-mentioned party.

(3) Where an order under subsection (1) above has been made with respect to a party to a marriage the parties to which have been legally separated, then, if the other party to the marriage dies while the legal separation is in force, the court shall not entertain an application under section 2 of this Act made by the first-mentioned party.

15B Restriction imposed in proceedings under Schedule 7 to the Civil Partnership Act 2004 on application under this Act

(1) On making an order under paragraph 9 of Schedule 7 to the Civil Partnership Act 2004 (orders for financial provision, property adjustment and pension-sharing following overseas dissolution etc. of civil partnership) the court, if it considers it just to do so, may, on the application of either of the civil partners, order that the other civil partner shall not on the death of the applicant be entitled to apply for an order under section 2 of this Act.

(2) In subsection (1) above 'the court' means the High Court or the family court.

(3) Where an order under subsection (1) above has been made with respect to one of the civil partners in a case where a civil partnership has been dissolved or annulled, then, on

the death of the other civil partner, the court shall not entertain an application under section 2 of this Act made by the surviving civil partner.

(4)   Where an order under subsection (1) above has been made with respect to one of the civil partners in a case where civil partners have been legally separated, then, if the other civil partner dies while the legal separation is in force, the court shall not entertain an application under section 2 of this Act made by the surviving civil partner.

16   Variation and discharge of secured periodical payments orders made under Matrimonial Causes Act 1973

(1)   Where an application for an order under section 2 of this Act is made to the court by any person who was at the time of the death of the deceased entitled to payments from the deceased under a secured periodical payments order made under the Matrimonial Causes Act 1973 or Schedule 5 to the Civil Partnership Act 2004, then, in the proceedings on that application, the court shall have power, if an application is made under this section by that person or by the personal representative of the deceased, to vary or discharge that periodical payments order or to revive the operation of any provision thereof which has been suspended under section 31 of that Act of 1973 or Part 11 of that Schedule.

(2)   In exercising the powers conferred by this section the court shall have regard to all the circumstances of the case, including any order which the court proposes to make under section 2 or section 5 of this Act and any change (whether resulting from the death of the deceased or otherwise) in any of the matters to which the court was required to have regard when making the secured periodical payments order.

(3)   The powers exercisable by the court under this section in relation to an order shall be exercisable also in relation to any instrument executed in pursuance of the order.

17   Variation and revocation of maintenance agreements

(1)   Where an application for an order under section 2 of this Act is made to the court by any person who was at the time of the death of the deceased entitled to payments from the deceased under a maintenance agreement which provided for the continuation of payments under the agreement after the death of the deceased, then, in the proceedings on that application, the court shall have power, if an application is made under this section by that person or by the personal representative of the deceased, to vary or revoke that agreement.

(2)   In exercising the powers conferred by this section the court shall have regard to all the circumstances of the case, including any order which the court proposes to make under section 2 or section 5 of this Act and any change (whether resulting from the death of the deceased or otherwise) in any of the circumstances in the light of which the agreement was made.

(3)   If a maintenance agreement is varied by the court under this section the like consequences shall ensue as if the variation had been made immediately before the death of the deceased by agreement between the parties and for valuable consideration.

(4)   In this section 'maintenance agreement', in relation to a deceased person, means any agreement made, whether in writing or not and whether before or after the commencement of this Act, by the deceased with any person with whom he formed a marriage or civil partnership, being an agreement which contained provisions governing the rights and liabilities towards one another when living separately of the parties to that marriage or of the civil partners (whether or not the marriage or civil partnership has been dissolved or annulled) in respect of the making or securing of payments or the disposition or use of any property, including such rights and liabilities with respect to the maintenance or education of any child, whether or not a child of the deceased or a

person who was treated by the deceased as a child of the family in relation to that marriage or civil partnership.

18 Availability of court's powers under this Act in applications under ss.31 and 36 of the Matrimonial Causes Act 1973

(1) Where –

    (a) a person against whom a secured periodical payments order was made under the Matrimonial Causes Act 1973 has died and an application is made under section 31(6) of that Act for the variation or discharge of that order or for the revival of the operation of any provision thereof which has been suspended, or

    (b) a party to a maintenance agreement within the meaning of section 34 of that Act has died, the agreement being one which provides for the continuation of payments thereunder after the death of one of the parties, and an application is made under section 36(1) of that Act for the alteration of the agreement under section 35 thereof,

the court shall have power to direct that the application made under the said section 31(6) or 36(1) shall be deemed to have been accompanied by an application for an order under section 2 of this Act.

(2) Where the court gives a direction under subsection (1) above it shall have power, in the proceedings on the application under the said section 31(6) or 36(1), to make any order which the court would have had power to make under the provisions of this Act if the application under the said section 31(6) or 36(1), as the case may be, had been made jointly with an application for an order under the said section 2; and the court shall have power to give such consequential directions as may be necessary for enabling the court to exercise any of the powers available to the court under this Act in the case of an application for an order under section 2.

(3) Where an order made under section 15(1) of this Act is in force with respect to a party to a marriage, the court shall not give a direction under subsection (1) above with respect to any application made under the said section 31(6) or 36(1) by that party on the death of the other party.

18A Availability of court's powers under this Act in applications under paragraphs 60 and 73 of Schedule 5 to the Civil Partnership Act 2004

(1) Where–

    (a) a person against whom a secured periodical payments order was made under Schedule 5 to the Civil Partnership Act 2004 has died and an application is made under paragraph 60 of that Schedule for the variation or discharge of that order or for the revival of the operation of any suspended provision of the order, or

    (b) a party to a maintenance agreement within the meaning of Part 13 of that Schedule has died, the agreement being one which provides for the continuation of payments under the agreement after the death of one of the parties, and an application is made under paragraph 73 of that Schedule for the alteration of the agreement under paragraph 69 of that Schedule,

the court shall have power to direct that the application made under paragraph 60 or 73 of that Schedule shall be deemed to have been accompanied by an application for an order under section 2 of this Act.

(2) Where the court gives a direction under subsection (1) above it shall have power, in the proceedings on the application under paragraph 60 or 73 of that Schedule, to make any order which the court would have had power to make under the provisions of this Act if

the application under that paragraph had been made jointly with an application for an order under section 2 of this Act; and the court shall have power to give such consequential directions as may be necessary for enabling the court to exercise any of the powers available to the court under this Act in the case of an application for an order under section 2.

(3) Where an order made under section 15ZA(1) of this Act is in force with respect to a civil partner, the court shall not give a direction under subsection (1) above with respect to any application made under paragraph 60 or 73 of that Schedule by that civil partner on the death of the other civil partner.

Miscellaneous and supplementary provisions

19 Effect, duration and form of orders

(1) Where an order is made under section 2 of this Act then for all purposes, including the purposes of the enactments relating to capital transfer tax, the will or the law relating to intestacy, or both the will and the law relating to intestacy, as the case may be, shall have effect and be deemed to have had effect as from the deceased's death subject to the provisions of the order.

(2) Any order made under section 2 or 5 of this Act in favour of –

   (a) an applicant who was the former spouse or former civil partner of the deceased,

   (b) an applicant who was the husband or wife of the deceased in a case where the marriage with the deceased was the subject of a decree of judicial separation and at the date of death the decree was in force and the separation was continuing, or

   (c) an applicant who was the civil partner of the deceased in a case where, at the date of death, a separation order under Chapter 2 of Part 2 of the Civil Partnership Act 2004 was in force in relation to their civil partnership and the separation was continuing,

   shall, in so far as it provides for the making of periodical payments, cease to have effect on the formation by the applicant of a subsequent marriage or civil partnership, except in relation to any arrears due under the order on the date of the formation of the subsequent marriage or civil partnership.

(3) A copy of every order made under this Act other than an order made under section 15(1) or 15ZA(1) of this Act shall be sent to the principal registry of the Family Division for entry and filing, and a memorandum of the order shall be endorsed on, or permanently annexed to, the probate or letters of administration under which the estate is being administered.

20 Provisions as to personal representatives

(1) The provisions of this Act shall not render the personal representative of a deceased person liable for having distributed any part of the estate of the deceased, after the end of the period of six months from the date on which representation with respect to the estate of the deceased is first taken out, on the ground that he ought to have taken into account the possibility –

   (a) that the court might permit the making of an application for an order under section 2 of this Act after the end of that period, or

   (b) that, where an order has been made under the said section 2, the court might exercise in relation thereto the powers conferred on it by section 6 of this Act,

   but this subsection shall not prejudice any power to recover, by reason of the making of an order under this Act, any part of the estate so distributed.

(2) Where the personal representative of a deceased person pays any sum directed by an order under section 5 of this Act to be paid out of the deceased's net estate, he shall not be under any liability by reason of that estate not being sufficient to make the payment, unless at the time of making the payment he has reasonable cause to believe that the estate is not sufficient.

(3) Where a deceased person entered into a contract by which the agreed to leave by his will any sum of money or other property to any person or by which he agreed that a sum of money or other property would be paid or transferred to any person out of his estate, then, if the personal representative of the deceased has reason to believe that the deceased entered into the contract with the intention of defeating an application for financial provision under this Act, he may, notwithstanding anything in that contract, postpone the payment of that sum of money or the transfer of that property until the expiration of the period of six months from the date on which representation with respect to the estate of the deceased is first taken out or, if during that period an application is made for an order under section 2 of this Act, until the determination of the proceedings on that application.

21

[*Repealed*]

22

[*Repealed*]

23 Determination of date on which representation was first taken out

(1) The following are to be left out of account when considering for the purposes of this Act when representation with respect to the estate of a deceased person was first taken out –

   (a) a grant limited to settled land or to trust property,
   (b) any other grant that does not permit any of the estate to be distributed,
   (c) a grant limited to real estate or to personal estate, unless a grant limited to the remainder of the estate has previously been made or is made at the same time,
   (d) a grant, or its equivalent, made outside the United Kingdom (but see subsection (2) below).

(2) A grant sealed under section 2 of the Colonial Probates Act 1892 counts as a grant made in the United Kingdom for the purposes of this section, but is to be taken as dated on the date of sealing.

24 Effect of this Act on s.46(1)(vi) of Administration of Estates Act 1925

Section 46(1)(vi) of the Administration of Estates Act 1925, in so far as it provides for the devolution of property on the Crown, the Duchy of Lancaster or the Duke of Cornwall as bona vacantia, shall have effect subject to the provisions of this Act.

25 Interpretation

(1) In this Act –

   'beneficiary', in relation to the estate of a deceased person, means –
      (a) a person who under the will of the deceased or under the law relating to

intestacy is beneficially interested in the estate or would be so interested if an order had not been made under this Act, and

(b)   a person who has received any sum of money or other property which by virtue of section 8(1) or 8(2) of this Act is treated as part of the net estate of the deceased or would have received that sum or other property if an order had not been made under this Act;

'child' includes an illegitimate child and a child en ventre sa mère at the death of the deceased;

'the court' means unless the context otherwise requires the High Court, or where the county court has jurisdiction by virtue of section 25 of the County Courts Act 1984, the county court;

'former civil partner' means a person whose civil partnership with the deceased was during the lifetime of the deceased either –

(a)   dissolved or annulled by an order made under the law of any part of the British Islands, or

(b)   dissolved or annulled in any country or territory outside the British Islands by a dissolution or annulment which is entitled to be recognised as valid by the law of England and Wales;

'former spouse' means a person whose marriage with the deceased was during the lifetime of the deceased either –

(a)   dissolved or annulled by a decree of divorce or a decree of nullity of marriage granted under the law of any part of the British Islands, or

(b)   dissolved or annulled in any country or territory outside the British Islands by a divorce or annulment which is entitled to be recognised as valid by the law of England and Wales;

'net estate', in relation to a deceased person, means –

(a)   all property of which the deceased had power to dispose by his will (otherwise than by virtue of a special power of appointment) less the amount of his funeral, testamentary and administration expenses, debts and liabilities, including any capital transfer tax payable out of his estate on his death;

(b)   any property in respect of which the deceased held a general power of appointment (not being a power exercisable by will) which has not been exercised;

(c)   any sum of money or other property which is treated for the purposes of this Act as part of the net estate of the deceased by virtue of section 8(1) or (2) of this Act;

(d)   any property which is treated for the purposes of this Act as part of the net estate of the deceased by virtue of an order made under section 9 of the Act;

(e)   any sum of money or other property which is, by reason of a disposition or contract made by the deceased, ordered under section 10 or 11 of this Act to be provided for the purpose of the making of financial provision under this Act;

'property' includes any chose in action;

'reasonable financial provision' has the meaning assigned to it by section 1 of this Act;

'valuable consideration' does not include marriage or a promise of marriage;

'will' includes codicil.

(2)   For the purposes of paragraph (a) of the definition of 'net estate' in subsection (1) above a person who is not of full age and capacity shall be treated as having power to dispose by will of all property of which he would have had power to dispose by will if he had been of full age and capacity.

(3) Any reference in this Act to provision out of the net estate of a deceased person includes a reference to provision extending to the whole of that estate.

(4) For the purposes of this Act any reference to a spouse, wife or husband shall be treated as including a reference to a person who in good faith entered into a void marriage with the deceased unless either –

    (a) the marriage of the deceased and that person was dissolved or annulled during the lifetime of the deceased and the dissolution or annulment is recognised by the law of England and Wales, or

    (b) that person has during the lifetime of the deceased formed a subsequent marriage or civil partnership.

(4A) For the purposes of this Act any reference to a civil partner shall be treated as including a reference to a person who in good faith formed a void civil partnership with the deceased unless either –

    (a) the civil partnership between the deceased and that person was dissolved or annulled during the lifetime of the deceased and the dissolution or annulment is recognised by the law of England and Wales, or

    (b) that person has during the lifetime of the deceased formed a subsequent civil partnership or marriage.

(5) Any reference in this Act to the formation of, or to a person who has formed, a subsequent marriage or civil partnership includes (as the case may be) a reference to the formation of, or to a person who has formed, a marriage or civil partnership which is by law void or voidable.

(5A) The formation of a marriage or civil partnership shall be treated for the purposes of this Act as the formation of a subsequent marriage or civil partnership, in relation to either of the spouses or civil partners, notwithstanding that the previous marriage or civil partnership of that spouse or civil partner was void or voidable.

(6) Any reference in this Act to an order or decree made under the Matrimonial Causes Act 1973 or under any section of that Act shall be construed as including a reference to an order or decree which is deemed to have been made under that Act or under that section thereof, as the case may be.

(6A) Any reference in this Act to an order made under, or under any provision of, the Civil Partnership Act 2004 shall be construed as including a reference to anything which is deemed to be an order made (as the case may be) under that Act or provision.

(7) Any reference in this Act to any enactment is a reference to that enactment as amended by or under any subsequent enactment.

26 Consequential amendments, repeals and transitional provisions.

(1) [*Repealed*]

. . .

(3) The repeal of the said enactments shall not affect their operation in relation to any application made thereunder (whether before or after the commencement of this Act) with reference to the death of any person who died before the commencement of this Act.

(4) Without prejudice to the provisions of section 38 of the Interpretation Act 1889 (which relates to the effect of repeals) nothing in any repeal made by this Act shall affect any order made or direction given under any enactment repealed by this Act, and, subject to the provisions of this Act, every such order or direction (other than an order made under section 4A of the Inheritance Family Provision Act 1938 or section 28A of the Matrimonial Causes Act 1965) shall, if it is in force at the commencement of this Act or is made by virtue of subsection (3) above, continue in force as if it had been made under

section 2(1)(a) of this Act, and for the purposes of section 6(7) of this Act the court in exercising its powers under that section in relation to an order continued in force by this subsection shall be required to have regard to any change in any of the circumstances to which the court would have been required to have regard when making that order if the order had been made with reference to the death of any person who died after the commencement of this Act.

27 Short title, commencement and extent.

(1) This Act may be cited as the Inheritance (Provision for Family and Dependants) Act 1975.

(2) This Act does not extend to Scotland or Northern Ireland.

(3) This Act shall come into force on 1st April 1976.

Intestate Succession (Interest and Capitalisation) Order 1977, SI 1977/1491

1 Citation and interpretation

(1) This Order may be cited as the Intestate Succession (Interest and Capitalisation) Order 1977 and shall come into operation on 15th September 1977.

(2) The Interpretation Act 1889 shall apply to the interpretation of this Order as it applies to the interpretation of an Act of Parliament.

2 Interest on statutory legacy

For the purposes of section 46(1)(i) of the Administration of Estates Act 1925, as it applies both in respect of persons dying before 1953 and in respect of persons dying after 1952, the specified rate of interest shall be 6 per cent. per annum.

3 Capitalisation of life interests

(1) Where after the coming into operation of this Order an election is exercised in accordance with subsection (6) or (7) of section 47A of the Administration of Estates Act 1925, the capital value of the life interest of the surviving spouse or civil partner shall be reckoned in accordance with the following provisions of this article.

(2) There shall be ascertained, by reference to the index compiled by the Financial Times, The Institute of Actuaries and the Faculty of Actuaries, the gross redemption yield on fifteen-year Government Stocks at the date on which the election was exercised or, if the index was not complied on that date, by reference to the index on the last date before that date on which it was complied; and the column which corresponds to that yield in whichever of the Tables set out in the Schedule hereto is applicable to the sex of the surviving spouse or civil partner shall be the appropriate column for the purposes of paragraph (3) of this article.

(3) The capital value for the purposes of paragraph (1) of this article is the product of the part of the residuary estate (whether or not yielding income) in respect of which the election was exercised and the multiplier shown in the appropriate column opposite the age which the surviving spouse or civil partner had attained at the date on which the election was exercised.

SCHEDULE

Table 1 [see pp. **185–189**]

Multiplier to be applied to the part of the residuary estate in respect of which the election is exercised to obtain the capital value of the life interest of a surviving husband or a surviving male civil partner when the gross redemption yield on fifteen year Government Stocks is at the rate shown.

Age last birthday of husband or male civil partner	Less than 2.5%	2.5% or between 2.5% and 3.5%	3.5% or between 3.5% and 4.5%	4.5% or between 4.5% and 5.5%	5.5% or between 5.5% and 6.5%	6.5% or between 6.5% and 7.5%	7.5% or between 7.5% and 8.5%	8.5% or between 8.5% and 9.5%	9.5% or between 9.5% and 10.5%	10.5% or between 10.5% and 11.5%	11.5% or more
16	0.630	0.761	0.836	0.881	0.907	0.922	0.932	0.938	0.942	0.944	0.946
17	0.625	0.756	0.833	0.878	0.905	0.921	0.931	0.937	0.941	0.944	0.945
18	0.620	0.752	0.829	0.875	0.903	0.920	0.930	0.936	0.941	0.943	0.945
19	0.615	0.747	0.825	0.872	0.901	0.918	0.929	0.936	0.940	0.943	0.945
20	0.610	0.743	0.822	0.870	0.899	0.917	0.928	0.935	0.939	0.942	0.945
21	0.604	0.738	0.818	0.867	0.896	0.915	0.927	0.934	0.939	0.942	0.944
22	0.599	0.733	0.814	0.863	0.894	0.913	0.925	0.933	0.938	0.941	0.944
23	0.594	0.728	0.809	0.860	0.891	0.911	0.924	0.932	0.937	0.941	0.943
24	0.588	0.723	0.805	0.857	0.889	0.909	0.922	0.931	0.936	0.940	0.943
25	0.582	0.717	0.801	0.853	0.886	0.907	0.921	0.930	0.936	0.940	0.942
26	0.577	0.712	0.796	0.849	0.883	0.905	0.919	0.928	0.935	0.939	0.942
27	0.571	0.706	0.791	0.846	0.880	0.903	0.917	0.927	0.934	0.938	0.941
28	0.565	0.701	0.786	0.842	0.877	0.900	0.915	0.926	0.932	0.937	0.940
29	0.559	0.695	0.781	0.837	0.874	0.898	0.913	0.924	0.931	0.936	0.940
30	0.553	0.689	0.776	0.833	0.870	0.895	0.911	0.922	0.930	0.935	0.939
31	0.546	0.683	0.771	0.829	0.867	0.892	0.909	0.920	0.928	0.934	0.938
32	0.540	0.676	0.765	0.824	0.863	0.889	0.907	0.918	0.927	0.933	0.937
33	0.533	0.670	0.759	0.819	0.859	0.886	0.904	0.916	0.925	0.931	0.936
34	0.527	0.663	0.753	0.814	0.854	0.882	0.901	0.914	0.923	0.930	0.935
35	0.520	0.657	0.747	0.809	0.850	0.879	0.898	0.912	0.922	0.928	0.933

Age last birthday of husband or male civil partner	Less than 2.5%	2.5% or between 2.5% and 3.5%	3.5% or between 3.5% and 4.5%	4.5% or between 4.5% and 5.5%	5.5% or between 5.5% and 6.5%	6.5% or between 6.5% and 7.5%	7.5% or between 7.5% and 8.5%	8.5% or between 8.5% and 9.5%	9.5% or between 9.5% and 10.5%	10.5% or between 10.5% and 11.5%	11.5% or more
36	0.514	0.650	0.741	0.803	0.845	0.875	0.895	0.909	0.919	0.927	0.932
37	0.507	0.643	0.734	0.798	0.841	0.871	0.892	0.907	0.917	0.925	0.931
38	0.500	0.636	0.728	0.792	0.836	0.867	0.888	0.904	0.915	0.923	0.929
39	0.493	0.628	0.721	0.785	0.830	0.862	0.885	0.901	0.912	0.921	0.927
40	0.485	0.621	0.714	0.779	0.825	0.858	0.881	0.897	0.910	0.918	0.925
41	0.478	0.613	0.706	0.773	0.819	0.853	0.877	0.894	0.907	0.916	0.923
42	0.471	0.605	0.699	0.766	0.813	0.847	0.872	0.890	0.903	0.913	0.921
43	0.463	0.597	0.691	0.759	0.807	0.842	0.867	0.886	0.900	0.910	0.918
44	0.456	0.589	0.683	0.751	0.800	0.836	0.863	0.882	0.896	0.907	0.916
45	0.448	0.580	0.675	0.744	0.794	0.830	0.857	0.877	0.893	0.904	0.913
46	0.440	0.572	0.666	0.736	0.786	0.824	0.852	0.873	0.888	0.900	0.910
47	0.432	0.563	0.658	0.728	0.779	0.817	0.846	0.868	0.884	0.896	0.906
48	0.424	0.554	0.649	0.719	0.771	0.811	0.840	0.862	0.879	0.892	0.903
49	0.416	0.545	0.640	0.711	0.763	0.803	0.834	0.856	0.874	0.888	0.899
50	0.408	0.536	0.630	0.702	0.755	0.796	0.827	0.850	0.869	0.883	0.895
51	0.400	0.526	0.621	0.692	0.746	0.788	0.820	0.844	0.863	0.878	0.890
52	0.392	0.517	0.611	0.683	0.738	0.780	0.812	0.837	0.857	0.873	0.885
53	0.383	0.507	0.601	0.673	0.728	0.771	0.804	0.830	0.851	0.867	0.880
54	0.375	0.497	0.591	0.663	0.719	0.762	0.796	0.823	0.844	0.861	0.875
55	0.366	0.487	0.580	0.653	0.709	0.753	0.788	0.815	0.837	0.855	0.869

Age last birthday of husband or male civil partner	Less than 2.5%	2.5% or between 2.5% and 3.5%	3.5% or between 3.5% and 4.5%	4.5% or between 4.5% and 5.5%	5.5% or between 5.5% and 6.5%	6.5% or between 6.5% and 7.5%	7.5% or between 7.5% and 8.5%	8.5% or between 8.5% and 9.5%	9.5% or between 9.5% and 10.5%	10.5% or between 10.5% and 11.5%	11.5% or more
56	0.357	0.477	0.569	0.642	0.698	0.743	0.779	0.807	0.829	0.848	0.863
57	0.349	0.467	0.558	0.631	0.688	0.733	0.769	0.798	0.821	0.840	0.856
58	0.340	0.456	0.547	0.620	0.677	0.723	0.759	0.789	0.813	0.833	0.849
59	0.331	0.445	0.536	0.608	0.665	0.712	0.749	0.779	0.804	0.824	0.841
60	0.322	0.435	0.524	0.596	0.654	0.701	0.738	0.769	0.795	0.816	0.833
61	0.313	0.424	0.512	0.584	0.641	0.689	0.727	0.759	0.785	0.806	0.825
62	0.304	0.413	0.500	0.571	0.629	0.677	0.716	0.748	0.774	0.797	0.815
63	0.295	0.401	0.488	0.558	0.616	0.664	0.704	0.736	0.764	0.786	0.806
64	0.286	0.390	0.475	0.545	0.603	0.651	0.691	0.724	0.752	0.776	0.796
65	0.277	0.379	0.462	0.532	0.590	0.638	0.678	0.712	0.740	0.765	0.785
66	0.268	0.367	0.450	0.519	0.576	0.624	0.665	0.699	0.728	0.753	0.774
67	0.259	0.356	0.437	0.505	0.562	0.610	0.651	0.685	0.715	0.740	0.762
68	0.250	0.344	0.424	0.491	0.547	0.596	0.637	0.671	0.701	0.727	0.750
69	0.240	0.333	0.410	0.476	0.533	0.581	0.622	0.657	0.687	0.714	0.737
70	0.231	0.321	0.397	0.462	0.517	0.565	0.606	0.642	0.673	0.699	0.723
71	0.222	0.309	0.383	0.447	0.502	0.549	0.590	0.626	0.657	0.684	0.708
72	0.213	0.297	0.369	0.432	0.486	0.533	0.574	0.610	0.641	0.669	0.693
73	0.204	0.285	0.355	0.417	0.470	0.516	0.557	0.593	0.624	0.652	0.677
74	0.195	0.273	0.341	0.401	0.453	0.499	0.540	0.575	0.607	0.635	0.660
75	0.186	0.261	0.327	0.385	0.436	0.482	0.522	0.557	0.589	0.617	0.642

Age last birthday of husband or male civil partner	Less than 2.5%	2.5% or between 2.5% and 3.5%	3.5% or between 3.5% and 4.5%	4.5% or between 4.5% and 5.5%	5.5% or between 5.5% and 6.5%	6.5% or between 6.5% and 7.5%	7.5% or between 7.5% and 8.5%	8.5% or between 8.5% and 9.5%	9.5% or between 9.5% and 10.5%	10.5% or between 10.5% and 11.5%	11.5% or more
76	0.177	0.249	0.313	0.370	0.419	0.464	0.503	0.539	0.570	0.598	0.624
77	0.168	0.237	0.299	0.354	0.402	0.446	0.485	0.519	0.551	0.579	0.604
78	0.159	0.225	0.284	0.337	0.385	0.427	0.465	0.500	0.531	0.559	0.585
79	0.150	0.214	0.270	0.321	0.367	0.409	0.446	0.480	0.510	0.538	0.564
80	0.142	0.202	0.256	0.305	0.349	0.390	0.426	0.459	0.490	0.517	0.543
81	0.133	0.191	0.242	0.289	0.332	0.371	0.406	0.439	0.468	0.496	0.521
82	0.125	0.179	0.228	0.273	0.314	0.352	0.386	0.418	0.447	0.473	0.498
83	0.117	0.168	0.215	0.257	0.297	0.333	0.366	0.397	0.425	0.451	0.475
84	0.109	0.157	0.201	0.242	0.279	0.314	0.346	0.376	0.403	0.429	0.453
85	0.102	0.147	0.188	0.227	0.262	0.296	0.326	0.355	0.381	0.406	0.429
86	0.095	0.137	0.176	0.212	0.246	0.278	0.307	0.334	0.360	0.384	0.406
87	0.088	0.127	0.164	0.198	0.230	0.260	0.288	0.314	0.339	0.362	0.384
88	0.081	0.118	0.152	0.185	0.215	0.243	0.270	0.295	0.318	0.340	0.362
89	0.075	0.110	0.142	0.172	0.200	0.227	0.252	0.276	0.299	0.320	0.340
90	0.070	0.102	0.132	0.160	0.187	0.212	0.236	0.259	0.280	0.301	0.320
91	0.065	0.094	0.122	0.149	0.174	0.198	0.221	0.242	0.263	0.282	0.301
92	0.060	0.088	0.114	0.139	0.162	0.185	0.207	0.227	0.247	0.265	0.283
93	0.056	0.082	0.106	0.130	0.152	0.173	0.194	0.213	0.231	0.249	0.266
94	0.052	0.076	0.099	0.121	0.142	0.162	0.181	0.200	0.217	0.234	0.251
95	0.048	0.071	0.092	0.113	0.133	0.152	0.170	0.188	0.204	0.221	0.236

Age last birthday of husband or male civil partner	Less than 2.5%	2.5% or between 2.5% and 3.5%	3.5% or between 3.5% and 4.5%	4.5% or between 4.5% and 5.5%	5.5% or between 5.5% and 6.5%	6.5% or between 6.5% and 7.5%	7.5% or between 7.5% and 8.5%	8.5% or between 8.5% and 9.5%	9.5% or between 9.5% and 10.5%	10.5% or between 10.5% and 11.5%	11.5% or more
96	0.045	0.066	0.086	0.106	0.124	0.143	0.160	0.176	0.192	0.208	0.223
97	0.042	0.062	0.081	0.099	0.117	0.134	0.150	0.166	0.181	0.196	0.210
98	0.039	0.058	0.075	0.093	0.109	0.125	0.141	0.156	0.170	0.184	0.198
99	0.037	0.054	0.071	0.087	0.102	0.118	0.132	0.146	0.160	0.173	0.186
100 and over	0.034	0.050	0.066	0.081	0.096	0.110	0.124	0.137	0.150	0.163	0.175

Table 2 [see pp.**191–4**]

Multiplier to be applied to the part of the residuary estate in respect of which the election is exercised to obtain the capital value of the life interest of a surviving wife or a surviving female civil partner when the gross redemption yield on fifteen year Government Stocks is at the rate shown.

Age last birthday of wife or female civil partner	Less than 2.5%	2.5% or between 2.5% and 3.5%	3.5% or between 3.5% and 4.5%	4.5% or between 4.5% and 5.5%	5.5% or between 5.5% and 6.5%	6.5% or between 6.5% and 7.5%	7.5% or between 7.5% and 8.5%	8.5% or between 8.5% and 9.5%	9.5% or between 9.5% and 10.5%	10.5% or between 10.5% and 11.5%	11.5% or more
16	0.650	0.779	0.851	0.892	0.916	0.929	0.937	0.942	0.944	0.946	0.947
17	0.645	0.775	0.848	0.890	0.914	0.928	0.936	0.941	0.944	0.946	0.947
18	0.640	0.771	0.845	0.888	0.912	0.927	0.936	0.941	0.944	0.946	0.947
19	0.636	0.767	0.842	0.885	0.911	0.926	0.935	0.940	0.944	0.946	0.947
20	0.631	0.762	0.838	0.883	0.909	0.925	0.934	0.940	0.943	0.945	0.947
21	0.626	0.758	0.835	0.880	0.907	0.923	0.933	0.939	0.943	0.945	0.947
22	0.621	0.753	0.831	0.878	0.905	0.922	0.932	0.938	0.942	0.945	0.946
23	0.615	0.749	0.828	0.875	0.903	0.921	0.931	0.938	0.942	0.944	0.946
24	0.610	0.744	0.824	0.872	0.901	0.919	0.930	0.937	0.941	0.944	0.946
25	0.605	0.739	0.820	0.869	0.899	0.917	0.929	0.936	0.941	0.944	0.946
26	0.599	0.734	0.816	0.866	0.897	0.916	0.928	0.935	0.940	0.943	0.945
27	0.594	0.729	0.812	0.863	0.894	0.914	0.926	0.934	0.939	0.943	0.945
28	0.588	0.724	0.807	0.859	0.892	0.912	0.925	0.933	0.939	0.942	0.945
29	0.582	0.719	0.803	0.856	0.889	0.910	0.924	0.932	0.938	0.942	0.944
30	0.577	0.713	0.798	0.852	0.886	0.908	0.922	0.931	0.937	0.941	0.944
31	0.571	0.708	0.794	0.848	0.883	0.906	0.920	0.930	0.936	0.940	0.943
32	0.565	0.702	0.789	0.844	0.880	0.903	0.919	0.929	0.935	0.940	0.943
33	0.559	0.696	0.784	0.840	0.877	0.901	0.917	0.927	0.934	0.939	0.942
34	0.552	0.690	0.778	0.836	0.874	0.898	0.915	0.926	0.933	0.938	0.941
35	0.546	0.684	0.773	0.832	0.870	0.896	0.913	0.924	0.932	0.937	0.941
36	0.540	0.678	0.767	0.827	0.866	0.893	0.910	0.922	0.930	0.936	0.940

Age last birthday of wife or female civil partner	Less than 2.5%	2.5% or between 2.5% and 3.5%	3.5% or between 3.5% and 4.5%	4.5% or between 4.5% and 5.5%	5.5% or between 5.5% and 6.5%	6.5% or between 6.5% and 7.5%	7.5% or between 7.5% and 8.5%	8.5% or between 8.5% and 9.5%	9.5% or between 9.5% and 10.5%	10.5% or between 10.5% and 11.5%	11.5% or more
37	0.533	0.671	0.762	0.822	0.862	0.890	0.908	0.920	0.929	0.935	0.939
38	0.527	0.664	0.756	0.817	0.858	0.886	0.905	0.918	0.927	0.934	0.938
39	0.520	0.658	0.750	0.812	0.854	0.883	0.902	0.916	0.926	0.932	0.937
40	0.513	0.651	0.743	0.807	0.849	0.879	0.900	0.914	0.924	0.931	0.936
41	0.506	0.644	0.737	0.801	0.845	0.875	0.896	0.911	0.922	0.929	0.935
42	0.499	0.636	0.730	0.795	0.840	0.871	0.893	0.909	0.920	0.927	0.933
43	0.492	0.629	0.723	0.789	0.835	0.867	0.890	0.906	0.917	0.926	0.932
44	0.485	0.621	0.716	0.783	0.829	0.862	0.886	0.903	0.915	0.924	0.930
45	0.477	0.613	0.708	0.776	0.823	0.858	0.882	0.899	0.912	0.921	0.928
46	0.470	0.605	0.701	0.769	0.817	0.852	0.878	0.896	0.909	0.919	0.926
47	0.462	0.597	0.693	0.762	0.811	0.847	0.873	0.892	0.906	0.916	0.924
48	0.454	0.589	0.685	0.754	0.805	0.841	0.868	0.888	0.902	0.913	0.922
49	0.447	0.580	0.676	0.747	0.798	0.835	0.863	0.883	0.899	0.910	0.919
50	0.439	0.572	0.668	0.739	0.791	0.829	0.858	0.879	0.895	0.907	0.916
51	0.431	0.563	0.659	0.730	0.783	0.823	0.852	0.874	0.891	0.903	0.913
52	0.422	0.553	0.650	0.722	0.775	0.816	0.846	0.868	0.886	0.899	0.910
53	0.414	0.544	0.640	0.713	0.767	0.808	0.839	0.863	0.881	0.895	0.906
54	0.406	0.534	0.631	0.703	0.758	0.800	0.832	0.857	0.876	0.890	0.902
55	0.397	0.525	0.620	0.694	0.749	0.792	0.825	0.850	0.870	0.885	0.897
56	0.388	0.515	0.610	0.684	0.740	0.784	0.817	0.843	0.864	0.880	0.893
57	0.379	0.504	0.600	0.673	0.730	0.775	0.809	0.836	0.857	0.874	0.888

Age last birthday of wife or female civil partner	Less than 2.5%	2.5% or between 2.5% and 3.5%	3.5% or between 3.5% and 4.5%	4.5% or between 4.5% and 5.5%	5.5% or between 5.5% and 6.5%	6.5% or between 6.5% and 7.5%	7.5% or between 7.5% and 8.5%	8.5% or between 8.5% and 9.5%	9.5% or between 9.5% and 10.5%	10.5% or between 10.5% and 11.5%	11.5% or more
58	0.371	0.494	0.589	0.663	0.720	0.765	0.800	0.828	0.850	0.868	0.882
59	0.361	0.483	0.577	0.652	0.709	0.755	0.791	0.820	0.843	0.861	0.876
60	0.352	0.472	0.566	0.640	0.698	0.745	0.782	0.811	0.835	0.854	0.869
61	0.343	0.461	0.554	0.628	0.687	0.734	0.771	0.802	0.826	0.846	0.862
62	0.334	0.450	0.542	0.616	0.675	0.722	0.761	0.792	0.817	0.837	0.854
63	0.324	0.438	0.529	0.603	0.662	0.710	0.749	0.781	0.807	0.828	0.846
64	0.315	0.427	0.517	0.590	0.649	0.698	0.737	0.770	0.797	0.819	0.837
65	0.305	0.415	0.504	0.577	0.636	0.685	0.725	0.758	0.786	0.808	0.828
66	0.295	0.403	0.490	0.563	0.622	0.671	0.712	0.746	0.774	0.797	0.817
67	0.286	0.391	0.477	0.549	0.608	0.657	0.698	0.732	0.761	0.786	0.806
68	0.276	0.378	0.463	0.534	0.593	0.642	0.684	0.719	0.748	0.773	0.795
69	0.266	0.366	0.449	0.519	0.578	0.627	0.669	0.704	0.734	0.760	0.782
70	0.256	0.353	0.435	0.504	0.562	0.611	0.653	0.689	0.720	0.746	0.769
71	0.246	0.340	0.420	0.488	0.545	0.595	0.637	0.673	0.704	0.731	0.754
72	0.236	0.327	0.405	0.472	0.529	0.578	0.620	0.656	0.688	0.715	0.739
73	0.226	0.314	0.390	0.455	0.512	0.560	0.602	0.639	0.671	0.698	0.723
74	0.216	0.301	0.375	0.439	0.494	0.542	0.584	0.621	0.653	0.681	0.706
75	0.206	0.288	0.359	0.422	0.476	0.524	0.565	0.602	0.634	0.662	0.688
76	0.196	0.275	0.344	0.404	0.457	0.504	0.546	0.582	0.614	0.643	0.669
77	0.186	0.262	0.328	0.387	0.439	0.485	0.526	0.562	0.594	0.623	0.649
78	0.176	0.248	0.312	0.369	0.420	0.465	0.505	0.541	0.573	0.602	0.628

Age last birthday of wife or female civil partner	Less than 2.5%	2.5% or between 2.5% and 3.5%	3.5% or between 3.5% and 4.5%	4.5% or between 4.5% and 5.5%	5.5% or between 5.5% and 6.5%	6.5% or between 6.5% and 7.5%	7.5% or between 7.5% and 8.5%	8.5% or between 8.5% and 9.5%	9.5% or between 9.5% and 10.5%	10.5% or between 10.5% and 11.5%	11.5% or more
79	0.166	0.235	0.296	0.351	0.400	0.444	0.484	0.519	0.551	0.580	0.606
80	0.156	0.222	0.281	0.334	0.381	0.424	0.462	0.497	0.529	0.557	0.583
81	0.147	0.209	0.265	0.316	0.361	0.403	0.440	0.474	0.506	0.534	0.560
82	0.138	0.197	0.250	0.298	0.342	0.382	0.418	0.451	0.482	0.510	0.536
83	0.129	0.184	0.234	0.280	0.322	0.361	0.396	0.428	0.458	0.485	0.511
84	0.120	0.172	0.219	0.263	0.303	0.340	0.374	0.405	0.434	0.461	0.486
85	0.111	0.160	0.205	0.246	0.284	0.320	0.352	0.382	0.410	0.436	0.460
86	0.103	0.149	0.191	0.230	0.266	0.299	0.330	0.359	0.386	0.411	0.435
87	0.095	0.138	0.177	0.214	0.248	0.280	0.309	0.337	0.363	0.387	0.410
88	0.088	0.127	0.164	0.198	0.230	0.261	0.289	0.315	0.340	0.363	0.385
89	0.081	0.118	0.152	0.184	0.214	0.242	0.269	0.294	0.318	0.340	0.361
90	0.075	0.109	0.140	0.170	0.199	0.225	0.251	0.274	0.297	0.318	0.338
91	0.069	0.100	0.130	0.158	0.184	0.210	0.233	0.256	0.277	0.297	0.317
92	0.063	0.093	0.120	0.146	0.171	0.195	0.217	0.238	0.259	0.278	0.297
93	0.059	0.086	0.111	0.136	0.159	0.181	0.202	0.222	0.242	0.260	0.278
94	0.054	0.079	0.103	0.126	0.148	0.169	0.189	0.207	0.226	0.243	0.260
95	0.050	0.073	0.096	0.117	0.137	0.157	0.176	0.194	0.211	0.228	0.244
96	0.046	0.068	0.089	0.109	0.128	0.146	0.164	0.181	0.197	0.213	0.228
97	0.043	0.063	0.083	0.101	0.119	0.137	0.153	0.169	0.185	0.200	0.214
98	0.040	0.059	0.077	0.094	0.111	0.127	0.143	0.158	0.173	0.187	0.201
99	0.037	0.055	0.071	0.088	0.104	0.119	0.134	0.148	0.162	0.175	0.188

Age last birthday of wife or female civil partner	Less than 2.5%	2.5% or between 2.5% and 3.5%	3.5% or between 3.5% and 4.5%	4.5% or between 4.5% and 5.5%	5.5% or between 5.5% and 6.5%	6.5% or between 6.5% and 7.5%	7.5% or between 7.5% and 8.5%	8.5% or between 8.5% and 9.5%	9.5% or between 9.5% and 10.5%	10.5% or between 10.5% and 11.5%	11.5% or more
100 and over	0.034	0.051	0.066	0.082	0.097	0.111	0.125	0.138	0.152	0.164	0.177

Inheritance Tax Act 1984 (extracts)

[1984 c.51]

...

PART II   EXEMPT TRANSFERS

Chapter I   General

...

29A   Abatement of exemption where claim settled out of beneficiary's own resources

(1) This section applies where –

    (a) apart from this section the transfer of value made on the death of any person is an exempt transfer to the extent that the value transferred by it is attributable to an exempt gift, and

    (b) the exempt beneficiary, in settlement of the whole or part of any claim against the deceased's estate, effects a disposition of property not derived from the transfer.

(2) The provisions of this Act shall have effect in relation to the transfer as if –

    (a) so much of the relevant value as is equal to the following amount, namely the amount by which the value of the exempt beneficiary's estate immediately after the disposition is less than it would be but for the disposition, or

    (b) where that amount exceeds the relevant value, the whole of the relevant value,

were attributable to such a gift to the exempt beneficiary as is mentioned in subsection (3) below (instead of being attributable to a gift with respect to which the transfer is exempt).

(3) The gift referred to in subsection (2) above is a specific gift with respect to which the transfer is chargeable, being a gift which satisfies the conditions set out in paragraphs (a) and (b) of section 38(1) below.

(4) In determining the value of the exempt beneficiary's estate for the purposes of subsection (2) above –

    (a) no deduction shall be made in respect of the claim referred to in subsection (1)(b) above, and

    (b) where the disposition referred to in that provision constitutes a transfer of value –

        (i) no account shall be taken of any liability of the beneficiary for any tax on the value transferred, and

        (ii) sections 104 and 116 below shall be disregarded.

(5) Subsection (1)(b) above does not apply in relation to any claim against the deceased's estate in respect of so much of any liability as is, in accordance with this Act, to be taken into account in determining the value of the estate.

(6) In this section –

'exempt gift', in relation to a transfer of value falling within subsection (1)(a) above, means –

- (a) a gift with respect to which the transfer is (apart from this section) exempt by virtue of the provisions of any section 18 and 23 to 28A above, or
- (b) where (apart from this section) the transfer is so exempt with respect to a gift up to a limit, so much of the gift as is within that limit;

'the exempt beneficiary', in relation to an exempt gift, means any of the following, namely –

- (a) where the gift is exempt by virtue of section 18 above, the deceased's spouse or civil partner,
- (b) where the gift is exempt by virtue of section 23 above, any person or body –

    - (i) whose property the property falling within subsection (1) of that section becomes, or
    - (ii) by whom that property is held on trust for charitable purposes,

- (c) where the gift is exempt by virtue of section 24 or 25 above, any body whose property the property falling within subsection (1) of that section becomes,
- (d) where the gift is exempt by virtue of section 24A above, any body to whom the land falling within subsection (1) of that section is given, and
- (e) where the gift is exempt by virtue of section 27, 28 or 28A above, the trustees of any settlement in which the property falling within subsection (1) of that section becomes comprised;

'gift' and 'specific gift' have the same meaning as in Chapter III of this Part; and

'the relevant value', in relation to a transfer of value falling within subsection (1)(a) above, means so much of the value transferred by the transfer as is attributable to the gift referred to in that provision.

…

PART III   SETTLED PROPERTY

…

Chapter II   Interests in posessesion, reversionary interests and settlement powers

49   Treatment of interest in possession

(1) A person beneficially entitled to an interest in possession in settled property shall be treated for the purposes of this Act as beneficially entitled to the property in which the interest subsists.

(1A) Where the interest in possession mentioned in subsection (1) above is one to which the person becomes beneficially entitled on or after 22nd March 2006, subsection (1) above applies in relation to that interest only if, and for so long as, it is –

- (a) an immediate post-death interest,
- (b) a disabled person's interest, or
- (c) a transitional serial interest,

or falls within section 5(1B) above.

(1B) Where the interest in possession mentioned in subsection (1) above is one to which the person became beneficially entitled before 22nd March, subsection (1) above does not apply in relation to that interest at any time when section 71A below applies to the property in which the interest subsists.

(2) Where a person becomes entitled to an interest in possession in settled property as a

result of a disposition for a consideration in money or money's worth, any question whether and to what extent the giving of the consideration is a transfer of value or chargeable transfer shall be determined without regard to subsection (1) above.

(3) [*Repealed*]

49A   Immediate post-death interest

(1) Where a person ('L') is beneficially entitled to an interest in possession in settled property, for the purposes of this Chapter that interest is an 'immediate post-death interest' only if the following conditions are satisfied.

(2) Condition 1 is that the settlement was effected by will or under the law relating to intestacy.

(3) Condition 2 is that L became beneficially entitled to the interest in possession on the death of the testator or intestate.

(4) Condition 3 is that –

   (a)   section 71A below does not apply to the property in which the interest subsists, and

   (b)   the interest is not a disabled person's interest.

(5) Condition 4 is that Condition 3 has been satisfied at all times since L became beneficially entitled to the interest in possession.

49B   Transitional serial interests

Where a person is beneficially entitled to an interest in possession in settled property, for the purposes of this Chapter that interest is a 'transitional serial interest' only –

(a)   if section 49C or 49D below so provides, or

(b)   if, and to the extent that, section 49E below so provides.

49C   Transitional serial interest: interest to which person becomes entitled during period 22nd March 2006 to 5th October 2008

(1) Where a person ('B') is beneficially entitled to an interest in possession in settled property ('the current interest'), that interest is a transitional serial interest for the purposes of this Chapter if the following conditions are met.

(2) Condition 1 is that–

   (a)   the settlement commenced before 22nd March 2006, and

   (b)   immediately before 22nd March 2006, the property then comprised in the settlement was property in which B, or some other person, was beneficially entitled to an interest in possession ('the prior interest').

(3) Condition 2 is that the prior interest came to an end at a time on or after 22nd March 2006 but before 6th October 2008.

(4) Condition 3 is that B became beneficially entitled to the current interest at that time.

(5) Condition 4 is that –

   (a)   section 71A below does not apply to the property in which the interest subsists, and

   (b)   the interest is not a disabled person's interest.

49D Transitional serial interest: interest to which person becomes entitled on death of spouse or civil partner on or after 6th October 2008

(1) Where a person ('E') is beneficially entitled to an interest in possession in settled property ('the successor interest'), that interest is a transitional serial interest for the purposes of this Chapter if the following conditions are met.

(2) Condition 1 is that –

    (a) the settlement commenced before 22nd March 2006, and

    (b) immediately before 22nd March 2006, the property then comprised in the settlement was property in which a person other than E was beneficially entitled to an interest in possession ('the previous interest').

(3) Condition 2 is that the previous interest came to an end on or after 6th October 2008 on the death of that other person ('F').

(4) Condition 3 is that, immediately before F died, F was the spouse or civil partner of E.

(5) Condition 4 is that E became beneficially entitled to the successor interest on F's death.

(6) Condition 5 is that –

    (a) section 71A below does not apply to the property in which the successor interest subsists, and

    (b) the successor interest is not a disabled person's interest.

49E Transitional serial interest: contracts of life insurance

(1) Where –

    (a) a person ('C') is beneficially entitled to an interest in possession in settled property ('the present interest'), and

    (b) on C's becoming beneficially entitled to the present interest, the settled property consisted of, or included, rights under a contract of life insurance entered into before 22nd March 2006,

the present interest so far as subsisting in rights under the contract, or in property comprised in the settlement that directly or indirectly represents rights under the contract, is a 'transitional serial interest' for the purposes of this Chapter if the following conditions are met.

(2) Condition 1 is that –

    (a) the settlement commenced before 22nd March 2006, and

    (b) immediately before 22nd March 2006 –

        (i) the property then comprised in the settlement consisted of, or included, rights under the contract, and

        (ii) those rights were property in which C, or some other person, was beneficially entitled to an interest in possession ('the earlier interest').

(3) Condition 2 is that –

    (a) the earlier interest came to an end at a time on or after 6th October 2008 ('the earlier-interest end-time') on the death of the person beneficially entitled to it and C became beneficially entitled to the present interest –

        (i) at the earlier-interest end-time, or

        (ii) on the coming to an end, on the death of the person beneficially entitled to it, of an interest in possession to which that person became beneficially entitled at the earlier-interest end-time, or

        (iii) on the coming to an end of the second or last in an unbroken sequence of two or more consecutive interests in possession to the first of which a person became beneficially entitled at the earlier-interest end-time and each of which ended on the death of the person beneficially entitled to it, or

(b) C became beneficially entitled to the present interest –

  (i) on the coming to an end, on the death of the person entitled to it, of an interest in possession that is a transitional serial interest under section 49C above, or

  (ii) on the coming to an end of the second or last in an unbroken sequence of two or more consecutive interests in possession the first of which was a transitional serial interest under section 49C above and each of which ended on the death of the person beneficially entitled to it.

(4) Condition 3 is that rights under the contract were comprised in the settlement throughout the period beginning with 22nd March 2006 and ending with C's becoming beneficially entitled to the present interest.

(5) Condition 4 is that–

  (a) section 71A below does not apply to the property in which the present interest subsists, and

  (b) the present interest is not a disabled person's interest.

50 Interests in part, etc.

(1) Where the person referred to in section 49(1) above is entitled to part only of the income (if any) of the property, the interest shall be taken to subsist in such part only of the property as bears to the whole the same proportion as the part of the income to which he is entitled bears to the whole of the income.

(2) Where the part of the income of any property to which a person is entitled is a specified amount (or the whole less a specified amount) in any period, his interest in the property shall be taken, subject to subsection (3) below, to subsist in such part (or in the whole less such part) of the property as produces that amount in that period.

(3) The Treasury may from time to time by order prescribe a higher and a lower rate for the purposes of this section; and where tax is chargeable in accordance with subsection (2) above by reference to the value of the part of a property which produces a specified amount or by reference to the value of the remainder (but not where chargeable transfers are made simultaneously and tax is chargeable by reference to the value of that part as well as by reference to the value of the remainder) the value of the part producing that specified amount –

  (a) shall, if tax is chargeable by reference to the value of that part, be taken to be not less than it would be if the property produced income at the higher rate so prescribed, and

  (b) shall, if tax is chargeable by reference to the value of the remainder, be taken to be not more than it would be if the property produced income at the lower rate so prescribed;

but the value to be taken by virtue of paragraph (a) above as the value of part of a property shall not exceed the value of the whole of the property

(4) The power to make orders under subsection (3) above shall be exercisable by statutory instrument, which shall be subject to annulment in pursuance of a resolution of the House of Commons.

(5) Where the person referred to in section 49(1) above is not entitled to any income of the property but is entitled, jointly or in common with one or more other persons, to the use and enjoyment of the property, his interest shall be taken to subsist in such part of the

property as corresponds to the proportion which the annual value of his interest bears to the aggregate of the annual values of his interest and that or those of the other or others.

(6) Where, under section 43(3) above, a lease of property is to be treated as a settlement, the lessee's interest in the property shall be taken to subsist in the whole of the property less such part of it as corresponds to the proportion which the value of the lessor's interest (as determined under Part VI of this Act) bears to the value of the property.

51 Disposal of interest in possession

(1) Where a person beneficially entitled to an interest in possession in settled property disposes of his interest the disposal –

(a) is not a transfer of value, but

(b) shall be treated for the purposes of this Chapter as the coming to an end of his interest;

and tax shall be charged accordingly under section 52 below.

(1A) Where the interest disposed of is one to which the person became beneficially entitled on or after 22nd March 2006, subsection (1) above applies in relation to the disposal only if the interest is –

(a) an immediate post-death interest,

(b) a disabled person's interest within section 89B(1)(c) or (d) below, or

(c) a transitional serial interest,

or falls within section 5(1B) above.

(1B) Where the interest disposed of is one to which the person became beneficially entitled before 22nd March 2006, subsection (1) above does not apply in relation to the disposal if, immediately before the disposal, section 71A or 71D below applies to the property in which the interest subsists.

(2) Where a disposition satisfying the conditions of section 11 above is a disposal of an interest in possession in settled property, the interest shall not by virtue of subsection (1) above be treated as coming to an end.

(3) References in this section to any property or to an interest in any property include references to part of any property or interest.

52 Charge on termination of interest in possession

(1) Where at any time during the life of a person beneficially entitled to an interest in possession in settled property his interest comes to an end, tax shall be charged, subject to section 53 below, as if at that time he had made a transfer of value and the value transferred had been equal to the value of the property in which his interest subsisted.

(2) If the interest comes to an end by being disposed of by the person beneficially entitled to it and the disposal is for a consideration in money or money's worth, tax shall be chargeable under this section as if the value of the property in which the interest subsisted were reduced by the amount of the consideration; but in determining that amount the value of a reversionary interest in the property or of any interest in other property comprised in the same settlement shall be left out of account.

(2A) Where the interest mentioned in subsection (1) or (2) above is one to which the person became beneficially entitled on or after 22nd March 2006, that subsection applies in relation to the coming to an end of the interest only if the interest is –

(a) an immediate post-death interest,

(b) a disabled person's interest, or

(c) a transitional serial interest,

or falls within section 5(1B) above.

(3)   Where a transaction is made between the trustees of the settlement and a person who is, or is connected with, –

   (a)   the person beneficially entitled to an interest in the property or

   (b)   a person beneficially entitled to any other interest in that property or to any interest in any other property comprised in the settlement, or

   (c)   a person for whose benefit any of the settled property may be applied,

   and, as a result of the transaction, the value of the first-mentioned property is less than it would be but for the transaction, a corresponding part of the interest shall be deemed for the purposes of this section to come to an end, unless the transaction is such that, were the trustees beneficially entitled to the settled property, it would not be a transfer of value.

(3A) Where the interest mentioned in paragraph (a) of subsection (3) above is one to which the person mentioned in that paragraph became beneficially entitled on or after 22nd March 2006, that subsection applies in relation to the transaction only if the interest is –

   (a)   an immediate post-death interest,

   (b)   a disabled person's interest, or

   (c)   a transitional serial interest,

   or falls within section 5(1B) above.

(4)   References in this section or section 53 below to any property or to an interest in any property include references to part of any property or interest; and –

   (a)   the tax chargeable under this section on the coming to an end of part of an interest shall be charged as if the value of the property (or part) in which the interest subsisted were a corresponding part of the whole; and

   (b)   if the value of the property (or part) to which or to an interest in which a person becomes entitled as mentioned in subsection (2) of section 53 below is less than the value on which tax would be chargeable apart from that subsection, tax shall be chargeable on a value equal to the difference.

...

54A   Special rate of charge where settled property affected by potentially exempt transfer

(1)   If the circumstances fall within subsection (2) below, this section applies to any chargeable transfer made –

   (a)   under section 52 above, on the coming to an end of an interest in possession in settled property during the life of the person beneficially entitled to it, or

   (b)   on the death of a person beneficially entitled to an interest in possession in settled property;

   and in the following provisions of this section the interest in possession mentioned in paragraph (a) or paragraph (b) above is referred to as 'the relevant interest'.

(1A) Where a person becomes beneficially entitled on or after 22nd March 2006 to an interest in possession in settled property, subsection (1)(b) above applies in relation to the person's death only if the interest is –

   (a)   a disabled person's interest, or

   (b)   a transitional serial interest.

(2)   The circumstances referred to in subsection (1) above are –

(a) that the whole or part of the value transferred by the transfer is attributable to property in which the relevant interest subsisted and which became settled property in which there subsisted an interest in possession (whether the relevant interest or any previous interest) on the making by the settlor of a potentially exempt transfer at any time on or after 17th March 1987 and within the period of seven years ending with the date of the chargeable transfer; and

(b) that the settlor is alive at the time when the relevant interest comes to an end; and

(c) that, on the coming to an end of the relevant interest, any of the property in which that interest subsisted becomes settled property in which no qualifying interest in possession (as defined in section 59 below) subsists . . . ; and

(d) that, within six months of the coming to an end of the relevant interest, any of the property in which that interest subsisted has neither –

    (i) become settled property in which a qualifying interest in possession subsists . . . , nor

    (ii) become property to which an individual is beneficially entitled.

(3) In the following provisions of this section 'the special rate property', in relation to a chargeable transfer to which this section applies, means the property in which the relevant interest subsisted or, in a case where –

(a) any part of that property does not fall within subsection (2)(a) above, or

(b) any part of that property does not become settled property of the kind mentioned in subsection (2)(c) above,

so much of that property as appears to the Board or, on appeal, to the tribunal to be just and reasonable.

(4) Where this section applies to a chargeable transfer (in this section referred to as 'the relevant transfer'), the tax chargeable on the value transferred by the transfer shall be whichever is the greater of the tax that would have been chargeable apart from this section and the tax determined in accordance with subsection (5) below.

(5) The tax determined in accordance with this subsection is the aggregate of –

(a) the tax that would be chargeable on a chargeable transfer of the description specified in subsection (6) below, and

(b) so much (if any) of the tax that would, apart from this section, have been chargeable on the value transferred by the relevant transfer as is attributable to the value of property other than the special rate property.

(6) The chargeable transfer postulated in subsection (5)(a) above is one –

(a) the value transferred by which is equal to the value transferred by the relevant transfer or, where only part of that value is attributable to the special rate property, that part of that value;

(b) which is made at the time of the relevant transfer by a transferor who has in the preceding seven years made chargeable transfers having an aggregate value equal to the aggregate of the values transferred by any chargeable transfers made by the settlor in the period of seven years ending with the date of the potentially exempt transfer; and

(c) for which the applicable rate or rates are one-half of the rate or rates referred to in section 7(1) above.

(7) This section has effect subject to section 54B below.

…

Chapter III   Settlements without interests in posessesion, and certain settlements in which interests in possession subsist

Interpretation

58   Relevant property

(1)   In this Chapter 'relevant property' means settled property in which no qualifying interest in possession subsists, other than –

    (a)   property held for charitable purposes only, whether for a limited time or otherwise;

    (b)   property to which section 71, 71A, 71D, 73, 74 or 86 below applies (but see subsection (1A) below);

    (c)   property held on trusts which comply with the requirements mentioned in paragraph 3(1) of Schedule 4 to this Act, and in respect of which a direction given under paragraph 1 of that Schedule has effect;

    (d)   property which is held for the purposes of a registered pension scheme, a qualifying non-UK pension scheme or a section 615(3) scheme;

    (e)   property comprised in a trade or professional compensation fund; . . .

    (ea)   property comprised in an asbestos compensation settlement;

    (eb)   property comprised in a decommissioning security settlement; and

    (f)   excluded property.

(1A)   Settled property to which section 86 below applies is 'relevant property' for the purposes of this Chapter if –

    (a)   an interest in possession subsists in that property, and

    (b)   that interest falls within subsection (1B) or (1C) below.

(1B)   An interest in possession falls within this subsection if –

    (a)   an individual is beneficially entitled to the interest in possession,

    (b)   the individual became beneficially entitled to the interest in possession on or after 22nd March 2006, and

    (c)   the interest in possession is –

        (i)   not an immediate post-death interest,

        (ii)   not a disabled person's interest, and

        (iii)   not a transitional serial interest.

(1C)   An interest in possession falls within this subsection if –

    (a)   a company is beneficially entitled to the interest in possession,

    (b)   the business of the company consists wholly or mainly in the acquisition of interests in settled property,

    (c)   the company has acquired the interest in possession for full consideration in money or money's worth from an individual who was beneficially entitled to it,

    (d)   the individual became beneficially entitled to the interest in possession on or after 22nd March 2006, and

    (e)   immediately before the company acquired the interest in possession, the interest in possession was neither an immediate post-death interest nor a transitional serial interest.

(2)   The reference in subsection (1)(d) above to property which is held for the purposes of a

scheme does not include a reference to a benefit which, having become payable under the scheme, becomes comprised in a settlement.

(2A) For the purposes of subsection (1)(d) above –

    (a)   property applied to pay lump sum death benefits within section 168(1) of the Finance Act 2004 in respect of a member of a registered pension scheme is to be taken to be held for the purposes of the scheme from the time of the member's death until the payment is made, and

    (b)   property applied to pay lump sum death benefits in respect of a member of a qualifying non-UK pension scheme or a section 615(3) scheme is to be taken to be so held if the benefits are paid within the period of two years beginning with the earlier of the day on which the member's death was first known to the trustees or other persons having the control of the fund and the day on which they could first reasonably be expected to have known of it.

(3)   In subsection (1)(e) above 'trade or professional compensation fund' means a fund which is maintained or administered by a representative association of persons carrying on a trade or profession and the only or main objects of which are compensation for or relief of losses or hardship that, through the default or alleged default of persons carrying on the trade or profession or of their agents or servants, are incurred or likely to be incurred by others.

(4)   In subsection (1)(ea) above 'asbestos compensation settlement' means a settlement –

    (a)   the sole or main purpose of which is making compensation payments to or in respect of individuals who have, or had before their death, an asbestos-related condition, and

    (b)   which is made before 24 March 2010 in pursuance of an arrangement within subsection (5) below.

(5)   An arrangement is within this subsection if it is –

    (a)   a voluntary arrangement that has taken effect under Part 1 of the Insolvency Act 1986 or Part 2 of the Insolvency (Northern Ireland) Order 1989,

    (b)   a compromise or arrangement that has taken effect under section 425 of the Companies Act 1985, Article 418 of the Companies (Northern Ireland) Order 1986 or Part 26 of the Companies Act 2006, or

    (c)   an arrangement or compromise of a kind corresponding to any of those mentioned in paragraph (a) or (b) above that has taken effect under, or as a result of, the law of a country or territory outside the United Kingdom.

(6)   For the purposes of subsection (1)(eb) above a settlement is a 'decommissioning security settlement' if the sole or main purpose of the settlement is to provide security for the performance of obligations under an abandonment programme.

(7)   In subsection (6) –

'abandonment programme' means an abandonment programme approved under Part 4 of the Petroleum Act 1998 (including such a programme as revised);

'security' has the same meaning as in section 38A of that Act.

59   Qualifying interest in possession

(1)   In this Chapter 'qualifying interest in possession' means –

    (a)   an interest in possession –

        (i)   to which an individual is beneficially entitled, and

        (ii)   which, if the individual became beneficially entitled to the interest in possession on or after 22nd March 2006, is an immediate post-death interest, a disabled person's interest or a transitional serial interest, or

(b) an interest in possession to which, where subsection (2) below applies, a company is beneficially entitled.

(2) This subsection applies where –

(a) the business of the company consists wholly or mainly in the acquisition of interests in settled property, and

(b) the company has acquired the interest for full consideration in money or money's worth from an individual who was beneficially entitled to it, and

(c) if the individual became beneficially entitled to the interest in possession on or after 22nd March 2006, the interest is an immediate post-death interest, or a disabled person's interest within section 89B(1)(c) or (d) below or a transitional serial interest, immediately before the company acquires it.

(3) Where the acquisition mentioned in paragraph (b) of subsection (2) above was before 14th March 1975 –

(a) the condition set out in paragraph (a) of that subsection shall be treated as satisfied if the business of the company was at the time of the acquisition such as is described in that paragraph, and

(b) that condition need not be satisfied if the company is an insurance company (within the meaning of Part 2 of the Finance Act 2012) and has permission –

(i) under Part 4A of the Financial Services and Markets Act 2000, or

(ii) under paragraph 15 of Schedule 3 to that Act (as a result of qualifying for authorisation under paragraph 12(1) of that Schedule),

to effect or carry out contracts of long-term insurance.

(4) In subsection (3)(b) above 'contracts of long-term insurance' means contracts which fall within Part II of Schedule 1 to the Financial Services and Markets Act 2000 (Regulated Activities) Order 2001.

60 Commencement of settlement

In this Chapter references to the commencement of a settlement are references to the time when property first becomes comprised in it.

61 Ten-year anniversary

(1) In this Chapter 'ten-year anniversary' in relation to a settlement means the tenth anniversary of the date on which the settlement commenced and subsequent anniversaries at ten-yearly intervals, but subject to subsections (2) to (4) below.

(2) The ten-year anniversaries of a settlement treated as made under section 80 below shall be the dates that are (or would but for that section be) the ten-year anniversaries of the settlement first mentioned in that section.

(3) No date falling before 1st April 1983 shall be a ten-year anniversary.

(4) Where –

(a) the first ten-year anniversary of a settlement would apart from this subsection fall during the year ending with 31st March 1984, and

(b) during that year an event occurs in respect of the settlement which could not have occurred except as the result of some proceedings before a court, and

(c) the event is one on which tax was chargeable under Chapter II of Part IV of the

Finance Act 1982 (or, apart from Part II of Schedule 15 to that Act, would have been so chargeable),

the first ten-year anniversary shall be taken to be 1st April 1984 (but without affecting the dates of later anniversaries).

62   Related settlements

(1)   For the purposes of this Chapter two settlements are related if and only if –

(a)   the settlor is the same in each case, and
(b)   they commenced on the same day,

but subject to subsection (2) below.

(2)   Two settlements are not related for the purposes of this Chapter if all the property comprised in one or both of them was immediately after the settlement commenced held for charitable purposes only without limit of time (defined by a date or otherwise).

62A   Same-day additions

(1)   For the purposes of this Chapter, there is a 'same-day addition', in relation to a settlement ('settlement A'), if –

(a)   there is a transfer of value by a person as a result of which the value immediately afterwards of the property comprised in settlement A is greater than the value immediately before,
(b)   as a result of the same transfer of value, or as a result of another transfer of value made by that person on the same day, the value immediately afterwards of the property comprised in another settlement ('settlement B') is greater than the value immediately before,
(c)   that person is the settlor of settlement A and settlement B,
(d)   at any point in the relevant period, all or any part of the property comprised in settlement A was relevant property, and
(e)   at that point, or at any other point in the relevant period, all or any part of the property comprised in settlement B was relevant property.

For exceptions, see section 62B.

(2)   Where there is a same-day addition, references in this Chapter to its value are to the difference between the two values mentioned in subsection (1)(b).

(3)   'The relevant period' means –

(a)   in the case of settlement A, the period beginning with the commencement of settlement A and ending immediately after the transfer of value mentioned in subsection (1)(a), and
(b)   in the case of settlement B, the period beginning with the commencement of settlement B and ending immediately after the transfer of value mentioned in subsection (1)(b)).

(4)   The transfer or transfers of value mentioned in subsection (1) include a transfer or transfers of value as a result of which property first becomes comprised in settlement A or settlement B; but not if settlements A and B are related settlements.

(5)   For the purposes of subsection (1) above, it is immaterial whether the amount of the property comprised in settlement A or settlement B (or neither) was increased as a result of the transfer or transfers of value mentioned in that subsection.

62B   Same day additions: exceptions

(1)   There is not a same-day addition for the purposes of this Chapter if any of the following conditions is met –

    (a)   immediately after the transfer of value mentioned in section 62A(1)(a) all the property comprised in settlement A was held for charitable purposes only without limit of time (defined by a date or otherwise),

    (b)   immediately after the transfer of value mentioned in section 62A(1)(b) all the property comprised in settlement B was so held,

    (c)   either or each of settlement A and settlement B is a protected settlement (see section 62C), and

    (d)   the transfer of value, or either or each of the transfers of value, mentioned in section 62A(1)(a) and (b) –

        (i)   results from the payment of a premium under a contract of life insurance the terms of which provide for premiums to be due at regular intervals of one year or less throughout the contract term, or

        (ii)   is made to fund such a payment.

(2)   If the transfer of value, or each of the transfers of value, mentioned in section 62A(1) is not the transfer of value under section 4 on the settlor's death, there is a same-day addition for the purposes of this Chapter only if conditions A and B are met.

(3)   Condition A is that –

    (a)   the difference between the two values mentioned in section 62A(1)(a) exceeds £5,000, or

    (b)   in a case where there has been more than one transfer of value within section 62A(1)(a) on the same day, the difference between –

        (i)   the value of the property comprised in settlement A immediately before the first of those transfers, and

        (ii)   the value of the property comprised in settlement A immediately after the last of those transfers,

    exceeds £5,000.

(4)   Condition B is that –

    (a)   the difference between the two values mentioned in section 62A(1)(b) exceeds £5,000, or

    (b)   in a case where there has been more than one transfer of value within section 62A(1)(b), the difference between –

        (i)   the value of the property comprised in settlement B immediately before the first of those transfers, and

        (ii)   the value of the property comprised in settlement B immediately after the last of those transfers,

    exceeds £5,000.

62C   Protected settlements

(1)   For the purposes of this Chapter, a settlement is a 'protected settlement' if it commenced before 10 December 2014 and either condition A or condition B is met.

(2)   Condition A is met if there have been no transfers of value by the settlor on or after 10 December 2014 as a result of which the value of the property comprised in the settlement was increased.

(3)   Condition B is met if –

    (a)   there has been a transfer of value by the settlor on or after 10 December 2014 as a result of which the value of the property comprised in the settlement was increased, and

    (b)   that transfer of value was the transfer of value under section 4 on the settlor's death before 6 April 2017 and it had the result mentioned by reason of a protected testamentary disposition.

(4)   In subsection (3)(b) 'protected testamentary disposition' means a disposition effected by provisions of the settlor's will that at the settlor's death are, in substance, the same as they were immediately before 10 December 2014.

63   Minor interpretative provisions

In this Chapter, unless the context otherwise requires –

'payment' includes a transfer of assets other than money;
'quarter' means period of three months.

Principal charge to tax

64   Charge at ten-year anniversary

(1)   Where immediately before a ten-year anniversary all or any part of the property comprised in a settlement is relevant property, tax shall be charged at the rate applicable under sections 66 and 67 below on the value of the property or part at that time.

(1A)   For the purposes of subsection (1) above, property held by the trustees of a settlement immediately before a ten-year anniversary is to be regarded as relevant property comprised in the settlement at that time if –

    (a)   it is income of the settlement,

    (b)   the income arose before the start of the five years ending immediately before the ten-year anniversary,

    (c)   the income arose (directly or indirectly) from property comprised in the settlement that, when the income arose, was relevant property, and

    (d)   when the income arose, no person was beneficially entitled to an interest in possession in the property from which the income arose.

(1B)   Where the settlor of a settlement was not domiciled in the United Kingdom at the time the settlement was made, income of the settlement is not to be regarded as relevant property comprised in the settlement as a result of subsection (1A) above so far as the income –

    (a)   is situated outside the United Kingdom, or

    (b)   is represented by a holding in an authorised unit trust or a share in an open-ended investment company.

(1C)   Income of the settlement is not to be regarded as relevant property comprised in the settlement as a result of subsection (1A) above so far as the income –

    (a)   is represented by securities issued by the Treasury subject to a condition of the kind mentioned in subsection (2) of section 6 above, and

    (b)   it is shown that all known persons for whose benefit the settled property or income from it has been or might be applied, or who are or might become beneficially entitled to an interest in possession in it, are persons of a description specified in the condition in question.

(2) For the purposes of subsection (1) above, a foreign-owned work of art which is situated in the United Kingdom for one or more of the purposes of public display, cleaning and restoration (and for no other purpose) is not to be regarded as relevant property.

65 Charge at other times

(1) There shall be a charge to tax under this section –

 (a) where the property comprised in a settlement or any part of that property ceases to be relevant property (whether because it ceases to be comprised in the settlement or otherwise); and
 (b) in a case in which paragraph (a) above does not apply, where the trustees of the settlement make a disposition as a result of which the value of relevant property comprised in the settlement is less than it would be but for the disposition.

(2) The amount on which tax is charged under this section shall be –

 (a) the amount by which the value of relevant property comprised in the settlement is less immediately after the event in question than it would be but for the event, or
 (b) where the tax payable is paid out of relevant property comprised in the settlement immediately after the event, the amount which, after deducting the tax, is equal to the amount on which tax would be charged by virtue of paragraph (a) above.

(3) The rate at which tax is charged under this section shall be the rate applicable under section 68 or 69 below.

(4) Subsection (1) above does not apply if the event in question occurs in a quarter beginning with the day on which the settlement commenced or with a ten-year anniversary.

(5) Tax shall not be charged under this section in respect of –

 (a) a payment of costs or expenses (so far as they are fairly attributable to relevant property), or
 (b) a payment which is (or will be) income of any person for any of the purposes of income tax or would for any of those purposes be income of a person not resident in the United Kingdom if he were so resident,

or in respect of a liability to make such a payment.

(6) Tax shall not be charged under this section by virtue of subsection (1)(b) above if the disposition is such that, were the trustees beneficially entitled to the settled property, section 10 or section 16 above would prevent the disposition from being a transfer of value.

(7) Tax shall not be charged under this section by reason only that property comprised in a settlement ceases to be situated in the United Kingdom and thereby becomes excluded property by virtue of section 48(3)(a) above.

(7A) Tax shall not be charged under this section by reason only that property comprised in a settlement becomes excluded property by virtue of section 48(3A)(a) (holding in an authorised unit trust or a share in an open-ended investment company is excluded property unless settlor domiciled in UK when settlement made).

(8) If the settlor of a settlement was not domiciled in the United Kingdom when the settlement was made, tax shall not be charged under this section by reason only that property comprised in the settlement is invested in securities issued by the Treasury subject to a condition of the kind mentioned in section 6(2) above and thereby becomes excluded property by virtue of section 48(4)(b) above.

(9)   For the purposes of this section trustees shall be treated as making a disposition if they omit to exercise a right (unless it is shown that the omission was not deliberate) and the disposition shall be treated as made at the time or latest time when they could have exercised the right.

…

PART V   MISCELLANEOUS RELIEFS

…

Chapter V   Miscellaneous

…

Changes in distribution of deceased's estate, etc.

142   Alteration of dispositions taking effect on death

(1)   Where within the period of two years after a person's death –

(a)   any of the dispositions (whether effected by will, under the law relating to intestacy or otherwise) of the property comprised in his estate immediately before his death are varied, or

(b)   the benefit conferred by any of those dispositions is disclaimed,

by an instrument in writing made by the persons or any of the persons who benefit or would benefit under the dispositions, this Act shall apply as if the variation had been effected by the deceased or, as the case may be, the disclaimed benefit had never been conferred.

(2)   Subsection (1) above shall not apply to a variation unless the instrument contains a statement, made by all the relevant persons, to the effect that they intend the subsection to apply to the variation.

(2A) For the purposes of subsection (2) above the relevant persons are –

(a)   the person or persons making the instrument, and

(b)   where the variation results in additional tax being payable, the personal representatives.

Personal representatives may decline to make a statement under subsection (2) above only if no, or no sufficient, assets are held by them in that capacity for discharging the additional tax.

(3)   Subsection (1) above shall not apply to a variation or disclaimer made for any consideration in money or money's worth other than consideration consisting of the making; in respect of another of the dispositions, of a variation or disclaimer to which that subsection applies.

(3A) Subsection (1) does not apply to a variation by virtue of which any property comprised in the estate immediately before the person's death becomes property in relation to which section 23(1) applies unless it is shown that the appropriate person has been notified of the existence of the instrument of variation.

(3B) For the purposes of subsection (3A) 'the appropriate person' is –

(a)   the charity or registered club to which the property is given, or

(b)   if the property is to be held on trust for charitable purposes or for the purposes of registered clubs, the trustees in question.

(4)   Where a variation to which subsection (1) above applies results in property being held in trust for a person for a period which ends not more than two years after the death, this Act shall apply as if the disposition of the property that takes effect at the end of the period had had effect from the beginning of the period; but this subsection shall not affect the application of this Act in relation to any distribution or application of property occurring before that disposition takes effect.

(5)   For the purposes of subsection (1) above the property comprised in a person's estate includes any excluded property but not any property to which he is treated as entitled by virtue of section 49(1) above or section 102 of the Finance Act 1986.

(6)   Subsection (1) above applies whether or not the administration of the estate is complete or the property concerned has been distributed in accordance with the original dispositions.

(7)   In the application of subsection (4) above to Scotland, property which is subject to a proper liferent shall be deemed to be held in trust for the liferenter.

…

144   Distribution etc. from property settled by will

(1)   Subsection (2) below applies where property comprised in a person's estate immediately before his death is settled by his will and, within the period of two years after his death and before any interest in possession has subsisted in the property, there occurs –

   (a)   an event on which tax would (apart from subsection (2) below) be chargeable under any provision, other than section 64 or 79, of Chapter III of Part III of this Act, or

   (b)   an event on which tax would be so chargeable but for section 65(4), 75, 75A or 76 above or paragraph 16(1) of Schedule 4 to this Act.

(1A) Where the testator dies on or after 22nd March 2006, subsection (1) above shall have effect as if the reference to any interest in possession were a reference to any interest in possession that is–

   (a)   an immediate post-death interest, or

   (b)   a disabled person's interest.

(2)   Where this subsection applies by virtue of an event within paragraph (a) of subsection (1) above, tax shall not be charged under the provision in question on that event; and in every case in which this subsection applies in relation to an event, this Act shall have effect as if the will had provided that on the testator's death the property should be held as it is held after the event.

(3)   Subsection (4) below applies where –

   (a)   a person dies on or after 22nd March 2006,

   (b)   property comprised in the person's estate immediately before his death is settled by his will, and

   (c)   within the period of two years after his death, but before an immediate post-death interest or a disabled person's interest has subsisted in the property, there occurs an event that involves causing the property to be held on trusts that would, if they had in fact been established by the testator's will, have resulted in –

      (i)   an immediate post-death interest subsisting in the property, or

      (ii)   section 71A or 71D above applying to the property.

(4)   Where this subsection applies by virtue of an event –

   (a)   this Act shall have effect as if the will had provided that on the testator's death the property should be held as it is held after the event, but

(b)   tax shall not be charged on that event under any provision of Chapter 3 of Part 3 of this Act.

(5)   Subsection (4) above also applies where –

(a)   a person dies before 22nd March 2006,

(b)   property comprised in the person's estate immediately before his death is settled by his will,

(c)   an event occurs –

(i)   on or after 22nd March 2006, and

(ii)   within the period of two years after the testator's death,

that involves causing the property to be held on trusts within subsection (6) below,

(d)   no immediate post-death interest, and no disabled person's interest, subsisted in the property at any time in the period beginning with the testator's death and ending immediately before the event, and

(e)   no other interest in possession subsisted in the property at any time in the period beginning with the testator's death and ending immediately before 22nd March 2006.

(6)   Trusts are within this subsection if they would, had they in fact been established by the testator's will and had the testator died at the time of the event mentioned in subsection (5)(c) above, have resulted in –

(a)   an immediate post-death interest subsisting in the property, or

(b)   section 71A or 71D above applying to the property.

145

[*Repealed*]

146   Inheritance (Provision for Family and Dependants) Act 1975

(1)   Where an order is made under section 2 of the Inheritance (Provision for Family and Dependants) Act 1975 ('the 1975 Act') in relation to any property forming part of the net estate of a deceased person, then, without prejudice to section 19(1) of that Act, the property shall for the purposes of this Act be treated as if it had on his death devolved subject to the provisions of the order.

(2)   Where an order is made under section 10 of the 1975 Act requiring a person to provide any money or other property by reason of a disposition made by the deceased, then –

(a)   if that disposition was a chargeable transfer and the personal representatives of the deceased make a claim for the purpose not more than 4 years after the date on which the order is made –

(i)   tax paid or payable on the value transferred by that chargeable transfer (whether or not by the claimants) shall be repaid to them by the Board or, as the case may be, shall not be payable, and

(ii)   the rate or rates of tax applicable to the transfer of value made by the deceased on his death shall be determined as if the values previously transferred by chargeable transfers made by him were reduced by that value;

(b)   the money or property shall be included in the deceased's estate for the purpose of the transfer of value made by him on his death.

(3)   Where the money or other property ordered to be provided under section 10 of the 1975

Act is less than the maximum permitted by that section, subsection (2)(a) above shall have effect in relation to such part of the value there mentioned as is appropriate.

(4) The adjustment in consequence of the provisions of this section or of section 19(1) of the 1975 Act of the tax payable in respect of the transfer of value made by the deceased on his death shall not affect –

(a) the amount of any deduction to be made under section 8 of that Act in respect of tax borne by the person mentioned in subsection (3) of that section, or

(b) the amount of tax to which regard is to be had under section 9(2) of that Act;

and where a person is ordered under that Act to make a payment or transfer property by reason of his holding property treated as part of the deceased's net estate under section 8 or 9 and tax borne by him is taken into account for the purposes of the order, any repayment of that tax shall be made to the personal representatives of the deceased and not to that person.

(5) Tax repaid under paragraph (a)(i) of subsection (2) above shall be included in the deceased's estate for the purposes of the transfer of value made by him on his death; and tax repaid under that paragraph or under subsection (4) above shall form part of the deceased's net estate for the purposes of the 1975 Act.

(6) Anything which is done in compliance with an order under the 1975 Act or occurs on the coming into force of such an order, and which would (apart from this subsection) constitute an occasion on which tax is chargeable under any provision, other than section 79, of Chapter III of Part III of this Act, shall not constitute such an occasion; and where an order under the 1975 Act provides for property to be settled or for the variation of a settlement, and (apart from this subsection) tax would be charged under section 52(1) above on the coming into force of the order, section 52(1) shall not apply.

(7) In subsections (2)(a) and (5) above references to tax include references to interest on tax.

(8) Where an order is made staying or dismissing proceedings under the 1975 Act on terms set out in or scheduled to the order, this section shall have effect as if any of those terms which could have been included in an order under section 2 or 10 of that Act were provisions of such an order.

(9) In this section any reference to, or to any provision of, the 1975 Act includes a reference to, or to the corresponding provision of, the Inheritance (Provision for Family and Dependants) (Northern Ireland) Order 1979.

…

Taxation of Chargeable Gains Act 1992, s.62

62 Death: general provisions

(1) For the purposes of this Act the assets of which a deceased person was competent to dispose –

  (a) shall be deemed to be acquired on his death by the personal representatives or other person on whom they devolve for a consideration equal to their market value at the date of the death, but
  (b) shall not be deemed to be disposed of by him on his death (whether or not they were the subject of a testamentary disposition).

(2) Allowable losses sustained by an individual in the year of assessment in which he dies may, so far as they cannot be deducted from chargeable gains accruing in that year, be deducted from chargeable gains accruing to the deceased in the 3 years of assessment preceding the year of assessment in which the death occurs, taking chargeable gains accruing in a later year before those accruing in an earlier year.

(2A) Amounts deductible from chargeable gains for any year in accordance with subsection (2) above shall not be so deductible from any such gains so far as they are –

  (a) gains that are treated as accruing by virtue of section 87 or 89(2) (read, where appropriate, with section 10A), or
  (b) NRCGT gains (see section 57B and Schedule 4ZZB).

(2AA) Where allowable NRCGT losses (see section 57B and Schedule 4ZZB) are sustained by an individual in the year of assessment in which the individual dies, the losses may, so far as they cannot be deducted from chargeable gains accruing to the individual in that year, be deducted from any gains such as are mentioned in subsection (2A)(b) that accrued to the deceased in the 3 years of assessment preceding the year of assessment in which the death occurs, taking chargeable gains accruing in a later year before those accruing in an earlier year.

. . .

(3) In relation to property forming part of the estate of a deceased person the personal representatives shall for the purposes of this Act be treated as being a single and continuing body of persons (distinct from the persons who may from time to time be the personal representatives), and that body shall be treated as having the deceased's residence and domicile at the date of death.

(4) On a person acquiring any asset as legatee (as defined in section 64) –

  (a) no chargeable gain shall accrue to the personal representatives, and
  (b) the legatee shall be treated as if the personal representatives' acquisition of the asset had been his acquisition of it.

(4A) The Treasury may by regulations make provision having effect in place of subsection (4)(b) above in a case where there has been a time when the personal representatives –

(a)   held the asset acquired by the legatee, and

(b)   would, if they had disposed of the asset at that time –

    (i)   by way of a bargain at arm's length, and

    (ii)   otherwise than to a legatee,

have been entitled as a result of regulations under section 151 (investments under plans) to relief from capital gains tax in respect of any chargeable gain accruing on the disposal.

(4B) Provision made by regulations under subsection (4A) above may (in particular) treat a person who acquires an asset as legatee as doing so at a time or for a consideration, or at a time and for a consideration, ascertained as specified by the regulations.

(5)   Notwithstanding section 17(1) no chargeable gain shall accrue to any person on his making a disposal by way of donatio mortis causa.

(6)   Subject to subsections (7) and (8) below, where within the period of 2 years after a person's death any of the dispositions (whether effected by will, under the law relating to intestacy or otherwise) of the property of which he was competent to dispose are varied, or the benefit conferred by any of those dispositions is disclaimed, by an instrument in writing made by the persons or any of the persons who benefit or would benefit under the dispositions –

(a)   the variation or disclaimer shall not constitute a disposal for the purposes of this Act, and

(b)   this section shall apply as if the variation had been effected by the deceased or, as the case may be, the disclaimed benefit had never been conferred.

(7)   Subsection (6) above does not apply to a variation unless the instrument contains a statement by the persons making the instrument to the effect that they intend the subsection to apply to the variation.

(8)   Subsection (6) above does not apply to a variation or disclaimer made for any consideration in money or money's worth other than consideration consisting of the making of a variation or disclaimer in respect of another of the dispositions.

(9)   Subsection (6) above applies whether or not the administration of the estate is complete or the property has been distributed in accordance with the original dispositions.

(10) In this section references to assets of which a deceased person was competent to dispose are references to assets of the deceased which (otherwise than in right of a power of appointment or of the testamentary power conferred by statute to dispose of entailed interests) he could, if of full age and capacity, have disposed of by his will, assuming that all the assets were situated in England and, if he was not domiciled in the United Kingdom, that he was domiciled in England, and include references to his severable share in any assets to which, immediately before his death, he was beneficially entitled as a joint tenant.

Civil Procedure Rules 1998, SI 1998/3132, Parts 21, 57 and 64 with Practice Directions

PART 21   CHILDREN AND PROTECTED PARTIES

Scope of this Part

21.1 (1)   This Part –

     (a)   contains special provisions which apply in proceedings involving children and protected parties;

     (b)   sets out how a person becomes a litigation friend; and

     (c)   does not apply to –

         (i)   proceedings under Part 75;

         (ii)   enforcement of specified debts by taking control of goods; or

         (iii)   applications in relation to enforcement of specified debts by taking control of goods,

     where one of the parties to the proceedings is a child.

   (2)   In this Part –

     (a)   'the 2005 Act' means the Mental Capacity Act 2005;

     (b)   'child' means a person under 18;

     (c)   'lacks capacity' means lacks capacity within the meaning of the 2005 Act;

     (d)   'protected party' means a party, or an intended party, who lacks capacity to conduct the proceedings;

     (e)   'protected beneficiary' means a protected party who lacks capacity to manage and control any money recovered by him or on his behalf or for his benefit in the proceedings;

     (f)   'specified debts' has the same meaning as in rule 75.1(2)(e); and

     (g)   'taking control of goods' means using the procedure to take control of goods contained in Schedule 12 to the Tribunals, Courts and Enforcement Act 2007.

(Rules 6.13 and 6.25 contain provisions about the service of documents on children and protected parties.)

(Rule 46.4 deals with costs where money is payable by or to a child or protected party.)

Requirement for a litigation friend in proceedings by or against children and protected parties

21.2 (1) A protected party must have a litigation friend to conduct proceedings on his behalf.

(2) A child must have a litigation friend to conduct proceedings on his behalf unless the court makes an order under paragraph (3).

(3) The court may make an order permitting a child to conduct proceedings without a litigation friend.

(4) An application for an order under paragraph (3) –

(a) may be made by the child;

(b) if the child already has a litigation friend, must be made on notice to the litigation friend; and

(c) if the child has no litigation friend, may be made without notice.

(5) Where –

(a) the court has made an order under paragraph (3); and

(b) it subsequently appears to the court that it is desirable for a litigation friend to conduct the proceedings on behalf of the child,

the court may appoint a person to be the child's litigation friend.

Stage of proceedings at which a litigation friend becomes necessary

21.3 (1) This rule does not apply where the court has made an order under rule 21.2(3).

(2) A person may not, without the permission of the court –

(a) make an application against a child or protected party before proceedings have started; or

(b) take any step in proceedings except –

(i) issuing and serving a claim form; or

(ii) applying for the appointment of a litigation friend under rule 21.6,

until the child or protected party has a litigation friend.

(3) If during proceedings a party lacks capacity to continue to conduct proceedings, no party may take any further step in the proceedings without the permission of the court until the protected party has a litigation friend.

(4) Any step taken before a child or protected party has a litigation friend has no effect unless the court orders otherwise.

Who may be a litigation friend without a court order

21.4 (1) This rule does not apply if the court has appointed a person to be a litigation friend.

(2) A deputy appointed by the Court of Protection under the 2005 Act with power to conduct proceedings on the protected party's behalf is entitled to be the litigation friend of the protected party in any proceedings to which his power extends.

(3) If nobody has been appointed by the court or, in the case of a protected party, has been appointed as a deputy as set out in paragraph (2), a person may act as a litigation friend if he –

(a) can fairly and competently conduct proceedings on behalf of the child or protected party;

(b) has no interest adverse to that of the child or protected party; and

(c) where the child or protected party is a claimant, undertakes to pay any costs which the child or protected party may be ordered to pay in relation to the proceedings, subject to any right he may have to be repaid from the assets of the child or protected party.

How a person becomes a litigation friend without a court order

21.5 (1) If the court has not appointed a litigation friend, a person who wishes to act as a litigation friend must follow the procedure set out in this rule.

(2) A deputy appointed by the Court of Protection under the 2005 Act with power to conduct proceedings on the protected party's behalf must file an official copy of the order of the Court of Protection which confers his power to act either –

(a) where the deputy is to act as a litigation friend for a claimant, at the time the claim is made; or

(b) where the deputy is to act as a litigation friend for a defendant, at the time when he first takes a step in the proceedings on behalf of the defendant.

(3) Any other person must file a certificate of suitability stating that he satisfies the conditions specified in rule 21.4(3) either –

(a) where the person is to act as a litigation friend for a claimant, at the time when the claim is made; or

(b) where the person is to act as a litigation friend for a defendant, at the time when he first takes a step in the proceedings on behalf of the defendant.

(4) The litigation friend must –

(a) serve the certificate of suitability on every person on whom, in accordance with rule 6.13 (service on a parent, guardian etc.), the claim form should be served; and

(b) file a certificate of service when filing the certificate of suitability.

(Rules 6.17 and 6.29 set out the details to be contained in a certificate of service.)

How a person becomes a litigation friend by court order

21.6 (1) The court may make an order appointing a litigation friend.

(2) An application for an order appointing a litigation friend may be made by –

(a) a person who wishes to be the litigation friend; or

(b) a party.

(3) Where –

(a) a person makes a claim against a child or protected party;

(b) the child or protected party has no litigation friend;

(c) the court has not made an order under rule 21.2(3) (order that a child can conduct proceedings without a litigation friend); and

(d) either –

(i) someone who is not entitled to be a litigation friend files a defence; or

(ii) the claimant wishes to take some step in the proceedings,

the claimant must apply to the court for an order appointing a litigation friend for the child or protected party.

(4) An application for an order appointing a litigation friend must be supported by evidence.

(5) The court may not appoint a litigation friend under this rule unless it is satisfied that the person to be appointed satisfies the conditions in rule 21.4(3).

Court's power to change a litigation friend and to prevent person acting as a litigation friend

21.7 (1) The court may –

(a) direct that a person may not act as a litigation friend;

(b) terminate a litigation friend's appointment; or

(c) appoint a new litigation friend in substitution for an existing one.

(2) An application for an order under paragraph (1) must be supported by evidence.

(3) The court may not appoint a litigation friend under this rule unless it is satisfied that the person to be appointed satisfies the conditions in rule 21.4(3).

Appointment of a litigation friend by court order – supplementary

21.8 (1) An application for an order under rule 21.6 or 21.7 must be served on every person on whom, in accordance with rule 6.13 (service on parent, guardian etc.), the claim form must be served.

(2) Where an application for an order under rule 21.6 is in respect of a protected party, the application must also be served on the protected party unless the court orders otherwise.

(3) An application for an order under rule 21.7 must also be served on –

(a) the person who is the litigation friend, or who is purporting to act as the litigation friend, when the application is made; and

(b) the person who it is proposed should be the litigation friend, if he is not the applicant.

(4) On an application for an order under rule 21.6 or 21.7, the court may appoint the person proposed or any other person who satisfies the conditions specified in rule 21.4(3).

Procedure where appointment of a litigation friend ceases

21.9 (1) When a child who is not a protected party reaches the age of 18, the litigation friend's appointment ceases.

(2) Where a protected party regains or acquires capacity to conduct the proceedings, the litigation friend's appointment continues until it is ended by court order.

(3) An application for an order under paragraph (2) may be made by –

(a) the former protected party;

(b) the litigation friend; or

(c) a party.

(4) The child or protected party in respect of whom the appointment to act has ceased must serve notice on the other parties –

(a) stating that the appointment of his litigation friend to act has ceased;

(b) giving his address for service; and

(c) stating whether or not he intends to carry on the proceedings.

(5) If the child or protected party does not serve the notice required by paragraph (4) within 28 days after the day on which the appointment of the litigation friend

ceases the court may, on application, strike out any claim brought by or defence raised by the child or protected party.

(6) The liability of a litigation friend for costs continues until –

    (a) the person in respect of whom his appointment to act has ceased serves the notice referred to in paragraph (4); or

    (b) the litigation friend serves notice on the parties that his appointment to act has ceased.

Compromise etc. by or on behalf of a child or protected party

21.10(1) Where a claim is made –

    (a) by or on behalf of a child or protected party; or

    (b) against a child or protected party,

no settlement, compromise or payment (including any voluntary interim payment) and no acceptance of money paid into court shall be valid, so far as it relates to the claim by, on behalf of or against the child or protected party, without the approval of the court.

(2) Where –

    (a) before proceedings in which a claim is made by or on behalf of, or against, a child or protected party (whether alone or with any other person) are begun, an agreement is reached for the settlement of the claim; and

    (b) the sole purpose of proceedings is to obtain the approval of the court to a settlement or compromise of the claim,

the claim must –

    (i) be made using the procedure set out in Part 8 (alternative procedure for claims); and

    (ii) include a request to the court for approval of the settlement or compromise.

(3) In proceedings to which Section II or Section III of Part 45 applies, the court will not make an order for detailed assessment of the costs payable to the child or protected party but will assess the costs in the manner set out in that Section.

(Rule 46.4 contains provisions about costs where money is payable to a child or protected party.)

Control of money recovered by or on behalf of a child or protected party

21.11(1) Where in any proceedings –

    (a) money is recovered by or on behalf of or for the benefit of a child or protected party; or

    (b) money paid into court is accepted by or on behalf of a child or protected party,

the money will be dealt with in accordance with directions given by the court under this rule and not otherwise.

(2) Directions given under this rule may provide that the money shall be wholly or partly paid into court and invested or otherwise dealt with.

(3) Where money is recovered by or on behalf of a protected party or money paid into court is accepted by or on behalf of a protected party, before giving directions in accordance with this rule, the court will first consider whether the protected party is a protected beneficiary.

21.11A [. . .]

Expenses incurred by a litigation friend

21.12 (1) Subject to paragraph (1A), in proceedings to which rule 21.11 applies, a litigation friend who incurs costs or expenses on behalf of a child or protected party in any proceedings is entitled on application to recover the amount paid or payable out of any money recovered or paid into court to the extent that it –

    (a) has been reasonably incurred; and

    (b) is reasonable in amount.

(1A) Costs recoverable under this rule are limited to –

    (a) costs incurred by or on behalf of a child and which have been assessed by way of detailed assessment pursuant to rule 46.4(2); or

    (b) costs incurred by or on behalf of a child by way of success fee under a conditional fee agreement or sum payable under a damages based agreement in a claim for damages for personal injury where the damages agreed or ordered to be paid do not exceed £25,000, where such costs have been assessed summarily pursuant to rule 46.4(5).

(2) Expenses may include all or part of –

    (a) a premium in respect of a costs insurance policy (as defined by section 58C(5) of the Courts and Legal Services Act 1990); or

    (b) interest on a loan taken out to pay a premium in respect of a costs insurance policy or other recoverable disbursement.

(3) No application may be made under this rule for costs or expenses that –

    (a) are of a type that may be recoverable on an assessment of costs payable by or out of money belonging to a child or protected party; but

    (b) are disallowed in whole or in part on such an assessment.

(Costs and expenses which are also 'costs' as defined in rule 44.1(1) are subject to rule 46.4(2) and (3).)

(4) In deciding whether the costs or expenses were reasonably incurred and reasonable in amount, the court will have regard to all the circumstances of the case including the factors set out in rule 44.4(3) and rule 46.9.

(5) When the court is considering the factors to be taken into account in assessing the reasonableness of the costs or expenses, it will have regard to the facts and circumstances as they reasonably appeared to the litigation friend or to the child's or protected party's legal representative when the cost or expense was incurred.

(6) Subject to paragraph (7), where the claim is settled or compromised, or judgment is given, on terms that an amount not exceeding £5,000 is paid to the child or protected party, the total amount the litigation friend may recover under paragraph (1) must not exceed 25% of the sum so agreed or awarded, unless the court directs otherwise. Such total amount must not exceed 50% of the sum so agreed or awarded.

(7) The amount which the litigation friend may recover under paragraph (1) in respect of costs must not (in proceedings at first instance) exceed 25% of the amount of the sum agreed or awarded in respect of –

    (a) general damages for pain, suffering and loss of amenity; and

    (b) damages for pecuniary loss other than future pecuniary loss, net of any sums recoverable by the Compensation Recovery Unit of the Department for Work and Pensions.

(8) Except in a case in which the costs payable to a child or protected party are fixed by these rules, no application may be made under this rule for a payment out of the money recovered by the child or protected party until the costs payable to the child or protected party have been assessed or agreed.

Appointment of a guardian of a child's estate

21.13 (1) The court may appoint the Official Solicitor to be a guardian of a child's estate where –

    (a) money is paid into court on behalf of the child in accordance with directions given under rule 21.11 (control of money received by a child or protected party);

    (b) the Criminal Injuries Compensation Authority notifies the court that it has made or intends to make an award to the child;

    (c) a court or tribunal outside England and Wales notifies the court that it has ordered or intends to order that money be paid to the child;

    (d) the child is absolutely entitled to the proceeds of a pension fund; or

    (e) in any other case, such an appointment seems desirable to the court.

(2) The court may not appoint the Official Solicitor under this rule unless –

    (a) the persons with parental responsibility (within the meaning of section 3 of the Children Act 1989) agree; or

    (b) the court considers that their agreement can be dispensed with.

(3) The Official Solicitor's appointment may continue only until the child reaches 18.

PRACTICE DIRECTION 21 – CHILDREN AND PROTECTED PARTIES

This Practice Direction supplements CPR Part 21

General

1.1 In proceedings where one of the parties is a protected party, the protected party should be referred to in the title to the proceedings as 'A.B. (a protected party by C.D. his litigation friend)'.

1.2 In proceedings where one of the parties is a child, where –

    (1) the child has a litigation friend, the child should be referred to in the title to the proceedings as 'A.B. (a child by C.D. his litigation friend)'; or

    (2) the child is conducting the proceedings on his own behalf, the child should be referred to in the title as 'A.B. (a child)'.

1.3 A settlement of a claim by a child includes an agreement on a sum to be apportioned to a dependent child under the Fatal Accidents Act 1976.

The litigation friend

2.1 A person may become a litigation friend –

    (a) without a court order under rule 21.5, or

    (b) by a court order under rule 21.6.

2.2   A person who wishes to become a litigation friend without a court order pursuant to rule 21.5(3) must file a certificate of suitability in Practice Form N235 –

(a)   stating that he consents to act,

(b)   stating that he knows or believes that the [claimant] [defendant] [is a child][lacks capacity to conduct the proceedings],

(c)   in the case of a protected party, stating the grounds of his belief and, if his belief is based upon medical opinion or the opinion of another suitably qualified expert, attaching any relevant document to the certificate,

(d)   stating that he can fairly and competently conduct proceedings on behalf of the child or protected party and has no interest adverse to that of the child or protected party, and

(e)   where the child or protected party is a claimant, undertaking to pay any costs which the child or protected party may be ordered to pay in relation to the proceedings, subject to any right he may have to be repaid from the assets of the child or protected party.

2.3   The certificate of suitability must be verified by a statement of truth.

(Part 22 contains provisions about statements of truth.)

2.4   The litigation friend is not required to serve the document referred to in paragraph 2.2(c) when he serves a certificate of suitability on the person to be served under rule 21.5(4)(a).

Application for a court order appointing a litigation friend

3.1   Rule 21.6 sets out who may apply for an order appointing a litigation friend.

3.2   An application must be made in accordance with Part 23 and must be supported by evidence.

3.3   The evidence in support must satisfy the court that the proposed litigation friend –

(1)   consents to act,

(2)   can fairly and competently conduct proceedings on behalf of the child or protected party,

(3)   has no interest adverse to that of the child or protected party, and

(4)   where the child or protected party is a claimant, undertakes to pay any costs which the child or protected party may be ordered to pay in relation to the proceedings, subject to any right he may have to be repaid from the assets of the child or protected party.

3.4   Where it is sought to appoint the Official Solicitor as the litigation friend, provision must be made for payment of his charges.

Procedure where the need for a litigation friend has come to an end

4.1   Rule 21.9 deals with the situation where the need for a litigation friend comes to an end during the proceedings because either –

(1)   a child who is not also a protected party reaches the age of 18 (full age) during the proceedings, or

(2)   a protected party regains or acquires capacity to conduct the proceedings.

4.2   A child on reaching full age must serve on the other parties to the proceedings and file with the court a notice –

(1)   stating that he has reached full age,

(2)   stating that his litigation friend's appointment has ceased,

(3)   giving an address for service, and

(4)   stating whether or not he intends to carry on with or continue to defend the proceedings.

4.3   If the notice states that the child intends to carry on with or continue to defend the proceedings he must subsequently be described in the proceedings as 'A.B. (formerly a child but now of full age)'.

4.4   Whether or not a child having reached full age serves a notice in accordance with rule 21.9(4) and paragraph 4.2 above, a litigation friend may, at any time after the child has reached full age, serve a notice on the other parties that his appointment has ceased.

4.5   Where a protected party regains or acquires capacity to conduct the proceedings, an application under rule 21.9(3) must be made for an order under rule 21.9(2) that the litigation friend's appointment has ceased.

4.6   The application must be supported by the following evidence –

(1)   a medical report or other suitably qualified expert's report indicating that the protected party has regained or acquired capacity to conduct the proceedings,

(2)   a copy of any relevant order or declaration of the Court of Protection, and

(3)   if the application is made by the protected party, a statement whether or not he intends to carry on with or continue to defend the proceedings.

4.7   An order under rule 21.9(2) must be served on the other parties to the proceedings. The former protected party must file with the court a notice –

(1)   stating that his litigation friend's appointment has ceased,

(2)   giving an address for service, and

(3)   stating whether or not he intends to carry on with or continue to defend the proceedings.

Settlement or compromise by or on behalf of a child or protected party before the issue of proceedings

5.1   Where a claim by or on behalf of a child or protected party has been dealt with by agreement before the issue of proceedings and only the approval of the court to the agreement is sought, the claim must, in addition to containing the details of the claim and satisfying the requirements of rule 21.10(2), include the following –

(1)   subject to paragraph 5.3, the terms of the settlement or compromise or have attached to it a draft consent order in Practice Form N292;

(2)   details of whether and to what extent the defendant admits liability;

(3)   the age and occupation (if any) of the child or protected party;

(4)   the litigation friend's approval of the proposed settlement or compromise,

(5)   a copy of any financial advice relating to the proposed settlement; and

(6)   in a personal injury case arising from an accident –

(a)   details of the circumstances of the accident,

(b)   medical and quantum reports and joint statements material to the opinion required by paragraph 5.2,

(c)   where appropriate, a schedule of any past and future expenses and losses claimed and any other relevant information relating to the personal injury as set out in Practice Direction 16 (statements of case), and

(d)   where considerations of liability are raised –

(i)   any evidence or reports in any criminal proceedings or in an inquest, and

(ii)   details of any prosecution brought.

5.2

    (1)   An opinion on the merits of the settlement or compromise given by counsel or solicitor acting for the child or protected party must, except in very clear cases, be obtained.

    (2)   A copy of the opinion and, unless the instructions on which it was given are sufficiently set out in it, a copy of the instructions, must be supplied to the court.

5.3   Where in any personal injury case a claim for damages for future pecuniary loss is settled, the provisions in paragraphs 5.4 and 5.5 must in addition be complied with.

5.4   The court must be satisfied that the parties have considered whether the damages should wholly or partly take the form of periodical payments.

5.5   Where the settlement includes provision for periodical payments, the claim must –

    (1)   set out the terms of the settlement or compromise; or

    (2)   have attached to it a draft consent order,

which must satisfy the requirements of rules 41.8 and 41.9 as appropriate.

5.6   Applications for the approval of a settlement or compromise will normally be heard by –

    (1)   a Master or a district judge in proceedings involving a child; and

    (2)   a Master, designated civil judge or his nominee in proceedings involving a protected party.

(For information about provisional damages claims see Part 41 and Practice Direction 41A.)

Settlement or compromise by or on behalf of a child or protected party after proceedings have been issued

6.1   Where in any personal injury case a claim for damages for future pecuniary loss, by or on behalf of a child or protected party, is dealt with by agreement after proceedings have been issued, an application must be made for the court's approval of the agreement.

6.2   The court must be satisfied that the parties have considered whether the damages should wholly or partly take the form of periodical payments.

6.3   Where the settlement includes provision for periodical payments, an application under paragraph 6.1 must –

    (1)   set out the terms of the settlement or compromise; or

    (2)   have attached to it a draft consent order,

which must satisfy the requirements of rules 41.8 and 41.9 as appropriate.

6.4   The court must be supplied with –

    (1)   an opinion on the merits of the settlement or compromise given by counsel or solicitor acting for the child or protected party, except in very clear cases; and

    (2)   a copy of any financial advice; and

    (3)   documentary evidence material to the opinion referred to at paragraph 6.4(1).

6.5   Applications for the approval of a settlement or compromise, except at the trial, will normally be heard by –

    (1)   a Master or a district judge in proceedings involving a child; and

    (2)   a Master, designated civil judge or his nominee in proceedings involving a protected party.

Apportionment under the Fatal Accidents Act 1976

7.1 A judgment on or settlement in respect of a claim under the Fatal Accidents Act 1976 must be apportioned between the persons by or on whose behalf the claim has been brought.

7.2 Where a claim is brought on behalf of a dependent child or children, any settlement (including an agreement on a sum to be apportioned to a dependent child under the Fatal Accidents Act 1976) must be approved by the court.

7.3 The money apportioned to any dependent child must be invested on the child's behalf in accordance with rules 21.10 and 21.11 and paragraphs 8 and 9 below.

7.4 In order to approve an apportionment of money to a dependent child, the court will require the following information:

(1) the matters set out in paragraphs 5.1(2) and (3), and

(2) in respect of the deceased –

    (a) where death was caused by an accident, the matters set out in paragraphs 5.1(6)(a), (b) and (c), and

    (b) his future loss of earnings, and

(3) the extent and nature of the dependency.

Control of money recovered by or on behalf of a child or protected party

8.1 When giving directions under rule 21.11, the court –

(1) may direct the money to be paid into court for investment,

(2) may direct that certain sums be paid direct to the child or protected beneficiary, his litigation friend or his legal representative for the immediate benefit of the child or protected beneficiary or for expenses incurred on his behalf, and

(3) may direct that the application in respect of the investment of the money be transferred to a local district registry.

8.2 The court will consider the general aims to be achieved for the money in court (the fund) by investment and will give directions as to the type of investment.

8.3 Where a child also lacks capacity to manage and control any money recovered by him or on his behalf in the proceedings, and is likely to remain so on reaching full age, his fund should be administered as a protected beneficiary's fund.

8.4 Where a child or protected beneficiary is in receipt of publicly funded legal services the fund will be subject to a first charge under section 10 of the Access to Justice Act 1999 (statutory charge) and an order for the investment of money on the child's or protected beneficiary's behalf must contain a direction to that effect.

Investment on behalf of a child

9.1 At the hearing of an application for the approval of a settlement or compromise the litigation friend or his legal representative must provide, in addition to the information required by paragraphs 5 and 6 –

(1) a CFO form 320 (initial application for investment of damages) for completion by the judge hearing the application; and

(2) any evidence or information which the litigation friend wishes the court to consider in relation to the investment of the award for damages.

9.2 Following the hearing in paragraph 9.1, the court will forward to the Court Funds Office a request for investment decision (form 212) and the Court Funds Office will make the appropriate investment.

9.3 Where an award for damages for a child is made at trial, unless paragraph 9.7 applies, the trial judge will –

    (1) direct the money to be paid into court and placed into the special investment account until further investment directions have been given by the court;

    (2) direct the litigation friend to make an application to a Master or district judge for further investment directions; and

    (3) give such other directions as the trial judge thinks fit, including a direction that the hearing of the application for further investment directions will be fixed for a date within 28 days from the date of the trial.

9.4 The application under paragraph 9.3(2) must be made by filing with the court –

    (1) a completed CFO form 320; and

    (2) any evidence or information which the litigation friend wishes the court to consider in relation to the investment of the award for damages.

9.5 The application must be sent in proceedings in the Royal Courts of Justice to the Masters' Support Unit (Room E16) at the Royal Courts of Justice.

9.6 If the application required by paragraph 9.3(2) is not made to the court, the money paid into court in accordance with paragraph 9.3(1) will remain in the special investment account subject to any further order of the court or paragraph 9.8.

9.7 If the money to be invested is very small the court may order it to be paid direct to the litigation friend to be put into a building society account (or similar) for the child's use.

9.8 If the money is invested in court, it must be paid out to the child on application when he reaches full age.

Investment on behalf of a protected beneficiary

10.1 The Court of Protection has jurisdiction to make decisions in the best interests of a protected beneficiary. Fees may be charged for the administration of funds and these must be provided for in any settlement.

10.2 (1) Where the sum to be invested for the benefit of the protected beneficiary is £50,000 or more, (save where under paragraph 10.2A the Court of Protection has authorised a sum of £50,000 or more to be dealt with under subparagraph (2) below), unless a person with authority as –

    (a) the attorney under a registered enduring power of attorney;

    (b) the donee of a lasting power of attorney; or

    (c) the deputy appointed by the Court of Protection,

to administer or manage the protected beneficiary's financial affairs has been appointed, the order approving the settlement will contain a direction to the litigation friend to apply to the Court of Protection for the appointment of a deputy, after which the fund will be dealt with as directed by the Court of Protection; or

    (2) Where the sum to be invested for the benefit of the protected party is under £50,000, or such sum as may be authorised by the Court of Protection under paragraph 10.2A, it may be retained in court and invested in the same way as the fund of a child.

10.2A The Court of Protection may authorise a sum of £50,000 or more to be retained in court and invested it the same way as the fund of a child under subparagraph 10.2(2), either of its own initiative or at the request of the judge giving investment directions in respect of the protected beneficiary.

10.3 A form of order transferring the fund to the Court of Protection is set out in practice form N292.

10.4 In order for the Court Funds Office to release a fund which is subject to the statutory charge, the litigation friend or his legal representative or the person with authority referred to in paragraph 10.2(1) must provide the appropriate regional office of the Legal Services Commission with an undertaking in respect of a sum to cover their costs, following which the regional office will advise the Court Funds Office in writing of that sum, enabling them to transfer the balance to the Court of Protection on receipt of a CFO form 200 payment schedule authorised by the court.

10.5 The CFO form 200 should be completed and presented to the court where the settlement or trial took place for authorisation, subject to paragraphs 10.6 and 10.7.

10.6 Where the settlement took place in the Royal Courts of Justice the CFO form 200 must be completed and presented for authorisation –

    (1)   on behalf of a child, in the Masters' Support Unit, Room E105, and

    (2)   on behalf of a protected beneficiary, in the Judgment and Orders Section in the Action Department, Room E17.

10.7 Where the trial took place in the Royal Courts of Justice, the CFO form 200 is completed and authorised by the court officer.

Costs or expenses incurred by a litigation friend

11.1 A litigation friend may make a claim for costs or expenses under rule 21.12(1) –

    (1)   where the court has ordered an assessment of costs under rule rule 46.4(2), at the detailed assessment hearing;

    (1A) where the court has assessed the costs to be paid by the child by way of summary assessment under rule 46.4(5)(b), at the conclusion of the hearing at which damages to be paid to the child are assessed or at the hearing to approve the compromise or settlement under Part 21, or at any time thereafter;

    (2)   where the litigation friend's expenses are not of a type which would be recoverable as costs on an assessment of costs between the parties, to the Master or district judge at the hearing to approve the settlement or compromise under Part 21 (the Master or district judge may adjourn the matter to the costs judge); or

    (3)   where an assessment of costs under Part rule 46.4(2) is not required, and no approval under Part 21 is necessary, by a Part 23 application supported by a witness statement to a Costs Judge or district judge as appropriate.

11.2 In all circumstances, the litigation friend must support a claim for payment out in relation to costs or expenses by filing a witness statement setting out –

    (1)   the nature and amount of the costs or expense; and

    (2)   the reason the costs or expense were incurred.

11.3 Where the application is for payment out of the damages in respect of costs pursuant to rule 21.12(1A) the witness statement must also include (or be accompanied by) –

    (1)   a copy of the conditional fee agreement or damages based agreement;

    (2)   the risk assessment by reference to which the success fee was determined;

    (3)   the reasons why the particular funding model was selected;

    (4)   the advice given to the litigation friend in relation to funding arrangements;

    (5)   details of any costs agreed, recovered or fixed costs recoverable by the child; and

    (6)   confirmation of the amount of the sum agreed or awarded in respect of –

        (a)   general damages for pain, suffering and loss of amenity; and

        (b)   damages for pecuniary loss other than future pecuniary loss, net of any sums recoverable by the Compensation Recovery Unit of the Department for Work and Pensions.

Guardian's account

12   Paragraph 8 of Practice Direction 40A deals with the approval of the accounts of a guardian of assets of a child.

Payment out of funds in court

13.1 Applications to a Master or district judge

(1)   for payment out of money from the fund for the benefit of the child, or
(2)   to vary an investment strategy,

may be dealt with without a hearing unless the court directs otherwise.

13.2 When the child reaches full age –

(1)   where his fund in court is a sum of money, it will be paid out to him on application; or
(2)   where his fund is in the form of investments other than money (for example shares or unit trusts), the investments will on application be

(a)   sold and the proceeds of sale paid out to him; or
(b)   transferred into his name.

13.3 Where the fund is administered by the Court of Protection, any payment out of money from that fund must be in accordance with any decision or order of the Court of Protection.

13.4 If an application is required for the payment out of money from a fund administered by the Court of Protection, that application must be made to the Court of Protection.

(For further information on payments out of court, see Practice Direction 37.)

PART 57   PROBATE, INHERITANCE AND PRESUMPTION OF DEATH

Scope of this Part and definitions

57.1 (1)   This Part contains rules about –

    (a)   probate claims;

    (b)   claims for the rectification of wills; . . .

    (c)   claims and applications to –

        (i)   substitute another person for a personal representative; or

        (ii)   remove a personal representative; . . .

    (d)   claims under the Inheritance (Provision for Family and Dependants) Act 1975; and

    (e)   proceedings under the Presumption of Death Act 2013.

  (2)   In this Part:

    (a)   'probate claim' means a claim for –

        (i)   the grant of probate of the will, or letters of administration of the estate, of a deceased person;

        (ii)   the revocation of such a grant; or

        (iii)   a decree pronouncing for or against the validity of an alleged will;

    not being a claim which is non-contentious (or common form) probate business;

    (Section 128 of the Senior Courts Act 1981 defines non-contentious (or common form) probate business.)

    (b)   'relevant office' means –

        (i)   in the case of High Court proceedings in a Chancery district registry, that registry;

        (ii)   in the case of any other High Court proceedings, Chancery Chambers at the Royal Courts of Justice, Strand, London, WC2A 2LL; and

        (iii)   in the case of County Court proceedings, the office of the County Court hearing centre in question;

    (c)   'testamentary document' means a will, a draft of a will, written instructions for a will made by or at the request of, or under the instructions of, the testator, and any document purporting to be evidence of the contents, or to be a copy, of a will which is alleged to have been lost or destroyed;

    (d)   'will' includes a codicil.

I   PROBATE CLAIMS

General

57.2 (1)   This Section contains rules about probate claims.

  (2)   Probate claims in the High Court are assigned to the Chancery Division.

  (3)   Probate claims in the County Court must only be started by sending the claim to, or making the claim at –

    (a)   a County Court hearing centre where there is also a Chancery district registry; or

    (b)   the County Court at Central London.

(4)   All probate claims are allocated to the multi-track.

How to start a probate claim

57.3 A probate claim must be commenced –

(a)   in the relevant office; and
(b)   using the procedure in Part 7.

Acknowledgment of service and defence

57.4 (1)   A defendant who is served with a claim form must file an acknowledgment of service.

(2)   Subject to paragraph (3), the period for filing an acknowledgment of service is –

(a)   if the defendant is served with a claim form which states that particulars of claim are to follow, 28 days after service of the particulars of claim; and
(b)   in any other case, 28 days after service of the claim form.

(3)   If the claim form is served out of the jurisdiction under rule 6.32 or 6.33, the period for filing an acknowledgment of service is 14 days longer than the relevant period specified in rule 6.35 or Practice Direction 6B.

(4)   Rule 15(4) (which provides the period for filing a defence) applies as if the words 'under Part 10' were omitted from rule 15.4(1)(b).

Lodging of testamentary documents and filing of evidence about testamentary documents

57.5 (1)   Any testamentary document of the deceased person in the possession or control of any party must be lodged with the court.

(2)   Unless the court directs otherwise, the testamentary documents must be lodged in the relevant office –

(a)   by the claimant when the claim form is issued; and
(b)   by a defendant when he acknowledges service.

(3)   The claimant and every defendant who acknowledges service of the claim form must in written evidence –

(a)   describe any testamentary document of the deceased of which he has any knowledge or, if he does not know of any such testamentary document, state that fact, and
(b)   if any testamentary document of which he has knowledge is not in his possession or under his control, give the name and address of the person in whose possession or under whose control it is or, if he does not know the name or address of that person, state that fact.

(A specimen form for the written evidence about testamentary documents is annexed to Practice Direction 57.)

(4)   Unless the court directs otherwise, the written evidence required by paragraph (3) must be filed in the relevant office –

(a)   by the claimant, when the claim form is issued; and
(b)   by a defendant when he acknowledges service.

(5)   Except with the permission of the court, a party shall not be allowed to inspect the

testamentary documents or written evidence lodged or filed by any other party until he himself has lodged his testamentary documents and filed his evidence.

(6) The provisions of paragraphs (2) and (4) may be modified by a practice direction under this Part.

Revocation of existing grant

57.6 (1) In a probate claim which seeks the revocation of a grant of probate or letters of administration every person who is entitled, or claims to be entitled, to administer the estate under that grant must be made a party to the claim.

(2) If the claimant is the person to whom the grant was made, he must lodge the probate or letters of administration in the relevant office when the claim form is issued.

(3) If a defendant has the probate or letters of administration under his control, he must lodge it in the relevant office when he acknowledges service.

(4) Paragraphs (2) and (3) do not apply where the grant has already been lodged at the court, which in this paragraph includes the Principal Registry of the Family Division or a district probate registry.

Contents of statements of case

57.7 (1) The claim form must contain a statement of the nature of the interest of the claimant and of each defendant in the estate.

(2) If a party disputes another party's interest in the estate he must state this in his statement of case and set out his reasons.

(3) Any party who contends that at the time when a will was executed the testator did not know of and approve its contents must give particulars of the facts and matters relied on.

(4) Any party who wishes to contend that –

(a) a will was not duly executed;

(b) at the time of the execution of a will the testator lacked testamentary capacity; or

(c) the execution of a will was obtained by undue influence or fraud,

must set out the contention specifically and give particulars of the facts and matters relied on.

(5) (a) A defendant may give notice in his defence that he does not raise any positive case, but insists on the will being proved in solemn form and, for that purpose, will cross- examine the witnesses who attested the will.

(b) If a defendant gives such a notice, the court will not make an order for costs against him unless it considers that there was no reasonable ground for opposing the will.

Counterclaim

57.8 (1) A defendant who contends that he has any claim or is entitled to any remedy relating to the grant of probate of the will, or letters of administration of the estate, of the deceased person must serve a counterclaim making that contention.

(2) If the claimant fails to serve particulars of claim within the time allowed, the defendant may, with the permission of the court, serve a counterclaim and the probate claim shall then proceed as if the counterclaim were the particulars of claim.

Probate counterclaim in other proceedings

57.9 (1) In this rule 'probate counterclaim' means a counterclaim in any claim other than a probate claim by which the defendant claims any such remedy as is mentioned in rule 57.1(2)(a).

(2) Subject to the following paragraphs of this rule, this Part shall apply with the necessary modifications to a probate counterclaim as it applies to a probate claim.

(3) A probate counterclaim must contain a statement of the nature of the interest of each of the parties in the estate of the deceased to which the probate counterclaim relates.

(4) Unless an application notice is issued within 7 days after the service of a probate counterclaim for an order under rule 3.1(2)(e) or 3.4 for the probate counterclaim to be dealt with in separate proceedings or to be struck out, and the application is granted, the court will order the transfer of the proceedings to either –

(a) the Chancery Division (if it is not already assigned to that Division) and to either the Royal Courts of Justice or a Chancery district registry (if it is not already proceeding in one of those places); or

(b) if the County Court has jurisdiction, to a County Court hearing centre where there is also a Chancery District Registry or the County Court at Central London.

(5) If an order is made that a probate counterclaim be dealt with in separate proceedings, the order shall order the transfer of the probate counterclaim as required under paragraph (4).

Failure to acknowledge service or to file a defence

57.10(1) A default judgment cannot be obtained in a probate claim and rule 10.2 and Part 12 do not apply.

(2) If any of several defendants fails to acknowledge service the claimant may –

(a) after the time for acknowledging service has expired; and

(b) upon filing written evidence of service of the claim form and (if no particulars of claim were contained in or served with the claim form) the particulars of claim on that defendant;

proceed with the probate claim as if that defendant had acknowledged service.

(3) If no defendant acknowledges service or files a defence then, unless on the application of the claimant the court orders the claim to be discontinued, the claimant may, after the time for acknowledging service or for filing a defence (as the case may be) has expired, apply to the court for an order that the claim is to proceed to trial.

(4) When making an application under paragraph (3) the claimant must file written evidence of service of the claim form and (if no particulars of claim were contained in or served with the claim form) the particulars of claim on each of the defendants.

(5) Where the court makes an order under paragraph (3), it may direct that the claim be tried on written evidence.

Discontinuance and dismissal

57.11 (1) Part 38 does not apply to probate claims.

(2) At any stage of a probate claim the court, on the application of the claimant or of any defendant who has acknowledged service, may order that –

(a)   the claim be discontinued or dismissed on such terms as to costs or otherwise as it thinks just; and

(b)   a grant of probate of the will, or letters of administration of the estate, of the deceased person be made to the person entitled to the grant.

II   RECTIFICATION OF WILLS

Rectification of wills

57.12 (1)   This Section contains rules about claims for the rectification of a will.

(Section 20 of the Administration of Justice Act 1982 provides for rectification of a will. Additional provisions are contained in rule 55 of the Non-Contentious Probate Rules 19872.)

(2)   Every personal representative of the estate shall be joined as a party.

(3)   Practice Direction 57 makes provision for lodging the grant of probate or letters of administration with the will annexed in a claim under this Section.

III   SUBSTITUTION AND REMOVAL OF PERSONAL REPRESENTATIVES

Substitution and removal of personal representatives

57.13 (1)   This Section contains rules about claims and applications for substitution or removal of a personal representative.

(2)   Claims under this Section must be brought in the High Court and are assigned to the Chancery Division.

(Section 50 of the Administration of Justice Act 1985 gives the High Court power to appoint a substitute for, or to remove, a personal representative.)

(3)   Every personal representative of the estate shall be joined as a party.

(4)   Practice Direction 57 makes provision for lodging the grant of probate or letters of administration in a claim under this Section.

(5)   If substitution or removal of a personal representative is sought by application in existing proceedings, this rule shall apply with references to claims being read as if they referred to applications.

IV   CLAIMS UNDER THE INHERITANCE (PROVISION FOR FAMILY AND DEPEND-ANTS) ACT 1975

Scope of this Section

57.14 This Section contains rules about claims under the Inheritance (Provision for Family and Dependants) Act 1975 ('the Act').

Proceedings in the High Court

57.15 (1)   Proceedings in the High Court under the Act shall be issued in either –

(a)   the Chancery Division; or

(b)   the Family Division.

(2)   The Civil Procedure Rules apply to proceedings under the Act which are brought

in the Family Division, except that the provisions of the Family Procedure Rules 2011 relating to the drawing up and service of orders apply instead of the provisions in Part 40 and Practice Direction 40B.

Procedure for claims under section 1 of the Act

57.16 (1) A claim under section 1 of the Act must be made by issuing a claim form in accordance with Part 8.

(2) Rule 8.3 (acknowledgment of service) and rule 8.5 (filing and serving written evidence) apply as modified by paragraphs (3) to (5) of this rule.

(3) The written evidence filed and served by the claimant with the claim form must, except in the circumstances specified in paragraph (3A), have exhibited to it an official copy of –

(a) the grant of probate or letters of administration in respect of the deceased's estate; and

(b) every testamentary document in respect of which probate or letters of administration were granted.

(3A) Where no grant has been obtained, the claimant may make a claim without naming a defendant and may apply for directions as to the representation of the estate. The written evidence must –

(a) explain the reasons why it has not been possible for a grant to be obtained;

(b) be accompanied by the original or a copy (if either is available) of the will or other testamentary document in respect of which probate or letters of administration are to be granted; and

(c) contain the following information, so far as known to the claimant –

(i) brief details of the property comprised in the estate, with an approximate estimate of its capital value and any income that is received from it;

(ii) brief details of the liabilities of the estate;

(iii) the names and addresses of the persons who are in possession of the documents relating to the estate; and

(iv) the names of the beneficiaries and their respective interests in the estate.

(3B) Where a claim is made in accordance with paragraph (3A), the court may give directions as to the parties to the claim and as to the representation of the estate either on the claimant's application or on its own initiative.

(Section 4 of the 1975 Act as amended confirms that nothing prevents the making of an application under the Act before representation with respect to the estate of the deceased person is taken out.).

(4) Subject to paragraph (4A), the time within which a defendant must file and serve –

(a) an acknowledgment of service; and

(b) any written evidence,

is not more than 21 days after service of the claim form on him.

(4A) If the claim form is served out of the jurisdiction under rule 6.32 or 6.33, the period for filing an acknowledgment of service and any written evidence is 7 days longer than the relevant period specified in rule 6.35 or Practice Direction 6B.

(5) A defendant who is a personal representative of the deceased must file and serve written evidence, which must include the information required by Practice Direction 57.

V PROCEEDINGS UNDER THE PRESUMPTION OF DEATH ACT 2013

Scope and interpretation

57.17 (1) This Section contains rules about proceedings under the Presumption of Death Act 2013.

(2) In this Section, terms used in the Presumption of Death Act 2013 Act have the meaning given by that Act, and –

(a) 'the 2013 Act' means the Presumption of Death Act 2013;

(b) 'a claim for a declaration of presumed death' means a claim under section 1 of the 2013 Act for a declaration that a missing person is presumed to be dead;

(c) 'a claim for a variation order' means a claim for an order under section 5 of the 2013 Act varying or revoking a declaration of presumed death.

Proceedings to be in the High Court

57.18 (1) Proceedings under the 2013 Act must be issued in the High Court in either –

(a) the Chancery Division; or

(b) the Family Division.

(2) The Civil Procedure Rules apply to proceedings under the 2013 Act which are brought in the Family Division, except that the provisions of the Family Procedure Rules 2010 relating to the drawing up and service of orders apply instead of the provisions in Part 40 and Practice Direction 40B.

Procedure for claims for a declaration of presumed death or a variation order

57.19 (1) A claim for a declaration of presumed death or for a variation order must be made by issuing a claim form in accordance with Part 8.

(2) In addition to the matters set out in rule 8.2 (contents of the claim form), the claim form must also include or be accompanied by the information required by Practice Direction 57B.

(3) Rules 8.2A, 8.3, 8.4 and 8.5 apply as modified by paragraphs (4) to (7) of this rule (and references elsewhere in these Rules to a defendant and to an acknowledgment of service are, where relevant, to be read as references to the substitute terms in rules 8.2A, 8.3, 8.4 and 8.5 as so modified).

(4) Rule 8.2A (issue of claim form without naming defendants) applies as if for 'without naming a defendant' in paragraph (1) there were substituted 'without serving notice on any person'.

(5) Rule 8.3 (acknowledgment of service) applies –

(a) as if, instead of referring to a defendant, it referred to a person giving notice of intention to intervene or applying for permission to intervene, as the case may be;

(b) as if, instead of referring to an acknowledgment of service, it referred to a notice of intention to intervene or an application for permission to intervene, as the case may be; and

(c) subject to paragraph (7), with the substitution of 21 days for 14 days as the time within which the notice of intention to intervene or application for permission to intervene must be filed and served.

(6) Rules 8.4 (consequence of not filing an acknowledgment of service) and 8.5 (filing and serving written evidence) apply –

    (a) as if, instead of referring to a defendant, they referred to a person giving notice of intention to intervene or applying for permission to intervene, as the case may be; and

    (b) as if, instead of referring to an acknowledgment of service, they referred to a notice of intention to intervene or an application for permission to intervene, as the case may be.

(7) If the claim form is served out of the jurisdiction under rule 6.32 or 6.33, the period for filing notice of intention to intervene or an application for permission to intervene, as the case may be, and any written evidence, is 7 days longer than the relevant period for serving an acknowledgement of service specified in rule 6.35 or Practice Direction 6B.

Giving notice of claim

57.20(1) Where the claim is for a declaration of presumed death, the claimant must give notice of the claim by serving a copy of it on the following persons (where not the claimant) –

    (a) the spouse or civil partner of the missing person;

    (b) any parent of the missing person;

    (c) any child of the missing person;

    (d) any sibling of the missing person;

    (e) if there are no persons within sub-paragraphs (a) to (d), the nearest relative of the missing person known to the claimant; and

    (f) any other person (including in particular any insurance company) appearing to the claimant to have an interest in the claim.

(2) Where the claim is for a variation order, the claimant must give notice of the claim by serving a copy of it on the following persons (where not the claimant) –

    (a) the person who was the claimant for the declaration of presumed death or (as the case may be) previous variation order which it is sought to have varied or revoked;

    (b) the spouse or civil partner of the missing person;

    (c) any parent of the missing person;

    (d) any child of the missing person;

    (e) any sibling of the missing person;

    (f) if there are no persons within sub-paragraphs (b) to (e), the nearest relative of the missing person known to the claimant; and

    (g) any other person (including in particular any insurance company) appearing to the claimant to have an interest in the claim.

(3) Notice under paragraph (1)(a) to (f) or paragraph (2)(a) to (g) must be given within 7 days after the claim is issued.

Advertisement of claim

57.21 (1) The claimant (whether the claim is for a declaration of presumed death or for a variation order) must, within 7 days of issue of the claim, ensure that notice of the claim is published –

(a) in a form which meets the requirements set out in Practice Direction 57B; and
(b) in at least one newspaper circulating in the vicinity of the last known address of the missing person.

(2) The claimant must, at least 5 days before the hearing, file a copy of the page of the newspaper bearing the advertisement of notice of the claim required by paragraph (1) and the date on which it was published.

Interveners

57.22 (1) The Attorney General, or a person who is entitled to intervene in proceedings under section 11(1), must first notify the court of the intention to intervene in accordance with the requirements of Practice Direction 57B.
(2) Any other person who wishes to intervene in such proceedings must submit an application for permission to intervene in accordance with the requirements of Practice Direction 57B.
(3) Where the court grants permission to intervene, it may do so on conditions and may give case management directions.
(4) The court may direct that a person who intervenes in proceedings, other than the Attorney General, be joined as a claimant or defendant.

Requirement to provide information

57.23 (1) An application for an order under section 12(1) of the 2013 Act must be supported by evidence and must in particular –

(a) specify or describe the information in respect of which the order is sought;
(b) set out the reasons why the person making the application believes that the person against whom the order is sought is likely to have such information; and
(c) include any further details, where known, of the missing person which are likely to assist in providing the information sought.

(2) The person making the application must serve a copy of the application notice on the person against whom the order is sought, and on every other party to the proceedings (within the meaning of section 20(2) of the 2013 Act), at least 14 days before the date fixed for the hearing of the application.
(3) An application for discharge or variation under section 12(6) of an order made under section 12(1) may be made without notice unless the court directs otherwise.

PRACTICE DIRECTION 57 – PROBATE

This Practice Direction supplements Part 57

I   PROBATE CLAIMS

General

1.1 This Section of this practice direction applies to contentious probate claims.
1.2 The rules and procedure relating to non-contentious probate proceedings (also known as 'common form') are the Non-Contentious Probate Rules 1987 as amended.

How to start a probate claim

2.1   A claim form and all subsequent court documents relating to a probate claim must be marked at the top 'In the estate of [name] deceased (Probate)'.

2.2   The claim form must be issued out of –

     (1)   Chancery Chambers at the Royal Courts of Justice; or

     (2)   one of the Chancery district registries; or

     (3)   if the claim is suitable to be heard in the County Court –

         (a)   a County Court hearing centre in a place where there is also a Chancery district registry; or

         (b)   the County Court at Central London.

There are Chancery district registries at Birmingham, Bristol, Caernarfon, Cardiff, Leeds, Liverpool, Manchester, Mold, Newcastle upon Tyne and Preston.

(Section 32 of the County Courts Act 1984 identifies which probate claims may be heard in the County Court.)

2.3   When the claim form is issued, the relevant office will send a notice to Leeds District Probate Registry, Coronet House, Queen Street, Leeds, LS1 2BA, DX 26451 Leeds (Park Square), telephone 0113 243 1505, requesting that all testamentary documents, grants of representation and other relevant documents currently held at any probate registry are sent to the relevant office.

2.4   The commencement of a probate claim will, unless a court otherwise directs, prevent any grant of probate or letters of administration being made until the probate claim has been disposed of.

(Rule 45 of the Non-Contentious Probate Rules 1987 makes provision for notice of the probate claim to be given, and section 117 of the Senior Courts Act 1981 for the grant of letters of administration pending the determination of a probate claim. Paragraph 8 of this practice direction makes provision about an application for such a grant.)

Testamentary documents and evidence about testamentary documents

3.1   Unless the court orders otherwise, if a testamentary document is held by the court (whether it was lodged by a party or it was previously held at a probate registry) when the claim has been disposed of the court will send it to the Leeds District Probate Registry.

3.2   The written evidence about testamentary documents required by this Part –

     (1)   should be in the form annexed to this practice direction; and

     (2)   must be signed by the party personally and not by his solicitor or other representative (except that if the party is a child or protected party the written evidence must be signed by his litigation friend).

3.3   In a case in which there is urgent need to commence a probate claim (for example, in order to be able to apply immediately for the appointment of an administrator pending the determination of the claim) and it is not possible for the claimant to lodge the testamentary documents or to file the evidence about testamentary documents in the relevant office at the same time as the claim form is to be issued, the court may direct that the claimant shall be allowed to issue the claim form upon his giving an undertaking to the court to lodge the documents and file the evidence within such time as the court shall specify.

Case management

4   In giving case management directions in a probate claim the court will give considera-
     tion to the questions –

   (1)   whether any person who may be affected by the claim and who is not joined as a
        party should be joined as a party or given notice of the claim, whether under rule
        19.8A or otherwise; and

   (2)   whether to make a representation order under rule 19.6 or rule 19.7.

Summary judgment

5.1   If an order pronouncing for a will in solemn form is sought on an application for
       summary judgment, the evidence in support of the application must include written
       evidence proving due execution of the will.

5.2   If a defendant has given notice in his defence under rule 57.7(5) that he raises no
       positive case but –

   (1)   he insists that the will be proved in solemn form; and

   (2)   for that purpose he will cross-examine the witnesses who attested the will;

any application by the claimant for summary judgment is subject to the right of that
defendant to require those witnesses to attend court for cross-examination.

Settlement of a probate claim

6.1   If at any time the parties agree to settle a probate claim, the court may –

   (1)   order the trial of the claim on written evidence, which will lead to a grant in
        solemn form;

   (2)   order that the claim be discontinued or dismissed under rule 57.11, which will
        lead to a grant in common form; or

   (3)   pronounce for or against the validity of one or more wills under section 49 of the
        Administration of Justice Act 1985.

(For a form of order which is also applicable to discontinuance and which may be
adapted as appropriate, see Practice Form No. CH38)

(Section 49 of the Administration of Justice Act 1985 permits a probate claim to be
compromised without a trial if every 'relevant beneficiary', as defined in that section,
has consented to the proposed order. It is only available in the High Court.)

6.2   Applications under section 49 of the Administration of Justice Act 1985 may be heard
       by a master or district judge and must be supported by written evidence identifying the
       relevant beneficiaries and exhibiting the written consent of each of them. The written
       evidence of testamentary documents required by rule 57.5 will still be necessary.

Application for an order to bring in a will, etc.

7.1   Any party applying for an order under section 122 of the Senior Courts Act 1981 ('the
       1981 Act') must serve the application notice on the person against whom the order is
       sought.

(Section 122 of the 1981 Act empowers the court to order a person to attend court for
examination, and to answer questions and bring in documents, if there are reasonable
grounds for believing that such person has knowledge of a testamentary document.
Rule 50(1) of the Non-Contentious Probate Rules 1987 makes similar provision where
a probate claim has not been commenced.)

7.2 An application for the issue of a witness summons under section 123 of the 1981 Act –

    (1)   may be made without notice; and

    (2)   must be supported by written evidence setting out the grounds of the application.

(Section 123 of the 1981 Act empowers the court, where it appears that any person has in his possession, custody or power a testamentary document, to issue a witness summons ordering such person to bring in that document. Rule 50(2) of the Non-Contentious Probate Rules makes similar provision where a probate claim has not been commenced.)

7.3 An application under section 122 or 123 of the 1981 Act should be made to a master or district judge.

7.4 A person against whom a witness summons is issued under section 123 of the 1981 Act who denies that the testamentary document referred to in the witness summons is in his possession or under his control may file written evidence to that effect.

Administration pending the determination of a probate claim

8.1 An application under section 117 of the Senior Courts Act 1981 for an order for the grant of administration pending the determination of a probate claim should be made by application notice in the probate claim.

8.2 If an order for a grant of administration is made under section 117 of the 1981 Act –

    (1)   Rules 69.4 to 69.7 shall apply as if the administrator were a receiver appointed by the court;

    (2)   if the court allows the administrator remuneration under rule 69.7, it may make an order under section 117(3) of the 1981 Act assigning the remuneration out of the estate of the deceased; and

    (3)   every application relating to the conduct of the administration shall be made by application notice in the probate claim.

8.3 An order under section 117 may be made by a master or district judge.

8.4 If an order is made under section 117 an application for the grant of letters of administration should be made to the Principal Registry of the Family Division, First Avenue House, 42–49 High Holborn, London WC1V 6NP.

8.5 The appointment of an administrator to whom letters of administration are granted following an order under section 117 will cease automatically when a final order in the probate claim is made but will continue pending any appeal.

II RECTIFICATION OF WILLS

Scope of this Section

9. This Section of this practice direction applies to claims for the rectification of a will.

Lodging the grant

10.1 If the claimant is the person to whom the grant was made in respect of the will of which rectification is sought, he must, unless the court orders otherwise, lodge the probate or letters of administration with the will annexed with the court when the claim form is issued.

10.2 If a defendant has the probate or letters of administration in his possession or under his control, he must, unless the court orders otherwise, lodge it in the relevant office within 14 days after the service of the claim form on him.

Orders

11. A copy of every order made for the rectification of a will shall be sent to the Principal Registry of the Family Division for filing, and a memorandum of the order shall be endorsed on, or permanently annexed to, the grant under which the estate is administered.

III   SUBSTITUTION AND REMOVAL OF PERSONAL REPRESENTATIVES

Scope of this Section

12. This Section of this practice direction applies to claims and applications for substitution or removal of a personal representative. If substitution or removal of a personal representative is sought by application in existing proceedings, this Section shall apply with references to the claim, claim form and claimant being read as if they referred to the application, application notice and applicant respectively.

Starting the claim

13.1 The claim form must be accompanied by –

    (1)   either –

        (a)   a sealed or certified copy of the grant of probate or letters of administration, or

        (b)   where the claim is to substitute or remove an executor and is made before a grant of probate has been issued, the original or, if the original is not available, a copy of the will; and

    (2)   written evidence containing the grounds of the claim and the following information so far as it is known to the claimant –

        (a)   brief details of the property comprised in the estate, with an approximate estimate of its capital value and any income that is received from it;

        (b)   brief details of the liabilities of the estate;

        (c)   the names and addresses of the persons who are in possession of the documents relating to the estate;

        (d)   the names of the beneficiaries and their respective interests in the estate; and

        (e)   the name, address and occupation of any proposed substituted personal representative.

13.2 If the claim is for the appointment of a substituted personal representative, the claim form must be accompanied by –

    (1)   a signed or (in the case of the Public Trustee or a corporation) sealed consent to act; and

    (2)   written evidence as to the fitness of the proposed substituted personal representative, if an individual, to act.

Production of the grant

14.1 On the hearing of the claim the personal representative must produce to the Court the grant of representation to the deceased's estate.

14.2 If an order is made substituting or removing the personal representative, the grant (together with a sealed copy of the order) must be sent to and remain in the custody of the Principal Registry of the Family Division until a memorandum of the order has been endorsed on or permanently annexed to the grant.

14.3 Where the claim is to substitute or remove an executor and the claim is made before a grant of probate has been issued, paragraphs 14.1 and 14.2 do not apply. Where in such a case an order is made substituting or removing an executor a sealed copy of the order must be sent to the Principal Registry of the Family Division where it will be recorded and retained pending any application for a grant. An order sent to the Principal Registry in accordance with this paragraph must be accompanied by a note of the full name and date of death of the deceased, if it is not apparent on the face of the order.

IV CLAIMS UNDER THE INHERITANCE (PROVISIONS FOR FAMILY AND DEPEND-ANTS) ACT 1975

Acknowledgment of service by personal representative – rule 57.16(4)

15. Where a defendant who is a personal representative wishes to remain neutral in relation to the claim, and agrees to abide by any decision which the court may make, he should state this in Section A of the acknowledgment of service form.

Written evidence of personal representative – rule 57.16(5)

16. The written evidence filed by a defendant who is a personal representative must state to the best of that person's ability –

    (1) full details of the value of the deceased's net estate, as defined in section 25(1) of the Act;

    (2) the person or classes of persons beneficially interested in the estate, and –

        (a) the names and (unless they are parties to the claim) addresses of all living beneficiaries; and

        (b) the value of their interests in the estate so far as they are known.

    (3) whether any living beneficiary (and if so, naming him) is a child or a person who lacks capacity (within the meaning of the Mental Capacity Act 2005); and

    (4) any facts which might affect the exercise of the court's powers under the Act.

Separate representation of claimants

17. If a claim is made jointly by two or more claimants, and it later appears that any of the claimants have a conflict of interests –

    (1) any claimant may choose to be represented at any hearing by separate solicitors or counsel, or may appear in person; and

    (2) if the court considers that claimants who are represented by the same solicitors or counsel ought to be separately represented, it may adjourn the application until they are.

Production of the grant

18.1 On the hearing of a claim the personal representative must produce to the court the original grant of representation to the deceased's estate.

18.2 If the court makes an order under the Act, the original grant (together with a sealed copy of the order) must be sent to the Principal Registry of the Family Division for a memorandum of the order to be endorsed on or permanently annexed to the grant in accordance with section 19(3) of the Act.

18.3 Every final order embodying terms of compromise made in proceedings under the Act, whether made with or without a hearing, must contain a direction that a memorandum of the order shall be endorsed on or permanently annexed to the probate or letters of administration and a copy of the order shall be sent to the Principal Registry of the Family Division with the relevant grant of probate or letters of administration for endorsement.

ANNEX: A form of witness statement or affidavit about testamentary documents

(CPR rule 57.5)

(Title of the claim)

I [name and address] the claimant/defendant in this claim state [on oath] that I have no knowledge of any document –

(i)   being or purported to be or having the form or effect of a will or codicil of [name of deceased] whose estate is the subject of this claim;
(ii) being or purporting to be a draft or written instructions for any such will or codicil made by or at the request of or under the instructions of the deceased;
(iii) being or purporting to be evidence of the contents or a copy of any such will or codicil which is alleged to have been lost or destroyed,

except . . . [describe any testamentary document of the deceased, and if any such document is not in your control, give the name and address of the person who you believe has possession or control of it, or state that you do not know the name and address of that person] . . .

[I believe that the facts stated in this witness statement are true] [or jurat for affidavit]

(NOTE: 'testamentary document' is defined in CPR rule 57.1)

PRACTICE DIRECTION 57B – PROCEEDINGS UNDER THE PRESUMPTION OF DEATH ACT 2013

This Practice Direction supplements CPR Part 57

Procedure for claims – Rule 57.19

Claim for declaration of presumed death – claim form

1.1   The claim form for a claim for a declaration of presumed death must include or be accompanied by the following (where known) –

(1)   Information about the claimant

(a)   the claimant's name and address;
(b)   the relationship of the claimant to the missing person; and
(c)   if the claimant is not the missing person's spouse, civil partner, parent, child or sibling, details of the claimant's interest in the determination of the application;

(2)   Information about the missing person

     (a)   the missing person's name and surname, and any other names by which the missing person is or has formerly been known;

     (b)   the missing person's gender;

     (c)   the missing person's maiden surname (if any);

     (d)   the missing person's date and place of birth;

     (e)   the occupation of the missing person;

     (f)   the occupation, name and surname of –

          (i)   the missing person's spouse or civil partner (or late spouse or civil partner if the marriage or civil partnership ended on death);

          (ii)   where the missing person was under 16 years of age, the missing person's parents;

     (g)   the missing person's National Insurance number;

     (h)   the date on which missing person is thought to have died, or on which the missing person was last known have been alive;

     (i)   on which of the grounds in section 1(4) of the 2013 Act the court is considered to have jurisdiction to entertain the claim;

     (j)   the usual or last known address of the missing person; and

     (k)   the name and address of the spouse or civil partner, parents, children or siblings of the missing person (if any, and if not the claimant);

(3)   Information about steps taken to trace the missing person

     (a)   details of any enquiries made or other steps taken to trace the missing person or confirm when the missing person was last known to be alive; and

     (b)   details of the results of such enquiries or other steps;

(4)   Information about the missing person's property

     (a)   an estimate of the total value of the assets of the missing person;

     (b)   details of property owned by the missing person; and

     (c)   details of the interest of any other person in the missing person's property which it is sought to have determined by the court; and

(5)   Information about advertisement and recipients of notice of the claim

     (a)   details of the newspaper in which the claimant proposes to advertise the claim; and

     (b)   details of the persons to whom the claimant is giving notice of the claim and, where notice is being given to a person under rule 57.20(1)(f), the nature of that person's interest in the claim.

Claim for variation order

1.2 The claim form for a variation order must include or be accompanied by the following (where known) –

(1)   Information about the claimant

     (a)   the claimant's name and address;

     (b)   the relationship of the claimant to the missing person; and

     (c)   details of the claimant's interest in the determination of the application;

(2)   Information about previous claim and missing person's property

     (a)   details of the declaration of presumed death or (as the case may be) previous variation order which it is sought to have varied or revoked;

(b)   details of the circumstances which are claimed to justify a variation order, and evidence of the enquiries made and other steps taken to verify them and their outcomes; and

(c)   details of any interest in property acquired as a result of the declaration of presumed death or (as the case may be) previous variation order which it is sought to have varied or revoked; and

(3)   Information about advertisement and recipients of notice of the claim

(a)   details of the newspaper in which the claimant proposes to advertise the claim; and

(b)   details of the persons to whom the claimant is giving notice of the claim and, where notice is being given to a person under rule 57.20(2)(g), the nature of that person's interest in the claim.

Issue of claim form without serving notice on any person

1.3   For the purposes of rule 8.2A as modified by rule 57.19, an application for permission to issue a claim form, whether the claim is for a declaration or presumed death or for a variation order, may be made only where the claimant believes there to be no person within paragraph (1)(a) to (f) or paragraph (2)(a) to (g) of rule 57.20. The application must explain why the claimant believes that there is no such person.

Case management – first directions hearing

1.4   A claim (whether for a declaration of presumed death or for a variation order) must be listed for case management directions either –

(a)   more than 28 days (but where practicable no more than 56 days) after issue; or

(b)   where the claim form has been served outside the jurisdiction, more than 7 days (but where practicable no more than 35 days) after the period forfiling provided for by rule 57.19(7), to allow for time for those served with notice of the claim or who respond to the advertisement of the claim to file notice of intention to intervene or an application for permission to intervene as the case may be.

1.5   The court must notify all those who have filed notice of intention to intervene or an application for permission to intervene of the date of the directions hearing.

Advertisement of claim – Rule 57.21

2.1   The advertisement of the claim required by section 9(2) of the 2013 Act and rule 57.21(1)(a) must be in the form set out below, or contain the equivalent information about the claim and the possibility of applying, and where and by when to apply, to the Court –

IN THE HIGH COURT OF JUSTICE
[CHANCERY] [FAMILY] DIVISION
Case Number . . . . . .
IN THE MATTER OF AN APPLICATION FOR A DECLARATION OF THE PRESUMED DEATH OF (INSERT NAME)
A claim has been issued in the High Court of Justice, for a [declaration] [variation of a declaration] that (insert name), whose last known address was (insert address) is presumed to be dead. Any person having an interest may apply to the Court to intervene in the matter.

If you wish to apply to the Court, you should do so at [Court address] as soon as possible, and if possible within 21 days of the date of this notice. Delay may harm your prospects of being able to intervene.

[If the claimant is legally represented]

(Name)

Claimant's Legal Representative

(Address)

[If the claimant is not legally represented]

(Claimant's address for service)

Interveners – Rule 57.22

3.1 The Attorney General, or a person who is entitled to intervene in the proceedings by virtue of section 11(1) (the missing person's spouse, civil partner, parent, child or sibling) should notify the intention to intervene as early as possible by filing, and serving on the claimant, notice in writing, specifying –

    (a)   the intervener's name and address;

    (b)   the intervener's relationship to the missing person (where the intervener is not the Attorney General);

    (c)   the reasons for intervening; and

    (d)   particulars of any determination or order sought under section 11(4)(b) or (c) of the 2013 Act.

3.2 An application under rule 57.22(2) for permission to intervene must be served on the claimant and must specify –

    (a)   the applicant's relationship to the missing person or other interest in the proceedings;

    (b)   the reasons for seeking to intervene; and

    (c)   particulars of any determination or order sought under section 11(4)(b) or (c) of the 2013 Act.

PART 64   ESTATES, TRUSTS AND CHARITIES

General

64.1 (1)   This Part contains rules –

(a)   in Section I, about claims relating to –

(i)   the administration of estates of deceased persons, and
(ii)   trusts; and

(b)   in Section II, about charity proceedings.

(2)   In this Part and Practice Directions 64A and 64B, where appropriate, references to trustees include executors and administrators.

(3)   All proceedings in the High Court to which this Part applies must be brought in the Chancery Division.

I   CLAIMS RELATING TO THE ADMINISTRATION OF ESTATES AND TRUSTS

Scope of this Section

64.2 This Section of this Part applies to claims –

(a)   for the court to determine any question arising in –

(i)   the administration of the estate of a deceased person; or
(ii)   the execution of a trust;

(b)   for an order for the administration of the estate of a deceased person, or the execution of a trust, to be carried out under the direction of the court ('an administration order');

(c)   under the Variation of Trusts Act 1958; or

(d)   under section 48 of the Administration of Justice Act 19852

Claim form

64.3 A claim to which this Section applies must be made by issuing a Part 8 claim form.

Parties

64.4 (1)   In a claim to which this Section applies, other than an application under section 48 of the Administration of Justice Act 1985 –

(a)   all the trustees must be parties;

(b)   if the claim is made by trustees, any of them who does not consent to being a claimant must be made a defendant; and

(c)   the claimant may make parties to the claim any persons with an interest in or claim against the estate, or an interest under the trust, who it is appropriate to make parties having regard to the nature of the order sought.

(2)   In addition, in a claim under the Variation of Trusts Act 1958, unless the court directs otherwise any person who –

(a)   created the trust; or

(b)   provided property for the purposes of the trust,

must, if still alive, be made a party to the claim.

(The court may, under rule 19.2, order additional persons to be made parties to a claim.)

II CHARITY PROCEEDINGS

Scope of this Section and interpretation

64.5 (1) This Section applies to charity proceedings.

(2) In this Section –

(a) 'the Act' means the Charities Act 1993;

(b) 'charity proceedings' has the same meaning as in section 33(8) of the Act; and

(c) 'the Commission' means the Charity Commission for England and Wales.

Application for permission to take charity proceedings

64.6 (1) An application to the High Court under section 33(5) of the Act for permission to start charity proceedings must be made within 21 days after the refusal by the Commission of an order authorising proceedings.

(2) The application must be made by issuing a Part 8 claim form, which must contain the information specified in Practice Direction 64A.

(3) The Commission must be made defendants to the claim, but the claim form need not be served on them or on any other person.

(4) The judge considering the application may direct the Commission to file a written statement of their reasons for their decision.

(5) The court will serve on the applicant a copy of any statement filed under paragraph (4).

(6) The judge may either –

(a) give permission without a hearing; or

(b) fix a hearing.

PRACTICE DIRECTION 64A – ESTATES, TRUSTS AND CHARITIES

This Practice Direction supplements Part 64

I CLAIMS RELATING TO THE ADMINISTRATION OF ESTATES AND TRUSTS

Examples of claims under rule 64.2(a)

1 The following are examples of the types of claims which may be made under rule 64.2(a) –

(1) a claim for the determination of any of the following questions –

(a) any question as to who is included in any class of persons having –

(i) a claim against the estate of a deceased person;

(ii) a beneficial interest in the estate of such a person; or

(iii) a beneficial interest in any property subject to a trust;

(b) any question as to the rights or interests of any person claiming –

        (i)   to be a creditor of the estate of a deceased person;

        (ii)   to be entitled under a will or on the intestacy of a deceased person; or

        (iii)   to be beneficially entitled under a trust;

(2)   a claim for any of the following remedies –

    (a)   an order requiring a trustee –

        (i)   to provide and, if necessary, verify accounts;

        (ii)   to pay into court money which he holds in that capacity; or

        (iii)   to do or not to do any particular act;

    (b)   an order approving any sale, purchase, compromise or other transaction by a trustee (whether administrative or dispositive); or

    (c)   an order directing any act to be done which the court could order to be done if the estate or trust in question were being administered or executed under the direction of the court.

Determining certain claims under rule 64.2(a) without a hearing

1A.1 Where a claim is made by a trustee for a remedy within paragraph 1(2)(b) (including a case where the remedy sought is approval of a transaction affected by conflict of interests or duties), the court may be requested to determine the claim without a hearing.

1A.2 The claim form in such a case may be issued in accordance with rule 8.2A (Issue of claim form without naming defendants), and no separate application for permission under rule 8.2A need be made.

1A.3 The claim form must be accompanied by –

    (a)   a witness statement setting out the material facts justifying determination without a hearing and in particular –

        (i)   identifying those affected by the remedy sought and

        (ii)   detailing any consultation of those so affected and the result of that consultation;

    (b)   the advice of a lawyer having a 10-year High Court qualification within the meaning of section 71 of the Courts and Legal Services Act 1990 on the merits of the claim;

    (c)   a draft order for the remedy sought;

    (d)   a statement of costs.

1A.4 If the court considers that the case does not require an oral hearing, it will proceed to consider the claim on the papers.

1A.5 If the court considers that an oral hearing is required, it will give appropriate directions.

1A.6 If the court considers it appropriate, it will make the order sought and may direct that the claimant must –

    (a)   serve notice of the order on the interested parties in accordance with rule 19.8A, and

    (b)   file a certificate of service within 7 days of doing so.

Applications by trustees for directions

2   A separate practice direction contains guidance about applications by trustees for directions.

Administration orders – rule 64.2(b)

3.1 The court will only make an administration order if it considers that the issues between the parties cannot properly be resolved in any other way.

3.2 If, in a claim for an administration order, the claimant alleges that the trustees have not provided proper accounts, the court may –

(1) stay the proceedings for a specified period, and order them to file and serve proper accounts within that period; or

(2) if necessary to prevent proceedings by other creditors or persons claiming to be entitled to the estate or fund, make an administration order and include in it an order that no such proceedings are to be taken without the court's permission.

3.3 Where an administration order has been made in relation to the estate of a deceased person, and a claim is made against the estate by any person who is not a party to the proceedings –

(1) no party other than the executors or administrators of the estate may take part in any proceedings relating to the claim without the permission of the court; and

(2) the court may direct or permit any other party to take part in the proceedings, on such terms as to costs or otherwise as it thinks fit.

3.4 Where an order is made for the sale of any property vested in trustees, those persons shall have the conduct of the sale unless the court directs otherwise.

Applications under the Variation of Trusts Act 1958 – rule 64.2(c)

4.1 Where children or unborn beneficiaries will be affected by a proposed arrangement under the Act, the evidence filed in support of the application must –

(1) show that their litigation friends or the trustees support the arrangements as being in the interests of the children or unborn beneficiaries; and

(2) unless paragraph 4.3 applies or the court orders otherwise, be accompanied by a written opinion to this effect by the advocate who will appear on the hearing of the application.

4.2 A written opinion filed under paragraph 4.1(2) must –

(1) if it is given on formal instructions, be accompanied by a copy of those instructions; or

(2) otherwise, state fully the basis on which it is given.

4.3 No written opinion needs to be filed in support of an application to approve an arrangement under section 1(1)(d) of the Act (discretionary interests under protective trusts).

4.4 Where the interests of two or more children, or two or more of the children and unborn beneficiaries, are similar, only a single written opinion needs to be filed.

Applications under section 48 of the Administration of Justice Act 1985 – rule 64.2(d)

5 A Part 8 claim form for an application by trustees under section 48 of the Administration of Justice Act 1985 (power of High Court to authorise action to be taken in reliance on legal opinion) may be issued without naming a defendant, under rule 8.2A. No separate application for permission under rule 8.2A need be made.

Prospective costs orders

6.1 These paragraphs are about the costs of applications under rule 64.2(a).

6.2 Where trustees have power to agree to pay the costs of a party to such an application, and exercise such a power, rule 44.5 applies. In such a case, an order is not required and the trustees are entitled to recover out of the trust fund any costs which they pay pursuant to the agreement made in the exercise of such power.

6.3 Where the trustees do not have, or decide not to exercise, a power to make such an agreement, the trustees or the party concerned may apply to the court at any stage of proceedings for an order that the costs of any party (including the costs of the trustees) shall be paid out of the fund (a 'prospective costs order').

6.4 The court, on an application for a prospective costs order, may –

(a) in the case of the trustees' costs, authorise the trustees to raise and meet such costs out of the fund;

(b) in the case of the costs of any other party, authorise or direct the trustees to pay such costs (or any part of them, or the costs incurred up to a particular time) out of the trust fund to be assessed, if not agreed by the trustees, on the indemnity basis or, if the court directs, on the standard basis, and to make payments from time to time on account of such costs. A model form of order is annexed to this Practice Direction.

6.5 The court will always consider whether it is possible to deal with the application for a prospective costs order on paper without a hearing and in an ordinary case would expect to be able to do so. The trustees must consider whether a hearing is needed for any reason. If they consider that it is they should say so and explain why in their evidence. If any party to the application referred to in paragraph 6.1 above (or any other person interested in the trust fund) considers that a hearing is necessary (for instance because he wishes to oppose the making of a prospective costs order) this should be stated, and the reasons explained, in his evidence, if any, or otherwise in a letter to the court.

6.6 If the court would be minded to refuse the application on a consideration of the papers alone, the parties will be notified and given the opportunity, within a stated time, to ask for a hearing.

6.7 The evidence in support of an application for a prospective costs order should be given by witness statement. The trustees and the applicant (if different) must ensure full disclosure of the relevant matters to show that the case is one which falls within the category of case where a prospective costs order can properly be made.

6.8 The model form of order is designed for use in the more straightforward cases, where a question needs to be determined which has arisen in the administration of the trust, whether the claimants are the trustees or a beneficiary. The form may be adapted for use in less straightforward cases, in particular where the proceedings are hostile, but special factors may also have to be reflected in the terms of the order in such a case.

II CHARITY PROCEEDINGS

Role of Attorney-General

7 The Attorney-General is a necessary party to all charity proceedings, other than any commenced by the Charity Commissioners, and must be joined as a defendant if he is not a claimant.

Service on Charity Commissioners or Attorney-General

8 Any document required or authorised to be served on the Commissioners or the

Attorney-General must be served on the Treasury Solicitor in accordance with paragraph 2.1 of Practice Direction 66.

Applications for permission to take charity proceedings – rule 64.6

9.1 The claim form for an application under section 33(5) of the Act must state –

(1) the name, address and description of the applicant;

(2) details of the proceedings which he wishes to take;

(3) the date of the Commissioners' refusal to grant an order authorising the taking of proceedings;

(4) the grounds on which the applicant alleges that it is a proper case for taking proceedings; and

(5) if the application is made with the consent of any other party to the proposed proceedings, that fact.

9.2 If the Commissioners have given reasons for refusing to grant an order, a copy of their reasons must be filed with the claim form.

Appeals against orders of the Charity Commissioners

10 Part 52 applies to any appeal against an order of the Charity Commissioners. Section III of Practice Direction 52 contains special provisions about such appeals.

APPENDIX
Model form of prospective costs order

UPON THE APPLICATION etc.

AND UPON HEARING etc.

AND UPON READING etc.

AND UPON the Solicitors for the ..... Defendant undertaking to make the repayments mentioned in paragraph 2 below in the circumstances there mentioned

IT IS [BY CONSENT] ORDERED THAT:

1. The Claimants as trustees of ..... ('the [Settlement/Scheme]') do –

    (a) pay from the assets of the [Settlement/Scheme] the costs of and incidental to these proceedings incurred by the ..... Defendant such costs to be subject to a detailed assessment on the indemnity basis if not agreed and (for the avoidance of doubt) to –

        (i) include costs incurred by the ..... Defendant from and after [*date*] in anticipation of being appointed to represent any class of persons presently or formerly beneficially interested under the trusts of the [Settlement/ Scheme] irrespective of whether [he/she] is in fact so appointed; and

        (ii) exclude (in the absence of any further order) costs incurred in prosecuting any Part 20 claim or any appeal;

    (b) indemnify the ..... Defendant in respect of any costs which he may be ordered to pay to any other party to these proceedings in connection therewith.

2. Until the outcome of the detailed assessment (or the agreement regarding costs)

contemplated in paragraph 1 above, the Claimants as trustees do pay from the assets of the [Settlement/Scheme] to the Solicitors for the ..... Defendant monthly (or at such other intervals as may be agreed) such sums on account of the costs referred to in paragraph 1(a) of this Order as the Solicitors for the ..... Defendant shall certify –

(i)   to have been reasonably and properly incurred and not to exceed such amount as is likely in their opinion to be allowed on a detailed assessment on the indemnity basis; and

(ii) to have accured on account of the present proceedings in the period prior to the date of such certificate and not to have been previously provided for under this Order.

PROVIDED ALWAYS that the Solicitors for the ..... Defendant shall repay such sums (if any) as, having been paid to them on account, are disallowed on a detailed assessment or are otherwise agreed to be repaid and any such sums shall be repaid together with interest at 1% above the base rate for the time being of [Barclays] Bank plc from and including the date of payment to those Solicitors up to and including the date of repayment, such interest to accrue daily.

3.   Any party may apply to vary or discharge paragraphs 1 and 2 of this Order but only in respect of costs to be incurred after the date of such application.

Note: this form of order assumes that the trustees are the claimants. If the claimant is a beneficiary and the trustees are defendants, references to the parties need to be adapted accordingly.

PRACTICE DIRECTION 64B – APPLICATIONS TO THE COURT FOR DIRECTIONS BY TRUSTEES IN RELATION TO THE ADMINISTRATION OF THE TRUST

This Practice Direction supplements Section I of Part 64

1   This Practice Direction is about applications to the court for directions by trustees in relation to the administration of the trust.

Contents of the claim form

2   If confidentiality of the directions sought is important (for example, where the directions relate to actual or proposed litigation with a third party who could find out what directions the trustees are seeking through access to the claim form under CPR rule 5.4) the statement of the remedy sought, for the purposes of CPR rule 8.2(b), may be expressed in general terms. The trustees must, in that case, state specifically in the evidence what it is that they seek to be allowed to do.

Proceedings in private

3   The proceedings will in the first instance be listed in private (see paragraph 1.5 of Practice Direction 39A and rule 39.2(3)(f)). Accordingly the order made, as well as the other documents among the court records (apart from a claim form which has been served), will not be open to inspection by third parties without the court's permission (rule 5.4(2)). If the matter is disposed of without a hearing, the order made will be expressed to have been made in private.

Joining defendants or giving notice to those interested

4.1   Rule 64.4(1)(c) deals with the joining of beneficiaries as defendants. Often, especially in the case of a private trust, it will be clear that some, and which, beneficiaries need to be joined as defendants. Sometimes, if there are only two views of the appropriate course, and one is advocated by one beneficiary who will be joined, it may not be necessary for other beneficiaries to be joined since the trustees may be able to present the other arguments. Equally, in the case of pension trust, it may not be necessary for a member of every possible different class of beneficiaries to be joined.

4.2   In some cases the court may be able to assess whether or not to give the directions sought, or what directions to give, without hearing from any party other than the trustees. If the trustees consider that their case is in that category they may apply to the court to issue the claim form without naming any defendants under rule 8.2A. They must apply to the court before the claim form is issued (rule 8.2A(2)) and include a copy of the claim form that they propose to issue (rule 8.2A(3)(b)).

4.3   In other cases the trustees may know that beneficiaries need to be joined as defendants, or to be given notice, but may be in doubt as to which. Examples could include a case concerning a pension scheme with many beneficiaries and a number of different categories of interest, especially if they may be differently affected by the action for which directions are sought, or a private trust with a large class of discretionary beneficiaries. In those cases the trustees may apply to issue the claim form without naming any defendants under rule 8.2A. The application may be combined with an application to the court for directions as to which persons to join as parties or to give notice to under rule 19.8A.

4.4   In the case of a charitable trust the Attorney-General is always the appropriate defendant, and almost always the only one.

Case management directions

5.1   The claim will be referred to the master or district judge once a defendant has acknowledged service, or otherwise on expiry of the period for acknowledgment of service, (or, if no defendant is named, as soon as the claimants' evidence has been filed) to consider directions for the management of the case. Such directions may be given without a hearing in some cases; these might include directions as to parties or as to notice of proceedings, as mentioned in paragraph 4 above.

Proceeding without a hearing

6.1   (1)   The court will dispose of the application without a hearing if it considers that to do so will save time or expense, and that a hearing is not necessary. The trustees must therefore consider whether a hearing is necessary and, if so, explain why in their evidence.

(2)   When considering whether to hold a hearing, the court will take into account any dispute between the parties as to directions, but will not necessarily direct a hearing for that reason alone.

(3)   If a defendant considers that a hearing is needed, and that the need is not sufficiently explained in the trustees' evidence, that defendant should so state in evidence, giving reasons why.

6.2   Where the court deals with an application without a hearing, it will in any order give the parties an opportunity, within a stated time, to apply to vary or discharge the order at an oral hearing.

6.3   In charity cases, the master or district judge may deal with the case without a hearing on the basis of a letter by or on behalf of the Attorney-General that sets out his attitude to the application.

Evidence

7.1 The trustees' evidence should be given by witness statement. In order to ensure that, if directions are given, the trustees are properly protected by the order, they must ensure full disclosure of relevant matters, even if the case is to proceed with the participation of beneficiaries as defendants.

7.2 Applications for directions whether or not to take or defend or pursue litigation should be supported by evidence of the following matters –

(1) the advice of an appropriately qualified lawyer as to the prospects of success;

(2) an estimate in summary form of –

(a) the value or other significance to the trust estate of the issues in the proceedings;

(b) the costs likely to be incurred by the trustees in the proceedings, by reference to the principal stages in the proceedings; and

(c) the costs of other parties to the proceedings for which, if unsuccessful, the trustees may be exposed to liability;

(3) any known facts concerning the means of other parties to the proceedings; and

(4) any other factors relevant to the court's decision whether to give the directions sought.

7.3 References in this practice direction to an appropriately qualified lawyer mean one whose qualifications and experience are appropriate to the circumstances of the case. The qualifications should be stated. If the advice is given on formal instructions, the instructions should always be put in evidence as well, so that the court can see the basis on which the advice was given. If it is not, the advice must state fully the basis on which it is given.

7.4 In the case of a pension trust the evidence should include the latest actuarial valuation, and should describe the membership profile and, if a deficit on winding up is likely, the priority provisions and their likely effect.

7.5 On an application for directions about actual or possible litigation the evidence should also state whether (i) the Practice Direction (Pre-Action Conduct) or any relevant Pre-Action Protocol has been complied with; and (ii) the trustees have proposed or undertaken, or intend to propose, mediation by ADR, and (in each case) if not why not.

7.6 If a beneficiary of the trust is a party to the litigation about which directions are sought, with an interest opposed to that of the trustees, that beneficiary should be a defendant to the trustees' application, but any material which would be privileged as regards that beneficiary in the litigation should be put in evidence as exhibits to the trustees' witness statement, and should not be served on the beneficiary. However if the trustees' representatives consider that no harm would be done by the disclosure of all or some part of the material, then that material should be served on that defendant. That defendant may also be excluded from part of the hearing, including that which is devoted to discussion of the material withheld.

Consultation with beneficiaries

7.7 The evidence must explain what, if any, consultation there has been with beneficiaries, and with what result. In preparation for an application for directions in respect of litigation, the following guidance is to be followed:

(1) If the trust is a private trust where the beneficiaries principally concerned are not numerous and are all or mainly adult, identified and traceable, the trustees will be expected to have canvassed with all the adult beneficiaries the proposed or possible courses of action before applying for directions.

(2) If it is a private trust with a larger number of beneficiaries, including those not yet born or identified, or children, it is likely that there will nevertheless be some adult beneficiaries principally concerned, with whom the trustees must consult.

(3) In relation to a charitable trust the trustees must have consulted the Attorney-General, through the Treasury Solicitor, as well as the Charity Commissioners whose consent to the application will have been needed under section 33 of the Charities Act 1993.

(4) In relation to a pension trust, unless the members are very few in number, no particular steps by way of consultation with beneficiaries (including, where relevant, employers) or their representatives are required in preparation for the application, though the trustees' evidence should describe any consultation that has in fact taken place. If no consultation has taken place, the court could in some cases direct that meetings of one or more classes of beneficiaries be held to consider the subject matter of the application, possibly as a preliminary to deciding whether a member of a particular class ought to be joined as a defendant, though in a case concerning actual or proposed litigation, steps would need to be considered to protect privileged material from too wide disclosure.

7.8 (1) If the court gives directions allowing the trustees to take, defend or pursue litigation it may do so up to a particular stage in the litigation, requiring the trustees, before they carry on beyond that point, to renew their application to the court. What stage that should be will depend on the likely management of the litigation under the CPR. If the application is to be renewed after disclosure of documents, and disclosed documents need to be shown to the court, it may be necessary to obtain permission to do this from the court in which the other litigation is proceeding.

(2) In such a case the court will if possible deal with the matter without a hearing, and in deciding whether to do so will take into account the advice of an appropriately qualified lawyer supporting the continuation by the trustees of the pursuit or defence (as the case may be) of the proceedings.

7.9 In a case of urgency, such as where a limitation period or period for service of proceedings is about to expire, the court may be able to give directions on a summary consideration of the evidence to cover the steps which need to be taken urgently, but limiting those directions so that the application needs to be renewed on fuller consideration at an early stage.

7.10 In any application for directions where a child is a defendant, the court will expect to have put before it the instructions to and advice of an appropriately qualified lawyer as to the benefits and disadvantages of the proposed, and any other relevant, course of action from the point of view of the child beneficiary.

7.11 The master or district judge may give the directions sought though, if the directions relate to actual or proposed litigation, only if it is a plain case, and therefore the master or district judge may think it appropriate to give the directions without a hearing: see Practice Direction 2B, para 4.1 and para. 5.1(e), and see also paragraph 6 above. Otherwise the case will be referred to the judge.

7.12 Where a hearing takes place, if the advice of a lawyer has been put in evidence in accordance with paragraph 7.2 or 7.10, that lawyer should if possible appear on the hearing.

Forms and precedents

Letter of claim

Dear Sirs,

Re: [*name*] Deceased

Our client [*name*]

This is a formal letter of claim by which we give notice our client intends to make a claim under the Inheritance (Provision for Family and Dependants) Act 1975 for reasonable provision to be made for [him/her] from the estate of [*name deceased*]. Our client makes [his/her] claim as [*describe e.g. the deceased's spouse*] under section 1(1) [*complete*] of the Act.

[We enclose a statement from our client which will form the basis of his/her evidence in support of a claim. We also enclose a draft Part 8 claim form that will be issued in due course, unless the claim can be settled by agreement in the meantime.]

You are aware the court will consider the factors set out in section 3 of the Act in determining both the question whether there is reasonable provision for our client on the death of the deceased and the question what provision, if any, should be awarded by an order under section 2 of the Act. We will consider the relevant parts of section 3 further below, but would first comment as follows on the provision made for our client [on intestacy] [under the deceased's will dated [*date*]].

[*Complete description of provision made for client on deceased's death*]

[Our client will rely on the following [*complete facts to describe basis of claim*]]

SECTION 3 FACTORS

We consider below the factors in section 3 that we believe are relevant to our client's claim.

(a) The first of these is in section 3(1)(a) and concerns our client's present and future financial needs and resources. [You will see from our client's draft statement and Schedule of Assets that he/she has income [*complete*]. She has capital [*complete*]]. [*Describe client's income/expenditure/financial needs and resources, preferably by reference to schedules.*]

(b) We propose to consider the needs and resources of [the will/intestacy beneficiaries/ other applicants] (section 3(1)(b) and (c)) as far as they are known to us [*complete*].

(c) The needs and resources of our client and the [will/intestacy beneficiaries] [other applicants] must be considered in the light of the size of the net estate (section 3(1)(e)) upon which we have the following observations [*complete*].

(d) We now turn to section 3(1)(d) of the Act. The deceased owed an obligation to [*complete*]. The deceased owed a responsibility to [*complete*].

(e) [*Refer to the mental and/or physical disability of any applicant/beneficiary under section 3(1)(d).*]

(f) We would ask you to consider [*section 3(1)(g) – 'Other matters' – to be completed*].

(g) [*If spouse applicant*] Finally, we refer to section 3(2) of the Act. Our client is [*number*] years of age. The marriage lasted [*duration*]. Our client contributed to the welfare of the deceased and his family in the following respects [*complete*]. You will be aware that a spouse applicant under the Act is not limited to financial provision for maintenance but is entitled to such provision as is reasonable in all the circumstances. We consider [*go on to explain what would be reasonable in the circumstances and why*].

We enclose the following documents in support of our client's claim: [*list*].

We would ask you now to provide us with a formal letter of response within 21 days. We believe you have in your possession or control the following documents relevant to the claim [*list*] and request receipt of copies of the same from you with your letter of response. Included in this list are a number of documents marked with an asterisk. We invite you to provide copies of these to us within 14 days of your receipt of this letter or to give us your written authority, in the form enclosed, so that we may obtain them.

We have also sent this letter to [*complete*] and enclose a [copy/copies] of the same.

Yours faithfully

Letter of response from personal representatives

Dear Sirs,

Re: [*name*] Deceased

Our Client: [*name*]

Your Client: [*name*]

We write in response to your letter of [*date*] by which you advised us formally of your client's intended application under the Inheritance (Provision for Family and Dependants) Act 1975 for provision to be made for your client from the Deceased's estate. We act for the [executor(s)/person(s) entitled to a grant of letters of administration]. [As you are aware] a grant [has/has not] been issued [on [*date*] and a copy of the same is enclosed herewith [with the will].]

This letter is intended to address the matters relevant to personal representatives as parties to claims under the 1975 Act and therefore anticipates the requirements set out in CPR 1998 rule 57.16(5) and the Practice Direction paragraphs 15 and 16. This letter will not address the substantive merits of your client's claim, nor the defences that may be raised by the persons entitled to the Deceased's estate [under the will/on intestacy].

If proceedings are issued our client intends to acknowledge service and state that he/she/they will remain neutral and abide the outcome of the trial or the other parties' compromise of your claim.

The beneficiaries of the estate have been notified by us of your claim and we suggest that you communicate directly with them. Please advise us if you need details of who they are and how to contact them.

[The estimated gross value of the estate is £[*X*].] [We enclose copies of the Inland Revenue Account (and a corrective account)] [and a schedule of the capital assets in the estate, and its income. The values given are estimates where indicated.]

We note that the date for service of your claim form expires under section 4 of the 1975 Act [6 months after the issue of a grant of representation [which will be on [*date*]]. Please keep us advised of the progress of your claim.

[You have a caused a caveat to be entered to prevent the issue of a grant of representation for the estate. This is an inappropriate step to take. We invite you to withdraw your caveat forthwith. The estate will not be distributed pending the expiry of 6 months from the date any grant is obtained and will then be held to await the outcome of your client's claim if he/she chooses to pursue it.]

Yours faithfully,

B3

Claim form for all applicants with claims for extension of time[1] and joint property to be treated as part of net estate[2]

[For insertion on Part 8 Claim Form]

In the High Court of Justice

Family or Chancery Division[3]

BETWEEN:

AB	**Claimant**
– and –	
(1) CD	**Defendants**
(2) EF (A child by his litigation friend)[4]	

Are there any Human rights issues involved in this application?   No

BRIEF DETAILS OF CLAIM

1. Part 8 of the Civil Procedure Rules 1998 applies to this claim.
2. [*Choose description of the applicant from the following list*]

   - The Claimant was the husband/wife of the above-named deceased *or*
   - The Claimant was the civil partner of the above-named deceased *or*
   - The Claimant was the former husband/wife of the above-named deceased *or*
   - The Claimant was the former civil partner of the above-named deceased *or*
   - The Claimant lived with the above-named deceased during the whole of the period of 2 years ending immediately before the date when the deceased died in the same household as the deceased and as the husband/wife of the deceased *or*
   - The Claimant lived with the above-named deceased during the whole of the period of 2 years ending immediately before the date when the deceased died in the same household as the deceased and as the civil partner of the deceased *or*

---

[1]   See **Chapter 8**.
[2]   Section 9 of the Inheritance (Provision for Family and Dependants) Act 1975 (1975 Act). See **Chapter 7**.
[3]   The claim can be brought in either Division. Claims by spouses are perhaps better brought in the Family Division because of the judges' experience in relation to divorce. The heading in the Chancery Division will now be as for **B4**.
[4]   A child or a protected party must have a litigation friend (CPR rule 21.2).

- The Claimant is a child of the above-named deceased *or*
- The Claimant was treated by the deceased as a child of the family in relation to his marriage or civil partnership or family in which the deceased stood in the role of a parent *or*
- The Claimant was immediately before the death of the deceased being maintained, either wholly or partly, by the deceased.

3. The deceased died on [*date*] and a grant of letters of administration was issued to the First Defendant out of the [*location*] Probate Registry on [*date*] or a grant of probate issued to the First Defendants out of the [*location*] Probate Registry on [*date*].
4. The Second Defendant is the infant child of the deceased and entitled to share his estate on intestacy.
5. The Claimant seeks the following relief:

   (a) that provision be made for him/her out of the estate of the above-named deceased;
   (b) that permission be granted for bringing this application notwithstanding the fact that more than 6 months has elapsed since the making of the grant of probate;[5]
   (c) that the above-named deceased's severable share of [his] property known as [*details*], at the value thereof immediately before his death, shall, to such extent as appears to the court to be just in all the circumstances of the case, be treated for the purposes of the Inheritance (Provision for Family and Dependants) Act 1975 as part of the net estate of the above-named deceased.[6]
   (d) That provision be made for the costs of this application.

(5) This application is made under sections 1, 4 and 9 of the Inheritance (Provision for Family and Dependants) Act 1975.

I believe that the contents of this Claim Form are true

Signed: .... Dated: ....

---

[5] See 1975 Act, s.4 and **Chapter 8**.
[6] See 1975 Act, s.9 and **Chapter 8**.

B4

Witness statement in support of application by spouse for provision[1]

Claimant

Date

Exhibits

In the High Court of Justice

Business and Property Courts

Property Trusts and Probate List (ChD)

In the Estate of XY Deceased

In the Matter of the Inheritance (Provision For Family And Dependants) Act 1975

BETWEEN:

GH	**Claimant**
– and –	
(1) IJ	
(2) KL	**Defendants**

WITNESS STATEMENT IN SUPPORT OF APPLICATION FOR REASONABLE FINANCIAL PROVISION

I, GH of [*address*] WILL SAY as follows:

Background

1. I am the Claimant herein and I make this statement in support of my application for reasonable financial provision to be made for me out of the estate of XY ('the Deceased') who died on 18 September 2005.
2. The First and Second Defendants are the executors and trustees of the Will of the Deceased and a grant of probate was made to them out of the Principal Registry of the Family Division on 13 December 2005. I now refer to a copy of that grant and the Will marked 'GH1'.

---

[1] This is just an example of a witness statement in a particular case. It can be adapted for other classes of applicants.

3.   By his Will the Deceased provided for a legacy to me of £50,000 but otherwise left his estate to his sons from his first marriage, the First and Second Defendants.

History of the relationship

4.   I was born on 13 June 1961. I met the Deceased in 1991 and we started living together in December 1992. I moved into a house which he owned known as Dunromin, sold my own flat and used the monies to buy furniture for our new home. We were married on 14 April 2001 and I now refer to a copy of our marriage certificate marked 'GH2'. At that date I was aged 40 and the Deceased 53. There were no children of the marriage but the Defendants came to stay at weekends and holidays from the age of 5 and 9 and I cared for them.

5.   At the date when I started living with the Deceased I worked as a librarian. However once we married he suggested that I give up work. He supported me financially. He worked as a city accountant and was very successful. We had a very good lifestyle. We ate out at least twice a week. We had two cars and a housekeeper. We had a holiday home which we purchased near Sienna and we spent at least five weeks a year there.

6.   Shortly before he died, I discovered that the Deceased had been having an affair with his boss and was planning to leave me. It was when I confronted him with this that he suffered the heart attack which proved fatal.

Current financial needs and resources

7.   I am now aged 55. Although I used to work as a librarian, I have not worked since my marriage in 2001.

8.   At page [*number*] of 'GH3' is a schedule[2] I have prepared which shows my outgoings. There are other needs which I will have in the future. I suffer from arthritis and my mobility may become restricted as I get older. I anticipate that I may need to go into residential care earlier than might otherwise be expected.

Size of the estate

9.   I do not have a complete picture of the estate and what it consists of and I refer to a bundle of correspondence marked 'GH4' between my solicitors and the solicitors acting for the estate. This indicates that the estate is worth in the region of £3.2 million and Dunromin is worth about £700,000 of that sum. There is no valuation as yet of the house in Sienna.

The beneficiaries of the estate

10.   As set out above the Deceased left his estate to the Defendants apart from the legacy of £50,000 to me. The First Defendant is aged 33 and is a criminal barrister and unmarried. The Second Defendant is aged 29 and is a drummer in a rock band which has had some success. He is unmarried but has a child aged 2 whom he supports. I have no details of their financial position but both appear to be comfortable and were not dependent on their father.

---

[2]   This should set out outgoings in detail, income and capital, see the following sample schedule for a suggestion.

Extension of time

11. I appreciate that this claim has been brought just outside the 6 month time limit provided for in the 1975 Act and I seek permission of the Court to bring this claim notwithstanding the effluxion of time. I understand that the date for making this claim was recorded incorrectly on the computer at my solicitors, Messrs Sue Grabit and Run. Mr. Sue of that firm has signed a statement explaining the circumstances. My solicitors and I erroneously believed that we had until the end of December to make the claim. Solicitors for the administrators, Messrs Clueless & Co., have always been aware that this claim was to be made and I refer to correspondence passing between my solicitors and them marked 'GH5'. I do not believe that there has been any prejudice caused as a result of the short delay in issuing proceedings for which I apologise.[3]

Statement of truth

12. I believe that the facts set out in this statement are true. Signed etc.

Schedule of financial position[4]

[*name*]

Summary of schedules of annual income needs

Schedule		Schedule A	Schedule B
1	Housing	0.00	0.00
2	Housekeeping	0.00	0.00
3	Clothes and footwear	0.00	0.00
4	Cars	0.00	0.00
5	Personal expenditure	0.00	0.00
6	Holidays, entertainment, sports, hobbies	0.00	0.00
7	Miscellaneous	0.00	0.00
TOTAL		**£0.00**	**£0.00**

---

[3] This statement sets out circumstances which are almost an inadvertent failure to comply with the time limits. In cases where there has been a long delay the circumstances should be explained to the court in as much detail as possible by the claimant and/or her solicitor.

[4] This schedule will need to be adapted depending on client circumstances.

Schedule 1: Housing

Schedule A (£)		Schedule B (£)
0.00	Road maintenance	0.00
0.00	Council tax	0.00
0.00	Water rates	0.00
0.00	Insurance – buildings and contents	0.00
0.00	Gas	0.00
0.00	Electricity	0.00
0.00	Other fuel	0.00
0.00	Telephone – landline	0.00
0.00	Telephone – Internet	0.00
0.00	Telephone – fax	0.00
0.00	Telephone – mobile	0.00
0.00	TV – licence	0.00
0.00	TV – cable/satellite	0.00
0.00	Burglar alarm	0.00
0.00	Interior/exterior decoration	0.00
0.00	Maintenance of domestic machines/ central heating	0.00
0.00	Equipment insurance (including water and sewage pipes)	0.00
0.00	Repairs, cleaning, replacement of furniture/ machines/carpets/curtains (average over [5] years)	0.00
0.00	Sweep	0.00
0.00	Window cleaner	0.00
0.00	Garden (plants, seeds, sundries)	0.00
0.00	House plants and cut flowers	0.00
0.00	**TOTAL**	**0.00**

Schedule 2: Housekeeping

Schedule A (£)		Schedule B (£)
0.00	Food, wine and household goods	0.00
0.00	Chemist	0.00
0.00	Laundry/dry cleaning	0.00
0.00	Shoe repairs	0.00
0.00	Newspapers and magazines	0.00
0.00	Stationery and postage	0.00
0.00	Domestic help ([frequency])	0.00
0.00	Cleaner ([frequency])	0.00
0.00	Gardener ([frequency])	0.00

0.00	Wages: other ([description])	0.00
0.00	Pets ([description])	0.00
0.00	Food	0.00
0.00	Vet	0.00
0.00	Insurance	0.00
0.00	Kennels	0.00
0.00	**TOTAL**	**0.00**

Schedule 3: Clothes and footwear

Schedule A (£)		Schedule B (£)
0.00	Clothes (average over [5] years)	0.00
0.00	Footwear (average over [5] years)	0.00
0.00	Accessories (average over [5] years)	0.00
0.00	**TOTAL**	**0.00**

Schedule 4: Cars

Schedule A (£)	[Description of car]	Schedule B (£)
0.00	Road tax	0.00
0.00	Insurance	0.00
0.00	Servicing	0.00
0.00	Maintenance and repairs	0.00
0.00	MOT	0.00
0.00	Tyres	0.00
0.00	Petrol	0.00
0.00	Oil	0.00
0.00	Car wash/valet service	0.00
0.00	Parking expenses	0.00
0.00	AA or RAC subscriptions (or other)	0.00
0.00	Depreciation	0.00
0.00	**TOTAL**	**0.00**

Schedule 5: Personal expenses

Schedule A (£)		Schedule B (£)
0.00	Hairdressing	0.00
0.00	Cosmetics and toiletries	0.00
0.00	Optician	0.00
0.00	Dentist	0.00

0.00	Beautician	0.00
0.00	Health clubs and equipment	0.00
0.00	Tobacco	0.00
0.00	Taxis	0.00
0.00	Train fares/bus fares/underground	0.00
0.00	**TOTAL**	**0.00**

Schedule 6: Holidays, entertainment, sports and hobbies

Schedule A (£)		Schedule B (£)
0.00	Restaurants	0.00
0.00	Theatre, cinema, concerts	0.00
0.00	Other spectator events (e.g. sporting events)	0.00
0.00	Books	0.00
0.00	Videos, compact discs, DVDs	0.00
0.00	Subscriptions for clubs and societies	0.00
0.00	Holidays (average for past [5] years)	0.00
0.00	Weekend breaks (average for the past [5] years)	0.00
0.00	Christmas expenses	0.00
0.00	Birthday and other gifts, parties, etc.	0.00
0.00	Film developing	0.00
0.00	Sport ([description])	0.00
0.00	**TOTAL**	**0.00**

Schedule 7: Miscellaneous

Schedule A (£)		Schedule B (£)
0.00	Annual accountancy charges	0.00
0.00	Donations (e.g. to charities)	0.00
0.00	Covenants	0.00
0.00	Other items of expenditure not set out elsewhere (tips, etc.)	0.00
0.00	**TOTAL**	**0.00**

271

B5

Witness statement by personal representative setting out matters required by paragraph 16 of the Practice Direction to CPR Part 57[1]

First Defendant

Date

Exhibits

In the F(ChD)[2]

In the Estate Of XY Deceased

In the Matter of the Inheritance (Provision For Family And Dependants) Act 1975

BETWEEN:

GH   **Claimant**

– and –

(1) IJ   **Defendants**
(2) KL

WITNESS STATEMENT OF FIRST DEFENDANT

I, IJ of [*address*] WILL SAY as follows:

1.   I am the First Defendant herein and one of the executors of the estate of XY ('the Deceased') who was my father. I make this statement in respect of the claim which has been made under the Inheritance (Provision for Family and Dependants) Act 1975 by the Claimant who is my stepmother. I make this statement in my capacity as one of the executors of XY and I am duly authorised by the Second Defendant who is the other executor to provide the information in this statement in accordance with paragraph 57.16 to the Practice Direction to Part 57 of the Civil Procedure Rules 1998 on his behalf too.

---

[1]   CPR rule 57.16 deals with the contents required in the personal representatives' statement and para.16 of the Practice Direction expands that.

[2]   The heading in the Chancery Division will now be as for **B4**.

Details of the net estate

2. There are now produced to me marked 'IJ1' [interim estate accounts/a schedule of assets in estate] which show that the net estate after the payment of inheritance tax is worth £3.2million. The estate comprises the house in which the Deceased lived with the Claimant worth £700,000 and a property near Sienna which we have had valued at £200,000. The rest of the estate comprises a portfolio of stocks and shares.

Names and addresses of beneficiaries of the estate

3. As the Claimant states in her statement the Deceased left a legacy of £50,000 to her and the residue of his estate to be divided between the Second Defendant and me. There is also a small legacy to the Deceased's secretary not mentioned in the Claimant's statement which amounts to £5,000. She is called MN and lives at [*address*].[3]

Other matters

4. I take issue with the amount of outgoings which the Claimant provides for in her schedule of needs and resources. It seems very high. Also she paints a picture of an extravagant life led with the Deceased whereas in fact he was rather mean with his money. I do not recall them eating out regularly or taking expensive holidays.
5. The Deceased confided in me on many occasions during the last ten years that his marriage to the Claimant was an unhappy one. Certainly as a child I found the Claimant to be very uncaring towards me when I went to stay with the Deceased. She certainly did not look after me as she suggests.

My financial position[4]

6. I am a barrister practising in criminal work and I have been greatly affected financially by the cuts in legal aid. I am engaged to be married and expect to marry next year. My fiancée works for the Crown Prosecution Service. My income is £50,000 per annum. I own a flat worth £450,000 which is subject to a mortgage amounting to £350,000. My outgoings exceed my income considerably and I have an overdraft of £30,000.
7. My father assisted me financially while I was establishing my career at the bar and he has contributed £2,000 to help clear my overdraft every year at Christmas. Apart from my flat I have no other capital.

Extension of time

8. I accept that the delay in bringing these proceedings was only one week. However the Claimant was fully aware that the claim had to be brought within 6 months and I urge the Court not to extend time.
9. I believe that the facts set out in this statement are true.

Signed: .... Dated: ....

---

[3] There is only a need to include addresses of beneficiaries who are not parties.
[4] If the beneficiaries of the estate want their financial position to weigh against the claim then they need to disclose it. Sometimes beneficiaries may be reluctant to do so. In that case the court will assume against them that they are comfortable financially.

Tomlin order settling claim of spouse taking advantage of spouse exemption[1]

In the High Court of Justice

Business and Property Courts

Property Trusts and Probate List (ChD)

Chancery Division

[Name of Judge] [Date]

In the Estate of XY Deceased

In the Matter of the Inheritance (Provision For Family And Dependants) Act 1975

BETWEEN:

GH	**Claimant**
– and –	
(1) IJ	**Defendants**
(2) KL	

MINUTE OF ORDER

UPON the application of the Claimant for provision from the estate of the above mentioned Deceased under the Inheritance (Provision for Family and Dependants) Act 1975.

AND UPON the Claimant and the First and Second Defendants agreeing the terms set forth in the Schedule hereto.

---

[1] For tax considerations in respect of compromise of these claims see **Chapter 9**. The aim of this order is to provide the spouse with a lump sum which will be exempt from tax, to utilise the nil-rate band for inheritance tax to direct money to the children and then to create a short-term life interest in favour of the spouse which will attract spouse relief (even after the changes made in the Finance Act 2006 – it is an immediate post-death interest in possession within s.49(1A)(iii) of the Inheritance Tax Act 1984).

AND THE Court being satisfied that the disposition of the Deceased's estate effected by the Will is not such as to make reasonable financial provision for the Claimant.

BY CONSENT IT IS ORDERED THAT:

1. The original Grant in this Estate together with a sealed copy of this Order be sent to the Principal Registry of the Family Division by the Claimant and the Defendants for a memorandum of this Order to be endorsed on or permanently annexed to the Grant in accordance with section 19(3) of the Inheritance (Provision for Family and Dependants) Act 1975.[2]

2. The Claimant and the Defendants having agreed to the terms set out in the Schedule hereto all further proceedings herein be stayed except for the purpose of carrying into effect the terms set out in the said Schedule. Liberty to apply as to carrying such terms into effect.

3. The costs of these proceedings (including costs of mediation) of the Claimant be subject to a detailed assessment on the standard basis[3] if not agreed and the costs of the Defendants be subject to a detailed assessment on the indemnity basis if not agreed and the said costs be raised and paid out of the estate.

SCHEDULE

(1) The Terms of the Will be varied to make provision for the Claimant under section 2 of the Inheritance (Provision for Family and Dependants) Act 1975 by the substitution of the following provisions marked (A), (B) and (C) for clauses 2, 3 and 4 of the Will and the Claimant and the Defendants (as executors of the Deceased) do carry the terms of this Schedule into effect.

   (A) I GIVE to my children IJ and KL in equal shares such sum of money as is equal in value to the largest sum of cash which I can give without any inheritance tax becoming due in respect of the transfer of my estate which I am deemed to make immediately before my death.[4]

   (B) I GIVE the sum of £1,000,000 to my wife GH.

   (C) I GIVE all the residue of my estate (out of which shall be paid my funeral and testamentary expenses and my debts) and any property over which I have at my death any general power of appointment to my trustees to pay the income to my wife for her life or until 1 March 2008 whichever is the shorter period[5] and subject thereto for my children IJ and KL in equal shares absolutely.

(2) The Claimant agrees to co-operate with the Defendants or either of them in providing information and undertaking any medical examination required for the purpose of

---

[2] This should be included in the order as a reminder to the personal representatives to comply with s.19(3) of the Act.

[3] That would be the usual basis of assessment for parties not acting as personal representatives although it is not uncommon for parties to agree that assessment should be on the indemnity basis.

[4] Depending on the tax position of the deceased this is likely to be equal to the nil-rate band for inheritance tax at the date of his death.

[5] While HMRC looks suspiciously at any interest less than five years, any interest which terminates more than two years after the date of death should work.

effecting insurance on her life against any inheritance tax which may become due on the gift set out in clause (C) above.[6]

(3)   The above terms are in full and final settlement of all claims which any party may have arising out of these proceedings.

---

[6]   Provided that the trust comes to an end on the termination of the interest in possession during the lifetime of the spouse she will make a PET. The possibility she might not survive seven years thereafter and additional inheritance tax would become payable can be insured against.

Tomlin order settling claim by spouse: approval of court on behalf of her infant children[1]

In the High Court of Justice

Business and Property Courts

Property Trusts and Probate List (ChD)

[Judge]

[Date]

In the Estate of OP Deceased

In the Matter of the Inheritance (Provision For Family And Dependants) Act 1975

BETWEEN:

<table>
<tr><td>QR</td><td>**Claimant**</td></tr>
<tr><td>– and –</td><td></td></tr>
<tr><td>(1) ST
(2) UV
(3) WX (a child by his litigation friend)
(4) YZ (a child by his litigation friend)</td><td>**Defendants**</td></tr>
</table>

MINUTE OF ORDER

ON the application of the Claimant as the widow of the above named Deceased for reasonable financial provision from his estate under the Inheritance (Provision for Family and Dependants) Act 1975 ('the 1975 Act').

AND the Claimant agreeing to the terms of compromise set forth in a Schedule hereto and the First and Second Defendants as administrators of the estate agreeing to carry the said terms into effect.[2]

---

[1] Under Part 21 of the CPR.
[2] The children cannot, of course, agree.

AND the Court being satisfied that the disposition of the Deceased's estate on intestacy is not such as to make reasonable financial provision for the Claimant.

AND the Court being satisfied that the said terms of compromise are for the benefit of the Third and Fourth Defendants HEREBY APPROVES the said terms of compromise and requires the First and Second Defendants to carry the said terms into effect.

IT IS ORDERED THAT:

In the High Court of Justice

1. The original grant together with the sealed copy of this Order be sent to the Principal Registry of the Family Division by the First and Second Defendants for a memorandum of this Order to be endorsed on or permanently annexed to the Grant in accordance with Section 19(3) of the 1975 Act.
2. All further proceedings in this action except for the purpose of carrying this Order and the said terms into effect be stayed, and for that purpose the parties are to be at liberty to apply.
3. That there be assessed on an indemnity basis[3] all parties' costs of and incidental to the said application of the Claimant (including the costs of and incidental to the application pursuant to CPR 21.10), in the event of such costs not being agreed and such costs be raised and paid out of the estate in the course of administration.
4. That the litigation friend of the Third and Fourth Defendants be authorised to make agreement on behalf of the Third and Fourth Defendants in relation to all parties' costs.[4]

SCHEDULE

(1) These terms shall be in full and final settlement of all claims which the Claimant may have against the estate of the said Deceased.
(2) The disposition of the Deceased's estate on intestacy be varied to make provision for the Claimant under Section 2 of the Inheritance (Provision for Family and Dependants) Act 1975 by the substitution of the following provisions in place of the intestacy rules.
(3) The First and Second Defendants as the personal representatives of the Deceased shall hold the Deceased's net estate:

    (a) as to one half thereof for the Claimant absolutely;
    (b) as to the other half thereof on trust for the Third and Fourth Defendants to hold the same UPON TRUST for them upon their attaining the age of [18][5]

in equal shares absolutely PROVIDED always that if either WX or YZ shall die before attaining the age of 18 leaving a child or children living who shall attain the age of 18

---

[3] There is no reason why the parties cannot agree this even though most parties' costs would be assessed on the standard basis and the personal representatives' costs on the indemnity basis.

[4] It is useful to include this provision as there is some doubt otherwise as to whether they have authority.

[5] Parents often wish their children to have capital at a later age than 18. There are two possible problems. It is perhaps doubtful whether the court has power to approve a settlement which postpones the vesting of capital in a child who would otherwise be entitled at 18, although in practice judges often are prepared to approve on that basis. Secondly, the Finance Act 2006 introduced changes to the way in which accumulation and maintenance trusts are taxed. If children do not attain an absolute interest in capital at 18 there is an inheritance tax charge (albeit quite limited) between then and 25. However, sometimes the reasons for an 18-year-old not inheriting a substantial sum of capital if they inherit from their parent can outweigh the tax disadvantages.

such child or children shall take if more than one in equal shares absolutely the interest in the residuary estate which his or her parent would have taken at 18 and subject thereto for the Claimant absolutely.

ACTAPS guidance

ACTAPS Code – preliminary note[1]

Preliminary note regarding the interaction between the ACTAPS Practice Guidance and Notes regarding pre action behaviour in other cases

In general terms, the ACTAPS Practice Guidance Notes (hereafter referred to as 'The ACTAPS Code') are designed to promote the resolution of trust and probate disputes without the need for what are often bitter and very expensive court proceedings by encouraging careful use at an early stage of mediation processes and explaining how best to manage the difficulty, so often present in these cases, that not all parties can speak for themselves.

The ACTAPS Code is not part of the CPR but it is hoped that judicial regard will be given to appropriate attempts to comply with the Code in the spirit of the CPR.

The Code is designed to make specific provision for particular aspects of trust and probate disputes which have been found in practice to call for special care.

The Code lists a wide variety of disputes to which the Code may apply, and mentioning some to which it does not –

- by recommending and providing a precedent for a letter of claim encompassing and adaptable to various types of dispute or claim (eg Inheritance Act claims)
- by providing lists of evidential documents to be produced in different types of disputes
- by promoting the early production of medical and social security records and evidence and providing precedent letters to that end (including a letter to a testator's GP agreed with the BMA)
- by providing for early production of evidence of testamentary capacity and a precedent *Larke* v. *Nugus* letter to the testator's solicitor
- by suggesting reasonable time limits
- by providing for cooperation in obtaining joint and third party letters of authority to disclose evidence
- by reproducing the new CPR covering the representation of unborn, minor, unascertained and incapable parties
- by encouraging mediation on the footing that the outcome will be subject to the approval of the Court in those cases where such approval is indispensable, and
- by providing for those cases where Revenue considerations arise.

---

[1] © ACTAPS 2006. Reproduced here with the kind permission of ACTAPS (**www.actaps.com**).

C2

ACTAPS Practice Guidance for the Resolution of Probate and Trust Disputes ('The ACTAPS Code')[1]

Paragraph 4 of the Practice Direction on Protocols has been substantially amended. It states that 'in cases not covered by any protocol, the court will expect the parties to act reasonably in exchanging information and documents relevant to their claim and in trying to avoid the necessity for the start of proceedings'.

Moreover, with effect from 1 April 2003, the 30th update to the CPR imposes on all parties to a dispute (whatever its nature) an obligation to comply with specified procedures designed to avoid litigation commencing.

Practitioners will no doubt remember the dicta of the Court of Appeal in *Carlson* v. *Townsend* [2001] 3 All ER 663 where it stated the use of the protocol was not limited to fast track cases. The spirit if not the letter of the protocol was equally appropriate to some higher value claims. In accordance with the aims of the civil justice reforms, the courts expected to see the spirit of reasonable pre-action behaviour applied in all cases regardless of the existence of a specific protocol.

The Association of Contentious Trust and Probate Specialists 'ACTAPS' and the Trust Law Committee have, as many practitioners will be aware, given much thought to the possibility that a special pre-action protocol ought to be developed for disputes within their area of expertise. Indeed a draft has for some time been on the ACTAPS website (**www.actaps.com**) and has since been the subject of extensive discussions with representatives of the judiciary concerned.

It is now clear that no special protocol will be adopted, despite a recognition that the draft contains useful elements. It will be seen that it deals in particular with the following matters:

(a) appointment of a representative to act on behalf of beneficiaries who cannot be ascertained or traced;
(b) requirement for a letter of claim setting out the basis of claim;
(c) early disclosure of documents;
(d) use of joint experts where possible;
(e) a joint letter of request for medical records;
(f) a joint *Larke* v. *Nugus* letter; and
(g) a joint letter requesting details of deceased's capacity.

In these circumstances the committee of ACTAPS has concluded that it would be useful to encourage members to have regard to The ACTAPS Code as a means of developing best practices in areas where special problems may arise, for example the need to have representatives for persons who cannot speak for themselves in a context where others may feel that mediation would be desirable.

---

[1] © ACTAPS 2006. Reproduced here with the kind permission of ACTAPS (**www.actaps.com**).

It is understood that the judges who have considered The ACTAPS Code have expressed no concerns that it is out of line with the CPR objectives or that to follow its principles would give rise to unnecessary problems in practice. In particular it is thought that CPR Rule 19.7(3)(b) gives the necessary scope for securing the appointment of representatives of those who are absent, unborn, or members of a large class, as well before as after the commencement of proceedings.

It is also hoped that in the context of probate issues the common difficulty of medical practitioners considering that they may as a matter of professional confidence be restricted in releasing records can be overcome by joint application (and following discussions between ACTAPS and the BMA the latter has confirmed that its future guidance will facilitate disclosure in accordance with The ACTAPS Code). The ACTAPS Code contains an outline for such a letter.

In these circumstances it is suggested that practitioners in the areas of trust and probate law should seek to follow the approaches indicated in The ACTAPS Code, approved by the Trust Law Committee and ACTAPS, on the basis that it may serve to amplify the basic principles of the general protocols and indicate considered methods of carrying the objectives of the general protocols into effect in areas which may be found to give rise to special difficulties with which the general protocols do not grapple. In putting forward this suggestion the committee of ACTAPS believes that it has the support of all who have been concerned to consider the draft protocol; the rejection of the proposal that it be adopted as a special protocol owes nothing (so far as is known) to any perception of defects and merely reflects the belief that the public interest is best served by seeking, where possible, to avoid specific protocols and to develop best practices in areas where general protocols have to be supplemented to meet the needs of special situations.

With that in mind the committee of ACTAPS encourages members and other users to help move the search for best practices forward by commenting on any defects, inadequacies or other difficulties which may be found to arise in carrying the terms of The ACTAPS Code into effect. Please make any such comments to the ACTAPS Chairman's or the ACTAPS Secretary's e-mail address.

Practitioners will wish to bear in mind the need for trustees and executors to consider the adequacy of their powers to enter into any particular course of conduct and the possibility that they may need e.g. Beddoes type directions if they propose a course of conduct to which their beneficiaries might wish to raise objection (as for example where the trustees wish voluntarily to disclose confidential documents to third parties) or which may involve material burdens of costs (as for example the institution of a lengthy mediation). But of course in circumstances where the aim is to explore ways of reaching agreement or otherwise saving costs any necessary order might be expected to be forthcoming (within the appropriate limits) without difficulty on the basis that the Court would be being asked to facilitate a course of action essentially in accordance with the overriding objective.

1. INTRODUCTION

The Scope of The Code

1.1   This Code is intended to apply to disputes about:

- the devolution and administration of estates of deceased persons
- the devolution and administration of trust funds ('probate and trust disputes'). It is not intended to displace other protocols if in the circumstances of the case they can be seen to be more appropriate.

The main types of disputes within the ambit of this Code can be expected to be:

- challenges to the validity of a will, for example on grounds of want of capacity or knowledge and approval, undue influence or forgery
- claims under the Inheritance (Provision for Family and Dependants) Act 1975 ('the Inheritance Act')
- actions for the removal of an administrator or executor or trustee or the appointment of a judicial trustee
- actions for the rectification of a will or other document
- disputes as to the meanings of provisions in a will or a trust
- administration actions
- allegations of breach of trust.

The ACTAPS Code may also apply to certain types of dispute where the provisions of a trust or the devolution of an estate are of the essence, for example where a claimant seeks in the alternative to set aside or overturn a trust or to take advantage of rights under a trust.

The Code has two aims; to encourage the resolution of disputes without hostile litigation; and even where litigation may be necessary to ensure that it is simplified as far as possible by maximizing the scope for the exchange of relevant information before the litigation process has commenced.

The Code is in general terms unlikely to be appropriate for disputes which involve:

- disputes as to the rights appertaining under rules of forced heirships under the law of some foreign jurisdiction
- the need for emergency injunctions
- (except in so far as concerns pre-action exchange of information) the need for a binding precedent or a declaration by the Court as to the true construction of some trust instrument or testamentary disposition.

The Code is formed in general terms to cover the broad range of trust and probate disputes; but it is recognised that the appropriate investigations and exchange of information will vary according to the circumstances of the dispute. However one of its primary purposes is to provide for a special feature of disputes in this area, namely that there may be beneficiaries who cannot speak for themselves but whose interests must be protected.

1.2 In cases where the express terms of The Code is not appropriate parties will be expected to follow the spirit of The Code and seek to achieve its aims so far as practicable in the particular case.

1.3 It is also to be borne in mind that there are certain cases in which a trust or probate dispute seeks to fulfil some non-contentious purpose, as for example where a question of difficulty is identified to which the parties are agreed that the best solution lies in inviting the Court to approve constructive proposals by way of compromise or where the objective is simply to find the cheapest way of protecting trustees or personal representatives against the risks involved in the existence of some theoretical doubt. In such cases The Code is unlikely to have any role to play.

1.4 One of the principal features of trust and probate disputes is that they may affect the interests of persons not of full capacity, as yet unborn or unascertained, or interested as members of a large class of persons who have similar beneficial interests. The Code is thus designed to make express provision for the need to find mechanisms that assist despite the absence of such persons (providing in particular an expedited process for Court approval of agreements reached in mediation). It is thus wrong in principle to regard a dispute as not amenable to the use of The Code just because there are persons concerned who cannot speak for themselves.

2. PRINCIPAL GUIDELINES

Parties

2.1   The parties to the probate or trust dispute will usually be trustees (or personal representatives or persons claiming to be entitled as such) and beneficiaries of the trust or estate who are of full capacity, though The Code is designed also to be capable of being used in exterior/third party disputes where appropriate.

2.2   In the case where interests of unascertained persons, minors, unborns, mentally incapacitated persons or members of a large class (such that it is not appropriate for all members of the class to be made parties to the dispute) will be affected, the procedure to be adopted will be an application to the Court (see Annex A) whether or not a claim has yet been instituted before the Court.

Status of Letters of Claim and Response

2.3   A letter of claim or of response is not intended to have the same status as pleadings. Matters may come to light as a result of investigation after the letter of claim has been sent or after the defendant has responded. These investigations could result in the pleaded case of a party differing in some respects from the case outlined in that party's letter of claim or response. It would not be consistent with the spirit of The Code for a party to complain about this difference provided that there was no indication of any intention to mislead.

Disclosure of Documents

2.4   The aim of the early disclosure of documents by the defendant is not to encourage 'fishing expeditions' by the claimant, but to promote an early exchange of relevant information to help in clarifying or resolving issues in dispute. The claimant's solicitors can assist by identifying in the letter of claim or in a subsequent letter the particular documents or categories of documents which they consider are relevant, and by providing copies of these where appropriate.

2.5   All documents are disclosed on the basis that they are not to be disclosed to third parties (other than legal advisers) or used for any purpose other than the resolution of the dispute, unless otherwise agreed in writing or permitted by the court.

Experts

2.6   Expert evidence appropriate to probate and trust disputes may include in particular medical evidence, handwriting evidence, valuation evidence, tax- related or actuarial evidence.

2.7   The Code encourages joint selection of, and access to, experts. However, it maintains the flexibility for each party to obtain their own expert's report. It is for the court to decide whether the costs of more than one expert's report should be recoverable.

287

Costs

2.8   Where The Code provides for the initial cost of obtaining information or reports to be borne by one party, it shall not restrict the court's discretion in relation to ultimate liability for such costs.

Negotiations/Mediation

2.9   Parties and their legal representatives are encouraged to enter into discussions and/or negotiations prior to starting proceedings. The parties should bear in mind that the courts increasingly take the view that litigation should be a last resort, and that claims should not be issued prematurely when a settlement is in reasonable prospect. Mediation of probate and trust disputes may assist in achieving a compromise, particularly in relation to disputes between family members. The form of the mediation will be set out in the mediation agreement between the mediator and the parties.

2.10   Mediation can be used to try to achieve a compromise whenever negotiation is appropriate and can be used at any stage in a trust dispute. Typically mediation may be considered:

(i)   before proceedings have commenced but once the issues are fairly well defined and the parties affected by them are known;
(ii)   even after proceedings have commenced and the statements of case have been served so that the parties have a better appreciation of the issues;
(iii)   at any critical stage in the litigation such as after disclosure of documents, exchange of experts' reports, exchange of witness statements and in the lead up to the trial.

The parties should seek to conclude a mediation within 42 days of the appointment of the mediator.

2.11   Since mediation negotiations are treated by the Courts as without prejudice, points disclosed during an attempt to reach a settlement will be confidential between the parties and cannot be used as evidence in subsequent Court proceedings unless expressly agreed by the party who made the disclosure. The mediator will not divulge information without consent. Also he will not pass on such information to outside parties or act for either party to the dispute in subsequent proceedings.

2.12   A settlement reached pursuant to a mediation should be recorded in writing and signed by the parties or their authorised representative. In probate and trust disputes, if and insofar as the subject matter of the dispute requires the sanction and approval of the Court, any agreement achieved as a result of the mediation should be expressed to be subject to the approval of the Court.

2.13   In a probate or trust dispute where the position of the Inland Revenue may have some bearing on any compromise solution which may be reached, any agreement may be made conditional upon indications of the Inland Revenue's position or adjourned to enable clarification of its position to be sought.

3. THE CODE

Letters of Claim

3.1 The Claimant shall send a letter of claim to each of the deceased's personal representatives or to the trustees, as the case may be and, unless it is impractical (e.g. because there is a large class of beneficiaries or the beneficiaries are minors) to each beneficiary or potential beneficiary of the estate or trust fund likely to be adversely affected by the claim (referred to as 'the proposed Defendants'), as soon as sufficient information is available to substantiate a realistic claim which the Claimant has decided he is prepared to pursue.

3.2 The letter shall contain a clear summary of the claim and the facts upon which it is based and state the remedy sought by the claimant.

3.3 Solicitors are recommended to use a standard format for the claim letter. A sample letter is set out at Annex B; this can be amended to suit the particular case.

3.4 In claims under the Inheritance Act the claimant should give details to the best of his ability of the matters set out in Section 3 of the Inheritance Act as relevant to the exercise of the Court's discretion (see Annex B).

3.5 Copies of documents in the claimant's possession which he wishes to rely upon or which any other party is likely to wish to rely upon should be enclosed with the letter of claim. Examples of documents likely to be relevant in different types of dispute are set out at Annex C. These lists are not exhaustive. The letter of claim may specify classes of document considered relevant for early disclosure by the proposed defendants.

Letter of Response

3.6 Each of the proposed defendants should respond to the letter of claim within 21 days stating whether he admits or denies the claim, responding in outline to the matters of fact relied upon by the claimant and setting out any particular matters of fact upon which he relies. If a proposed defendant intends to make an answering claim on his own behalf, the letter of response should contain the same information and documents as a letter of claim in relation to the Part 20 claim. If a proposed defendant is unable to respond within the time limit on any particular matter, the letter of response should give the reasons for the absence of a full response and state when it will be available.

3.7 In claims under the Inheritance Act each proposed defendant should give details to the best of his ability of the matters set out in Section 3 of the Inheritance Act as relevant to the exercise of the Court's discretion (and set out in Annex B).

3.8 Copies of documents in the proposed defendant's possession which he wishes to rely upon or which any other party is likely to wish to rely upon should be enclosed with the letter of response. Examples of relevant documents in relation to different categories of disputes are set out at Annex C. These lists are not exhaustive.

Documents

3.9 In relation to the documents in Annex C, the personal representatives of the deceased (including executors named in the last alleged will of the deceased) or trustees as appropriate should provide copies of such documents (if available) to a party requesting a copy within 14 days of the date of a letter of request (or such other reasonable time as may be agreed between the parties) or, if a copy is only available from a third party with the consent of the personal representatives or trustees, provide to the party making the request written authority to the third party to provide a copy of the document to that party.

3.10 Trustees or personal representatives should not be inhibited from making full disclosure by the absence of litigation.

Applications for documents or information in control of third parties

3.11 In a probate dispute the release of medical notes may cast much light on the likely outcome and it should be assumed for the purposes of The Code that they ought to be disclosed at the outset absent special reason.

3.12 If so requested in writing by any party all parties shall (in the absence of good reason to withhold the relevant items) within 14 days of any such request (or such longer period as shall reasonably be agreed):

(1) Sign and return to the party making the request, a joint application for the provision of copies of the deceased's medical notes or social worker's reports to all parties. The notes and/or reports should be sent separately and directly to each party. A specimen joint application is at Annex D.
(2) Sign, and return to the party making the request, a joint application for a statement by the solicitor who prepared the will of the deceased setting out all the circumstances leading up to the preparation and making of the will. A specimen joint application is at Annex E.

3.13 The party making the request for a joint application for information or documents from a third party shall:

(1) Submit it to the third party within 7 days of receipt of the joint application completed by the other parties.
(2) On receipt of the information or documents from the third party check that they have been received by all other parties and, if not, provide them with copies within 7 days of receipt.

3.14 In cases where the mental capacity of a deceased at the date of a testamentary instrument is in issue, the party seeking to uphold the testamentary instrument should obtain a report as to the deceased's mental capacity from his GP as soon as possible after the issue is identified and send it to all other parties within 7 days of receipt. A specimen letter of request is at Annex F.

Experts

3.15 Parties should consider the use of jointly instructed experts so far as possible. Accordingly before any prospective party (the first party) instructs an expert he should (unless of the opinion that another party will want to instruct his own expert) give the other (second) party a list of the name(s) of one or more experts in the relevant discipline whom he considers are suitable to instruct.

3.16 Within 14 days the second party may indicate an objection to one or more of such experts and suggest alternatives. The first party should then instruct a mutually acceptable expert.

3.17 If an expert to be jointly instructed is not agreed, the parties may then instruct experts of their own choice. It would be for the court to decide subsequently, if proceedings are issued, whether either party had acted unreasonably. No party shall be entitled to instruct an expert proposed in a list of experts for joint instructions until it is clear that joint instructions cannot be agreed and thereafter the party who submitted the list of experts shall be entitled to nominate one of the experts on this list as his own chosen expert and no other party shall instruct any expert named on the list until such nomination has taken place.

3.18 If the second party does not object to an expert nominated, he shall not be entitled to rely on his own expert evidence within that particular discipline unless:

(1)   the court so directs, or
(2)   the first party's expert report has been amended and the first party is not prepared to disclose the original report.

3.19 Either party may send to the expert written questions on the report, relevant to the issues, via the first party's solicitors. The expert should send answers to the question separately and directly to each party.

3.20 The cost of the report from an agreed expert will usually be paid by the party first proposing that a joint expert be instructed. The costs of the expert replying to questions will usually be borne by the party asking the questions. The ultimate liability for costs will be determined by the Court.

ANNEX A

Representation in Estate or Trust Disputes of interested persons who cannot be ascertained etc.

(1)   In any estate or trust dispute concerning:

    (a)   property comprised in an estate or subject to a trust or alleged to be subject to a trust; or
    (b)   the construction of a written instrument; or
    (c)   a situation where the interests of beneficiaries may require separate representation

the Court, if satisfied that it is expedient to do so, and that one or more of the conditions specified in paragraph (2) are satisfied, may appoint one or more persons to represent any person (including a person under a disability, a minor or an unborn person) or class who is or may be interested (whether presently or for any future, contingent or unascertained interest) in or affected by the dispute.

(2)   The conditions for the exercise of the power conferred by paragraph (1) are as follows:

    (a)   that the person, the class or some member of the class cannot be ascertained or cannot be readily ascertained, or is not of full capacity; or
    (b)   that the person, the class or some member of the class, though ascertained, cannot be found; or
    (c)   that, though the person or the class and members thereof can be ascertained and

found, it appears to the Court expedient (regard being had to all the circumstances, including the amount at stake and the degree of difficulty of the point to be determined) to exercise the power for the purposes of saving expense or for any other reason.

(3) Where, in any case to which paragraph 1 applies, the Court exercises the power conferred by that paragraph, a judgment or order of the Court given or made when the person or persons appointed in exercise of that power are before the Court shall be binding on the person or class represented by the person or persons so appointed.

(4) Where, in any such case, a compromise is proposed and some of the persons who are interested in, or who may be affected by the compromise have not been consulted (including persons under a disability, minors or unborn or unascertained persons) but

(a) there is some other person in the same interest before the Court who assents to the compromise or on whose behalf the Court sanctions the compromise; or

(b) the absent persons are represented by a person appointed under paragraph (1) who so assents, the Court, if satisfied that the compromise will be for the benefit of the absent persons and that it is expedient to exercise this power, may approve the compromise and order that it shall be binding on absent persons, and they shall be bound accordingly except where the order has been obtained by fraud or non-disclosure of material facts.

ANNEX B

To

Defendant

Dear

Re:

The estate of [*name of deceased*]

The Settlement made by [*Settlor*] on [*date*]

We are instructed on behalf of [*claimant*] [*give details of relief sought, e.g.* to seek reasonable provision out of the estate of the above-named deceased; to set aside probate of the will of the above-named deceased dated [*date*]; to seek a declaration that upon a proper construction of the above settlement our client is entitled to . . .]

The basis of our clients claim is: [*brief outline*]

The facts upon which our client relies are as follows: [*set out material facts with sufficient clarity and detail for the proposed defendants to make a preliminary assessment of the claim*]

The details of matters to which the Court would have regard under Section 3 of the Inheritance (Provision for Family and Dependants) Act 1975 insofar as they are known to our client are:

(a) Financial resources and needs of claimant;
(b) Financial resources and needs of any other claimant;
(c) Financial resources and needs of beneficiaries;
(d) Obligations and responsibilities of deceased towards claimants and beneficiaries;
(e) Size and nature of estate;
(f) Disabilities of claimants and beneficiaries;

(g)   Any other matter; and if claimant spouse or co- habitee,

(h)   age of claimant, length of marriage/co-habitation and contribution to family welfare.

We enclose the following documents which are relevant to the claim:

[*list documents*]

In accordance with The ACTAPS Code for probate and trust disputes, we look forward to receiving a letter of response, enclosing the documents in your possession and relevant to the claim within [21] days. We believe that the following documents relevant to the claim are likely to be in your possession: [*list documents*]

Pursuant to The ACTAPS Code as [personal representatives of the deceased/trustees of the settlement] we invite you to furnish us within 14 days of the date of this letter with copies of the following documents or written authority, in the form enclosed, to obtain copies of such document(s): [*list asterisked documents required*]

We have also sent a letter of claim to [*name and address*] and a copy of that letter is enclosed.

Yours faithfully

ANNEX C

All documents upon which you rely or upon which the other party is likely to wish to rely including but not limited to the following categories:

1.   In disputes in which the assets of an estate/trust fund or the financial resources of an individual are relevant; eg claims under the Inheritance Act, breach of trust claims:

   –   The Inland Revenue Account and any Corrective Account;
   –   A schedule of the capital assets (with values, estimated where appropriate) and income of the estate, trust fund or individual as appropriate;
   –   Trust or Estate Accounts.

2.   In disputes in which the mental capacity or medical condition of an individual is relevant, eg challenges to testamentary capacity, Inheritance Act claims where disability is alleged:

   –   A copy of the medical records of the individual or, if appropriate, the written authority of the personal representatives of a deceased to obtain his medical records together with an office copy of the grant of probate or letters of administration or other proof of their status.

3.   In disputes as to the validity, construction or rectification of a will or other testamentary instrument of the deceased:

   –   A statement setting out details of any testamentary script (now in CPR called testamentary document) within the knowledge of the claimant or proposed defendant and details of the name and address of the person who, to the best of his knowledge, has possession or control of such script.

Nb1: The provision of the statement in 3 above is of vital importance to all parties in a dispute since it ensures that the correct testamentary documents are being considered. This will prevent the problem of a dispute over a later testamentary document being allowed to overshadow the existence of an intermediate testamentary document which would be upheld if the later testamentary document fails.

Also it helps identify the correct parties to the existing disputes.

Nb2: Following from Nb1 above, it is most important that the fullest and most exhaustive search for all testamentary documents is made. Accordingly while the following list is not exhaustive it is incumbent upon all parties to check:

(i) with all known solicitors of the deceased as to the existence of a testamentary document;
(ii) with all attesting witnesses to testamentary documents as to the existence of testamentary documents;
(iii) with all named executors of testamentary documents as to the existence of testamentary documents;
(iv) with immediate family members (brothers, sisters, parents and children of the deceased) as to the existence of testamentary documents.

Nb3: Definition of Testamentary Script (now in CPR called Testamentary document)

A will, a draft of a will, written instructions for a will made by or at the request of, or under the instructions of, the testator, and any document purporting to be evidence of the contents, or to be a copy, of a will which is alleged to have been lost or destroyed. The word 'will' includes a codicil.

ANNEX D

JOINT APPLICATION FOR MEDICAL NOTES OR SOCIAL WORKER'S REPORTS

To: The medical records officer/social services

Dear Sir

Re: [*Name*] Deceased of [address], [*date of birth*]

We the undersigned Messrs [*firm's name*] [*ref.*] of [*firm's address*], Solicitors for the Executors named in the Will of the late [*deceased's name*] of [*deceased's address*] who died on [*date of death*] and we, the undersigned Messrs [*firm's name*] of [*firm's address*], Solicitors for parties interested in his/her estate, hereby authorise you to forward [a full set of copies of the deceased's Medical Records] [all social workers reports and notes relating to the deceased] to each of the aforementioned firms.

We confirm that we will be responsible for your reasonable photocopying charges and your invoice in this regard should be sent to [*firm's name*] and marked for the attention of [*ref.*].

Dated [...] 200[...]

Signed ....

Signed ....

ANNEX E

JOINT APPLICATION LETTER TO SOLICITORS WHO PREPARED WILL REQUESTING LARKE V. NUGUS STATEMENT

Dear Sirs

[*Name of Deceased*] deceased

We, the undersigned Messrs [*firm's name*] [*ref.*] of [*firm's address*], solicitors for the Executors named in the Will of [*deceased's name*] of [*deceased's address*] and we, the undersigned Messrs [*firm's name*] [*ref.*] of [*firm's address*], solicitors for parties interested in his/her estate regret to inform you that [*deceased's name*] died on [*date of death*].

We understand that you drafted the deceased's last will dated [...].

You may be aware that in 1959 the Law Society recommended that in circumstances such as this the testator's solicitor should make available a statement of his or her evidence regarding instructions for the preparation and execution of the will and surrounding circumstances. This recommendation was endorsed by the Court of Appeal on 21st February 1979 in *Larke* v. *Nugus*.

The practice is also recommended at paragraph 24.02 of the Law Society's *Guide to the Professional Conduct of Solicitors*, 7th edition (page 387), and that advice was highlighted and supplementary information provided by the Law Society Practice Note of 6 October 2011, on disclosing such information, the consequences of failing to do so, and protecting the estate.

Accordingly, we hereby request and authorise you to forward to each of the aforementioned firms statements from all appropriate members of your firm on the following points:

- How long had you known the deceased?
- Who introduced you to the deceased?
- On what date did you receive instructions from the deceased?
- Did you receive instructions by letter? If so, please provide copies of any correspondence.
- If instructions were taken at a meeting, please provide copies of your contemporaneous notes of the meeting including an indication of where the meeting took place and who else was present at the meeting.
- How were the instructions expressed?
- What indication did the deceased give to you that he knew he was making a will?
- Were you informed or otherwise aware of any medical history of the deceased that might bear upon the issue of his capacity?
- Did the deceased exhibit any signs of confusion or loss of memory? If so, please give details.
- To what extent were earlier wills discussed and what attempts were made to discuss departures from his earlier will-making pattern? What reasons, if any, did the testator give for making any such departures?
- When the will had been drafted, how were the provisions of the will explained to the deceased?
- Who, apart from the attesting witnesses, was present at the execution of the will? Where, when and how did this take place?
- Please provide copies of any other documents relating to your instructions for the preparation and execution of the will and surrounding circumstances or confirm that you have no objection to us inspecting your relevant file(s) on reasonable notice.

We confirm that we will be responsible for your reasonable photocopying charges in this connection and your invoice in this regard should be sent to [*each firm's name etc.*] and marked for the attention of [*each firm's ref.*].

Dated this [...] day of [...] 200[...]

Signed ....

Signed ....

ANNEX F

LETTER TO DECEASED'S GP REQUESTING REPORT AS TO MENTAL CAPACITY

To: Deceased's GP

Dear Dr . . ....

Re: [*Name*] Deceased of [*address*], [*date of birth*]

We the undersigned Messrs [*firm's name*] [*ref.*] of [*firm's address*] are Solicitors for the Executors named in the Will of the late [*deceased's name*] of [*deceased's address*] who died on [*date of death*] and we, the undersigned Messrs [*firm's name*] of [*firm's address*], are Solicitors for parties interested in his/her estate.

We enclose a photocopy of the deceased's last Will. The clauses in the Will which cause particular concern are [*clause numbers*].

The question of the deceased's mental capacity at the time of the making of his/her last Will dated has now been raised.

The test of testamentary capacity remains that established in the case of *Banks* v. *Goodfellow* where it was said:

'It is essential that a testator (1) shall understand the nature of the act and its effects; (2) shall understand the extent of the property of which he is disposing; and (3) shall be able to comprehend and appreciate the claims to which he ought to give effect, and; with a view to the latter object, (4) that no disorder of mind shall poison his affections, pervert his sense of right or pervert the exercise of his natural faculties; (5) that no insane delusions shall influence his mind in disposing of his property and bring about a disposal of it which if his mind had been sound, would not have been made.' [We have added numbers for convenience].

[*Set out the nature of the Estate if complex.*]

We would therefore be grateful if you would kindly provide us with a report setting out:

1. Your medical qualifications and your experience in assessing mental states and capacity
2. For how long you were the deceased's GP, how well you knew the deceased and a summary of his/her medical condition, insofar as it may have bearing upon the deceased's mental capacity.
3. Your findings as to the deceased's mental capacity at and around the time of the date of his/her last will.
4. Please also deal with any mental disorder from which the deceased may have been suffering at the relevant time, and any medication which could have affected his/her capacity as detailed above.

5. Please also consider any issues of vulnerability or suggestibility at or around the date of the deceased's last Will

We confirm that we will be responsible for your reasonable fees in the preparation of your report which we look forward to receiving as soon as possible.

Dated this […] day of […] 200[…]

Signed .... [ref: …]

Signed .... [ref: …]

Index